By Design:

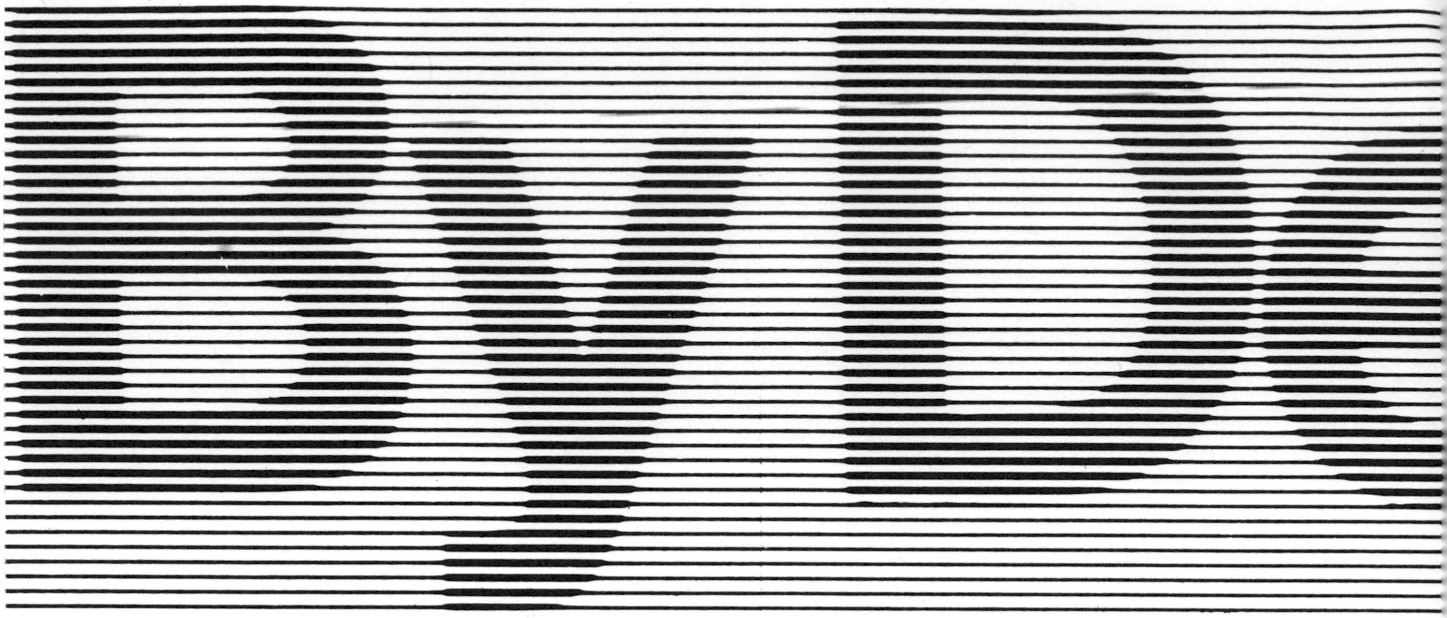

sign

A Graphics Sourcebook of Materials, Equipment and Services

by Jon Goodchild + Bill Henkin

quick fox

New York   London   Tokyo

In Great Britain:
Book Sales Ltd
78 Newman Street
London W1P 3LA

In Canada:
Gage Trade Publishing
Box 5000
164 Commander Blvd
Agincourt, Ontario M1S 3C7

In Japan:
Quick Fox
4-26-22 Jingumae
Shibuya-ku
Tokyo 150

International Standard Book
Number: 0-8256-3122-X
Library of Congress Catalog Card
Number: 78-68484

Book design copyright © Jon
Goodchild, 1980

Acknowledgements

Many thanks for all the help
provided by the many manufacturers
who kept us up to date with their
information, and to all those individuals who supplied little bits of
data — sometimes unknowingly.
We especially would like to thank
Flax Art Materials Store, San
Francisco, for all their courteous
assistance, and Charrette, Boston,
A I Friedman and Lee's Art Shop,
New York.

Thanks to Herb Wise for
his patience; to Malcolm Baker,
Richard Farson, Michael Schriven,
David Singer and Alan Rinzler for
their specialist knowledge; to
Guaranty Office Supplies and
Negatorium for their special
attentions.

And thanks to John Grissim,
Bill Johnson, Jim Anderson, *Com-
monweal,* Eugenia McNaughton,
Don Shandy, Jeanette Mall,
Bean Barnett, John C W Carroll,
Michael Harman, Debbie Holland,
Bryn Lea Pearson, Melinda Wentzell,
Bill Yenne, the *Graphic Artist's
Guild* and Stephen Gerstman for
various forms of support; and
special thanks to Craig DuMonte
and Janice Tweedy for putting up
with it all.

*Grateful acknowledgement is made
to the following individuals,
organizations and publishers:*

Design Council, London, England,
for permission to reprint the following
material from *Design* magazine:
"The Polluted Sea of Information" by
Phillip Thompson, and "How Wide
is a Degree" by Mark Brutton, editor,
copyright © 1977 by Design Council;
"Dreaming of a Humane and Busi-
nesslike Design School" by Arthur
Pulos, and "A Design Partnership"
by Colin Forbes of Pentagram, copyright © 1978 by Design Council.

Graphic Artists Guild, New York
and San Francisco, for permission
to reprint the following material from
the *Graphic Artists Guild Newsletter:*
"The Last Profession to Organize"
by Peter Kunz, "Affordable Necessary
Legal Help" by Ari Kopelman, and
"Beware the Work for Hire Clause,"
copyright © 1978 by Graphic
Artists Guild, Inc

Jan V White for permission to
print extracts from "Graphic Idea
Notebook," published in *Folio* magazine #80, copyright © 1979 by
Jan V White.

Gail Sheehey, for permission
to reprint extracts from *Life Times,*
published by the 1977 International
Design Conference Aspen, copyright
© 1977 by Gail Sheehey.

RitaSue Siegel, for permission
to reprint extracts from her address
at the Design Conference at Stanford,
copyright © 1977 by RitaSue Siegel.

International Typeface Corporation
for permission to reprint the following
material from *Upper and Lower Case:*
"'Similar to'-ism," copyright © 1977
by International Typeface Corporation,
and "The Mystery of the Graphic
Artist, or, Why 200,000,000 People
Need an Art Education," copyright
© 1978 by International Typeface
Corporation.

Jerzy Karo and Larry Levy

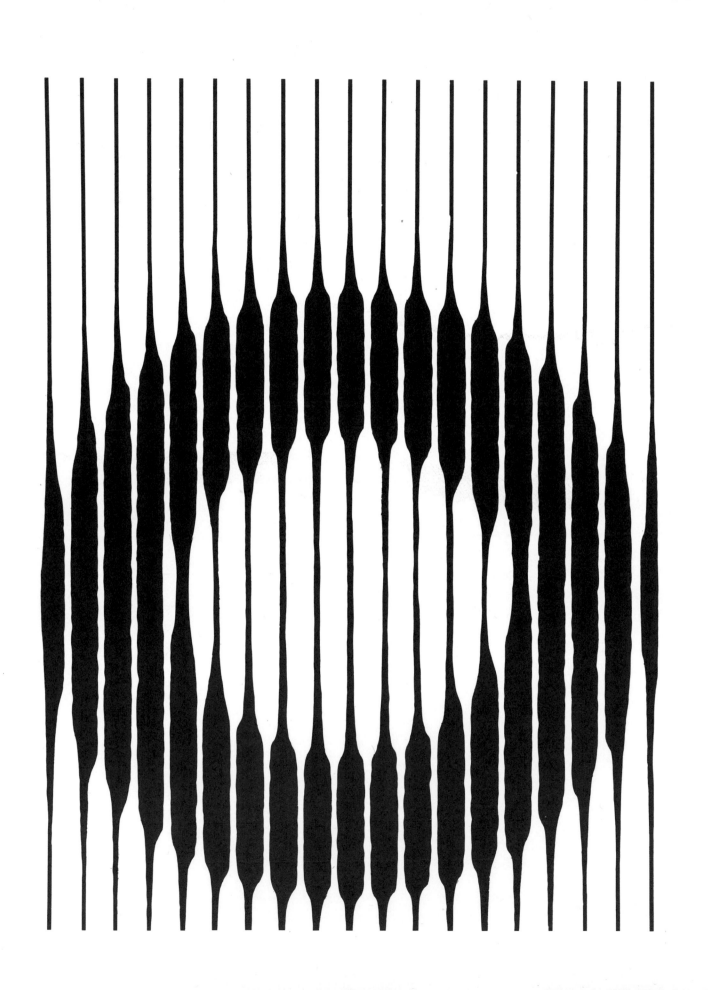

Contents

# Introduction

All problems of style, fashion or taste relate back to this problem of communication....

—John McConnell, "Jobbing Graphics," from *Living by Design,* by the partners of Pentagram.

This book has two overlapping purposes and, as such, is aimed at two overlapping audiences. First, it is intended to be an easy reference tool for the student or professional graphic artist. In this sense it is a tradesman's book, demonstrating a range of materials, services, and equipment useful to anyone involved in media communications, and doing so in a selective rather than a comprehensive fashion, highlighting those tools and services that are superior to others which may appear to be similar.

Secondly, it is intended to acquaint anyone with an overt or a covert creative flair with a catalog of sources, information, and useful items, some of which are never seen outside design studios and art supply stores, but which can easily find their place in any home or office.

Our theoretical observations and commentary notwithstanding, this is a reference book, not an instruction manual. While it can be a useful adjunct to a design course, it is in no way to be taken for the course itself, and we do presume the reader to have some passing familiarity, at least, with the processes of design. Nevertheless, in our approach to our material and in our selection and annotation of goods and services, we do intend to convey certain information about design as a profession.

The term *graphic designer* covers a broad territory and is ordinarily defined by the kind of basic training that was received. For our purposes *graphic design* entails all those aspects of design that are two-dimensional, including whatever is drawn, painted, written, or printed as it traditionally relates to printing, illustrating, advertising, promotion, and packaging: *information* and *identity* design. We exclude from our purview product and industrial design, environmental design, architectural design, interior design, and urban planning. Defined in this way, the graphics profession is easy to identify, and we have limited our attentions to the graphic arts only.

Throughout this book we are concerned with information that will be useful to anyone who communicates information, particularly through the medium of design. Since design necessarily entails aesthetic judgments, aesthetics inevitably play a part in our evaluations of goods and services and the milieu in which they exist. Thus, where all other factors are equal—for instance, in the comparison between two light tables—we will always prefer the model that is more attractive.

Insofar as graphics is a business that entails both service and product, as much information in this book derives from what is absent as from what is present. For instance, the attentive reader may discover that many items we have selected are of foreign origin. The best technical pens come from Germany and Switzerland; the best furniture and lighting units are Italian; the best dry transfer graphics system is British; and so forth. Certainly the United States is also capable of producing first-class design and design equipment. This country's technology is excellent, and its distribution and marketing systems are still the wonders of the modern business world.

Yet, American graphic standards—whether for tools and services or for design itself—tend to be quite low overall. The truly fine American graphics tools are the utilitarian and highly technical equipment used in the graphic arts *industry,* and are beyond the scope of this book—as they are beyond the needs of most designers. Truly fine American graphic design appears mostly in advertising, and does not extend very far into the rest of our culture.

Perhaps this is part of the reason that "commercial" art is often considered inferior to fine art, and seen as hack work undertaken for a pittance by failed Michelangelos. The problem for the graphic artist is compounded by the much more serious and erroneous assumptions, that the process of conveying information visually need not be understood by the people who buy it, use it, and respond to it; and that style, fashion, and taste are the only important issues of visual expression.

Ironically, these attitudes have long prevailed in the execution of some informational catalogs and brochures offered by design equipment distributors and manufacturers. Even when a product itself is wholly respectable, its promotional literature is often unorganized enough to reflect badly on the products. It can only be indicative of the general level of our cultural awareness that manufacturers who deal with the graphics community on a regular basis can circulate shoddy information design so casually to that very community.

Still, for all the problems in the field, the graphic arts are currently experiencing a great resurgence of interest and attention. Both the producers and the users of graphic design have become more sophisticated about the *results* good design can achieve; therefore, they are becoming increasingly aware of the processes and people through which those results are effected.

In *By Design* we present you with our selection of the best materials and services available for use in the graphic arts. But this book will have additional value for you if you keep in mind that what we think of as "the best," or what someone else calls "the best" may not be best for you. Assess your own needs carefully, and consider the longer term advantages of what you will get for what you will pay, and act accordingly.

We welcome any response from our readers, retailers or manufacturers regarding the information in this volume. If there are substantive errors in the text, or if there are items not included that ought to be, or if there are alternative recommendations to those listed here, please let us know. Write to Jon Goodchild, *By Design,* c/o Quick Fox, 33 West 60 Street, New York, NY 10023.

J. G., B. H. September 1979

A

The Working Environment

Light and Lighting

Temperature Control

Wall Space, Storage &
Shelving

Work Surfaces

Moveable Storage

Chairs and Other Items

CONVERTED WAREHOUSE STUDIO SPACE

In the beginning there is always space. Whether on the page or between four walls, space is an illusion precisely in that it comes to be defined. And space defined is space designed.

Setting up the space that constitutes your personal working environment has many of the same challenges and opportunities you encounter when working for clients. Maximum function and appropriate aesthetics will have to be balanced within the confines of form, budget, and a more or less restricted time frame.

How much time you allocate and money you budget for development of your studio make less difference than what you do with that time and money. If you took as long as you wanted and spent as much money as you needed to create your own perfect, ideal working environment, it probably would prove unsatisfactory when completed. Nothing is static, and your wants and needs are always in transition.

Obviously, the first step in defining your work environment is to choose the space that will become your studio. In large measure your selection of studio space defines other choices that you've already made, or which result from the location. You may locate in the city to be close to clients, suppliers, and associates; or you may locate in the country for pastoral peace. Your studio may be in your home or commercial building, barn or garage.

Your choices in these matters are effectively made for you by your particular line of work, or by the depth of your work experience. If you are an illustrator you can live pretty much where you like and work for magazines, book publishers, advertising agencies, and private clients. If you are a designer dependent on an advertising clientele, you will have to live in or near a major metropolitan area, and will almost certainly work in the agencies' offices. If you're new to the graphics business and just setting up shop, you should locate close to clients and suppliers. After you are well established as a free-lancer, with a certain and regular clientele, you can be farther removed from the seat of day-to-day commerce if you wish.

Your selection of a studio space—in your home or outside it, in the city, the suburbs, or the country—also affects and is affected by the way you live. Whether you regard yourself as an introverted loner or an extroverted party-goer, your profession can provide you with the trappings of your lifestyle and the means to support it or, by consuming your time, resources, and creative passions, can dominate it.

If you work for a company, the studio you are assigned may be nothing like the one you have in mind. In any case, you will find it useful to change your studio periodically, to gain fresh perspectives. Clearing out and cleaning up your environment, eliminating redundancies and changing routines, offer you the chance to reassess your work space and what you do there. Such a reassessment may equally reflect or presage shifts in your general attitude concerning your work or your life as a whole by helping you to be aware of the changes that have occurred while you thought everything was standing still.

The various ways in which you define and design your work environment make many statements about you. Like your graphic work, your studio speaks about your self-image and the image you wish to project. It speaks about your personal and professional preferences, your relationship to your work, its relationship to your life, and, above all else, your working space reflects your design sense.

Once your have made your choice of lifestyle and location, you will bring certain considerations to bear on your search and selection of a workspace. The single most important component in your entire studio, apart from the square footage, is access to available natural light. Such access is a given of any space. Unless you own the building and are prepared to undertake extensive and costly renovation, the natural light you see is the natural light you're going to be stuck with.

The second given of your studio space is access to temperature control. Sedentary work, such as designing or illustrating, demands a comfortable temperature for sustained concentration. For most people that temperature lies between 68° and 72°. If possible, you should be able to adjust the temperature in your studio to suit yourself. In a small building, temperature control is less likely to be a problem than in a large office building where central heating and air conditioning are almost sure to prevail.

The third given of your space is the efficiency of the layout itself: placement of windows, available wall space, ceiling height, odd little nooks and crannies, podiums, and storage areas.

Once you have the space that will become your studio, everything else in your working environment is likely to be provided by you. There are eight major areas of furniture and large hardware—apart from business machines, which are discussed in Section F, and smaller tools and equipment, which are discussed in Section B—with which you need concern yourself.

A CONVERTED TWO-STORY BRICK WAREHOUSE SPACE. LAWRENCE LEVY

A CONVENTIONAL STUDIO BOX IN A MODERN HIGHRISE. JODY CARAVAGLIA, BY PERMISSION OF BILL JOHNSON

Of the fundamental components in your studio, the first priority is ample lighting sources. We mentioned natural light previously, but both the quality and the quantity of that light are variable. Therefore, you must consider carefully both artificial illumination and controls for your natural light such as shutters, blinds, curtains, and window tints which will cut out the destructive heat and ultra-violet rays of sunlight that are so harmful to paper and ravage artwork.

Artificial Lighting

Never underestimate the importance of well-planned lighting in any work environment. In spite of all the propaganda put out by interested parties selling power and equipment, and all the articles, books, and exhortations devoted to the subject, little advance has been made over the austere lighting installations of the early twentieth century. The best lighting is still not readily available to the general public, partly because It's more difficult to sell lighting concepts than it is to sell lighting hardware.

Recently there has been a renaissance in office lighting prompted by the energy crisis and the popularity of the open-plan work environment—which has encouraged what is now known as Task/Ambient lighting. T/A lighting refers to a system that has long been used by artists and designers—localized and directional "task" lights, used with indirect, ambient lights that reflect off the ceiling and other surfaces. Besides being a personalized and cost effective approach to lighting, T/A adds enormously to eye comfort and a general sense of well-being. (See Appendix, "Lamp Selector Guide," pages 241–2).

Planning Your Lighting
[Derek Phillips]

A succinct and efficient Design Council (UK) book on lighting theory and practice, *Planning Your Lighting* is part of a series of practical design titles for professionals and laymen alike. The object of the book is to enhance the awareness, and improve the standards, of lighting in general; and, although it focuses on home lighting, its principles are equally applicable to working areas.

Cost: $4.00

Design Center Books

Perception and Lighting
[William M C Lam]

If you *really* want to study lighting, this is the book for you. *Perception and Lighting* is the basic text for lighting and interior designers. Lam explores all aspects of the subject, including peripheral and central vision, perception, color/mood effects, and even health concerns. He emphasizes the practicality of the European approach—combining low-level general illumination with specialized task lighting. As befits an exhaustive professional's reference work, Lam's book carries a "professional" price.

Cost: $27.95

Designer's Book Club

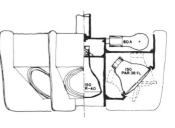

	RECESSED SURFACE	MOUNTED (ON CEILING OR WALL)	PENDANT	TABLE LAMP	FLOOR STANDARD
REFLECTOR SPOT					
TIN					
SHADE					

Lighting Hardware

In any lighting showroom, the choice of fittings appears limitless; but "appears" is the operative word, for the actual choice is strictly limited. Many of the fittings offered perform similarly when lit.

Lamps belonging to a single generic type distribute light in approximately equal proportions in all directions. The apparent differences are largely cosmetic. The main generic types can be listed according to the way in which they are supported in use:
1. Recessed into ceiling
2. Surface mounted on wall of ceiling.
3. Pendant
4. Table lamp
5. Floor standard

— From *Planning Your Lighting*

"It is not inconceivable that people in a few years time might be painting their walls with light in the same way that we use wallpaper. If such surfaces were to be activated electrically it is not too far fetched to think that both color and intensity might be varied at will . . . the most difficult barrier will be that of public acceptance.
— *Derek Phillips*

Sonneman

One of the better known manufacturers of lighting, Sonneman produces a constantly changing range of some 200 cleanly designed and relatively expensive light fixtures. Available in major metropolitan areas or by mail.

Lamp 8105

65½" adjustable chrome arm and adjustable, chrome bulb holder; dimmer switch; 150w flood spot.

Cost: $250.00

Lamp 5104

One version of the wall mounted swivel series; anodized bronze, black, or satin aluminum; 75 flood.

Cost: $89.00

Lamp 5109

18" flexible adjustable arm with wall mounting, chrome or black; 40w; t10 bulbs.

Cost: $49.50

Lamp 7080

11" high cantilevers; 23" long; 2" square brass tubing; plain or black. 60w.

Cost: $110.00

Robert Sonneman Associates Inc.

Lytespan

A flexible, easy to install, track lighting system with a large and fully adjustable range of some 25 snap-on units.

Starlet Series

Variations on a theme: a compact lampholder with different accessories — flexible accordian sleeve, reflector/cowl; parabolic reflector, white, brown, or black.

Basic Universal

Versatile housing with or without cords, matte white or bright aluminum; 75 or 100w.
Cost: $48.00 average per unit, without track.

Lightolier Inc

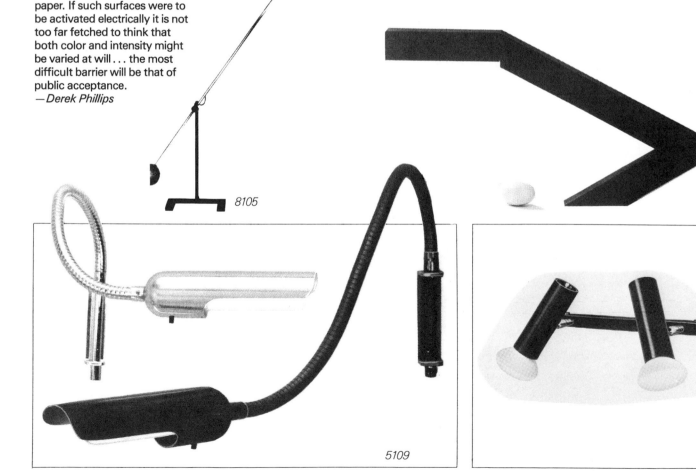

8105

7080

5109

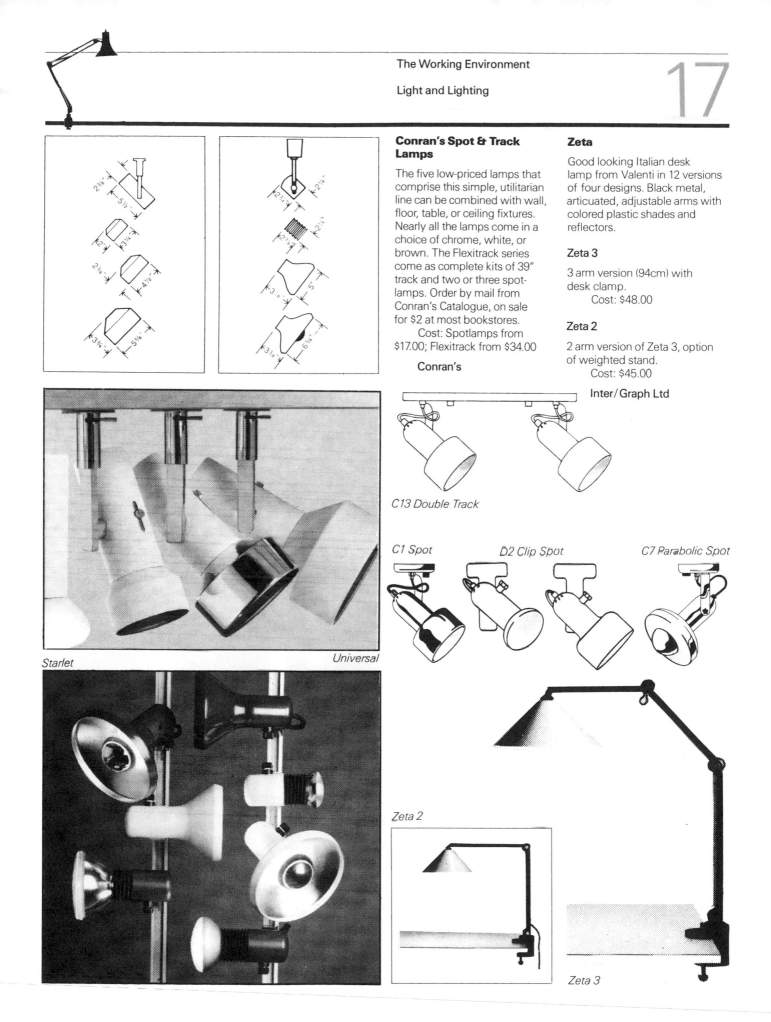

Conran's Spot & Track Lamps

The five low-priced lamps that comprise this simple, utilitarian line can be combined with wall, floor, table, or ceiling fixtures. Nearly all the lamps come in a choice of chrome, white, or brown. The Flexitrack series come as complete kits of 39" track and two or three spotlamps. Order by mail from Conran's Catalogue, on sale for $2 at most bookstores.
  Cost: Spotlamps from $17.00; Flexitrack from $34.00

Conran's

Zeta

Good looking Italian desk lamp from Valenti in 12 versions of four designs. Black metal, articuated, adjustable arms with colored plastic shades and reflectors.

Zeta 3

3 arm version (94cm) with desk clamp.
  Cost: $48.00

Zeta 2

2 arm version of Zeta 3, option of weighted stand.
  Cost: $45.00

Inter/Graph Ltd

C13 Double Track

C1 Spot

D2 Clip Spot

C7 Parabolic Spot

Starlet

Universal

Zeta 2

Zeta 3

Lucifer

A beautiful range of desk lights from A&E Designs, Sweden. Articulated arms and swivel fittings, although lamps always remain in the horizontal position. Brown, red, or white plastic construction with clamps; desk or floor stands, or wall mounts; 15w fluorescent. Not available in the US at press time.

Fagerhults Industri Ab

VitaLight

Advertised as "The Other Sunlight," these are fluorescent tubes that simulate the visible uv spectrum of natural outdoor light. The advantages of full spectrum lighting are proper color rendition, better black/white perception, and reduction of eye strain and fatigue. Available in 14w to 215w.
Cost: $15.70 (60w, 48" triple coil)

Jobec Inc

Light Inc

Minimal lighting in striking designs. Stark, architectural shapes softened by a wide choice of colors (epoxy over metal). Arched tube of light in a square base, fluorescent; available in New York.
Cost: $69.50

Light Inc

Luxo Lamps

The basic range of flexible arm, spring balanced desk lamps that swings, swivels, stretches and flexes up and down. Five models, fluorescent and incandescent, come in eight colors, including chrome, with a choice of brackets, bases, or stands. All models widely available.

LTR Series

The "designers choice" with original Luxo shade and standard 45" arm; 60w.
Cost: $45.00

Fluorescent/ FL Series

Basic 2 tube daylight fluorescent lamp; 45" arm; 15w.
Cost: $68.50

LFM-1 Magnifier

Circular magnifier 5" dia lens (alternate lenses available), with circular T9 fluorescent bulb.
Cost: $79.95

Luxo Lamp Corporation

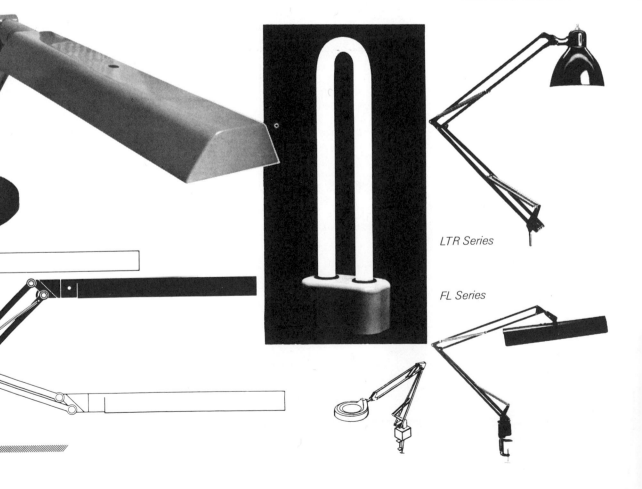

LTR Series

FL Series

MD Worklamp

All matte black with chrome shade, part of an attractive new range from MD Designs, England. A 48" articulated arm with swivel head; 60w. Available by mail order.

Cost: $54.50

Conran's

Vemcolite

A combination fluorescent/incandescent with telescoping arm, this lamp will maintain its position no matter how the slope of the working surface is varied. It will also clamp to most drafting machines. The telescopic arm extends from 26" to 46", and the lamp pivots and swivels as required. Black enamelled metal, 60w with 22w fluorescent circline. Available by mail.

Cost: $119.50

Vemco Corporation

Dazor Lamps

The well-known floating-arm lamps from the '50s, with finger tip control. Four basic models in bronze or gray baked enamel. Popular and widely available.

Universal Fluorescent/Incandescent Lamp

3-way lighting in one reflector that houses a 22w circline tube and a 60w bulb, to be used singly or together.

Cost: $55.75

Dazor Lamp Corporation

Cobra

Swedish lamp, fully adjustable with flexible metal coil neck sheathed in black plastic. The lamp shade has a built-in metal reflector and incorporates a black anti-glare ring. The lamps in this series are available with stand or clamp and come in brown, yellow, red, or white through-colored, impact resistant plastic. 75w. Limited availability.

Cost: $88.00

George Kovacs Inc

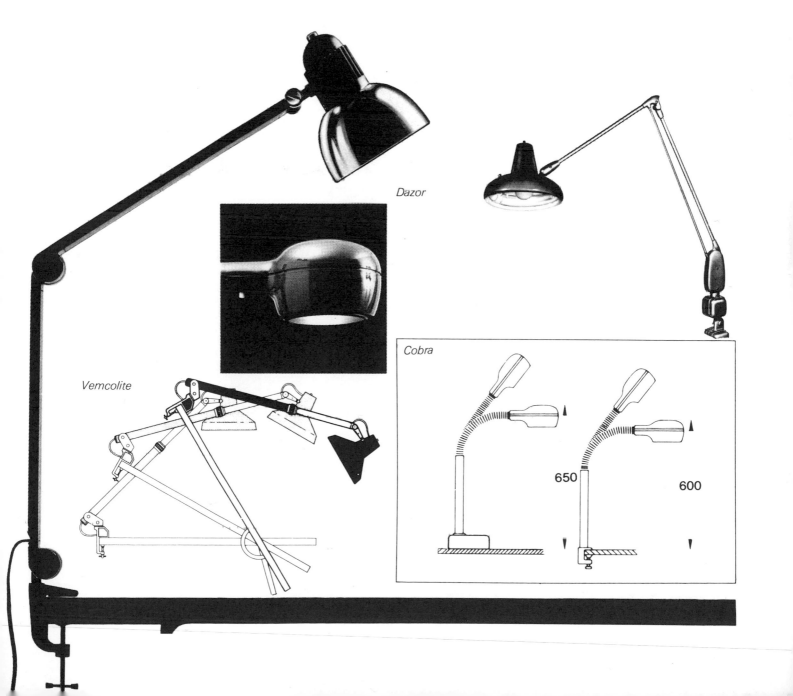

Dazor

Vemcolite

Cobra

650

600

Hardware Specials

Ordinary $1-$15 reflectors from a hardware store can be mounted on gooseneck sockets and used with spot or flood lamps for very effective and inexpensive task and general illumination.

Cost: approximately $25.00 per lamp unit.

Most hardware or building supply stores

Umbrella Lamps

The lights used by photographers have to be lightweight, portable, adjustable, and adaptable to many problems — attributes that make some of them ideal for other professional uses, or even for the home. The photographers folding umbrella is the perfect, functional reflector, available from all photo equipment supply stores.

Cost: $32.00 (with tripod)

Lowel-Light Manufacturing Co

Lamps

The lowest delivered price for any kind of lamp you are likely to ever need is offered by the mail-order lamp company, NAPSCO. They stock all lamps for an amazing variety of professional uses, and discount orders over $15 from 10%-40%. They will take off another 5% if you pre-pay.

Cost: See NAPSCO price list

Nationwide Photolamp Supply Co

(See "Lamp Selector Guide," pages 241-2).

Natural Light Control

3M Light Control

"Scotchtint" fade reducing film is an effective way to control the hazards of sunlight without elaborate blinds. Applied to the inside of the window, it will repel up to 99% of the sun's destructive ultraviolet rays. The film is transparent, not very noticeable from inside, and does not affect colors. Effectively, it becomes part of the glass and is a useful heat control in summer. Widely available from your local 3M Energy Control Center.

Cost: $1.50-$3.00 per sq ft, installed

3M Energy Control Centers

Modern Tint

A darker, polyester film version of "Scotchtint," this "reflecto shield" also completely filters out the uv rays. In fact, it turns your windows into insulated, one-way safety glass. Fully transparent (blue, gold, or bronze tint), heat from the sun is cut by 73%, and in winter heat is kept in. There is also a "Mosaic Tint" version that simulates stained glass. Available in California.

Cost: $1.25-$4.00 per sq ft, installed

Modern Tint

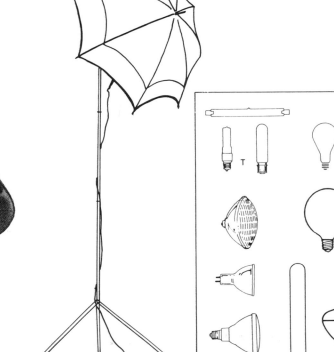

Brentwood Shutters

Custom-made shutters (1¼″ louvres in ¾″ frames) are a less effective but more aesthetic form of sunlight control than the tints. Made of California cedar, all joints are glued and doweled; assembled to your specifications, pre-finished and ready to install. Cost includes hanging strips, hinges and knobs, and choice of coloring; louvres can be horizontal or vertical.

Approximate cost: $177.00 (56″ x 30″, 4 panels)

Ohline Corporation

Riviera Blinds

A good-looking and effective window covering, these are narrow slat, metal blinds in a choice of over 100 colors, with many optional variations of fittings.

Sample cost: $55.36 (60″ x 30″, standard)

Levolor Lorentzen Inc

Thru-Vu Blinds

This is a floor to ceiling, vertical vane blind system, especially useful in larger studio or office environments. The hardware and vanes are custom tailored to exact size and ready to install, and are available in three sizes and many fabrics, aluminum, rigid PVC, or mirror-finish mylar.

Sample cost: $117.00 (60″ x 31″, 3½″ mylar vanes)

Ohline Corporation

Temperature Control

As with light, access to temperature control is a given of your studio space. However, temperature control is not always available from a thermostat on the wall, or a window, or a heating-duct cover. Depending on your geographical location and the structure of your building within that geography, you will have occasion to wish your studio were warmer or cooler at different times of the year. Most importantly, quick changes in temperature and humidity can cause considerable inconvenience, and alter the properties of some equipment such as rubber cement and rapidograph flow.

Heating and cooling equipment are best discussed with your local distributors of such hardware, and are really beyond the purview of this book. However, we will recommend some fans as a practical, low cost method of recirculating heated or cooled air in your studio. We also recommend you look into passive and active solar heating. In coming years, more and more Americans will attempt to use less and less energy, if for no other reason than that it will be increasingly expensive. As the cost of oil, gas, and electric heat continue to rise, so—consequently—will the popularity of alternative energy sources such as solar and wood heat.

Other Homes and Garbage
[Leckie, Masters, Whitehouse & Young]

The spate of general books on renewable energy sources has now given way to a new generation of literature which stresses practical application. If there is any possibility that you could convert to solar energy for your heating, it is now practical and relatively economic to do so, especially as some states offer a financial incentive as encouragement.

The four engineer-authors of *Other Homes And Garbage* cover such fundamentals as how solar technology operates; how to estimate the size of necessary collectors; sizing the storage systems; the economics of solar energy; and the fundamentals of energy conservation. The book, says *Smithsonian,* is a "remarkable achievement." Using simple arithmetic and abundant illustrations, it takes the reader through the design process step-by-step. Its practical orientation is impressive. For a nuts and bolts design book on solar energy, with the added bonus of sections on other aspects of self-sufficiency, this will be a standard text for some time to come.

Cost: $9.95

Sierra Club Books

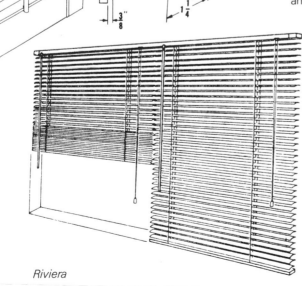

Brentwood

Riviera

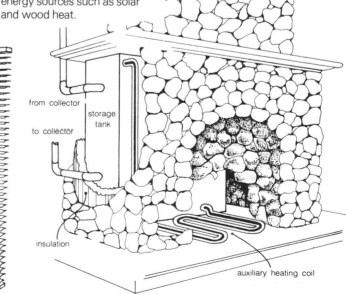

from collector

to collector

storage tank

insulation

auxiliary heating coil

Wood Heat

Wood is the only source of energy that grows, and new techniques in forestry are halving the length of time it takes for a tree to reach maturity. There is still plenty of wood around that is not useful except for burning and heating. Obviously, wood heating systems are not practical for inner cities; but with more and more offices locating in suburban and semi-rural areas, it is a viable alternative for some.

New designs in stoves have more than doubled the length of time it takes for wood to burn. In fact, wood properly burned and controlled is generally 22% cheaper than oil, 55% cheaper than natural gas, and 63% cheaper than electric heat. In the past few years a renaissance of interest in the wood burning stove has stimulated complete redesigns of the nineteenth century hardware for maximum efficiency.

Getting wood has also become more convenient than it used to be in a lot of areas, and a cord (4' x 4' x 8'-or, more precisely, 128 cu. ft.) will cost anywhere from $60 to $150 depending on locality and type of wood. Properly burned, its heat will equal approximately $313 worth of electricity (BTU value).

There are as many types of stoves on the market now as there are types of wood, but only the thermostatically controlled models are really practical. An efficient wood heater should have the following features: airtight construction, bi-metal thermostat; primary and secondary air intakes; firebrick lining; heavy gauge steel construction; large door access; and an ash removal cast-iron grate.

The R-76

One of the best wood stoves currently available, the R-76 comes with all the necessary features plus an optional two-speed 61w blower to maximize its efficiency. The cabinet is made of durable, baked-on black porcelain. It will burn for a full twelve hours in a single load because of the huge 26" firebox. Lift the top of the cabinet and you can even cook on it. 36" (height) x 35½" x 24" (depth); 280 lbs; shipped assembled from local dealer, available regionally.
Cost: $355.00

Shenandoah Manufacturing Co Inc

R76

The Fire Grate

If you have an efficiently designed fireplace, this motorized fire grate will put three times the normal amount of heat from your fire back into the room (normally nearly 90% goes up the chimney). Cool air is drawn evenly through 2" diameter tubes heated by the burning wood; baffles direct the hot air out from the tubes allowing smoke and gases to continue up the chimney. The grate requires no installation; simply attach the two-speed 61w blower. 24" height x 31" x 20" depth; 70 lbs; available regionally.
Cost: $167.90 (7 tube)

Shenandoah Manufacturing Co Inc

The Classic Ceiling Fan

Designed primarily to recirculate preheated factory air, these industrial fans are now used in many chic bars and restaurants. At slow speeds their gentle rhythm is very calming.
Cost: $182.00

Modern Supply Co; Patton Electric Co Inc

Safety Desk Fan

Elected to the Museum of Modern Art's Design Collection, this little Italian fan is quiet and inconspicuous. A metal stand adjusts the tilt, or becomes a handle; a bracket hangs the fan from the wall. Slotted plastic safety case in red or white.
Cost: $25.00

Museum of Modern Art Bookshop II

Portable Desk Fan

Well designed, ultra quiet, with a soft fan blade that is virtually harmless to straying fingers, this fan comes on a chrome stand for angling in any direction. About 8" high. White. Available by mail order.
Cost: $27.50

Brookstone Company

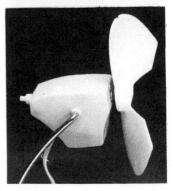

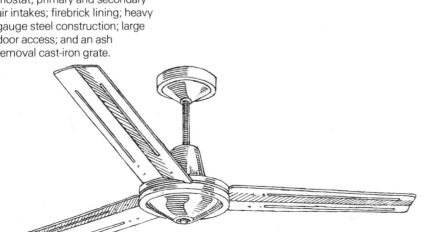

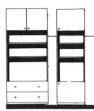

Wall Space, Storage & Shelving

Whether you are a designer, an illustrator, draftsperson, or any other person directly involved in the creation and production of graphics material, adequate wall space is essential. Apart from the areas devoted to the knick-knacks and visual poetry that tend to dot the walls around creative minds, a substantial portion of your wall space must be available to keep track of your current projects, and it is extremely convenient to have all such data immediately available to your eye.

Between art boards, artwork, paper stocks, correspondence, invoices, stationery, the tools and accoutrements of the trade we'll discuss in Section B, and the varieties of personal paraphernelia most people accumulate in their working environments, you will find that ample storage and shelving space is indispensable in your studio. Not only will you want to have as much storage space as possible, but also you will want to be sure it can accommodate the type of work you do. You certainly will need a flat file, or plan chest. If large quantities of oversized artwork pass through your studio you may need several of them. Beyond that, create your system according to your space — nothing defines the work environment more dramatically than your storage methods.

Fibreboard Panels

The cheapest, and probably the easiest, is fibreboard. This useful form of wall pinboard is available from all building supply stores. It's soft and easily cut with an Xacto knife. Usually sold in panels 8' x 4' x ¾" thick, with one side primed for painting.

Visual Scheduling Systems

Provided they are conscientiously maintained, wall display boards are an obvious and simple tool for keeping track of multiple projects. The easiest board to use is magnetic, and there are numerous types on the market, some of which are extremely complex. However, using a basic magnetic, square grid board, plus some simple accessories, you can tailor a system to your own needs. (illustration)
Cost example:
½" gridded magnetic board, gray lines on gray, 24" x 36"; cost: $38.00

Methods Research Corporation

Storage
[Melinda Davis]

The storage solutions collected in this *House & Garden* book are some of the most creative and ingenious around. The book covers the full storage spectrum from the simplest DIY shelving to integral built-in units. A comprehensive selection of this very specific design solution. 160pp, 8½" x 11", color.
Cost: $12.95

Pantheon Books

Build Yourself Towers

The wall towers shown here made of unfinished white birch plywood, hang together on a wall bar. The units have great flexibility with fully adjustable shelving and doors that swing open in two directions. The depths of the units vary, and drawers can be installed at any point. The units are also totally mobile.

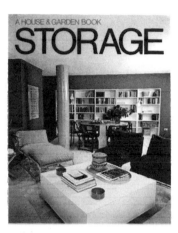

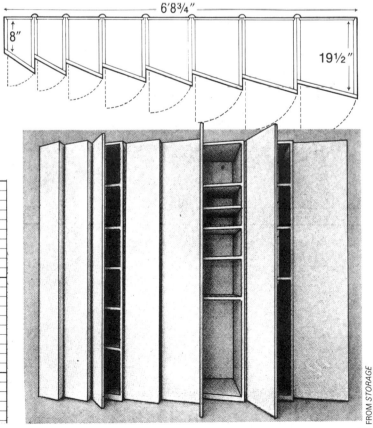

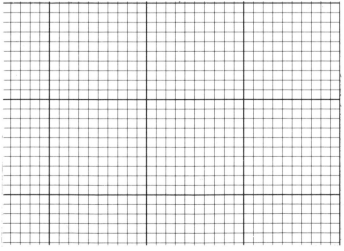

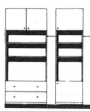

The Cube

One basic storage device, the cube, is multiplied to create the most traditional storage system of all, storage for books. Contemporary design turns the cubes on a diagonal, creating a dramatic effect with the diamond pattern. The bonus is that over-size or undersize books that seem out of place on ordinary shelves are no problem here, where the smooth, horizontal lines are no longer the controlling element. Designer Giovanni Patrini

Conran's Catalog

One of the fastest growing furnishing stores in the world, Conran's market-style retailing chain offers excellently designed products and low prices. The stores are stocked like warehouses and customers help themselves. Everything is packaged ready to be carried away — much of the furniture is marked "QA" (quick assembly), — and is available by mail order. Conran's does *not* offer charge accounts, "designer service," gift wrapping, or discounts. It's all very straightforward, unpretentious, stimulating and slick, as are the shelving units described below.
Cost: $2.00

Conran's; Mayflower Books Inc

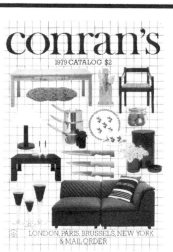

PDQ System

Adjustable, solid wood shelving of the simplest kind, with uprights drilled at 2" intervals, metal back brace, and five steel reinforced 15"D or 12"D shelves. Extension units also available. Height 73", width 36", supplied as knock-down kit.
Cost: $64.00;
extension: $49.25

Conran's

Mesh System

An attractive open storage system of upright wood frames with white, welded steel mesh. Five shelves of white melanine covered chipboard, the middle & bottom ones are fixed; metal back brace. Extension units available. 73" x 32" x 13", supplied as knock-down kit.
Cost: $110.00;
extension: $90.00

Conran's

PDQ System

Mesh System

An Open Shelf Room Divider

This is a do-it-yourself project
that is tailored for your specific
space. Using 18" width pine
boards for the floor to ceiling
dividers, the shelves can be
varied in their depths and quantity. Remember to work to a
module to simplify the carpentry
problems. Support the shelves
on simple 2" x 1" wood strip
brackets nailed to the uprights.

As a divider or set against a
wall beneath track spotlights,
most effective, low-cost storage
method. Using plywood or chipboard is cheaper still and looks
just as good if finished
and painted.

—from *Storage,* Melinda Davis

Open shelf room divider

Rolled Graphics Files

A steel stack file system
of square tubes that can be
expanded to any height or
width. The top of each unit has a
stacking rim that interlocks with
the unit below, and a fastener to
clip stacks together laterally.
Units come in 5" x 2⅛" squares
or 6" x 3⅜" squares, with seven
different depths for each.

Stack File

Three units of 2⅛" squares plus
two units of 3⅜" squares, with
cap and base.
Cost: $190.00

Storage Square Tube Files

Lightweight corrugated fibreboard version of the above. Each
unit has either eighteen 4" openings or thirty-two 3" openings
with two depths.
Cost: $25.00

Plan Hold

The Wireworks

Developed from in-store
window display systems, this
chrome wire furniture can be
used for airy, attractive storage
and shelving units, with or without wheels. All units are also
available with a large selection
of accessories, in galvanized or
stainless steel finish, and come
knocked down. Mail order.

FDM-07 Shelving

68" x 24" x 18", chrome.
Cost: $237.50

FDM-04 Shelving

74" x 24" x 13", chrome.
Cost: $110.00

**Sid Diamond Furniture
Design**

FDM-07

Britta System

A basic solid pine drawer and
divided cube, also solid pine,
comb-jointed and glued and
finished in clear lacquer. The
adjustable internal divisions
make four open shelves. Combinations of these two units
make a flexible system that
looks good anywhere.

Cost: drawer unit: $69.00;
cube units: $59.00

Conran's

〈使えない〉デザインの意味

This Japanese moveable
storage unit has impressive
structural qualities and cannot
be bought, but you could easily
make it yourself. The basic five-
sided cube can be adapted
endlessly. The cubes are glued
and screwed together at the
slight overlaps on their edges.
Build your own wall on wheels
from a series of plywood
9″ x 9″ x 9″ cubes.

Steel Box Lockers

Lockers are ubiquitous. They
turn up in schools, factories,
hospitals, terminals, and —
now — offices. Principally
available from industrial equipment manufacturers, they make
excellent storage units. The
eighteen-locker unit is one of the
more useful versions, and can,
of course, be extended endlessly;
each locker cube costs about
$13.00. Louvered doors, heavy
duty hinges, high grade enamel
in gray, tan, green, and red.
Locks optional. 72″ x 12″ x 12″.
Look for used ones.

Cost: $234.00

**National Business
Furniture; Lyon Metal
Products Inc**

$12⁵⁰ ✱
IN-STOCK

FDM-04

Clothing Exchange Locker

Designed for garment and linen
inventories, this steel locker has
ten compartments with separate,
lockable doors, all of which can
be opened with a single master
key. Gray enamel finish, but easily re-sprayed. 78" x 15" x 15".
    Cost: $281.00

**Global Equipment
Company**

Stacloc System

A handsome modular, flat-
shelf storage system that can be
expanded and modified easily as
your needs dictate. All units are
finished with clear, dull, vinyl,
and can be stacked up to six feet
high. There are four basic interchangeable units that are built
on two sizes of standard bases.
    Costs: 2-shelf unit, 12" x 47"
x 31": $65.00;
2-shelf unit, 12" x 36" x 24":
$50.00;
3-shelf unit, 12" x 47" x 32":
$85.00;
3-shelf unit, 12" x 36" x 24":
$65.00;
Base units: $23.00 and $25.00

Charrette Corporation

Singer's Knockdown Flatfiles

As you will notice, plan chests
or flat-files are costly pieces of
furniture; yet they are very difficult items to dispense with.
With a few basic woodworking
tools you can build your own for
under $100. Designer David
Singer's plans for an open,
sliding tray version has the
added convenience of knocking
down flat, with inside tray
dimensions of 2½" x 25". The
plans shown are for two eight-
tray cabinets set side by side to
create a useful benchtop space
of 31" x 62".
    Cost: approximately $110
(materials only).

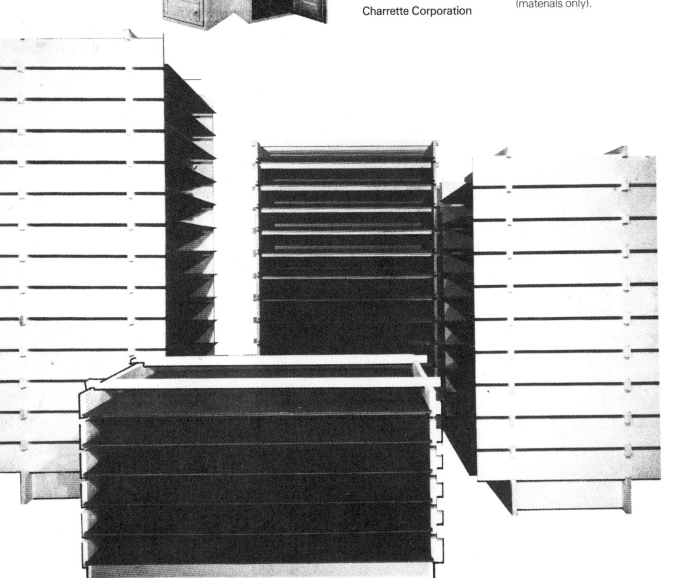

Stacloc System

Materials required:

6 29" 2" x 4" finished pine
4 31" 2" x 4" finished pine
4 ³/₄" 31" x 29" plywood panels
2 ³/₄" 38" x 29" plywood panels
28 25" 1" x 1" finished, oiled pine
2 ³/₄" 31" x 26¹/₂" plywood panels
14 ¹/₂" 25" x 26" fibreboard
panels
14 25" ¹/₂" x 2" pine endpieces
1 1¹/₂" 31" x 80" hollow door,
cut down)
Elmers glue
1¹/₂" panel nails
1¹/₂" narrow wood screws

Wood Plan Chests

All oak interlockable units
with mortise and tenon joints.
Drawers operate smoothly on
lubricated wood runners, and
wooden dowels align the five
drawer units in place when
stacked. Surprisingly inexpensive furniture when compared
with other flat file systems. Two
basic drawer sizes: 37⁵/₈" x25"
x 2" and 42¹/₂" x 32¹/₄" x 2".
Shipped from Wisconsin.
(illustration)
    Cost: $264 (small size +
base & cap unit)

Mayline

Stacor 25-Drawer Flat-File

Extremely useful, shallow-draw
cabinet of steel with nylon glides
and large rear hoods on all
drawers. Unfortunately, its high
price makes it a luxury item for
most small studios. Special
order only.
    Cost: $890.00

Flax stores

Fibreboard Flat Files

Walnut grained fibreboard with
metal frames that interlock when
stacked. An inexpensive and
durable five drawer unit in four
dimensions, all with 2" high
drawers. Widely available.
    Cost: $79 (22³/₄" x 27" x 2")

Banker's Box

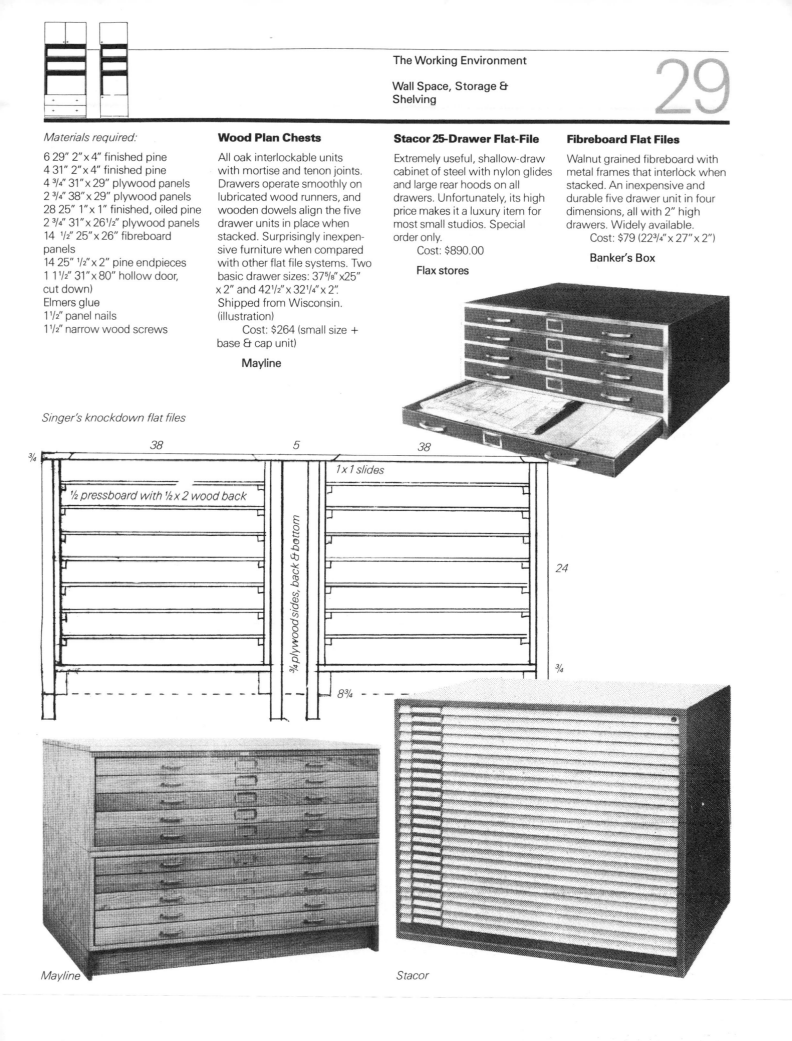

Singer's knockdown flat files

Mayline

Stacor

Steel Planchests

Heavy gauge steel five drawer
unit with integral cap and
optional base. Operates on ball-
bearing rollers, and each draw is
equipped with a rear hood and
hinged front compressors.
Available in gray, white or black
enamel finish, and in five
different sizes.

Cost: $329.00 (37" x 25"
x 2⅛" + base)

Charrette Corporation

Economical Flat File

Probably the least expensive
system on the market, this is a
tough, sturdy, corrugated fibreboard flat file with a hefty ¾" x
1½" wood frame that can ac-
comodate 30 drawers. Two
series are offered, 38½" x 24½"
x 1½" and 44½" x 30½" x 1½". The
files come in cartons of five only.

Cost: $330.00 (30 smaller
size files + 10-shelf frame)

**Global Equipment
Company**

Storage Cabinets

24 models of all-metal cabinets,
available in red, yellow, blue, or
white. Shown here, the 94
series, 67 series, and 33 series,
all 11" wide and 16" deep, with
two drawer heights.

Cost: range between
$50.00 and $100.00

Flax stores

Series 33

Series 67

Global flat files

Series 94

Cardboard Storage Systems

A corrugated fibreboard box
storage system developed for
bank records in 1917, this is an
economical way to store anything
not needed on a day-to-day
basis. Banker's Box have
expanded the original idea of a
filing/storage box into a vast
array of different storage
containers with a variety of steel
stacking frames.

Super Stor Drawer

The basic file comes in four
standard sizes: black and walnut, or black and white finish,
with coated drawers to reduce
friction. The "super" version is
steel reinforced with extra-
strength corrugated fibreboard.
The standard version will stack
five or six high with stability,
using metal interlock clips.
Supplied knocked down in
quantities of six.
Widely available.
    Cost: $8.95 ea. (black, letter
size)
$4.50 ea. (standard black and
white, letter size)

R-Kive #725

A simpler box with lid, it comes
in one size; will hold one cubic
foot of files. Walnut finish;
cartons of twelve, supplied flat.
    Cost: $1.95 ea.

Project Box

Keeps related files on current
or completed projects neatly
together. Two sizes of 5" capacity,
with handle, that fit standard filing cabinets; cartons of twelve,
supplied flat.
    Cost: $.95 ea.

    Banker's Box

Palaset

This stunningly simple cube
storage system from Finland
offers a variety of 13½" square
modular cubes and drawer that
allow considerable versatility in
building up your own unit.
Palaset is made of structural
foam, but unlike many plastic
products it is spray painted and
will not attract dust. Actually, the
cubes can be repainted, nailed,
sawn, and drilled just as wood
can. There are eleven components, any of which can be
bought singly, in a range of five
colors. They are connected with
plastic dowels. Widely available.
    Cost: $29.00 (two-shelf
cube); $240 (combination unit
shown below)

    Conran's, Inter/Graph Ltd

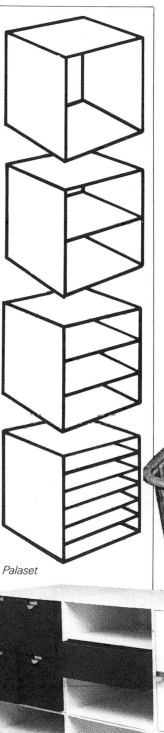

Palaset

Modular Plastic Box System

The standard industrial, molded
gray plastic box, with molded
grooves all around, that can be
adapted to a variety of office
uses. These boxes are designed
to carry objects within adjustable
compartments; they can be
stacked, affixed to wall spaces
with their dividers functioning as
shelves, or hung individually by
their lips as drawers. Twenty-
seven sizes, and they can be re-
sprayed to your color scheme.
    Cost: from $3.80 to
$14.50 each; dividers: from 13¢
to $1.70 each

    Global Equipment Company

Super-stor

Palaset

System 3

This versatile filing and storage system is designed primarily for the studio. It is based on gangable cabinets containing drawers that can be combined one, two, or four within a single larger cabinet. With connecting hardware, the cabinets assemble into freestanding blocks or roll-around units in any of three drawer depths. Each drawer unit divides into three, six, or twelve compartments. This Martin system, made of high impact resistant ABS plastic in light grey or brown, allows a static combination storage system, or a mobile unit of two, four, six, or eight cells. Very neat.

Cost: $295.80 (mobile unit shown below)

Martin Instrument Co.

Work Surfaces

It may be true, to paraphrase Parkinson's First Law, that work expands to fill the space available for its completion. Nonetheless, the designer has not yet been heard from who ever had too much tabletop or other flat surface space in a graphics studio, and the unwritten law of flat work space is, get as much as you can. The law applies to workspace in general.

To fill the work table need, any large, flat surface will suffice. Ordinarily you will want flat work surfaces at two different heights in a graphics studio — one about 29" from the floor for sitting work, and one at a comfortable standing height. Most of your standing work will be done at a drafting table, which should be adjustable both in height and tilt so that you can suit your personal needs. A draftperson's stool will provide a perch at the right height. In general, the tops of your flat working surfaces should be washable and easy to clean. Laminated plastic, wood, and PVC (poly vinyl chloride) all do quite nicely.

The Hollow Door

Most building suppliers or large hardware stores that sell lumber also sell hollow construction, lightweight doors of varying dimensions. This is probably the cheapest, substantial looking work surface that is readily available almost anywhere. All you have to do is finish it with two or three coats of clear polyurethane varnish, or cover it with Laminene.

Cost: $15 (approximately)

Vyco Laminene

This highly recommended drawing surface of five-ply vinyl not only protects all furniture surfaces, but provides a soft yet firm, self-sealing, and easily cleaned cover. One side is soft tint, non-glare green, the other a soft ivory. Affix with white glue or spray-mounts, depending on the surface you are covering. Available in seven widths of 10-yard rolls, or fourteen precut standard sizes, from all art stores.

Cost: $25.00 (36" x 72"); $105.00 (36" x 10 yds.)

Vyco Products

Saw Horses

The simplest trestle to suspend your work surface between is a pair of saw horses from a building supply center. The horses range from heavy-duty ready-mades to timber-and-hinge kits. Other, more elaborately crafted, are available from stores that sell unfinished wooden furniture. Make sure you get the height and width that is right for you.

Cost: $15.00 each, approximately

Do a Desk

A system of individually produced components that you put together however you like. You choose pedestal, base, and top. The combinations are endless, and you can have any item tailored to your own measurements. For example:

Desk: 6. 13. 19

Utilizes a metal three-drawer pedestal with white or chocolate file, oak saw horse base, and 1½" oak 24" x 60" top.

Cost: $140.00

Door Store

System 3

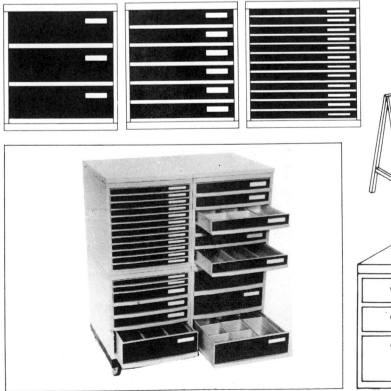

Desk 6. 13. 9

Table Tops

Oak edged drafting table with reversible putty/ivory vinyl top. An oak strip, 1½" x 1½" is all around, and 2" wide along top edge for easy attachment of lamp or parallel rule. Top comes in two sizes: 37½" x 60" and 37½" x 72". The oak trestles (¾" x 2" and 28" or 34" high) make sturdy bases and are finished in clear polyurethane. Available by mail.

Cost: $162.50 (37½" x 60" + 34" trestle)

Charrette Corporation

Stacloc Tables

A more sophisticated version of the basic board-across-two-trestles. The birch plywood trestles feature reversible edges for flat or sloped work surface, and have a shelf as part of their bottom support. Two sizes, supplied knocked down. Table top is 1" thick slab of birch plywood.

Cost: Trestles, $85 per pair (largest size); table top: $95.00

Charrette Corporation

Stacloc Special

The versatile 36" x 72" work table, supplied knocked down, is complete with a Stacloc trestle, a work top, and two of the Stacloc storage units mentioned earlier.

Cost: $270.00 (complete)

Charrette Corporation

Packing Assembly Table

A sturdy, low-cost, all-steel factory work table in standard grey enamel. Ten sizes in a choice of three heights and a useful optional end tray. Other optional extras include a low shelf, bench drawer, and a pressed wood work-top finish.

Cost: $145.50 (basic 36" x 72" table with end tray)

Global Equipment Company

Packing assembly table

Stacloc trestles

Stacloc

Altona Trestle Table

A very elegant ash veneer table top in natural or black finish, suspended on chromed steel trestle legs. 30" x 72" x 28".
 Cost: $180.00

Conran's

Logus Worktable

63" x 29½" x 28" white, laminate top and steel colored epoxy legs; French.
 Cost: $152.00

Design Research

Arredo

A modular line of plastic laminated desks and shelving units by Neolt, designed to create the total environment for the design studio. Standard color is white.
 Cost: see catalog

Sam Flax;
Martin Instrument Co

Pupil

A sturdy, minimal, drawing stand by Bieffe has a board top that can be adjusted at four different angles with three pivoting trays suspended from the frame. Chrome, white, yellow, red, or green. Board sizes: 28¾" x 49¼" or 23½" x 45¼", height 27½". Limited availability.
 Cost: $160.00

Inter/Graph Ltd.

Designer 1 Fold-A-Way

A design table that collapses neatly to a 5½" depth. Basic and simple metal frame in four colors with three top sizes: 24" x 36", 31" x 42", or 26" x 48".
 Cost: $102.00

Plan Hold

Planmaster

A semi-automatic drafting table with spring-loaded height adjustment, leveling floor glides, and a ratchet for pre-set board angles. Planmaster tables come in standard two-tone gray with several optional features: storage tray for under-top storage, locking tool drawer, pencil trough, and bookcase.
 Cost: $359.00 (fully equipped)

Plan Hold

Pupil

Designer 1 Fold-A-Way

Logus

Unigraph

A Bieffe version of the basic drawing table that is also available in foldaway style. Solid steel, stove enamelled stand that accommodates a board up to 31½" x 55" size. Adjustable height and angle. A tray and three swivel draws are optional extras.

Cost: $145.00 (12¼" x 18½" top, plus extras)

Flax stores; Inter/Graph Ltd

Duograph

Another simple Italian drawing table with spring loaded, manual angle and height adjustment. Stand available in four colors, with top in two sizes (30" x 42" or 31" x 47") of either laminated plastic, poplar wood, or PVC.

Cost: $145.00 (both sizes of wood top)

Flax stores; Inter/Graph Ltd

Ranger

A thrifty, traditional, four-post table with steel end cleat top that tilts through an angle of 50.° Complete with tool drawer and wide shallow drawer. Standard desert sand finish. Four top sizes available: 37½" x 60", 37½" x 72", 42" x 72", and 42" x 84". Well known for its weight, and also available in wood.

Cost: $198.00 (37½" x 60")

Mayline

POP

A more sophisticated Bieffe design table, pneumatically counterbalanced and operated by a foot pedal. Takes boards of laminated plastic, poplar wood, or PVC in sizes up to 38" x 72". Stand in black or white only.

Cost: $345.00 (38" x 48", wood top)

Flax stores

Globus

A heavy, adjustable stand with foot operated oleopneumatic action. Board angle adjusted by lever, and takes boards up to 38" x 60" of laminated plastic, poplar wood, or PVC. Stand in black or white only.

Cost: $450.00 (38" x 48", wood top)

Flax stores

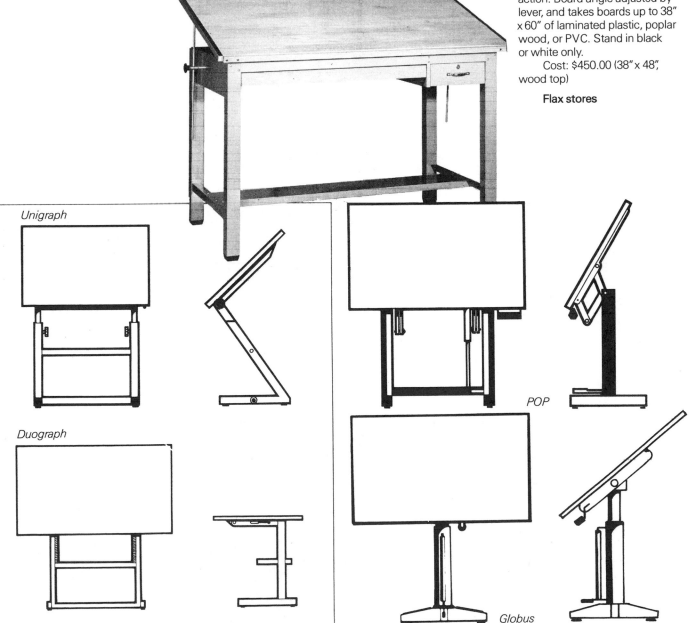

Ranger

Unigraph

Duograph

POP

Globus

Duolite

The ultimate in combination light box and drawing table, this Bieffe design is the smaller version (23½" x 29"). Comes in white only with fully adjustable light intensity and pneumatic stand. Limited availability.
   Cost: $990.00

   Flax stores

Aero/Core Drawing Boards

Very light, strong boards made of a tough multi-cell core laminated between a hard, kiln-dry wood. Boards constructed this way can be more durable than solid wood, and will not warp or crack. Available in three sizes: 24" x 36", 31" x 42", or 36" x 48", which will fit drafting table stands. There are seven other sizes, from 12" x 17" to 31" x 42" for portable use, and all ten sizes come with or without a metal edge.
   Cost: $29.50 (31" x 42", metal edge)

   Pickett Industries

Study

Another Italian drawing table from Neolt, with spring balanced height and tilt. Heavy gauge base includes bookshelf, and the formica top comes in three sizes. Not widely available.
   Cost: $288.25 (32" x 48")

   Sam Flax;
Martin Instrument Co

Bieffe Drawing Boards

Good quality boards available in five sizes (30" x 42" up to 38" x 72") with laminated plastic finish, poplar wood, or PVC.
   Cost: $65.00 (38" x 48", wood)

   Flax stores

Moveable Storage

As dentists and surgeons have long known, it's often easier to bring your tools to your work than the other way 'round. Trolleys that hold your basic implements allow flexibility in your work area — particularly in an open plan situation. There are many kinds of moveable work stations, and those built especially for designers tend to be the more expensive models. Other mobile carts are manufactured for use in hospitals, factories, restaurants, and home kitchens; most are intended to withstand heavy wear. We've selected a few of the most useful versions of this increasingly popular form of furniture.

Heavy Duty Casters

Truth to tell, you can add your own casters to nominally stable storage pieces without enormous difficulty. If you decide on such a course, we suggest you avoid the lightweight casters, which break rather easily. You needn't get the extra heavy duty casters either; but the normal heavy duty ones — hot-forged and capable of carrying over 400 lb. — will do most office or studio jobs with dispatch. Many sizes and specifications are available.
   Cost: $31.20 (2" wheel width, 7¼" high, mold-on rubber swivel type)

   Global Equipment Company

Duolite

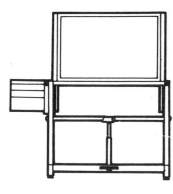

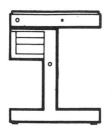

Multipurpose Steel Cart

Stainless steel, with adjustable shelves and additional drawer units available.
> Cost: $180.00

Market Forge

Portable Tool Chest

The basic sort of three-drawer roller mechanic's cabinet, with a large sliding door compartment 32½" x 26½" x 17" overall. Six-drawer chest without tool tray can be added on top. Everything is lockable.
> Cost: Cabinet: $152.00; chest: $120.00

Global Equipment Company

Mobile Work Bench

A superb heavy duty industrial chest/table/cabinet on wheels, accessible from both sides with drawers at both ends. Several optional features designed for machinists only. Nine-drawer model, 29" x 46" top.
> Cost: $850.00

Global Equipment Company

The Boby Taboret

A portable storage system made up of modular sections that add up to an ingeniously flexible unit. All versions incorporate swing-out trays, shelves, and a deep pocket with adjustable depth. Made of plastic by Bieffe, these taborets can be disassembled for cleaning. They are mounted on three parallel roll casters. Available in five colors and six versions, although all components are available separately.
> Cost: $175.00 (three-drawer) — $259.00

Inter/Graph Ltd

Stile Taboret

A four-drawer version multi-purpose cabinet from Neolt in ABS anti-static plastic. All units have a 17" x 16" top surface; 12" x 11" shelves; carpet casters, and adjustable deep pockets. Basically there are two units, 30" and 22" high, with or without drawers. An optional chart reference arm can be attached.
> Cost: $197.00 (30" high, 3-drawer)

**Sam Flax;
Martin Instrument Company**

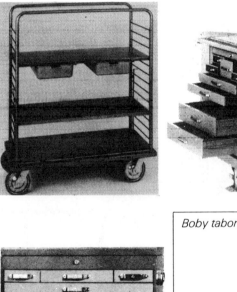

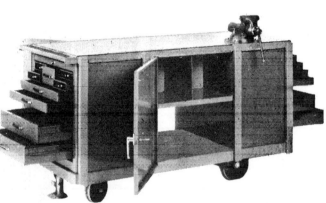

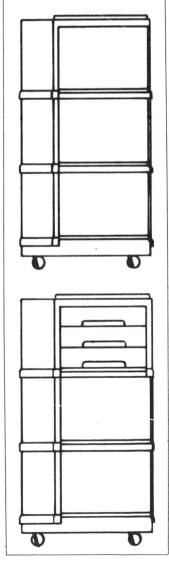

Stile taboret

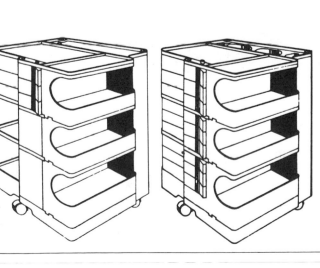

Boby taboret

Chairs

In the past few decades, most design innovation in seating has come from the commercial environment of contract furnishing, or from architects and industrial designers. Commercial specifications have given us the tilt, swivel, stacking, bentwood and steel tube varieties of chair. Seating for work is quite different, obviously, from seating for leisure although recently the former has found its way into homes for the latter use.

Wooden Stool

An inexpensive, durable, all purpose work stool made of birch wood, with 14" seat. Tongue and groove joinery, catalysed varnish finish. Fitted with nylon glides, the stool comes in three heights, 18", 24", and 30".
Cost: $32.95 (24")

Charrette Corporation

Wooden Steno Chair

A traditional specialist office chair that is both comfortable and well made. Fully adjustable with swivel.
Cost: $130.00

Jasper Seating Company

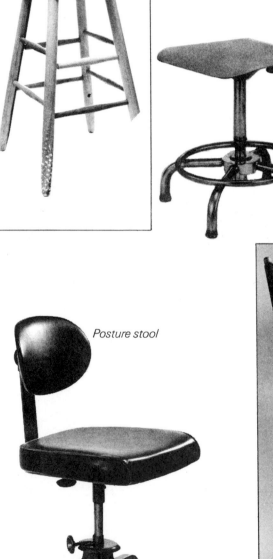

Laboratory Chair

Designed for the ultra-clean environment, this all-stainless steel swivel chair with a flexi-back is adjustable and also very comfortable.
Cost: $60

Adjusto Equipment Company

Posture Stool

Adjustable height from 17" to 23". Four way back adjustment with casters. Finished in gray enamel and upholstered in black vinyl.
Cost: $77.45

Flax stores

The Directors High Chair

A tall version of the popular collapsible canvas and wood directors chair. Again, a very comfortable seat for the drafting table.
Cost: $68

Sears/Roebuck

Steno chair

Posture stool

Vertebra

This advanced seating design from Italy is based on a telescopic forward movement and spring-loaded pivots for back tilting. For anyone who has to spend hours in a chair, all postures are "ideal" and any movement is automatic in all three versions shown.
Cost: see catalog

Krueger Corporation

The Old Office Chair

A particular favorite, the adjustable tilt-swivel-and-roll oak office chair was popular worka-day seating in the '40s. Although modern versions have been manufactured, they are seldom so well designed as the originals, due to misguided efforts to reduce costs by saving on materials. The hardy and often beautiful old ones are increas-ingly difficult to find. Old or new these chairs can be expensive — so you might as well go for the originals. You may still get a deal.
Cost: $60.00 and up

Used office furniture stores

Table Seating

Some of the simplest, best designed chairs around, including a Bauhaus and a Corbusier design. All available from one source, Conran's. All should be widely available in all locales.
Cost: From $40 to $129

Conran's Taylor & Ng

"Hard To Find Tools"

The Brookstone Catalog is a fascinating and useful tool in itself to have around—some people get addicted to it. It offers an extensive selection of rare and ingenious tools and equipment for all sorts of professional specializations. The catalog is published several times a year, and you never know what will turn up in there next.

Angle Lamp

A rugged, utility, counter-balanced lamp, fully adjustable. Ventilated shade for 75w bulb; 34½" reach; universal mounting clamp.
    Cost: $29.95

Magnifier

Strong 4" diameter lens mounted on flexible gooseneck will adjust to any angle or position. Heavy iron base, chrome plated ferrule and rim.
    Cost: $16.50

The Brookstone Company

Wood Files

If you really prefer wood to steel or plastic, you simply have to pay for it. Arenson manufactures a whole range of office type furniture entirely of wood with some metal finishing. Available regionally.

Drawer Files

Lateral or vertical cabinet in walnut with black trim, 2, 3, or 4 drawer, with floor glides. The backs are as finished as the fronts.
    Cost: $369.00 (36" x 19" x 52", 4-drawer, lateral)

Arenson Inc.

Security Devices

According to FBI statistics, 85% to 90% of all break-ins occur through side or back doors. The other 10% to 15% usually involve windows, but getting the loot out requires opening a door anyway. Usually, a burglar opens one or two doors immediately; just in case. Most businesses need to have at least their doorways protected, especially in ground level situations.

The L4 Wireless Radio System

This alarm counters the moves that most burglars must and do make to gain entry. The alarm is sounded by switches on all outside doors, and there is also a completely portable "panic button." A control unit receives the signal and activates a loud electronic siren. All the door transmitters (one per door) operate on transistor batteries, and the radio range is 150 ft.
    Sample cost: $217 (2 door transmitters, 2 magnetic switches and a control/receiver unit).

Mountain West Alarm Co.

Two good wired systems for the do-it-yourself installer can be obtained from:

Eico Electronic Instrument Company; Emerson Electric Company

Sound

To complete the office/studio environment, a sound system is an obvious necessity. Choosing from the vast array of hi-fidelity stereo components is a very personal matter of taste and pocketbook, and is beyond the scope of this book. We'll simply focus on the best designed system currently available for the hell of it—a system on permanent exhibition at the Museum of Modern Art.

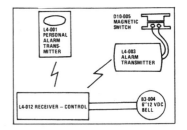

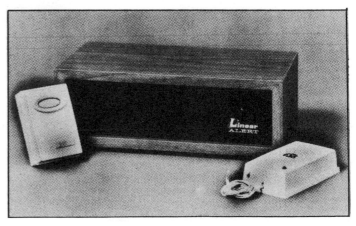

Bang & Olufsen

This small Danish audio manufacturer has developed a sound component system that is beautiful in its simplicity, both technically and aesthetically. It has won many international awards and the components have been designed for the non-technically minded. There are very few knobs and dials to play with, and the equipment is cheaper than it looks.

Beomaster 1900 Receiver

The bottom of the line B&O receiver has touch sensitive electronic controls switching with some controls hidden under the lift-up top. The tuner section is the part that has been acclaimed for its advanced technology. The 1900 is missing the remote control facilityt and modified front panel of the more sophisticted B&O receivers.
Cost: $495.00

Beogram 2400 Turntable

The cheaper of two turntable models that has no apparent controls — they are all incorporated in the supersensitive flush touch-panel. A machine with beautiful balance; MMC cartridge; electronic servo-drive; and pendulum suspension.
Cost: $325.00

Beovox P-30 Speakers

The second in a range of seven different speaker units, the P-30s do not use the phase link drive of the more expensive models, but eliminate distortion through a modified 6dB/octave filter technique.
Cost: $250.00 (per pair)

**Bang & Olufsen
of America Inc**

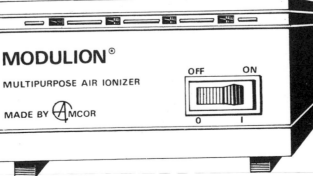

Modulion PR

Vitamins Of The Air

Research has shown that our moods, energy, and health can be markedly improved through control of the electrical charges in the air we breathe. Ionization is the modern method of refreshing and renewing air which has become oversaturated with positive ions. In the urban, air-conditioned environment, all sorts of pollution deplete the negative ions, creating an imbalance leading to fatigue, irritability, headaches, respiratory problems, etc. Negative ion enrichment helps restore freshness to the air in a way air-conditioning systems cannot do.

The Modulion PR Ionizer

To produce negative ions, by "high-voltage corona discharge effect," this ionizer converts 110 volts to 5000 volts, forcing out electrons at the rate of 250 billion per second. The discharging electrons attach themselves to oxygen molecules creating negative ions. Although this is a high energy device, its amperage is negligible and therefore quite safe. It is particularly effective in eliminating cigarette smoke. Available by mail order.
Cost: $79.95

California Air Environments

Arbitare

An excellent magazine of the interior environment, especially with regard to hardware, this import from Italy is printed in both English and Italian. A certain number of the products reviewed eventually find their way to the United States, and they embody a design and presentation attitude not widely prevalent in the States. The careful selection of advertisements alone is worth the price of the publication. Gravure, 96 pages. Becoming available at most good bookshops.

 Cost: $3.75

Arbitare

Attention To Detail
[Herbert H Wise]

A recent, luxurious paperback collects together the best of all the easily available options for the fixtures in the home or workplace. This very visual, full-color reference to lighting fixtures, storage systems, shelving concepts, tools, worksurfaces, handles, knobs and toilets is beautifully simple and eloquent. Almost in passing the photographs of interiors are full of interesting design solutions, and particularly useful is the lamp selector guide charts and index to manufacturers. One could almost see this format as the beginning of a series of popular interior design journals.

 Cost: $9.95

Quick Fox

Environmental Graphics

These are very large scale graphics designed to transform existing surroundings by creating visual illusion with wall space. The graphics for walls come in different sizes ranging from 6'6" x 8'8" to 8'9" x 24'5" in some 45 different concepts. There are also graphics for doors. Environmental Graphics are supplied in up to eight panels, mounted like wallpaper, and are washable. Some of the effects attained with the high quality lithographs are totally surreal.

 Cost: from $15 to $210

Environmental Graphics Inc

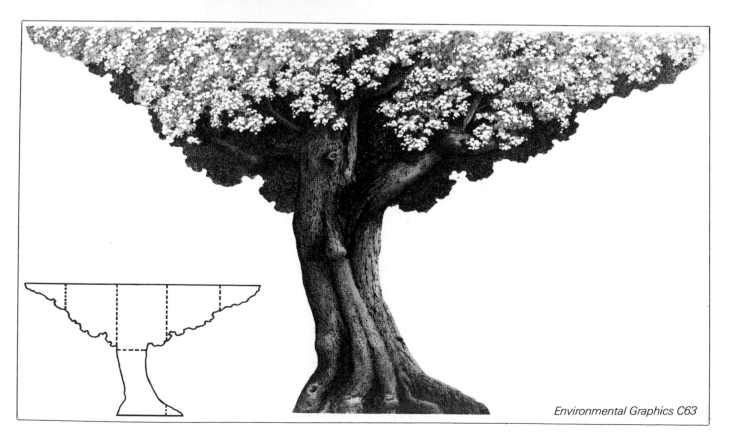

Environmental Graphics C63

Paper, Film & Boards

Drawing and Drafting Tools

Pens, Markers, Inks
& Pencils

Brushes and Airbrushes

Tapes and Adhesives

Color and Paints

Graphic Aids

Larger Equipment

FROM FLAX ART MATERIALS GIFT CATALOG, 1979

B

Even in the midst of recession, the business in graphic arts materials is booming. Improving their old stand-bys, and creating entirely new tools for the trade that accomplish more tasks better and more efficiently, the major manufacturers and suppliers have all increased the range of their products. Competition is fierce among them, of course, and many are developing new outlets for their wares, intending to supply the general public as well as the professional and dedicated amateur.

Whether as a cause or an effect of all this activity, large conglomerates—some newly evolved as if solely for this purpose—are taking over the field. Reckitt & Coleman has bought the old, established house of Winsor & Newton; Letraset has taken over Charles T. Bainbridge's Sons; CBS has acquired X-acto; Hunt has purchased such firms as Bienfang, Boston, and Lit-Ning; the huge Times-Mirror corporation now owns Chartpak and Grumbacher. Results of these mergers, take-overs, and purchases have included a great deal of product improvement, increased importing, more aggressive marketing strategies, and higher retail prices.

Even though the general public is now seen to be an important market for graphic arts supplies, the vast bulk of the industry's materials and equipment are selected and purchased by art directors, designers, and illustrators (71%)*; and even though new, general markets are being opened, most such supplies are purchased directly from art stores (81%) or from graphic arts catalogues (12%). In response to pressure from this major consuming group, particular improvements have been made in the quality of pressure graphics, markers, and technical pens. Quality, rather than dollar savings, has long been this market's prime concern, and in the past few years the industry has responded accordingly: prices are high, but in general so is quality. For a variety of reasons, the best equipment and material continues to originate in Europe.

In compiling the following selection of the best graphic tools and materials available, we considered, first, their creative usefulness; second, their overall quality; third, their value relative to other, similar items; fourth, price; and fifth, availability. Reflecting the rather bizarre economic picture that confronts the world at the beginning of the 1980s, prices are subject to considerable change. As a result, those prices cited herein should be seen as a comparative guide only, and not as definitive.

By quality, we refer not only to the quality of materials used in the manufacture of an item, but also the quality of its visual appearance and ergonomic design—aesthetics as *applied to function.* One indicator of quality now used by major suppliers is the "Art-Tec" mark, indicating that the product has been "designed and approved by professionals." While such a designation may be a helpful guide from time to time, it should be noted that the Art-Tec mark does not signify an independent appraisal from outside the industry, and it may serve on occasion as a marketing ploy only. Nonetheless, Art-Tec items are, ordinarily, unconditionally guaranteed against *any* defect.

Everything listed in this section is available, and addresses of all manufacturers and distributors are provided in the book's appendix. Major retail or mail order suppliers are named below. Some of the items here are available exclusively through specific retail outlets such as Sam Flax or Charrette; but often they are available elsewhere under a different brand name. When we list Charrette, for instance, as the major source of a product, we do so partly because it may be hard to find the item elsewhere as of our press date.

Graphics Today Survey, 1978

Mail Order Supplies

These are the major mail order supply companies for professional art materials; some of them also have retail outlets, and all produce annual catalogs. All addresses can be found in the appendix.

A. I. Friedman—New York
Alvin & Co Inc—Connecticut, California
Arthur Brown & Bro—New York
Charrette Corporation—Massachusetts, New York
Dick Blick—Illinois, Pennsylvania

Dot Paste-up Supply Co—Nebraska
Flax's—California, Arizona, Illinois
Martin Instrument Co—Michigan
Midwest Publishers Supply Co—Illinois
New York Central Supply Co—New York
Portage—Ohio
Sam Flax—New York, Georgia, Texas

Art Supplies and Health Hazards

It has been estimated that about 25 million artists, photographers, designers, and amateur and cottage-industry craftspeople are exposed daily to dangerous levels of asbestos and other toxic substances such as arsenic, lead, cadmium, mercury, benzene, tuolene, and xylene. Although warning labels concerning known carcinogens usually appear on bulk quantities of products containing them when they are shipped from manufacturers, distributors often leave off the warnings when repacking the products for retailers.

Similarly, many products containing dangerous chemicals do not offer directions about safe use. "Adequate ventilation," for example, may be understood to mean leaving a door or window open; but in fact, an exhaust fan may be necessary to keep toxic levels within safe limits, or to effect multiple air changes per hour.

Because no one has insisted that the art materials industry clean up its act until recently, it appears that many manufacturers and distributors have not seen fit to provide the least toxic alternatives possible when preparing or distributing their goods. But the general concern about toxic substances and health hazards, spurred by abuses in other industries, has finally reached the graphic arts. Concern surfaced at the first national conference on health hazards, held in 1979, sponsored by the Art Hazards Project at the Center for Occupational Hazards. At the conference it was shown that, unlike household products suppliers, suppliers to the arts are not regulated by any federal agency, and that this $2.7 billion industry has allowed numerous health hazards to go unchecked. Most people at the conference, in fact, were unaware just how toxic some of the ingredients in arts materials can be.

At last, legislation is under consideration that would require manufacturers to provide labels detailing product ingredients, precautions to be taken in their use, health problems that might result from misuse, and steps to take in the event of adverse effects. Beyond the medical desirability for access to such information, the legislation has significant legal implications as well, since artists and designers receive little protection under the law, and do not fall within the ambit of the Occupational Safety and Health Administration, which is the watchdog of workers' health in this country. The Graphic Artists Guild and some professional organizations are now inaugurating educational programs for artists to alert them to this occupational problem.

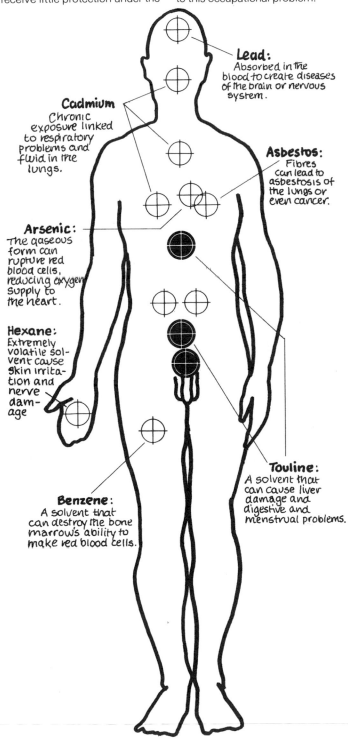

Lead: Absorbed in the blood to create diseases of the brain or nervous system.

Cadmium Chronic exposure linked to respiratory problems and fluid in the lungs.

Asbestos: Fibres can lead to asbestosis of the lungs or even cancer.

Arsenic: The gaseous form can rupture red blood cells, reducing oxygen supply to the heart.

Hexane: Extremely volatile solvent cause skin irritation and nerve damage

Benzene: A solvent that can destroy the bone marrow's ability to make red blood cells.

Touline: A solvent that can cause liver damage and digestive and menstrual problems.

Health Hazards Manual for Artists

[Michael McCann, PhD]

The range of dangerous materials used in art supplies is extremely broad, and some induce chronic effects that are hard to diagnose because the symptoms are vague and may not appear until long after exposure. McCann clearly details all the toxic substances in current use within the various art and design professions and crafts, as well as safety precautions and protective equipment necessary. He cites the example of chronic benzol poisoning whose symptoms include fatigue, dizziness, nausea, and loss of appetite — a condition easily mistaken for mild flu, until effects are serious and prolonged. He states that many toxicologists believe such chronic poisoning to be far more common among artists than is commonly believed.

First published in 1975, McCann's book received little notice until recent activism brought national attention to the problem of health hazards in the arts. But this updated edition is important to have around the studio; its fairly good index allows you to check suspect chemicals in the products you use, and at least get some idea of the potential hazards you are facing.

Cost: $3.50

Foundation for the Community of Artists

HEALTH HAZARDS MANUAL FOR ARTISTS
Michael McCann, PhD.

REVISED EDITION 3.50

Paper

All the art supply stores and mail order houses listed in this section offer complete ranges of paper stocks of all types; also, many different kinds of papers may carry specific retailers' brand names, and so be replicated under a variety of labels from one company to another. Therefore, we have limited our selection to the basic range necessary in the process of design, avoiding the wide array of specialty papers used for finished art, as well as those used expressly in various crafts. For your own use, examine the paper ranges carried by your local art materials store, and ask for any sample swatch booklets they may have. Overall, the most complete range of artist's papers will be found in the catalog of New York Central Supply Co, which specializes in unusual and/or handmade papers from all over the world.

The basic design studio range consists of vellum tracing, tracing, blue-gridded tracing, 100% rag bond, bond, marker, newsprint, and transfer papers, as well as colored pads, sheets, or rolls. Those listed below are not necessarily the best available, but they are papers we know to be good.

Most brand-named papers are pretty well comparable with each other; many have even originated from the same source. Because of the increasingly serious paper shortage (see Section C, "Support Systems"), paper prices are uniformly high everywhere, and promise to get a lot higher in the near future. Both prices and sizes indicated here are for comparison only.

Vellum Tracing

A good prepared tracing paper should be stable and strong; it should not yellow or oxidize and become brittle; it should be very transparent and smooth, with a "hard" surface for reproducible art rendered in either pen or pencil. The best is made of 100% long fibre, new white rag, and treated with resins to be waterproof. An average sheet thickness of medium weight is .0025;" usually there is a greater range available in rolls or single sheets than in the convenient pads.

Albanene is made to all the above specifications. It is available in packaged rolls in three thicknesses, single sheets, or five sizes of 50-sheet pads of .0025." Each pad comes with a board insert printed with 8" x 8" and 10" x 10" square grid guidelines.
Cost: $8.50 (14" x 17")

Keuffel & Esser Co

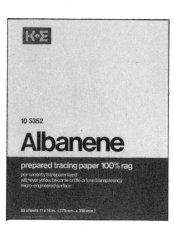

Vellum Drafting

One of the more popular tracing papers is the 1000H vellum, a white transparent paper with a plastic base which ensures a hard, smooth drawing and erasing surface. The 100% new cotton rag, non-glare paper with a blue-white tone is very strong and resistant to wear and tear. Available in single sheets, rolls of seven widths, and four sizes of 50-sheet pad.
Cost: $5.00 (11" x 14")

Clearprint Paper Company

Heavyweight Tracing

Similar in many ways to a good vellum, an extra heavyweight tracing paper is usually 25% rag, and therefore not quite as strong and durable as vellum, but a little cheaper. Otherwise, its transparency and ability to take pen and pencil is about the same. Thickness should be .0035," and these tracings are available in rolls, single sheets, and five sizes of 70-sheet pads. Flax's No51H is a good example.
Cost: $6.50 (14" x 17")

All Flax stores

Medium Tracing

A standard, all-purpose tracing paper has the same qualities as heavyweight tracing, but is more transparent and not quite as strong at .0025" thickness, and may have a tendency to yellow over a period of time. This quality of smooth tracing paper is the most popular, and the Art-Tec No. 38 is available everywhere.
Cost: $4.45 (14" x 17")

National Art Industries, Inc.

Thin Tissue Tracing

Inexpensive, cream or yellow finished tracing that is very transparent, used for all sorts of preliminary or intermediate layouts or sketches. This tracing is best bought in rolls—it is not always available in pads anyway—and usually comes in 50-yd. lengths in up to eight widths.

Both the yellow and the cream have surfaces that take pen and pencil, and neither is designed for long life. Cream-Trace 903 is one name for a tissue tracing.

Cost: $3.10 (14" x 50yds.)

Charrette Corporation

Gridded Tracing

Very useful for all sorts of layout, drawing, and typography, medium tracing paper comes ruled in fade-out blue grids in millimeters, 4x4, 5x5, 6x6, 8x8 and 10x10 cross sections. Normally available in rolls of four widths, all loose sheet sizes, and two sizes of 50-sheet pad: 8½" x 11" and 11"x17." Gridded tracing paper is always of a quality suitable for finished art.

Cost: $7.20 (11" x 17")

Clearprint Paper Company

Pro-form Tracing

Used for drawings or designs that may have to undergo several revisions, the pre-printed tracing paper forms help standardize whatever notes and information may be necessary for each drawing and revision. Available in seven sizes from 8½" x 11" to 30" x 42" on a Printfast vellum, in a single sheet, or packs of 25 and 100.

Cost: $12.10 (11" x 17"); or 22¢ per sheet.

Teledyne National Tracing Paper

Rag Bond Layout

A quality layout paper should be really white and fairly opaque, with a good enough surface to take pencil, pen, markers, and dry-brush applications. The Admaster is an adaptable paper made of 100% rag, and comes in a brilliant white with two different finishes, smooth (406S) and rough (406R). Admaster comes in two roll sizes, and seven sizes of both finishes in either 50 or 100 sheet pads.

Cost: $3.55 (11" x 14." 50 sheet)

Bienfang Paper Company

Bond Visual

A less expensive, lighter weight layout paper, white with medium-smooth finish is an all around medium for roughs, layouts, and comps. Art-Tec No. 73 is the medium transparent workaday quality in four pad sizes of 50 or 100 sheets.

Cost: $2.30 (11" x 14." 50 sheet)

National Art Industries, Inc.

Marker Bond

Felt tip markers will bleed through on many papers, and a lightly sized layout paper that has good translucency, holds sharp edges, and has a good color saturation level is necessary for their use. Art-Tec No. 212 is an inexpensive paper made for this very purpose, available in four 50 or 100-sheet pad sizes.

Cost: $2.65 (11" x 14." 50 sheet).

National Art Industries, Inc

Charrette 903 and 916H

All-purpose Bond

A thick, white, opaque, smooth, strong and durable bond ledger paper is another layout requirement, since it will adapt easily to wet media such as markers, gouache and inks. The bond of the Strathmore 400 series is a heavyweight and opaque ledger stock of proven quality, available in four size pads of three different weights of paper; 50 sheets per pad.
    Cost: $3.15 (11" x 14." 28 lb)

Strathmore Paper Co

Newsprint

The cheapest of all layout papers that has very little surface quality. Most art stores carry a version of a clean, white newsprint, either rough or smooth, for the most economical roughs, layouts, or sketches. Five sizes of 50-sheet pads.
    Cost: $1.25 (11" x 14." smooth)

All art materials stores

Transfer Paper

An impregnated transfer paper for transferring traced images. It produces a sharp, grease-free line and has an extremely eraseable surface. Available in 12½" x 12' rolls in graphite, white, blue, yellow, and red.
    Cost: $4.30

S B. Albertis; Charrette Corporation

Pantone Colored Papers

The most useful colored paper range for graphic designers is the selection color-matched to the standardized Pantone system. There is a range of 505 matte colors with a working surface that accepts virtually every medium, and resists creasing, marking, and other common abuses. The backs of the sheets are printed with a grid that makes a useful cutting guide, and with the Pantone code number at regular intervals. Each sheet has a guide along the top showing 20%, 30%, 40%, 50%, and 70% black tints over 20%, 30%, 40%, 50%, 70%, and 100% of the color. The guide also shows halftones on the color and its tints, and indicates black, reverse, and color printing on the different tints. Available as single sheets, 20" x 26."
    Cost: $1.40

Letraset USA, Inc

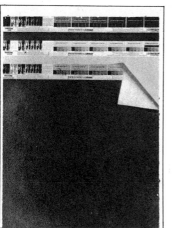

Film

Several sorts of plastic-type films are essential studio stock items; and again, understanding that quality does not vary much from brand to brand since retailers carry their own brands in most cases, we have selected a basic range.

Clear Acetate

Transparent plastic normally used as a protective covering or as a base to which overlay art is adhered. Useful in all applications where total see-through is necessary. Cannot be worked on with inks unless it has been "prepared," clear acetate comes in rolls, single sheets, and four pad sizes in two basic thicknesses: .003 and .005. Single sheets will often be available in four alternate thicknesses also. The 25-sheet paper-lined pads of .005 are the most convenient.
    Cost: $6.85 (11" x 14")

All Flax stores

Prepared Acetate

Clear plastic treated on both sides with a gelatine layer to take ink, paint, or dyes without anything having to be added to the medium. Corrections can be made by washing off without affecting the working qualities of the specially treated surfaces. Prepared acetate comes in single sheets or four sizes of 12-sheet pad of .005 thickness only, and is best bought in single sheets.
    Cost: $6.45 ((11" x 14," 12-sheet pad)

A I Friedman Inc

Plasti-Vellum

An all purpose acetate-type paper that is very transparent and smooth, and will take all media including color markers. Dimensionally stable, provides for perfect fidelity suitable for direct contacting into Ozalid or Technifax foil. Available in single sheets of 100-sheet packages in nine sizes of one thickness: .0015; or four sizes of pad.
    Cost: $6.45 (11" x 14," 25 sheet pad)

A I Friedman, Inc

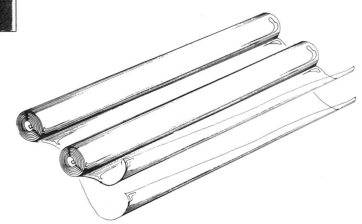

Herculene

A basic drafting material of excellent quality that is superb for pencil, ink, and paints. Herculene is a widely used, permanently transparent, prepared film for draftsmen, and comes in rolls of .003 thickness with the matte working surface on one or both sides.

Cost: $47.50 (36" x 20 yd; matte one side)

Keuffel & Esser Co

Amberlith

This is a masking film for overlay work: a thin amber film laminated to a clear mylar backing sheet which is completely transparent and dimensionally stable. The film cuts very easily and peels cleanly from the backing. A special adhesive permits removed portions to be replaced or transferred to other surfaces. The subtle adhesive always stays on the film. Amberlith is visually transparent but photographs black, and is more generally useful than Rubylith which is a deep transparent red. Two thicknesses are available: .003 and .005, in rolls, single sheets, and often 25-sheet pads of two sizes.

Cost: $16.50 (11" x 14." 25-sheet pad)

The Ulano Companies

Ulano Stripping Guide

Ulano manufactures a large range of films and graphic aid equipment, and produces this handy 16-page booklet, illustrated with step-by-step techniques on the various ways to use Amberlith. Discovering some of the tricks of the trade can be a real time saver, and knowing the correct procedures for preparing camera ready art will save a lot of money. The booklet comes with a special 5-sheet pad of Amberlith and Rubylith, a sample swatch book, Ulano's special peeling tool, plus a 24-page compendium of ideas and tips.

Cost: $9.95

The Ulano Companies

Transpaseal

A non-yellowing, protective covering for drawings, artwork, and printed material of all kinds. The self-adhesive, clear film adheres to the art smoothly, yet can be removed without leaving a residue or otherwise damaging the art. Transpaseal is stainproof and washable and available in boxed rolls of 20" x 25 yds.

Cost: $34.90

All Flax stores

Schemac Acetate

A very thin, matte acetate (.001) that has a special removable adhesive which is used to transfer images to another surface for positioning. You can draw or typeset directly onto this acetate, or print on it with copying or offset machines. Once applied to drafting papers, it will reproduce well on diazo, blueprint, or ozalid copiers. Available in 9" x 11" sheets.

Cost: $15.00 (50 sheets)

Morgan Adhesives Co

Pantone Colored Film

The transparent color/tint film overlays that match the Pantone color matching system papers and printing inks. Matte surfaced Letrafilm comes in self-adhesive sheets in a range of 108 colors, only 96 of which are Pantone matched. The parallel range of semi-gloss, self-adhesive film has a range of 210 Pantone matched colors, 58 of which are sheets containing four different tints.

Letrafilm Matte colors are translucent, even, and very strong in tone; they give excellent color results when used as reflective art. The colors are surface printed, and can therefore be scraped or thinned with solvent to achieve illustration effects, or used with instant lettering sheets to create typographic visuals of any color. The film cuts easily, and the low-tack adhesive allows for re-positioning, although once rubbed down it cannot be removed. The surface will take most art media, and all sheets are 10" x 15."

The semi-gloss Letracolor film is a more transparent self-adhesive sheet with a highly translucent backing sheet you can see through. The adhesive is easy to re-position and is also heat resistant. All these Pantone matched sheets are 20" x 26."

Costs: $2.25, Letrafilm; $4.95, Letracolor; $2.50, Letrafilm Solvent

Letraset USA, Inc

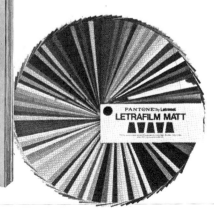

Pantone Color Selectors

All art material dealers now carry Pantone color sample guides (the major one, the Designers Edition tear-out sample book, is shown on page 132). Letraset markets a sample selector for Letrafilm, Letracolor overlay film, and their papers. Pantone's Printer's Edition is an ink match formula guide, a Pantone Tint Guide, and the Pantone Four Color Process Guide. These reference books link your artwork and the printer, and provide the basic standard reference system that is now generally used. Letraset and Pantone also market a complete range of matching color markers page 69).

Costs: $5.50, Matte Letrafilm Selector; $9.50, Letracolor Overlay Selector; $6.50, Color Paper Selector; $7.00, Printer's Edition; $15.00, Pantone Tint Guide; $110.00, Pantone Four Color Process Guide

**Pantone, Inc;
Letraset USA, Inc**

Board

Illustration boards are quality drawing papers mounted on stiff backing board; they are available in both single and double weight, and we suggest you experiment with the various surface finishes to find the ones best suited to your needs and budget. (Hot pressed is a hard, smooth surface; cold pressed has a slight texture.) All boards can be cut to your specifications, but this is an expensive option to be avoided where possible. It is best to purchase boards in factory-wrapped packages (usually 25 sheets) which keep them free from dirt and moisture.

Bristol board is used for general artwork and lettering, and can be used on both sides. At 1-5 ply, it has a greater range of thickness than most other boards. Mounting boards, which have a greater range yet, are used for all kinds of mounting and paste-up; basic mounting board is usually semi-gloss white on one side, and white or colored on the reverse.

As with other items discussed in this chapter, many identical boards are sold under different retailers' individual brand names. Once more, then, we list a range of board types generally used in the design studio, and do not include the multitude of variations commonly stocked, or the many special surface boards designed for specific types of illustration and graphic effects.

Hot Press Illustration Board

Among the several quality grades of hot pressed board, the median Art-Tec illustration board is versatile, economical, very white, dense fibered, and thoroughly sized. It is suitable for ink, pencil, felt markers, and water based paints. It is available in three sizes of double or single weight: 15" x 20," 20" x 30," and 30" x 40."

Cost: $1.30 (20" x 30," single weight)

National Art Industries, Inc

Cold Press Illustration Board

Essentially the same as the hot press board, except for its textured surface. The popular Bainbridge No. 80 has a high rag content, giving it the quality surface for all mediums. Three sizes, two weights.

Cost: $1.30 (20" x 30," SW)

Charles T Bainbridge's Sons, Inc

Rough Illustration Board

An extra rough, cold press board with a high rag content. Bainbridge No. 169 is suitable for all mediums and is available in two sizes and two weights.

Cost: $1.30 (20" x 30," SW)

Charles T Bainbridge's Sons, Inc

Bristol Drawing Board

A 100% cotton fiber board that has two hard-surfaced finishes: a semi-gloss smooth "plate," and a lightly textured vellum finish. The Strathmore 500 Bristol comes in two sheet sizes of up to 5 ply in both finishes, and is also available in 11" x 14" pads of 2 ply boards, 15 sheets each.

Cost: $1.80 (23" x 29." 3 ply)

Strathmore Paper Co

Prelined Artwork Board

An ideal type of board for paste-up and certain sorts of artwork. The Bristol or Illustration board is ruled in an 8 x 8 fade-out blue grid accented every inch and half-inch; it comes in one size (22" x 28"), single weight sheet, or in 11" x 14" pads of 24 sheets.

Cost: $1.50 (Illustration); 60¢ (Bristol)

Sam Flax

Mounting Board

The heavyweight Studio Mounting Board is a good example of an inexpensive all-purpose board intended primarily for mounting work for presentation, or for paste-up. It is glossy, white-coated on one side and dull white on the other. Not suitable for working on directly, but it will take linework fairly well. This board is available in 14 and 28 ply, and should be available in lighter weight versions of 4, 6, and 8 ply, all in at least five sizes.

Cost: 85¢ (22" x 28." 14 ply)

Sam Flax

Pantone Tint Guide

KENNETH DEWEY

Lightweight Mounting

A cheap, sturdy, lightweight mounting board with a smooth surface, useful for paste-up work, is the Index Bristol Board, versions of which are available everywhere. This 2 ply board comes in one size only, as a rule.
    Cost: 28¢ (22½" x 28½")

Sam Flax

Black Mounting

Known as "Railroad" board for some reason, this is a 4 or 6 ply mount board, black on both sides and ideal for mounting for presentation. Railroad boards come in a range of at least twenty-one other colors, and in one standard size of 22" x 28."
    Cost: 50¢

Charrette Corporation

Polystyrene Mount Board

A sandwich laminate of polystyrene foam between whitish clay-coated, smooth paper facings, this board's surface will take some mediums such as gouache and markers, and can be drawn on in ink. The advantages of "Fome-Cor" board are that it is extremely lightweight, even though it's as much as ½" thick; easy to slice through, and popular for mounting displays or shipping inexpensively. No. 327W is a useful ³/₁₆" thick with a white polystyrene in five sheet sizes.
    Cost: $1.82 (20" x 30")

Bienfang Paper Co

Drawing and Drafting Tools

It would be both impossible and pointless to attempt an exhaustive listing of these essentials. Our short list aims to cover the most useful knives, scissors, compasses, ruling pens, rules, drafting machines, triangles, templates, and magnifiers.

Knives

It's not the body, but the blades that cost you money over the years, and if you've used the standard No. 11, you know they don't last long at all. Our advice is to invest in surgical steel blades and a fine oilstone, and you can stop running out to the store for those endless packs of 100 ordinary blades.

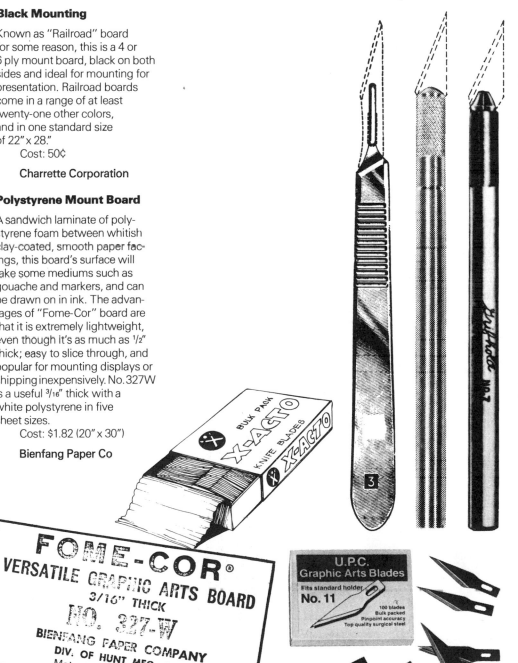

Surgeon's Scalpel

Obviously, this tool has been designed to be highly manipulatable and comfortable in the hand for prolonged and delicate work. Surgical handle No. 3 holds all the surgical blades normally used in graphic work — Nos. 10, 11, and 15. The Schein blades are extra sharp, flexible, and relatively durable — and you don't need the sterile versions.
    Cost: $2.45 (No. 3 handle); $13.75 (100 pack No. 11 blades)

Henry Schein, Inc

X-acto No. 1 Knife

The standard graphic arts tool that will accomplish most lightweight cutting work in the studio. A light aluminum handle takes the normal No. 11 blade, as well as the Nos. 10 and 16. There is a super No. 1 version that comes with blade shield and blade lock for easier blade changing, and a version with safety shield and hexagonal chuck two-thirds down that eases the grip and prevents the knife from rolling off the drawing board. Neither refinement is really necessary, but both are — well, cute. X-acto also produces six other kinds of handles to carry eleven other blade designs, most of which are specialist craft tools. Altrnatively, the Griffold No. 7 with the No. 7E blade is equally good and comparably priced.
    Cost: $1.00 (No. 1 handle); $10.00 (100 pack No. 11 blades)

**X-acto Corporation;
Griffin Manufacturing Co, Inc**

UPC No. 11 Blades

Surgical steel blades similar to the Schein type mentioned above, designed to fit standard holders like X-acto No. 1. Well worth the extra $2.00.
    Cost: $12.00 (100 pack)

Sam Flax; Al Friedman

The NT Cutter

A neat, well balanced knife usually used for the more intricate work, especially with film and film overlays. All the Japanese NT cutters use the snap-off blade system — blades that come in a long, pre-scored strip and snap off with a vinyl blade snapper; the most useful model is the D-500. The blade end can be inverted to store in the handle, and the other end is designed as a burnisher, or, unscrewed and reversed, a scriber point.

Cost: $3.50 (including blade strips)
$2.98 (packet of 10 blade strips)

All Flax stores

Uber Skiver

A high quality precision cutting knife with a rear activated "drawbar" for easy blade changing and blade stability, and a knurled grip and hex section body to prevent rolling. Blades are surgical stainless steel or chrome steel of five different types including the standard No. 11. A really fine tool.

Cost: $5.10 (K-2 handle);
$34.90 (100 Noll blades in packs of 6)

Charrette Corporation; Flax's

Swivel Knife

A weighted knife that needs little or no pressure, this precision, ball-bearing instrument is meant for cutting curves and complicated patterns; its swivel lock makes it adjustable to straight line cutting. Swivel knives are ideal for film, masks, screens, etc. The blades are hollow ground and razor sharp, and may have to be slightly blunted before use to prevent drag; they can be sharpened on a fine oilstone. The blade cover stores in the handle. Special blades are available for cutting along curve guides and straightedges.

Cost: $22.00;
$49.98 (100 blades in packs of 6)

The Ulano Companies

Utility Knife

An old favorite is the ubiquitous Stanley Knife. The Stanley 99 is the retractable version with a blade that adjusts to three cutting positions for scoring, cutting, and scraping. Lightweight aluminum handle stores extra blades of heavy or medium weight.

Cost: $2.50;
$14.98 (100 medium blade dispenser)

All art, craft and hardware stores

Arkansas Oilstone

Hard Novaculite from Arkansas deposits, used with mineral oil, is the best stone for honing a surgically sharp edge on a blade that is already sharp. It is the natural mineral used for finishing precision tools such as ruling pens, drawing instruments, and most blades.

Cost: $3.50

Charrette Corporation; Sam Flax

Scissors

Friskars Scissor

The precision ground surgical steel blades of this Finnish tool hold sharp edges for years. This is a lightweight version of tailor's shears, with molded plastic handles, available in 8" right or left hand models.

Cost: $8.95

Most art, craft, and hardware stores

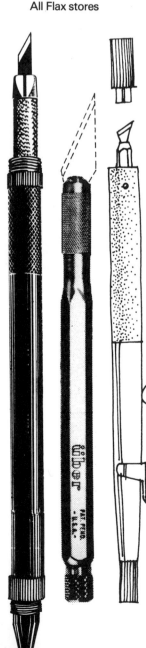

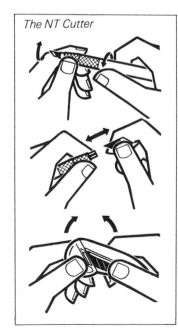

The NT Cutter

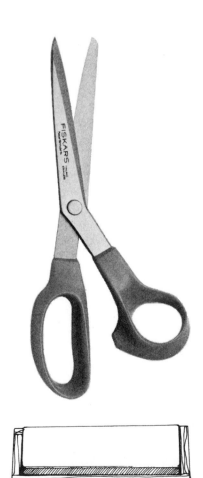

Wiss Paper Shears

A long bladed (12"), heavy duty trimmer with the finest quality, high carbon "inlaid" blades. Wiss shears have an adjusting screw, spring tension device, and black contoured handles.
Cost: $27.00

All Flax stores

Alex Scissor

A slimline, 7," stainless steel scissor that is inexpensive, comfortable, and very sharp. This Japanese tool has become very popular and is available everywhere.
Cost: $7.50

Yasatumo & Co

Drafting Instruments

Kern, Vemco, Mars, Pickett, Charrette, Alvin, and other good manufacturers all offer three qualities of drafting instrument— student, intermediate (or engineering), and professional — in three price ranges. The more expensive professional tools are intended for use by people who are engaged in drafting most of their time, and are not strictly necessary for others. Our basic selection mostly concerns the intermediate range, and our choices here of one brand over another do not imply superiority. Within a given price range, the brands are equally good, and your own selection will depend on what is available, and what feels and looks good to you. All brands have instrument kits of different combinations of tools, as well as the single units shown here. Most of these instruments come from Europe, especially Germany and Switzerland.

Small Bow Combination Compass

A sturdy precision tool with bar lock that has absolutely no play or "give." This Mars Super-bow is made of hard-drawn brass with a matte brushed finish; nylon fittings on moving parts virtually eliminate wear. The 4½" small bow comes with interchangeable pen, pencil, and divider parts, with a micro-setting up to 2¼" radius.
Cost: $9.95

J S Staedtler, Inc

Large Bow Combination Compass

The Kern T Series are copper alloy, nickel, and chromium plated. The compass "half set" has a precision self-centering head with adjustment screws under the plastic cap to adjust stiff or easy motion. The 6.3" compass unit with interchangeable pen and pencil points has a radius up to 11," plus a 3.9" lengthening bar that will take an adapter to hold a technical pen.
Cost: $32.50

Koh-I-Noor Rapidograph, Inc

Large Divider

Simple nautical 7" dividers made of brass with a brushed chrome finish and steel points. The basic, elegant tool.
Cost: $4.50

J S Staedtler, Inc

Proportional Divider

A divider that divides for you is an ideal. This 8" divider with rack movements, made of nickel silver with replaceable steel points, divides lines from 1½ to 10 units and circles from 6 to 36. Comes boxed with instructions.
Cost: $46.50

Charrette Corporation

Cross Joint Ruling Pen

In these days of the technical pen, a range of ruling pens is no longer necessary, but a good, sturdy pen with a large ink capacity that can be cleaned without the line width being altered, is a necessity. The 5.9" Kern "Border" pen with a swivel blade is a good example.
Cost: $17.50

Koh-I-Noor Rapidograph, Inc

Parallel Ruling Pen

Known as the "Railroad" pen, this precise instrument will draw adjustable width parallel lines. Hardened steel, fork spring action with octagon blades, 5¾" long.
Cost: $9.50

Alvin & Co, Inc

Precision Cutting Compass

A large, chrome steel compass, beautifully made and, with its special adapter, designed for cutting film using the Ulano swivel knife. Spring adjustment on the radius arm allows exact radius control up to 10," or up to 20" with an extension bar accessory. Accepts most Technical pen units.
Cost: $40.00

The Ulano Companies

Adjustable Dual Cutter

A simple tool for making parallel cuts quickly and easily. Adjustment to ½" at the turn of the precision screws.
Cost: $4.75

Griffin Manufacturing Co, Inc

Rules

Adjustable Steel T-Square

If you need a T-square, it is best to have the most adaptable version, made from stainless steel for use as a cutting edge as well as a drafting tool, and adjustable to at least 12 given angles. Wood and acrylic T-squares damage too easily. This is a particularly well made and accurate version, and comes in six different lengths: 18," 24," 30," 36," 42," and 48," without calibration.
Cost: $26.95 (36")

Pickett Industries

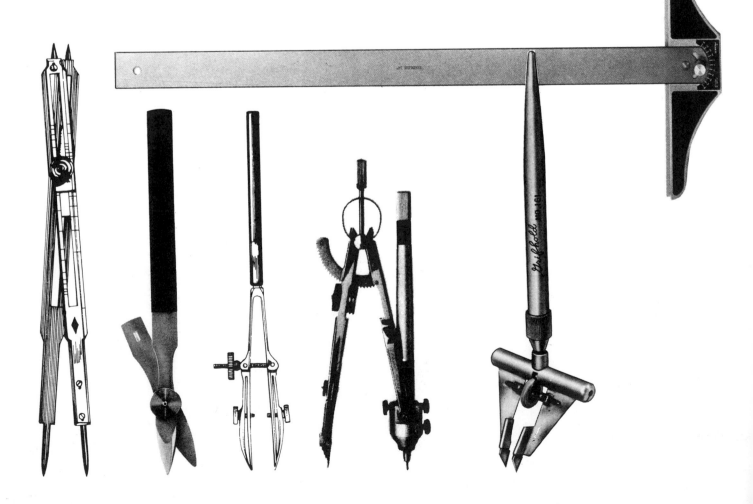

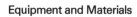
The Basic Steel Rule

A good, general purpose rule needs to be light, tempered stainless steel, at least two feet long, with some relevant calibrations. A zero centered rule is a useful addition to your collection, and the Gaebel 627 is completely zero center with one side marked in 16ths and 12ths, and the other in 10ths and picas.
Cost: $6.50 (24")

Arthur H Gaebel, Inc

Flexible Steel Rule

One of the more popular multi-use rules, this is flexible, made of high-tempered steel, and has a non-slip cork backing that raises the rule off the drawing surface —an essential attribute if you work in ink. Calibrated in inches and metric, or inches and picas, available in 6," 9," 12," 15," 18," and 24."
Cost: $4.90 (24")

Bates Manufacturing Co; Arthur H Gaebel, Inc

Pica/Agate Ruler

A good steel rule is an essential tool, and a designer needs it with inch and pica calibration. This is a clear, accurate version with picas and 6 & 12 pt scales on one side, and agates & inches in 16ths on the other. 18" or 24."
Cost: $3.95 (24")

Pickett Industries

The Printers Rule

The traditional rule used by printers and hot-metal type-setters, with a hook-type end originally intended to hook over the ends of type slugs. It is solid and accurate, graduated in 16ths on one side and agate on the other; and on the reverse in points and picas. Some versions also include 8 and 10 pt markings.
Cost: $4.00 (12")

Arthur H Gaebel, Inc

Parallel Rule

Usually associated with navigation, the parallel rule makes any series of parallel lines easy to render. The Staedtler is a thick, clear plastic with bevelled edges, aluminum brackets, chromed guide knobs, and non-slip friction pads. It comes in three lengths: 12," 15," and 18."
Cost: $3.50 (12")

J S Staedtler, Inc

Multidraft

An ingenious and simple tool that is very useful when your parallel motion drawing board is not convenient. This little drafting machine takes the place of a T-square, triangles, and protractor; it operates with a magnetic clutch system and includes push-button control. It tracks parallel, locks, turns in a circular motion, and adjusts to angular settings.
Cost: $16.50

Abbeon Cal, Inc

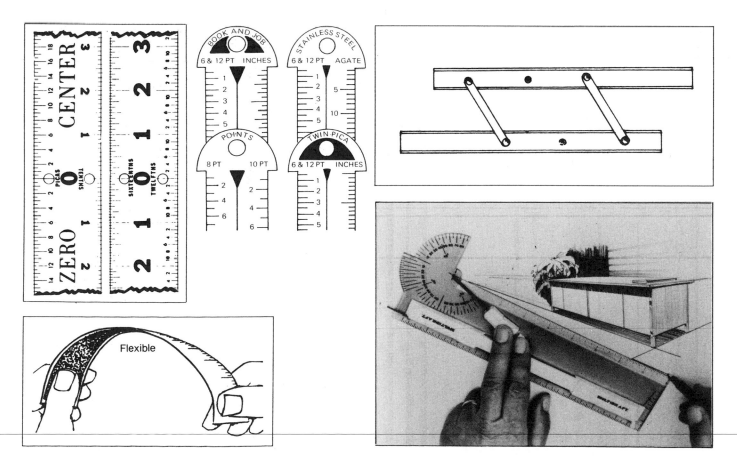

Flexible

Acu-Arc Ruler

An easily adjustable rule that will effect curves and arcs of any radius from $6\frac{1}{4}°$ to 200.° It can also determine the radius of any given curve, find center lines and center points, and determine the radius needed to connect existing points or lines. It effectively eliminates the need for a beam compass or a set of rigid curves.
    Cost: $22.35

Abbeon Cal, Inc

Circlometer

A digital drafting tool that allows precisely sized circles to be drawn quickly and accurately anywhere from $\frac{1}{2}$" to six inches. The circlometer comes in four different scales: fractional, decimal, $\frac{1}{4}$" and metric. The fractional circlometer, for example, has 161 circle diameters graduated in $\frac{1}{32}$" increments. It is operated simply by inserting a drafting pencil or technical pen into the required hole and rotating the circle template that swivels on a center pin. It really works.
    Cost: $4.95

Atlantic & Pacific Industries, Inc

Flexible Curve One

Good adjustable curves that hold their shape easily are an ideal alternative to the tedious search for the right french curve —providing you are not an engineering draftsperson. The Acu-Arc Ship Curve is one, formed of interlocking layers of butyrate plastic which are finger shaped to the desired curve plotting and held in position by friction. Apart from two sizes of Ship Curve (18" and 24"), there is also an Acu-Arc circular version that forms similarly to a french curve, and longer Spline Curves of 36" and 48."
    Cost: $7.50 (18")

Abbeon Cal, Inc

Flexible Curve Two

Slightly better type and a little more expensive than the Acu-Arc Ship Curve, the K + E flexible curve rule is made of soft, serrated plastic. It flexes along two clear xylonite bevel-type ruling edges, lies flat, and is as easy to use as a triangle. It comes in four sizes: 12," 18," 24," and 30."
    Cost: $9.90 (18")

Keuffel + Esser, Inc

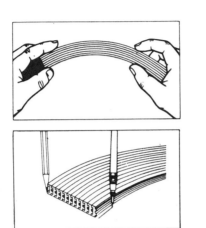

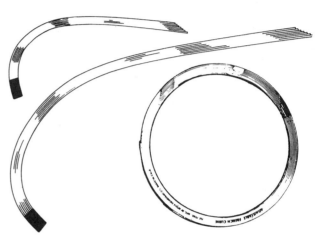

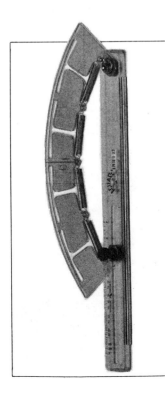

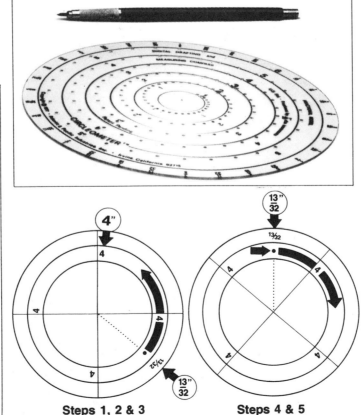

Steps 1, 2 & 3   **Steps 4 & 5**

Mayline Parallel Motion Rule

A traditionally standard piece of drafting equipment, parallel motion has been largely superseded by simplified versions of engineer/architect drafting machines. Nevertheless, parallel motion is still a popular option.

The Mayline E-Z grip type has stainless steel straightedges, and retractable rollers underneath for really smooth action. Made of a black phenolic laminate in seven sizes (30"-72"), the blade's steel edges are raised off the bottom slightly, and the small rollers underneath retract with the slightest pressure. The cable runs through the center of the E-Z Grip handle, and the mountings, cable, and delrin pulley glides are included.

Top mounting attachments are part of the standard kit, but we suggest you get the bottom mounting attachments instead so all that cable doesn't get in your way.

Cost: $60.00;(42")
$10.50 (under-board attachments)

Mayline Manufacturing Co

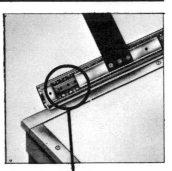

The Glideliner

Often, all you really need is a reliable, accurate parallel motion rule such as this one, which is an effective alternative to cable-type devices and expensive drafting machines. The Glideliner sticks or screws to any board or light table, and rolls smoothly on low-friction ball bearings. Its bevelled blade is made of a hard, anodized aluminum, and is hinged to move up off the board when you want it out of the way. A stop lever feature can fix the blade in position along the glide. The only drawback to parallel motion rules of this sort is their tendency to "give" at the place the rule attaches to the glide, and they have to be checked every so often to make sure the attachment is tight. The Glideliner X 290 is available in four sizes: 18" x 24," 24" x 30," 28" x 36," and 28" x 42."

Cost: $57.00 (28" x 42")

The Ulano Companies

Cross-section of Mayline E-Z mobile straightedge

Under-board attachment

Glideliner

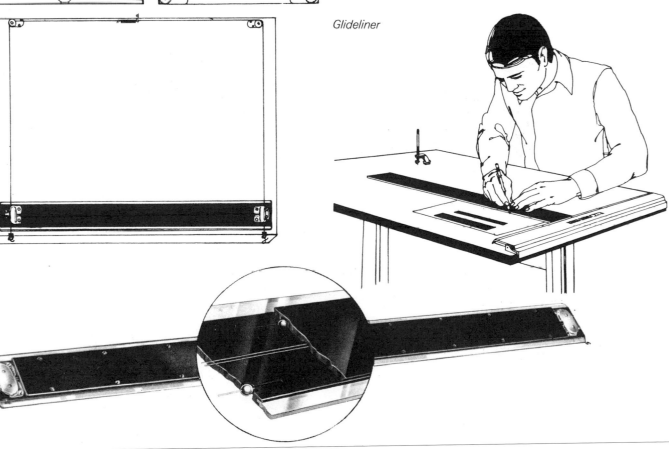

Designer Drafting

For general graphic work, this low cost, sturdy kind of machine has all the accuracy and conveniences of the big specialist machines. The Designer portable type is the most utilitarian of the available models. It has tubular nickel steel arms, counter spring balancing, a 135° protractor head with 15° indexing, a built-in hatching device, and pivotal tilt to lift the machine completely away from the board. Available with 16" or 18" arms, and with either 8" or 12" scales of various types of calibration.

Cost: $89.50 (18"; board coverage up to 31" x 42")

Alvin & Co, Inc

Compact Elbow Drafting

A slightly smaller version of the large professional engineer/architect models, the Vemco 3300 is a well-known drafting machine that suits the needs of most graphic artists — and even comes in a left-hand model. It is operated by continuous steel bands, with disc brakes for steadiness; has 15° indexing, free angle setting, and full circle baseline setting; and accepts all standard size scales in either plastic or aluminum. Available with 16," 18," 20," or 22" arms and three styles of mounting brackets.

Cost: $101.50 (22;" board coverage up to 37½" x 50")

Vemco Corporation

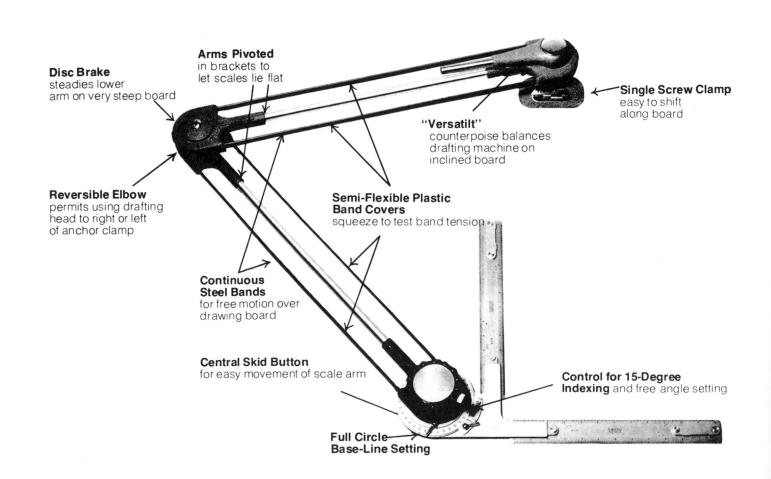

Disc Brake steadies lower arm on very steep board

Arms Pivoted in brackets to let scales lie flat

Single Screw Clamp easy to shift along board

"Versatilt" counterpoise balances drafting machine on inclined board

Reversible Elbow permits using drafting head to right or left of anchor clamp

Semi-Flexible Plastic Band Covers squeeze to test band tension

Continuous Steel Bands for free motion over drawing board

Central Skid Button for easy movement of scale arm

Control for 15-Degree Indexing and free angle setting

Full Circle Base-Line Setting

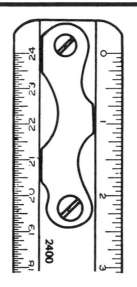

Junior Track Drafting

The most convenient type of drafting device, the tracking machines are better suited to angled than flat boards, and to large working areas. The Neolt "Lilly" is an inexpensive, smaller, less sophisticated track drafting machine which suits all general graphic work requirements. It features fingertip controlled vertical locking system, 15° indexing, freewheel device, intermediate angle locking, and a spring-loaded horizontal carriage. Available in three sizes: 24" x 36¹/₄," 29¹/₂" x 41¹/₄," and 37¹/₂" x 47¹/₄," with 12" scales which only fit this machine.

Cost: $144.50 (board coverage up to 37¹/₄" x 47¹/₄")

Martin Instrument Co

Mutoh Track Drafting

A full size, standard professional drafting machine, Model S has exceptionally smooth and silent action at any board angle. It also has all the usual features of a basic tracking machine including ball bearing nylon pulleys, horizontal brake release, hinged protractor head, 360° baseline setting, vernier clamp, dual action indexing control, a magnifier, and a micro adjusting device. A well designed machine at a reasonable price, available in one size.

Cost: $240.00 (board coverage up to 37¹/₂" x 60"

Consul & Mutoh, Ltd

Drafting Machine Scales

Fully divided scales usually come in three sizes: 9," 12," and 18," in either transparent plastic or satin aluminum. The Vemco selection will fit nearly all machines (Neolt excepted), and includes over twenty different types of calibration.

Cost: from $6.00 to $9.75 each

Vemco Corporation

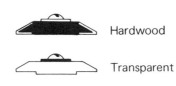

Hardwood

Transparent

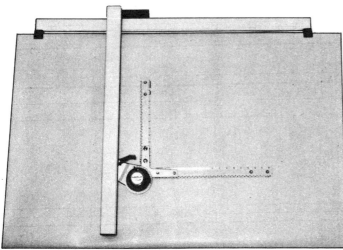

Triangles and Templates

Triangles

Good double thick triangles made of .080" clear acrylic, double layered with the bottom layer slightly smaller to provide raised ruling edge and fingerlift, are made by Staedtler. The Mars 964 series comes in 45° and 60° angles, seven sizes of each.

Cost: from $1.00 to $5.50

J S Staedtler, Inc

Adjustable Triangle

A thicker triangle (.100") of clear acrylic with bevelled edges. Protractor section is graduated in ½" degree increments from 0° to 90° with magnifier. Three sizes.

Cost: $12.00 (12")

J S Staedtler, Inc

Steel Triangles

Thick gauge, nickel steel triangles with open center, but without bevelled edges. Removable lifting knobs. 30°/60° and 45°/90° in three sizes each.

Cost: from $14.00 to $50.50

Arthur H Gaebel, Inc

Lettering Triangle

Clear plastic triangle designed to rule accurately spaced lines, particularly for lettering. Practically any desired spacing or guide lines may be obtained by inserting pencil point through proper hole and sliding triangle along a parallel rule. Includes a 67½° slot for obtaining uniform slope in lettering, and comes in 30°/60° and 45° two sizes each.

Cost: from $2.00 to $3.10

Charrette Corporation

Marabu Angle Square

A unique little clear plastic tool that gives most important angles, and serves as a template with some useful symbols. It provides a complete system for laying out guides for freehand lettering, plus 7° and 42° guide lines to serve as vanishing points. Two sizes.

Cost: $6.50 (10")

All Flax stores

Templates

There are hundreds of template patterns made for every possible use. Most have been superseded by pressure graphics, which are simpler and more convenient to work with; but templates work out cheaper since they constitute a one-time cost. Template designs are particularly necessary if you are involved with plans or diagrams requiring special coded symbolism, such as mechanical engineering drawings, architectural plans, computer diagramming, plumbing or electrical diagrams, or such arcane fields as fluid power, welding, heating and air conditioning, or chemical, highway, or general cartographic diagramming. Generally, designers use the all-purpose drawing guide templates such as a radius guide, parallel spacer, or isometric ellipsis guides.

There are several companies that specialize in good quality templates, and every art supply store will stock one brand or another.

Cost: from $1.00 to $10.00 each

Berol USA; Pickett Industries; Alvin & Co; C-Thru Graphics; Lietz

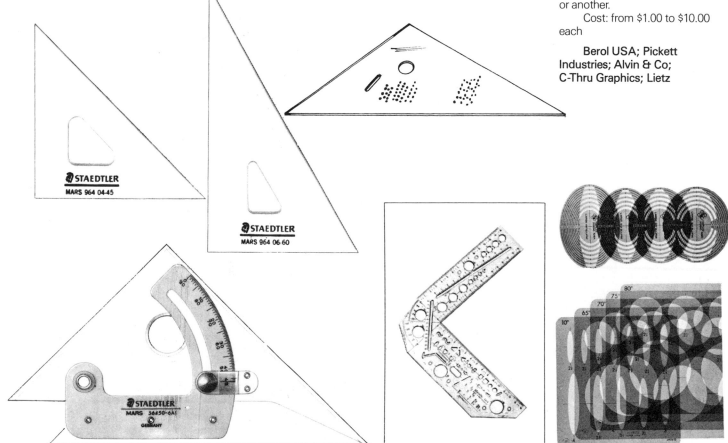

French Curve Templates

Every art supply store carries at least ten or so clear plastic french curves, usually marketed under the store's own brand name. Pickett produces a range of 13 irregular curves at .080" thickness, and a three-curve set of the most popular sizes. Such a set is useful to have around, in combination with the more convenient flexible curve shown above.

Cost: $4.50 (3-curve set)

Pickett Industries

Pantograph

An inexpensive instrument for making enlarged or reproduced copies for layouts and drawings; the aluminum type, which costs a little extra, is worth the investment because it is more durable and easier to use. The 26 ratios, set from 1½ to 8, are further adjustable with micrometer setting to any desired ratio. 21" long bars, ¾" wide, with an extra steel point. Comes assembled with accessories and instructions.

Cost: $19.00

**All Flax stores;
Charrette Corporation;
Arthur Brown & Bro**

Gooseneck Magnifier

A distortion-free magnifier is a great aid to your eyes for detail work; the most convenient type is the long 24" gooseneck shaft version with a board clamp and a 3" diameter lens with ball joint.

Cost: $16.50

All Flax stores

Luxo Magnifier Lamp

A much more expensive magnifier (LFM 1A), the gray Luxor lamp has a ring-style fluorescent tube and 3 diopter lens for shadowless illumination. Comes with standard A type bracket clamp.

Cost: $75.00

Luxo Lamp Corporation

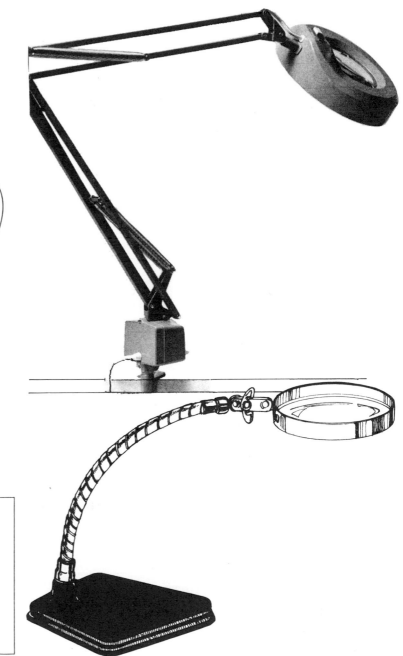

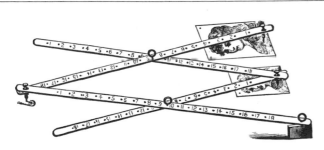

Technical and Fountain Pens

Since the days of the Rapidograph Technical Fountain Pen, these pen systems have improved tremendously, and they are now used in every area of graphic art. The major manufacturers (Koh-I-Noor, Faber-Castell, Staedtler-Mars, Standardgraph, Alvin, and Keuffel + Esser) vie with one another to produce the best, with the happy result that there is little to distinguish among them, and any one is a good piece of equipment.

All technical pens need care and attention if they are to continue working well. Despite some claims to the contrary, they *will* clog up if they are not used regularly, not stored in a humidifier, or, if not cleaned out prior to lying idle for a week or so. All these systems have the same basic components: barrel, reservoir, color-coded collar, drawing cone, cone extractor, cap, and hygro or dry seal inner cap.

Drawing cone points conform to a standard line-width designation number, ranging between 14 and .000000 (6x0), which equals approximately 6.00 mm to .11 mm; or else to the international metric line-width scale of nine sizes ranging from 2.00 to .13. This latter line-width designation is used principally by engineers and people involved with microfilm, and is based on a geometric progression of 1.414, or $\sqrt{2}$. Some points match both line-width systems, but in general you need concern yourself only with the first. Standard line-width designations are *not* comparative from brand to brand. In other words, Staedtler-Mars number 6 is a different line-width from FaberCastell number 6.

Every person who has reason to be involved with these pens comes sooner or later to have a favorite brand. While we do not recommend any one particularly above the others (except, perhaps, the FaberCastell TGH series), we do suggest that you stick with the single system you prefer since parts are not really interchangeable from make to make, and most retail outlets carry only two or three brands.

All the pen systems shown here have a complete range of accessories; most are made in Germany to very exact specifications; prices shown are for one complete pen.

FaberCastell TG System

The standard TG pen has a black barrel and uses stainless steel drawing points in a self-locking cone with no screw connection; it is easily removed and replaced. The cone's enlarged thermic compensating spiral eliminates ink seepage at the tip, and inhibits clogging. The ink reservoir does not have to be removed for filling and cleaning. The hygro element in the cap keeps the point moist and prevents ink drying in the cone. The collar is designed for use with most scribing or compass units.

The TGH range varies from the TG pens in that their drawing cone points are made of tungsten carbide—an extra-hard, polished point for use on abrasive polyester drafting films. TGH pens have green barrels for easy identification, though the cones will fit the standard TG barrels.

All pen parts are available separately; each pen comes with a box that has a "key hole" to hold the pen in an upright position by the cap, and with a cone

extractor. Both the TG and the TGH series are available in four barrel/four point sets, or two barrel/nine point sets with cone extractor, joint adaptor, ink bottle, and manual. A TG four barrel/seven point set is also available.

There are 11 drawing point sizes, which FaberCastell has rationalized so that the US size designations actually relate to the metric scale; thus they range from 7 (2.00 mm) to 000 (0.1 mm) in even 0.1 increments.

Cost: from $8.00 to $9.25 (TG pen, complete); from $14.50 to $18.50 (TGH pen, complete)

FaberCastell Corporation

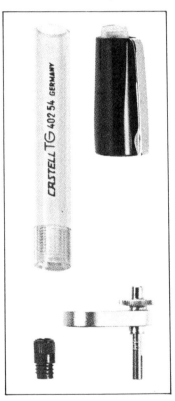

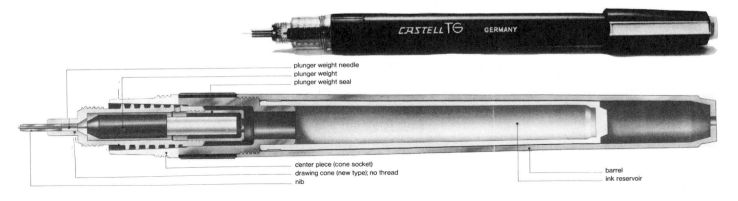

plunger weight needle
plunger weight
plunger weight seal

center piece (cone socket)
drawing cone (new type); no thread
nib

barrel
ink reservoir

Rapidograph SL, DCS System

The well known Koh-I-Noor technical pens come in four types: the technical fountain pen, the standard Rapidograph, the Rapidograph SL, and the Rapidometric. We have selected slimline Rapidograph SL series, which offers only twelve drawing point sizes out of a possible eighteen, but also offers the optional Dry Clamp Selector (DCS) modules. The DCS module is a dry short-term and extended storage system featuring an airtight double seal into which the pens can be clamped. Each pen module pivots up and down, and can be joined to other modules with a slide lock.

The drawing cone points are available in either the normal stainless steel, a jewel (synthetic sapphire), or tungsten carbide, the last two designed for drafting film. The pens are all a uniform gray with line-width color-coding on the dry-seal cap tops only. All Rapidograph SL pen parts are available separately,

and each pen can be bought separately or with a DCS module. The SL series come in sets of nine pens + modules or four pens + modules; both have an extra accessory module containing board clamp, ink, and cone extractor keys. Otherwise, SL pens come in standard boxed sets — without modules — of three, four, six, seven, eight, or nine pens including vertical storage key holes, cone extractor key, and ink.

The twelve drawing point sizes range from 6 (1.40 mm) through 6 x 0 (.11 mm).

Cost: from $9.50 to $13.50 (SL pen complete with module and steel point)

Koh-I-Noor Rapidograph, Inc

Mars 700 System

The comfortable Staedtler pen is a standard unit that accepts standard drawing points of three types (stainless steel, jewel, or tungsten carbide) in the nine metric line-widths. It has all the features of the three brands mentioned above, but with the cone extractor key inset into the top of the standard blue barrel. Line-width color coding is on the drawing cone only. The pens and the drawing points are available separately.

The Mars 700 sets are available in either standard or metric selection; both consist of either a three, four, seven, or nine pen unit with ink and special slots to store other accessories and spare drawing points. The boxes rest on a slope when opened, and all sets have a key hole facility allowing the pens to stand vertically while in use.

Cost: $7.00 to $10.00 (700 pen complete with steel point)

J S Staedtler, Inc

Pivotal action easily raises pen for immediate use, or lowers it into clamped airtight position to seal point away from air whenever pen is not in use.

Clamped position of pen.

Nib has cylindrical metal sleeve

safety screw

flow regulating device

point housing

Mars 700

The Leroy DCS System

This is the Keuffel + Esser version of the Rapidograph DCS system, and in fact it's pretty hard to tell them apart except in some coloring detail variations. Otherwise, all features of this pen and its Dry Clamp Selector units are as noted above.

The drawing cone points are available in either stainless steel or jewel tips; line-widths are in the nine metric sizes only (2.00 mm to 0.13 mm). The pen and module units come separately with cone extractor key, or in sets of nine pens + modules or four pens + modules; both sets have an extra accessory module containing board clamp, ink, and cone keys. Leroy sets are also available in the nine or four pen standard boxed sets with vertical storage holes, extractor key, and ink.

Cost: from $9.50 to $12.50 (pen + module and steel point)

Keuffel + Esser Co

The Stano-pen System

Standardgraph's brightly colored technical pen series can be likened to the Mars 700 above. It includes all the contemporary features such as hygro element caps, ventilation/labyrinth type drawing cones, key extractor inserted in the barrel, and drawing tips of either stainless steel or tungsten carbide. Cosmetically, the Stano-pen is unique in that it is color coded all over.

The drawing points have a range of 13 line-widths (6 to 5 x 0), nine of which conform to the metric scaled system. The pens come separately with a spare ink cartridge, in three-pen sets with cartridges, or in four-, seven-, and eight-pen sets that include key holes and ink. An extra four-pen set comes complete with ink, compass attachment, drop bow, masterbow, extension bar, and an adjustable joint.

Cost: from $8.95 to $11.95 (complete; steel point)

Martin Instrument Co

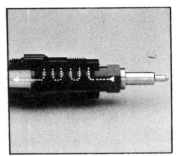

Leroy nine-pen set

The Polygraph System

The last of our technical pen systems, Alvin & Company's Polygraph, is comparable to any of the other systems. It has two ranges of pen, the black Combiscript and the green Micro series, both of which use chrome steel points. All basic features are otherwise the same as above; the main difference is cosmetic — the barrel design has finger grips.

The twelve sizes of drawing points, four of which match the metric scaling system, range from 2.00 to .004 and feature the ventilation labyrinth ink flow design. The caps are the dry-seal type.

Pens, pen parts, and accessories are available separately, or in five-size sets of three, four, eight, or fourteen reservoir sections with, annoyingly, only one pen holder. Each set contains either ink, some accessories, some reservoirs, or all three.

Cost: from $8.50 to $10.75 (Combiscript, complete).

Alvin & Co, Inc

Technical Pen Accessories

Each of the technical pen systems described above has complementary accessory items such as humidifier storage units, ultrasonic cleaner machines, cleaning fluids, cleaning pins, special erasers, templates, and specially formulated inks, all of which are interchangeable from system to system. Koh-I-Noor even has a miniature hygrometer for measuring humidity in the humidifiers, and a liquid humectant. Pens may fit each system's compass joint adaptor, but it is wise to use the same brand drafting implements that you do technical pen so that everything works together. And for that reason, as we suggested earlier, it's best to stick to one make of pen for all your needs.

Accessory items are shown throughout this section.

Ultrasonic Pen Cleaner

The most effective — and expensive — way to clean out technical pens quickly and neatly. High frequency sound waves release millions of energized, microscopic bubbles through a solution in the cleaning tank. Pens — or airbrushes and other drawing implements — are instantaneously scrubbed clean of all accumulated dried ink residue. Cast aluminum housing, stainless steel tank, and transistorized solid state circuitry. Supplied complete with ultrasonic cleaner compound and instruction booklet.

Cost: $110.00

FaberCastell Corporation

The Pelikan Graphos

A popular alternative to technical pens, the Graphos offers a more versatile drawing and writing system based on sixty easily interchangeable steel nibs of five basic types. The fountain pens are efficient in technical drawing, ruling and stenciling, freehand drawing, lettering, and calligraphy. The ink flow is continuous and uniform, and may be varied by using one of the three feed units.

Except the flexible "S" type, the rust-proof nibs are of a predetermined width not affected by varying pressure. A pivot device allows them to be easily and thoroughly cleaned. Nib types are shown in the chart below.

The penholder, including the ink reservoir, can be used in technical pen compasses and adaptors. Graphos is available in three sets: six nib and twelve nib, both with penholder, feed unit and ink; and a sixty nib set with penholder and three feed units. All parts are available separately.

Cost: $8.50 (penholder and feed unit); $1.00-$1.50 (nibs)

Koh-I-Noor Rapidograph, Inc

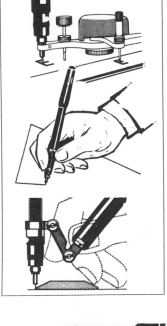

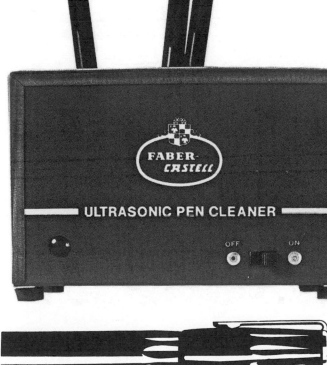

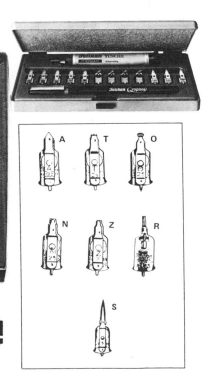

Technical Fountain Pen

The original technical pen, this versatile tool doubles as drawing, drafting, and lettering pen and uses regular drawing and writing inks. It is easy to use, has strong points, and is adaptable to any style of writing. The points come in eighteen color-coded sizes ranging from 14 through 6x0, and are available in stainless steel or jewel tips.

Cost: $16.00 (complete, stainless steel 2.0 point)

Koh-I-Noor Rapidograph, Inc

Koh-I-Noor Artpen

A new type of pen that's becoming popular, the Artpen features ultra-flexible nib units, screw plunger filling, and carefully controlled ink flow. Nibs are smooth and flexible with a quill-like touch, and are ideal for drawing and sketching. Six nib styles available.

Cost: $12.00 (complete with one nib unit)

Koh-I-Noor Rapidograph, Inc

Platinum Silverline Fountain Pen

The classic inexpensive fountain pen with squeeze filler bar and a range of sixteen nib units for all types of writing needs, from the usual fine, straight nibs to the broad oblique style, including two left handed types. Waterproof ink should not be used in these sorts of pens; rather, the Pelikan 4001 inks are recommended.

The Silverline is available separately, as a boxed italic set of pen plus five nib units, or as a boxed lettering set of pen and six nib units.

Cost: $3.50 (complete with one nib unit)

Pentalic Corporation

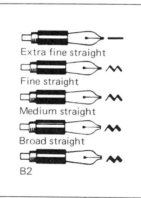

Silverline italic nib set

Mount Blanc Fountain Pen

From a range of thirty-six instruments in eleven styles of pen, pencil, and ballpoint, we have selected the Noblesse 1120 fountain pen. It is a beautifully designed writing instrument that uses ink cartridges, is easily converted to standard type filling from bottles, and has a refined steel nib and piston converter. White and black chromium plated.

Cost: $22.00

Koh-I-Noor Rapidograph, Inc

Metal Pen Holders

Balanced, lightweight aluminum penholders for either crowquills or lettering and writing nibs. Griffold #49 accepts all other nib styles. Nibs are locked vise-tight in the gripper heads to prevent any wobble.

Cost: $1.50 (47); $2.25 (49)

Griffin Manufacturing Co, Inc

Hunt Artist Nibs

Fine quality steel pen nibs for drawing, lettering, mapping, and fine line work, in a range of 15 styles for all requirements.

Cost: from 95¢ to $2.08 each

Charrette Corporation; all Flax stores

Mont Blanc — Extra Fine
Montblanc — Fine
Mont blanc — Medium
Moutblanc — Broad
Moutblanc — BBB (Wide)

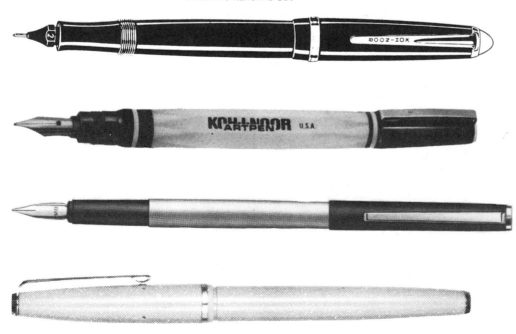

Marker Pens

Illustrator Pen

A relatively cheap artist's ballpoint with superfine carbide points that comes in three colors: India Ink black, India Ink red, and non-reproducing light blue.
Cost: 59¢ each

All Art Material stores

Shaeffer 2002

The best looking of the all-purpose ballpoints, with a fine rolling "tektor" point that writes smoothly with a blue or black liquid ink flow. A very smart writing implement that comes in a damn silly presentation case.
Cost: $5.00 each

Shaeffer Eaton

Pilot Razor Point

The most popular of the Pilot range of fineline marker pens has the "extreme" extra-fine point made of soft plastic (0.78mm tip). It lasts well and has a generous ink supply available in six colors.
Cost: 69¢ each

Pilot Corporation of America

Niji Stylist

An extra long-tipped, fineline pen suited to sketching and use with ruling equipment. Plastic tip in long metal shank is also long-lasting; range of twelve dense ink colors.
Cost: 50¢ each

Yasutomo & Co

Chisel Art Pens

Part of the well-known "Design" marker pen range from Eberhard Faber, the chisel point is a compatible addition to your studio pen selection. The nylon tip design produces a brush stroke or broad calligraphic effect, and makes an excellent writing or layout tool. Art pens come in three tip designs (fine, medium and chisel) and a range of twelve colors.
Cost: 50¢ each

Eberhard Faber, Inc

Flo-Master

A versatile drawing and writing marker "system" with a reuseable, chrome-plated brass barrel and special valve control. The pen is refillable with Flo-Master water-proof ink, and has six interchangeable felt wool nib styles. If you are careful, the nibs only need to be replaced occasionally, and the 4 ox. ink cans last a good while, making this a very economical marker pen system. The ADO Flo-Master comes with four assorted nibs, and uses either the eight colors of transparent ink or five colors of opaque ink.
Cost: $4.25 (without ink)

FaberCastell Corporation

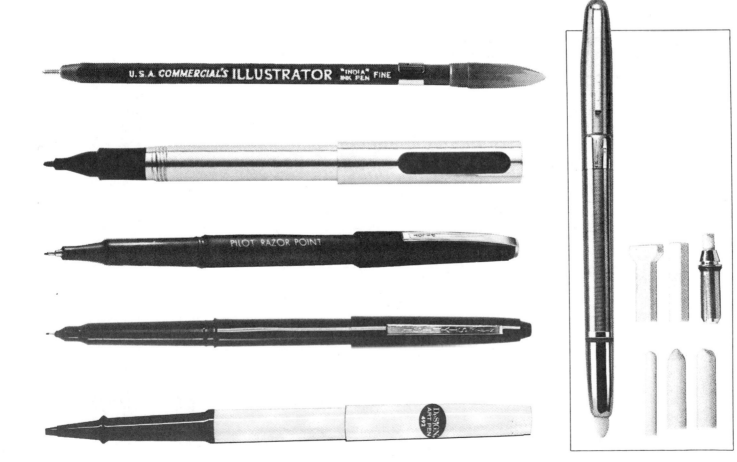

Pentel Signa

A heavy-duty marker that contains a lot of permanent ink. Stubby, durable, bullet-shaped, fiber-tipped point. Four colors.
Cost: 59¢ each

Pentel of America, Ltd

Colleen Scoop Double-ended Pen

There are four of these pens with different combinations of points, the two most useful being the black superfine point plus a broad, fluorescent yellow marker, and the black superfine point plus a red superfine point. The metal cased points are hard-wearing plastic.
Cost: $1.34 each

Itoya of America, Ltd

Niji Giant Markers

Extra broad, felt chisel-tipped permanent ink marker will draw in four line widths up to 1/2". Available in twelve colors with huge ink reservoirs, which, unfortunately, are not refillable.
Cost: $1.80 each

Yasutomo & Co

Pentel White Marker

On all types of surfaces, the best white line marker for opaque, waterproof, and quick-drying white lines. Two sizes, standard and fine.
Cost: $1.20 or $1.98 each

Pentel of America, Ltd

Non-Repro Blue Marker

An essential marker that will not reproduce on most reproducing equipment; good for notations on camera-ready art or layout planning. Medium-fine tip.
Cost: 59¢ each

Eberhard Faber, Inc

Lumocolor Markers

A marker pen system for drawing on acetate and similar materials for overhead projection. All the eight colors are available in either water-soluble or water-proof inks, and with two styles of polyester-fiber tip. They are available separately, or in sets of four or eight. Staedtler also supplies a special solvent marker to erase the inks, a Lumoplast eraser, a special compass, and Lumo-color AV technical pens.
Cost: 60¢ each

J S Staedtler, Inc

Opaquing Markers

A new application of the felt tip marker for working on film or negatives. Using one of the two tips — broad or fine — a solid line or area can be filled quickly with the dense opaque ink. Part of the Letraset "straight-through" marker pen system (see below).
Cost: $1.25 each

Letraset USA, Inc

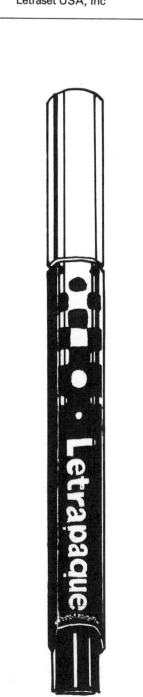

Letraset Pantone Markers

We have chosen these over the other brands for two major reasons: they are the state-of-the-art in marker pen design, and they are part of the Pantone color matching system (see page 000). Each Pantone marker barrel is color coded and bears the color code number. Broad nib versions are available in 120 permanent colors, and the fine tip in 48 colors.

The redesigned markers are elegant and slightly tapered for easy handling; tips are made of wool felt; a tight-fitting twist-off cap with an inner seal is coded white for broad tip, and black for fine tip, pens. The ink flow is very smooth and the colors full strength, including twenty-two grays and a double black.

All the markers are available separately, or in six-packs of various color combinations. There is also an "art director's" storage unit of sixty pens (free if you buy forty-eight pens), and a portable attache case kit containing 124 pens.

Cost: $1.20 each

Letraset USA, Inc

Letraset Marker Pads

A new series of special bleed-proof paper pads in the continental "A" paper sizes that are all in the golden mean proportion (see Paper, page 000). Lateral surface bleed is excellent and nothing soaks through; super-white; sizes: A2 (23.7" x 16.8"), A3 (16.8" x 11.8"), and A4 (11.8" x 8.4").

Cost: from $6.30 (A3)

Letraset USA, Inc

Magic Markers

For years, this alternative felt tip marker system has been a studio favorite with its extensive range of 186 permanent colors that are not Pantone matched. The famous barrel-type broad tip markers are available singly or in twelve unit sets of sixteen different color combinations. The fineline markers — a longer and slimmer design — come in seventy colors, and are available singly or in twelve unit sets of eight color combinations.

Magic Marker also produces an "introduction" desk-top stand set of thirty-six broad tip, twelve fine tip, and ten watercolor fine-line pens; and a "studio" desk-top unit of seventy-two broad tip, twenty-four fine tip, and ten watercolor pens; and the monster full spectrum studio set on a swivel-clamped stand containing 114 broad tips and thirty-six fine tips. There are even thirty-six spray cans of equivalent transparent marker colors for those really big areas — rather like a marker pen with a two-foot-wide tip.

Cost: 98¢ each
(39¢ for watercolor pens);
$2.75 (8 oz spray cans)

Magic Marker Corporation

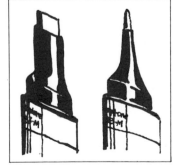

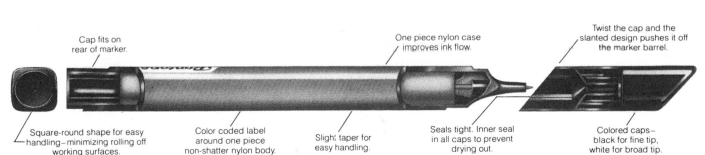

Cap fits on rear of marker.

One piece nylon case improves ink flow.

Twist the cap and the slanted design pushes it off the marker barrel.

Square-round shape for easy handling — minimizing rolling off working surfaces.

Color coded label around one piece non-shatter nylon body.

Slight taper for easy handling.

Seals tight. Inner seal in all caps to prevent drying out.

Colored caps — black for fine tip, white for broad tip.

Inks

All the manufacturers of technical pens supply their own brands of ink. Since these are all made to similar specifications, and for the same purpose, they are interchangeable. The best-known inks, Pelikan and Higgins, are matched by those offered by Artone, FW (Steig), Winsor & Newton, and Speedball.

Inks are formulated to be used on different surfaces and with different drawing implements; it is important, therefore, to select your ink type with care. Even so, since new plastic sheets with new properties are being introduced to the market regularly, you may find that your chosen ink does not work well on some plastic drafting surfaces. Polyester, particularly, requires special etching ink.

But in general, ink is not that complicated. Colored inks are the most versatile of mediums, and may be either transparent or opaque. Black India ink (water-proof) is very opaque, and, since its pigment is carbon, free of dye. All India inks can be diluted by adding aqua ammonia to pure water, four drops to the ounce. Drawing inks have a reasonable degree of permanence—if kept out of sunlight, and even out of strong diffused light. Since shellac is the usual waterproofing ingredient, it is essential that you clean pens, instruments, and brushes thoroughly after use; technical pens should in any case be cleaned out regularly.

Pelikan Drawing Inks

Pelikan offers a complete selection of inks for all uses in sixteen "transparent" colors and nine "opaque" shades that are well-known for the quality of their color and permanency. They can all be mixed with one another and diluted with distilled or boiled water. They come in round 29 ml (1 oz) bottles with pipette, square 10 ml bottles with quill filler, and three studio sizes of 9, 18, and 36 oz, but not all colors are available in all sizes.

Colors 1-18 (including a black, white, and light gray) are transparent—except for the white—and suitable for most *paper* surfaces. They dry waterproof and eraser-proof.

Six of these colors come in special formulations that are more free-flowing; they are the Type K colors which contain a solvent that slightly dissolves uncoated film surfaces and bonds with it, and affects all plastics. Obviously, these inks are not recommended for polyester base materials. Types T, TT, TN, and

C are special blacks for different surfaces; Type C only becomes waterproof after some time. Types T and TT are the most commonly used, and have special cleaning mediums that have to be used with them.

Shades 50-56 (including a special black) are dense, opaque colors formulated for technical pens and for use on most drafting films, as well as on all types of paper. The special black (#50) is a particularly good all-purpose ink, available in cartridges for the Technos pen (see above) and the 1 or 9 oz bottles only.

Pelikan Fount India ink is a free-flowing, deep black ink for use with ordinary fountain pens, and is almost waterproof when dry. It is available in a special 1 oz bottle or in a 9 oz bottle with rubber pouring spout. All the standard colors (1-18) can also be used in fountain pens.

Cost: $1.10 (1 oz, colors 1-18); $1.40 (1 oz, colors 50-56); $1.45 (1 oz, Types T and TT); $1.10 (Fount India)

Gunther Wagner Pelikan-Werke; Koh-I-Noor Rapidograph, Inc.

Higgins Drawing Inks

A broad range of good quality inks in seventeen colors and nine special color formulations for technical pens.

The non-waterproof range can be used with all equipment, pens, brushes, and airbrushes, and all seventeen colors can be mixed together or diluted to create a full spectrum of shades and hues. This range includes an opaque white that covers well and is free-flowing. An extra color, a non-waterproof intense black, can be added to produce a complete range of grays. The entire non-waterproof range is available in the distinctive one-ounce phial, in eight or 16 oz bottles, and in the gallon jug.

Higgins waterproof range replicates the non-waterproof range, but is better suited to technical pens and calligraphy. It can be used on all paper and some film surfaces. The black India ink is very dense and miscible.

The Higgins Pigmented colors are nine opaque shades that are permanent and lightfast;

they are specially formulated for use on drafting films, and with technical pens and airbrushes. Available in one- and three-ounce bottles.

Higgins Black Magic is a dense formulation intended for use on all drafting materials, including polyester; it adheres to the surface without cracking or peeling, and comes in the full range of bottle sizes as well as two small (23 ml and 38 ml) phials with long spouts.

FaberCastell also supplies complementary Artone inks: an ultra-opaque white for retouching; an extra dense matte black for drafting film; an exceptionally free-flowing black; and a non-waterproof sepia for fountain pens.

　　Cost: $1.00 (1 oz, waterproof or non-waterproof); $1.20 (1 oz, pigmented); $1.30 (1 oz, Black Magic)

FaberCastell Corporation

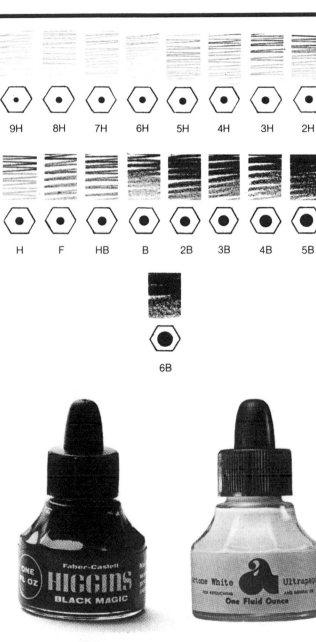

9H　8H　7H　6H　5H　4H　3H　2H

H　F　HB　B　2B　3B　4B　5B

6B

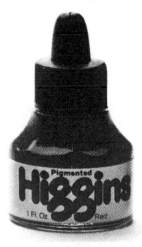

Pencils

Many art materials manufacturers make pencils, and there is an extraordinary variety of shapes, types, and sizes available. Very generally, pencils can be broken down into five types: black graphite, charcoal, colored, grease, and water soluble. There are also the various styles of leadholder and mechanical pencil that have enjoyed a minor renaissance of late. We have selected good quality examples in each category with the understanding that the same or similar pencils are invariably available under other brand names.

"Lead pencil" is a misnomer. The principal ingredient of most drawing pencils is graphite, a black mineral variety of carbon. In the best pencil, the graphite is bonded with a clay compound for point strength and even, slow wear, and the "leads" are often bonded to the wood to inhibit breakage and allow for smooth sharpening. The degree of hardness is indicated by a standard code; the chart above shows this seventeen degree gray scale (6B-9H) and the corresponding lead diameters.

Charcoal pencils make soft, jet black marks without gloss; both are used mainly for drawing or retouching. Grease or china-marking pencils are for all glossy surfaces, and rub off cleanly. Colored pencils contain more clay or polymers than other pencils, and the fine leads for mechanical pencils are usually made of a tempered graphite/polymer composition; they work best if grooved along their length for a firm grip by the mechanism. Like automobiles, leadholders come in every conceivable type of styling; and the differences among them are mostly cosmetic.

Usual breakage area now reinforced through bonding

Mongol Drawing

A top quality, all-purpose
pencil that comes in 10 grades;
hexagonal design, no eraser.
 Cost: $2.10 (dozen)

 Eberhard Faber, Inc

Wolff's Carbon Drawing (Royal Sovereign)

A favorite with artists, this is
an excellent layout pencil in six
grades; round, no eraser.
 Cost: $3.15 (dozen)

 J S Staedtler, Inc

Black Magic Drawing

Thick diameter, coal black
soft lead only; rounded black
finish; no eraser.
 Cost: $1.50 (dozen)

 FaberCastell, Inc

Oval Sketching

Extra wide lead for layout,
sketching, and lettering in three
grades; natural finish wood.
 Cost: $3.83 (dozen)

 Koh-I-Noor, Rapidograph,
Inc

Black Flyer Drawing

Jet black lead in five grades;
round cedarwood black finish;
with eraser.
 Cost: $2.70 (dozen)

 FaberCastell, Inc

Mars Dynagraph Drawing

Plastic-based lead for drawing
on drafting films in three grades;
blue hexagonal case.
 Cost: $4.50 (dozen)

 J S Staedtler, Inc

Eagle Verithin Non-Repro Blue

Strong, thin lead that takes
a needle point; it won't smear or
reproduce; round, no eraser.
 Cost: $2.50 (dozen)

 Berd USA

Unique Col-erase Blue

Easily erased medium blue
for all copy marking; hexagonal
blue case; special eraser.
 Cost: $2.50 (dozen)

 FaberCastell, Inc

Charcoal Sketching

100% pure charcoal with
no grease in three soft grades;
round black case.
 Cost: $4.80 (dozen)

 Koh-I-Noor, Rapidograph,
Inc

Eagle Prismacolors

Smooth, large diameter, soft-leaded range of sixty colors in round color-coded cases; waterproof and light resistant.

The hexagonal cased Verithin version that takes a needle point is available in thirty-nine waterproof colors.
Cost: $4.50 (Prismacolor, dozen); $2.50 (Verithin, dozen)

Berol, USA

Peel-off China Marker

Nine colors of crayon type lead that writes on all glossy surfaces. Very thick diameter leads, paper wrapped with pull-string.
Cost: $4.50 (dozen)

FaberCastell, Inc

Carb-Othello Pastel Pencils

A neat way to use pastels; thick diameter pastels in pencil form for easy sharpening; good spreading and blending; range of 60 colors.
Cost: $6.00 (set of 12)

Most art supply stores

Stabilo "All" Pencils

Water soluble pencils mark clearly and densely on all surfaces when dampened, and can be sharpened to a very fine point; hexagonal, color coded; range of nine colors.
Cost: $6.00 (dozen)

Flax stores;
Charrette Corporation

Eagle Turquoise 3375 Leadholder

A well-designed and styled leadholder, with all the necessary features: jeweler's chuck gripper without push-button action; unbreakable black plastic barrel with silver metal cap and grip; colored buttons for lead identification; takes all grades of standard leads.
Cost: $3.60

Berol USA

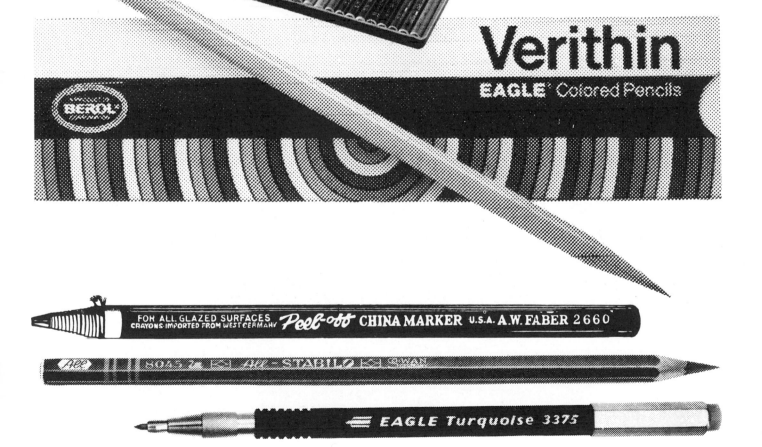

TK-Fine Mechanical Pencils

The best of the mechanical holders have long (5mm) telescopic sleeves for the lead points which retract as you draw. The TK's long sleeve is a half-slide version whose sleeve retracts to expose fresh lead, while remaining constant at 3.5mm in relation to the instrument. Comes with grade indicator, automatic lead feed, built-in eraser, cleaning wire, and lead storage. Very fine graphite and polymers have been blended to produce strong, dense points on a lead that requires no sharpening. Made for plastic film as well as all papers, and also available in red and blue, the leads come in four diameters — 0.9mm, 0.7mm, 0.5mm, and 0.3mm — of which the 0.5mm has the greatest grade range.

The TK pencil, therefore, comes in four sleeves and three models. The 0.5mm Professional pencil is beautifully styled in silver and green with grade indicator on the barrel.
Cost: $5.95 (leads: 70¢, pack of 12)

FaberCastell, Inc

Mars Lumograph Drawing Leads

Distinguished by the metal ferrule on the end of each lead to prevent it from falling out of the holder, Lumograph 2mm leads are strong, fine quality, grooved, and supplied in nineteen grades. Each lead is 5⅛", and printed with the grade in four places along its length. Each box of twelve leads is color coded, and includes a color coded button to be inserted in the top of the leadholder, if it has such a facility. Leads also available in twinpack tubes.
Cost: $3.84 (box of 12)

J S Staedtler, Inc

Pencil Accessories

Boston Vacuum Mount 1068

An inexpensive manual sharpener with self-feeder pencil guide that accommodates eight different sizes of pencil. Steel double bearing gears and twinmilling cutters stop automatically when the point is sharpened. Nickel chrome receptcle on gray or black stand with rubber air-suction cap that adheres to smooth surfaces. An efficient, utilitarian machine.
Cost: $9.25

Hunt Manufacturing Co

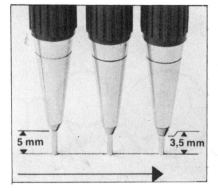

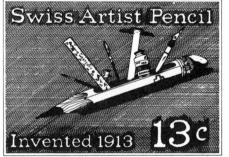

Dahle 166

A more sophisticated manual model with self-feeder, auto-stop, and "select-a-point" facility. Single, left-helix cutting head wtihin an orange/black receptacle with transparent reservoir draw. Excellent for drafting or soft coloring leads.
   Cost: $15.95

   Dahle USA, Inc

Panasonic Pana Point

Fully automatic, heavy duty, electric pencil sharpener with atuo-stop and transparent shaving receptacle. Non-skid suction caps; available in two colors: orange or tan.
   Cost: $21.95

   Panasonic Corporation

Eagle No. 17 Lead Pointer

Makes a needle point with a few revolutions against a 60 edge steel cutting wheel. Two-tone gray, complete with desk clamp, lead cleaning pads, and 4 guides for different size lead holders.
   Cost: $7.98

   Berol USA

Behrens Electric Lead Pointer

Precision made, high speed electric lead pointer for both pencils and leads. Carbide cutting wheel starts and stops automatically, activated by slight pressure. Walnut finished box and solid brass fittings mounted on rubber feet.
   Cost: $25.95

   Charrette Corporation;
A I Friedman

Mars Sandpaper Lead Pointer

Twelve sheets of extra fine sandpaper, padded and mounted on a handle—a convenient way to keep a pointed lead while concentrating on drawing or drafting. Something you can make yourself, in fact.
   Cost: 40¢

   J S Staedtler, Inc

Dry Cleaning Powder

A grit-free powder (Pounce) for sprinkling over a drawing surface before working, to remove any traces of grease and to keep the surface clean and free from smudges. Usually used with special cleaning pad.
   Cost: $1.25

   Keuffel + Esser Co

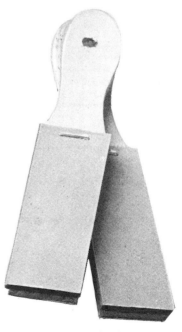

Erasers

There are several different kinds of erasers for different uses, and the major point to remember is never to use a plastic type for anything other than plastic films. We have chosen our selection from Eberhard Faber, makers of the famous "Pink Pearl" soft eraser for all pencil work. You will also need a kneaded rubber eraser for chalks, charcoal, and pastel as well as soft pencils; a gum eraser for cleaning off art-work and erasing over newly inked lines; and one or more plastic erasers, either hard, soft, or both. In addition to its usual block form, "Pink Pearl" also comes in a handy paper-wrapped stick and in a plastic tube with clutch, and can be sharpened like a pencil.

Cost: from 2.00 to $4.00 (dozen)

Eberhard Faber, Inc

Brunning Electric Eraser

Commonly used by draftspersons and architects for accurate detail erasing, the Brunning holds like a pencil and is vibration- and maintenance-free. Motor stalls if too much pressure is applied. Available with standard ring-type chuck, retractable hanger, and 7' cord; black finish. A cordless version is a little more expensive.

Cost: $38.00

All Flax stores; Charrette Corporation, A I Friedman

Dusting Brush

Pure gray horsehair brush, wax-set in a lacquered handle; 13" long.

Cost: $4.00

M Grumbacher, Inc

Studio Tissue

Strong, high quality tissue that absorbs better than any sponge and leaves no lint or smears.

Cost: $2.25 (dispenser of 75)

Arthur Brown & Bro, Inc

Tool Organizer

A desk-top item for holding
your immediate project's working
tools. A soft flocked foam organizer set in a black and white heavy
plastic base, 8¹/₂" long; four
foam colors: black, rust,
dark blue, red.
        Cost: $8.00

Charrette Corporation

Foam Cube Organizer

With one-inch-square cubes of
foam mounted to a one-inch-wide
strip of wood or plastic, you can
make your own handy desk-top
tool organizer for nothing.

"Set-up" Dentistry Trays

Ideal for keeping all your drafting tools easily accessible and
neatly stored, the high-impact
plastic and stainless steel tray
holder will take about eight high-
impact plastic flat trays or set-up
trays with compartments and
instrument slots. A tray holder
with dust cover (12¹/₂" x 9¹/₂"
x 9") plus six mixed trays is a
complete package.
        Cost: $38.50
(extra trays: $3.50 each)

Henry Schein, Inc

Girex Rotating Tray

This ubiquitous item that
collects dust easily is available
everywhere. An artist's lazy susan
that holds everything you will
need for the day's work within its
10" circle. Three tool holder depths
and seven trays in six colors.
        Cost: $10.00

Keuffel + Esser Co

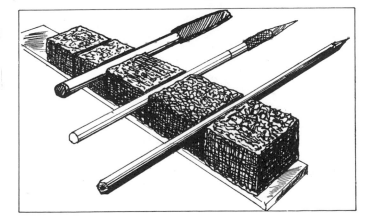

Stac-A-Drawer

Very useful styrene, high-impact drawers that come in sets of three and can be added to, one unit at a time. Gray frame 10" x 12" x 5¾" with drawers in a choice of three colors.

Cost: $8.95 (3-drawer unit)

A I Friedman, Sam Flax

Mecanorma Drawer Unit

A slim, five-drawer unit designed to hold pressure graphic sheets; also makes ideal tool storage trays, or trays for holding any papers, roughs, drawings-in-progress, etc. Durable, lightweight plastic in white or orange; comes with cap and base; two or more units can be stacked one above the other; 13" x 17" x 9".

Cost: $48.50 (5-drawer unit)

Keuffel + Esser Co

Bieffe Tablotte

A table-top extension unit, compartmentalized to hold a whole range of working tools, including inks, drafting tools, and such, at your side and off the board. It even has a humidifier container for technical pens. Easily fitted with screws to either the right or left hand side, and can be used at an angle.

Cost: $28.00

Inter/Graph Ltd;
all Flax stores

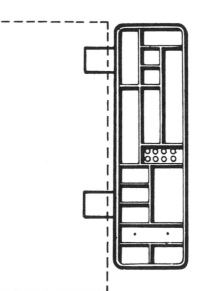

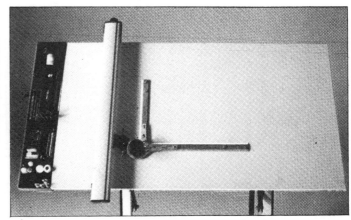

Brushes and Airbrushes

Brushes

A brush consists of three parts: the hair, the ferrule, and the handle. Most important is the hair, the highest grade of which is known as red sable. Other grades are: ox hair, black sable, "camel" hair, fitch hair, badger hair, and goat hair.

The best brushes are made from Kolinsky fox tails, commonly known as the Red Tartar marten. Carefully selected and properly prepared, this hair is soft textured and resilient, and has a natural taper from root to tip. The price of red sable increases substantially as its length increases slightly, which explains the expense of the large size red sable brushes. Black sable comes from the Stone marten, a very durable but scarce hair that comes from tails of the Canadian civet-cat. Black sable is best suited to oil colors.

Ox hair, from the ears of oxen, comes in many qualities; they are all soft, with great tensile strength, and will take a lot of abuse. So-called "camel" hair is also soft; the name is applied in-discriminately to the hair of squirrels and ponies; camel hair is the most common general purpose brush used in graphic arts. Fitch hair comes from either the Russian fitch *(Iltus)* or the North American skunk; it is a very soft hair not suitable for water based colors. The Eastern European badger hair makes a good, resilient, soft brush; goat hair is both coarser and cheaper.

Bristle-type brushes are mainly used for oil painting; the hair comes from hogs and boars. Brushes made of nylon are for use with acrylic (polymer) paints.

The best brushes are made partly by hand; the hair is tied and inserted into the ferrule, then pulled out to the required length. In the final steps of brushmaking, setting compound is placed in the ferrule; they are vulcanized or "cured," and the handle is inserted, crimped, and stamped.

We are dealing with brushes made for watercolor and polymer use, and include four basic brush shapes: pointed, oval, flat, and round. We have selected our basic range from Grumbacher's large collection, and included only those of use to the graphic artist. Illustrators, specifically, will use a much wider selection for all kinds of special effects.

It is important to clean brushes thoroughly after every use, with cold water and mild soap for water colors, benzine or turpentine, and lukewarm water and mild soap for oil-based colors, squeezing out from the ferrule to the tip. They should then be shaped and stored flat, or upright resting on their handles.

The size of a brush is indicated by number, usually from 1 on up; the larger the number the larger the brush. Some sizes are given in inches and fractions.

Grumbacher Series 177

A range of eleven graphic arts brushes of selected red sable, with long-tapered, needle-sharp points. Slimline design with nickel plated seamless ferrules fastened to black handles. The top quality brushes for all water colors and inks, from size 000 to 8.
Cost: from $2.50 to $20.00

Grumbacher Series 178

A short-haired sable brush range with needle points for all kinds of detail work. Slimline nickel plated ferrules and ivory handles; sizes 00000 to 5.
Cost: from $1.15 to $2.40

Pointed   Oval   Flat   Round

Grumbacher 926B Flats

Straight, square-edged red sable brushes with nickel plated ferrules and black handles. Sizes 0 to 12.

Cost: from $1.10 to $5.60

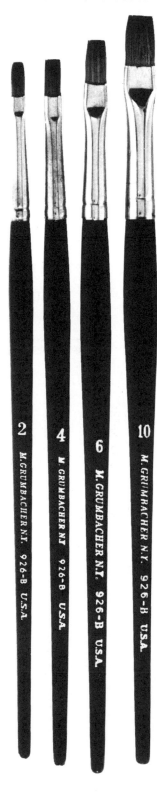

Grumbacher Series 4567 Acrylic

Fine white nylon brushes that last much longer than others with polymer paints. Nickel plated ferrules on tan handles; sizes 1 to 12 in either of three brush shapes: bright (short-haired flats), flat, or round.

Cost: from $1.05 to $2.75

M Grumbacher, Inc

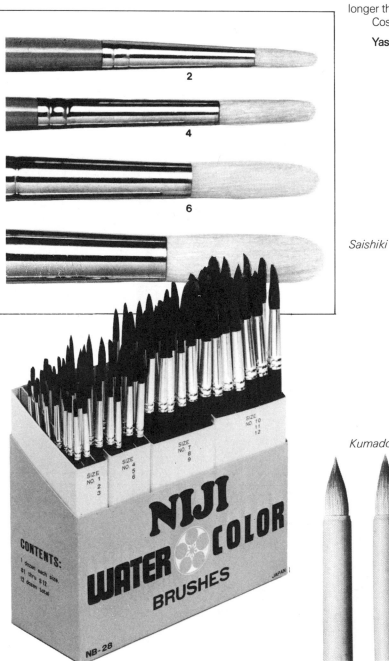

Niji Watercolor Round Brushes

Made of "camel" hair in aluminum ferrules, these are inexpensive, medium length, rounded brushes for all graphic work; sizes 1 to 12.

Cost: from 30¢ to $1.10

Yasutomo & Co

Sumi Brushes

Japanese sumi brushes come in a variety of styles and forms; two that are particularly useful are called Saishiki and Kumadori. Without going into the complexities of sumi, you need Sabaki type brushes: brushes free of starch, made of stiff hair surrounded by soft hair. The two Sabaki state brushes have specially tapered hairs inserted in wooden handles; Kumadori (five sizes) are broader and longer than Saishiki (three sizes).

Cost: from $2.50 to $10.00

Yasutomo & Co

Saishiki

Kumadori

Airbrushes

The airbrush is designed to apply color as an atomized spray by means of air pressure. Fundamentally, an airbrush consists of two valves in the body of the brush, a needle valve at the nozzle, and an air valve controlling air velocity which in turn regulates the amount of color drawn from the reservoir. Through a combination of air pressure and needle valve opening, the operator has full control of the instrument. In double action brushes, the two valves are controlled by the same lever; in the single action type, the lever only controls the air valve, and the needle valve is set in a separate adjustment.

Paasche AB Type Airbrush

A model for the experienced professional, the AB type draws the finest hairline or dot to a gradually widening pattern. It is used primarily for fine detail work, and is excellent for retouching. This is a double action airbrush powered by an air turbine, which permits the brush to use all types of watercolor and inks without clogging. Comes with adjustable color cup, one dozen needles, and basic tools, hanger, and hose coupling.
    Cost: $152.80

Paasche Airbrush Co

Badger 100L Standard Illustration

A much less expensive, general illustration airbrush, this has a wider spray pattern than the Paasche, but is still capable of fine line work. The large reservoir allows a large area to be covered, and will handle thinned down lacquers and enamels as well as watercolors. It is a double action airbrush that comes with interchangeable color cups, one extra needle, wrench, and coupling.
    Cost: $55.00

Badger Air-Brush Co

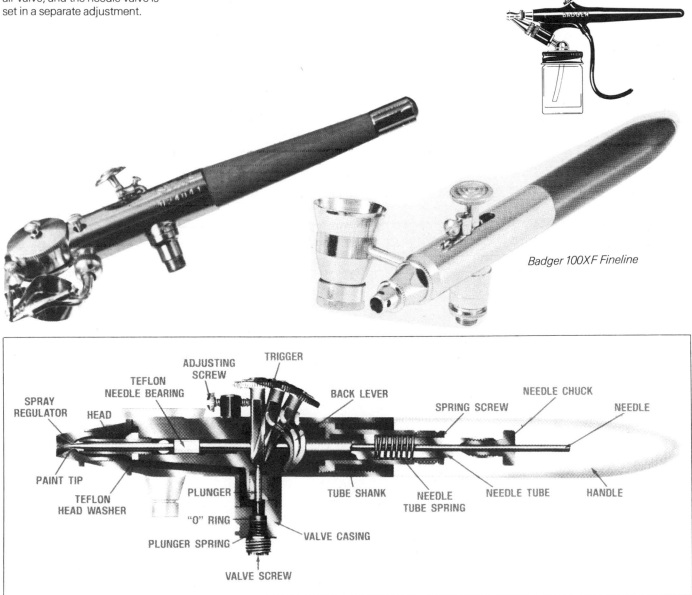

Badger 100XF Fineline

Paasche Type H Airbrush

A less sophisticated all-purpose airbrush capable of a wide range of color effects. It has three sizes of interchangeable color and air cap parts: H1 for light colors and fine detail; H3 for medium tone colors and less detail; and H5 for heavier colors and faster spray. The Type H can use any liquid color, varnish, or lacquer. It is a single action airbrush and comes with reservoir cup and bottle, H3 adjuster part, and hanger.
Cost: $25.15

Paasche Airbrush Co

Single Diaphragm Air Compressor

To operate an airbrush you need some type of air pressure system that delivers pressure up to thirty pounds. The Paasche D1 (¼ hp) is the smallest of the heavy duty air compressors to suit most requirements. It is light, portable, and quiet; its rubber diaphragm will last for 500 hours and is easily replaced. Two-tone green, 110 v, 60 cycle, 1 phase motor, ac only. Comes with extra diaphragm, 10 feet of cord, and plug.
Cost: $110.88

Paasche Airbrush Co

Carbonic Gas Cylinders

A pressure system for those who use a limited amount of compressed air. The 10 lb LCT gas (CO_2) unit with simple attachments for airbrush and air regulator is ideal where electricity may not be available. Weighs 27 lb when full, with valve; refills are available locally from places like soda fountain suppliers.
Cost: $93 (complete with air regulator and gauge)

Paasche Airbrush Co

The Complete Airbrush Book

There are many techniques and tricks which will maximize your skills with an airbrush; and if you are new to painting with air, a good manual will be a great help. The *Airbrush Book* is a clear, basic text on the step-by-step use of the artist's airbrush; techniques, care and maintenance, rendering, retouching, and designing with air, are all covered with 425 illustrations.
Cost: $12.95

Paasche Airbrush Co

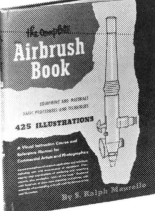

Airbrush Paints

Airbrushes will take all water-based mediums with no problem as long as they are of the correct consistency, and some will also accept acrylics and lacquers (see "Inks and Color & Paints" in this section). However, there are special retouch colors in the complete gray scale from white to black that are particularly suited for airbrush retouch work. Gamma Neutral Grays are equivalent to photographic tonal values from No 1 to No 6, as are warm or cool grays. Misket is a liquid masking frisket used with watercolors and easily removed by peeling or rubbing.

Cost: 85¢ each (Gamma Neutral Grays); 90¢ (Gamma Warm and Cool Grays); $1.75 (Misket)

M Grumbacher, Inc

Copyon Frisket Film

Unprinted, self-adhesive, matte acetate film .0012" thick, for masking out any area while retaining complete visibility. Heat resistant sheets have low-tack adhesive which is very easily removed. The film can also be drawn or typed upon if necessary.

Cost: 60¢ (10 x 14)

Graphic Products Corporation

The Atomiser

A mouth-operated spray tool for use with watercolors, fixatives, and some varnishes, this tool allows you to duplicate certain airbrush effects such as stippling. Seamless nickel-brass folding tube, 5" long. But be careful. You are dangerously near your medium and some inks, paints, and fixatives are toxic.

Cost: 95¢

M Grumbacher, Inc

Adhesives and Tapes

Adhesives

The abundance of adhesives on the market — rubber and latex cements, wax, dry-mount sheets, low-tack position mounting sheets, and aerosol spray adhesives — have myriad applications within the graphic arts, depending on the situation and purpose. Although the spray adhesives are superior to rubber cement and some other adhesives because a uniformity of depth can easily be achieved with them, they require extra care in both maintenance and application to guard against their fumes.

One-Coat Rubber Cement

Although many of the applications for rubber cement have been usurped by other types of adhesives, this is still a mainstay of the graphic arts professions, and is widely used for such paper-to-paper adhesions as mechanicals, layouts, type proofs, and the assemblage of photostats. A good-quality, naturally white rubber cement such as Best-Test provides stable adhesion, yet can be removed easily without leaving traces; it will not wrinkle, curl, or shrink the thinnest paper. Usually available in quart or gallon containers.

Cost: $8.95 (gallon)

Union Rubber & Asbestos Co

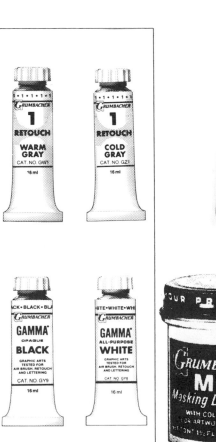

Bestine Rubber Cement Solvent

Essential for thinning or reducing rubber cement, and for removing mounted material. Non-toxic, non-staining, and evaporates very quickly. Available in pints, quarts, and gallons.
Cost: $2.25 (quart)

Union Rubber & Asbestos Co

Rubber Cement Dispenser

Natural, standard grade polyethylene of about 1-pint capacity. A non-breakable container with metal brush cap and attached brush.
Cost: $3.00

Most art supply stores

Valvespout Solvent Dispenser No 45

A metal, cone-type leakproof, dispenser for use with cement solvent or similar volatile fluids, or with water. A twisting brass valve and double diaphragm keep the liquid from evaporating, and permit one drop of steady flow. Holds 6 fl oz.
Cost: $5.25

Most art supply stores

Rubber Cement Pick-up

A small square of crepe rubber is necessary for removing excess rubber cement completely and cleanly.
Cost: 50¢

All art supply stores

Elmer's Glue-All

The handy latex-type water-based glue that dries clear, and holds fast when completely set. Not recommended as a paper adhesive, but excellent for mounting to boards, wood, cloth, and all porous materials. Non-toxic and non-flammable; plastic squeeze bottles of 1½ oz, 4 oz, 8 oz, 16 oz, and 22 oz, or quart bottle and gallon jug.
Cost: $2.75 (16 oz)

All hardware and art supply stores

Elmer's Contact Cement

A latex-based adhesive for hard-to-glue areas, which bonds all porous and non-porous surfaces instantly on contact. Heat resistant, non-toxic, and waterproof, it cleans up with water while wet. Available in 1 oz and 3 oz tube, or pint and quart cans.
Cost: $1.27 (3 oz)

All hardware and craft stores

Artwax

A polymer adhesive white wax that melts at the low temperature of 143°F. Artwax is the ideal adhesive medium for pasteup and mechanicals because it allows elements to be re-positioned as frequently as necessary, yet will stick firmly when burnished. Artwax should not be melted at higher than 160°F for efficient use; and is suitable for most waxing machines. Packed in 10 lb box of 40 bars, or 5 lb box of twenty bars, individually wrapped.
Cost: $18.90 (10 lb)

Portage

'Lectro-Stik Waxer

The smallest waxing unit available, this hand-held waxing roller with heated reservoir can be used anywhere. Holds two bars of any type wax in a rein-forced plastic body; rubber-tired roller; 120 v. Lays down a strip 1" wide. Lectro-Stik requires no adjustment and little upkeep, pro-viding you never have it plugged in empty. Since it takes an hour to heat up, it is best to keep the waxer "on" all the time. Comes with wax, replacement tires, and film seats; all the parts are available separately.
Cost: $32.50

Lectro-Stik Corporation

The Artwaxer 111

An inexpensive waxing machine encased in reinforced plastic with open-ended rollers that will cover an 11" width with wax stripes. All parts easily accessi-ble for cleaning; 115 v; comes complete with footswitch, artwax, art burnisher, artbrayer, extra parts packet, and instructions.
Cost: $269.00

Portage

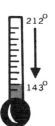

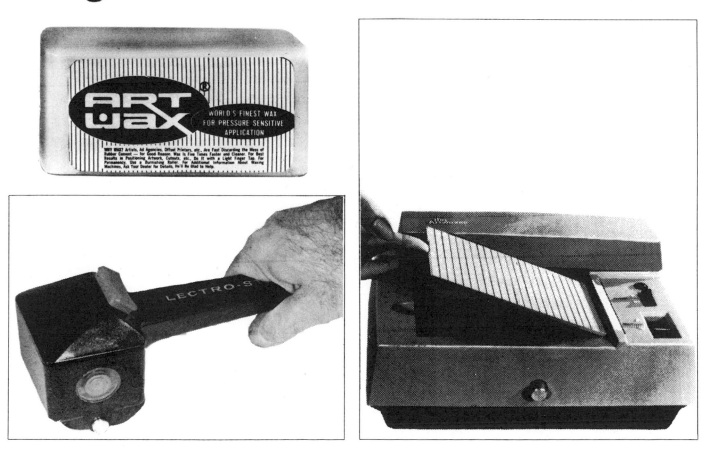

Schaefer Wax Coater

If your volume of waxing is such that you require a heavy-duty, industrial-type machine, you may as well get a wide 14" model. The Schaefer is a proven, sturdy, metal machine that lays down a smooth layer of wax, and has a calibrated dial so you can adjust the wax layer you need. Direct motor drive, temperature control, thermostat, adjustable heated strippers, and pressure roller; 110 v; 1000 watts; footswitch is an optional extra.

Cost: $465.00 (14")

Schaefer Machine Co, Inc

Twin-Tak Mounting Sheets

A double-sided, self-adhesive, transparent dry-mounting cellulose sandwiched between two heavy release papers. Mounts anything to anything quickly, cleanly, and permanently. Available in sizes 18 x 24 and 24 x 36.

Cost: $1.50 (18 x 24)

The Ulano Companies

Scotch Positionable Mounting Adhesive

A dry-mounting adhesive contained between two sheets of release paper allows material to be repositioned for proper alignment. Once burnished it forms a high-strength bond, but it has to be burnished hard and evenly. Ideal for photo mounting, paste-ups, layouts, and so on. Three sizes of 25-sheet boxes: 8 x 10, 11 x 14, and 16 x 20.

Cost: $6.94 (8 x 10)

3M Company

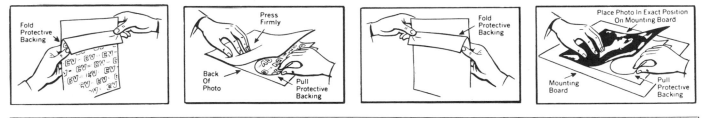

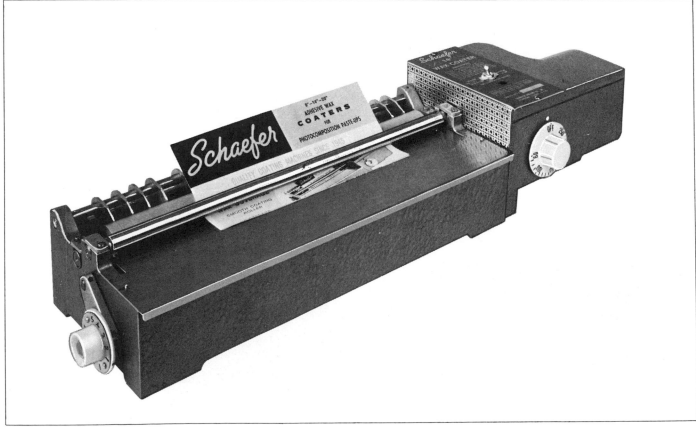

Fusion 4000

A dry-mounting adhesive in thermoplastic sheet form for use with a dry mount press. It bonds without bubbles or bleed-through, and is 100% Ph balanced. Since the adhesive liquefies completely, it can be patched, overlapped, and pieced together without difficulty or waste. Useful for all problem materials such as resin-coated paper, plastic-coated stats, foils, or fabrics, and even Fome-Cor, Masonite, formica, particle board, plywood, etc. However, it requires a hot press. Available in 100-sheet boxes in four sizes, and in six roll sizes.
Cost: $8.50 (8 x 10)

Seal Art Materials Group

Seal Dry Mount Press 210

A dry mount press is an expensive piece of equipment, and for the money it is wisest to get a large enough machine to cover all needs, including lamination. The Commercial 210 has an 18½ x 23" platen that takes work up to 36" wide by any length in sections. Easy to operate, the manual 210 reaches operational temperature fast with minimal heat loss at the edges; durable steel cantilevers, free-floating platen, optional thermostatic control. 115 v, 1300 watts (adapts to 220 v).
Cost: $488.00

Seal Art Materials Group

Technal TKR Rollamount

An inexpensive dry-mounting device that will handle most basic dry mounting. Hand operated; heated rollers; built-in thermostatic temperature control. 115 v.
Cost: $50.00

All Flax stores

Uhu Glue Stick

A compact stick of rub-on, dry glue that operates like lipstick; clean and convenient for quick tacking at the drafting table, it is for use mainly on paper, but adheres well to fabric, photographs, and polystyrene.

Cost: 80¢

FaberCastell, Inc

Spray Mount Adhesive

There are several all-purpose spray glues among which the most practical for use in the graphic arts is 3M's Spray Mount (No 6065). It is a clear, one-surface adhesive that is repositionable for several hours, and will not soak through, stain, or wrinkle. Like all aerosol sprays, this one has to be taken care of if it is to stay in working condition, and must be shaken vigorously before use. Read the instructions, and beware of overspray.

Cost: $4.17 (11 oz can)

3M Company

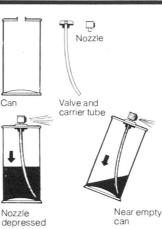

Nozzle

Can

Valve and carrier tube

Nozzle depressed

Near empty can

hisssss . . .

Tapes

All the tapes listed below are from the 3M range, and all are pressure-sensitive; most come in both one- and three-inch sizes. In all cases we suggest the larger, in 60- or 72-yard rolls suitable for commercial dispensers. They are cheaper per inch of tape, and more convenient. We also recommend rolls that are 3/4" wide for most uses.

No 810 Magic Transparent Tape

The general-purpose Scotch tape that supersedes the stronger No 600 transparent PVC tape for most graphic purposes. It's more expensive, but it is almost invisible and can be written on. Offers matte finish with good adhesion, and is water repellent. The 72-yd rolls are available in three widths: 1/2", 3/4", and 1".
Cost: $2.78 (3/4")

No 230 Drafting Tape

Another all-purpose tape to hold things together temporarily while you work. Supersedes No 202 masking tape which will discolor, stain, and leave adhesive residue upon ageing. A crepe paper drafting tape with a low-tack adhesive more economically bought in bulk rather than in its cutter-edge dispenser box. 60-yd rolls in 1/2", 3/4", and 1" widths.
Cost: $1.10

No 256 White Paper Tape

Smooth, matte white surface takes ink, markers, and pencil, and is ideal for pasteup work, mounting, etc. Firm adhesive, easy edge-tear, and removes cleanly. 60-yd rolls in 1/4", 1/2", 3/4", 1", 2", and 3" widths.
Cost: $2.50

No 235 Black Crepe Tape

A totally opaque, flexible tape for masking, mounting, and many other uses. Black, rubber saturated with low-tack adhesive; usually comes in a cutter-edge dispenser box, but best bought in bulk. 60 yd in 1/2", 3/4", and 1" widths.
Cost: $3.65

No 400 Double-Coated Tape

An opaque paper tissue-coated on both sides with a heavy-duty adhesive that bonds well to a variety of surfaces. Removable crepe paper liner between each two layers of tape. Excellent for mounting purposes. 36-yd rolls of 1/4", 1/2", 3/4", 1", and 2" widths.
Cost: $3.05

No 924 Adhesive Transfer Tape

A film of acrylate adhesive on a silicone-coated glassine paper with no liner. This is a version of No 465 designed for use with a special dispenser that transfers the adhesive easily to any smooth surface. A handy mounting medium that works and rubs off like rubber cement. 36-yd rolls of 1/2" and 3/4".
Cost: $3.86

Scotch ATG 750 Dispenser

For use only with No 924 transfer tape. A fast one-handed operation with trigger.
Cost: $19.00

No 898 Glass Filament Tape

An exceptionally strong and flexible tape with instant adhesion and maximum holding power: 300 lb tensile strength per inch width. Perfect for wrapping, and for any bond that needs strength. 60-yd rolls of 1/2", 3/4", and 1".
 Cost: $3.50

No 255 Package Sealing Tape

A natural-colored Kraft paper tape with a high-tack adhesive, stronger and heavier-weight than masking tapes. Mainly for sealing packages and large envelopes, or for mounting uses. 60-yd roll of 1 1/2" width only.
 Cost: $3.72

No 393 Gaffer's Cloth Tape

An exceptionally sticky and strong plastic-coated cloth tape with silver-gray finish. For all sorts of studio purposes like taping cables to the floor or walls, sealing and attaching things to surfaces. Peels off cleanly, but may take loose paint or other finish with it. 60-yd roll is 2" wide.
 Cost: $5.80

All the above tapes from 3M Company

P-54W Mainline Tape Dispenser

A multiple 3" core tape roll holder for tapes 1/4" to 4" wide. Portable, but weighted for desk-top use.
 Cost: $17.00

3M Company

C22 Heavy-Duty Dispenser

A 3" core two-tape roll metal holder either for two tapes up to 1" wide or one tape 2" wide. Heavily weighted dispenser with foam rubber base.
 Cost: $13.75

3M Company

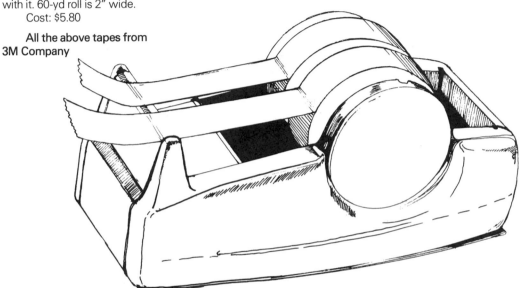

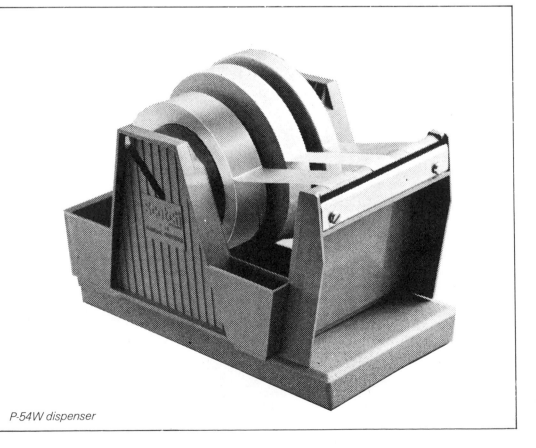

P-54W dispenser

M73 Bracket Dispenser

A dispenser that mounts on the side of a working table or cabinet, with screws. Holds 3" core tapes up to 1" wide.
Cost: $2.95

3M Company

204HD Multiple Tape Bracket

Dispenses all kinds and widths of tape up to 4" wide, or three 1" tapes, with 3" cores. Bracket clamps rigidly to desk or table.
Cost: $8

All art material stores

Colors and Paints

Of the four types of color mediums — oil, alkyd resin, acrylic (polymer emulsion), and water-based — acrylic and water-based are the most convenient for use in the graphic arts. Watercolors may be either transparent or opaque; gouache, cassein, and tempera are opaque colors. Many polymer colors are also water-based, and can be mixed with wet watercolors; but acrylic polymers dry with a tough, durable plastic film. The popularity of the new alkyd resin (spirit-based) colors is partly attributable to the fact that they have the disadvantages of neither oils nor acrylics. Other color mediums include the soft pastels, Cray-Pas (a pastel/crayon compound that blends and mixes like oils), aerosol spray paints, marker liquids (very liquid watercolors that resemble inks), and inks and markers (see pages 67–71).

Pre-Tested Oil Colors

A high-quality range of pure, brilliant, permanent oils available in 47 colors and 3 whites in 1 x 4" tubes. The whites are also available in 1½" x 6" tubes. The whole range of color vehicles or mediums — Cobalt Drier (linoleate) poppyseed oil, linseed oil, turpentine, and so on — are part of the Grumbacher series.
Cost: $1.00 to $3.00 (tube)

M Grumbacher, Inc

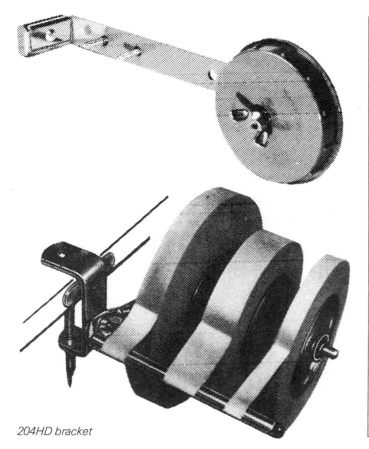

204HD bracket

W & N Alkyd Colors

A range of thirty colors most of which correspond to oil color pigments. Alkyds are neither oil color nor acrylic, and fall somewhere in between. They are a spirit-based resin color medium that has most of the properties of oils; they dry much faster than oils, but not as fast as acrylics. Colors are thinned with white spirit or turpentine, and there are three vehicles to modify the paint quality: Liquin, Win-Gel and Oleopasto, all based on alkyd resin. All colors come in 1 x 4'' tubes; whites also come in 1½ x 5½" tubes.

Cost: $1.80 to $10.00 (per tube)

Winsor & Newton, Inc

Acrylic Polymer Colors, Series 1045

Thirty-nine fast drying and completely permanent colors that thin and clean-up with water. The acrylic, or plastic resin, bonding agent creates a durable gloss film that is highly adhesive and water-resistant. Water and other mediums such as Gel or Gesso (a modeling paste and drying retarder) extend the versatility of the paints. Series 1045 comes in tubes of 1⅛ x 5". (Series 1047 is composed of two blacks and a white in 1½ tubes.)

Cost: $1.15 to $2.75 (per tube)

Liquitex

Speedball White Polymer Gesso

An excellent medium for covering large areas of dense, opaque white. Dries fast and waterproof. Used to prepare all sorts of surfaces for color work, it can be applied with brush, roller, or squeegee. Gesso can also be tinted with any acrylic color. 8 oz, pint, quart, or gallon sizes.

Cost: $2.75 (pint)

Hunt Manufacturing Co

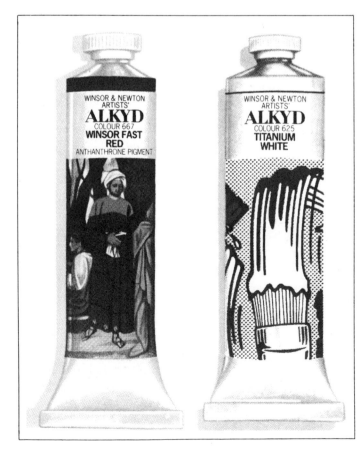

W & N Gouache Watercolor

A brilliant, superfine (gouache) watercolor with very smooth flow and great opacity. Can be used with transparent watercolors to produce combinations of transparency and opacity, and can be thinned for use in airbrushes and instruments, or as a wash. Designer's Gouache comes in three degrees of pigment permanency: type A colors are largely permanent; type B is moderately fast to light; and type C is called "fugitive." The eighty-three colors are divided into four series indicating pigments of different prices; ³/₄ x 2³/₄" tubes.

    Cost: $1.00 to $2.40

    Winsor & Newton, Inc

Pelikan Tempera Color

A glue-tempera that dries to a smooth, densely opaque matte finish. The brilliant shades of the sixty-nine colors are suitable for work on paper, cardboard, wood, and similar materials. Suitable for application with airbrush and instruments. This tempera adheres very well and dries waterproof. Four metallic colors are also available. Comes in tubes (³/₄ x 5", 1¹/₄ x 6¹/₄") or ³/₄ oz jars.

    Cost: $1.50 (1¹/₄ x 6¹¹/₄" tube)

    Koh-I-Noor Rapidograph, Inc

Pelikan Plaka Cassein Emulsion

A ready-to-use, waterproof formulation that has exceptional covering power. It dries matte and adheres to all kinds of surfaces. Supplied in 1³/₄ oz jars or 12¹/₂ oz cans, cassein emulsion can be diluted with water outside its container. The Plaka assortment comprises twenty-five colors plus three bronzes and seven fluorescent shades, and is also available in 10 oz aerosol spray cans.

    Cost: $1.75 to $3.50 (1³/₄ oz jar); $6.15 to $13.50 (spray cans)

    Koh-I-Noor Rapidograph, Inc

Steig Luma Water Colors

Applied full-strength, these eighty brilliant colors in liquid form equal tempera in depth and intensity. They are luminous, can be diluted with water to produce an infinite range of hues, and can be "erased" with bleach. Supplied in 2 oz bottles with eye-dropper stopper, and 8 oz, 16 oz, and 32 oz bottles.

Cost: $1.90 (2 oz bottle)

Sam Flax; A l Friedman

Blair Instant Color

Spray colors are a useful addition to any color inventory. Apart from marker spray colors (Spray Mark, see page 69), Blair produces high-quality and durable aerosol colors especially for paper and for use on wood, cloth, metal, glass, some plastics, and styrofoam. The colors dry very quickly to a matte surface that takes and holds a good top-coat. Nineteen colors plus four metallics in the 8 oz cans, and matte white and black also in the 16 oz cans.

Cost: $1.69 (8 oz)

Blair Art Products

Marabu Retouch Grays

These retouch sets are considered to be the best retouching medium. The eighteen cakes retouch grays and brown/gray, and come one at a time, or in metal palette boxes in sets of twelve or twenty four. Very smooth in consistency, they work up quickly to brushing condition, and are suitable for airbrushes.

Cost: $22.95 (24 cake set)

Loew Cornell, Inc

Nupastel Color Sticks

Square sticks of solid color that are firmer and stronger than conventional pastel sticks. Nupastels resist crumbling, and are firm and clean to use; perfect for toning, delicate shades, blends, and detail work. Wide range of ninety-six strong colors that take fixative without discoloration. Available in six sets of eight sizes containing from twelve to twenty-four colors, plus one set of all grays.

Cost: $10.80 (set of 36 sticks)

Eberhard Faber, Inc

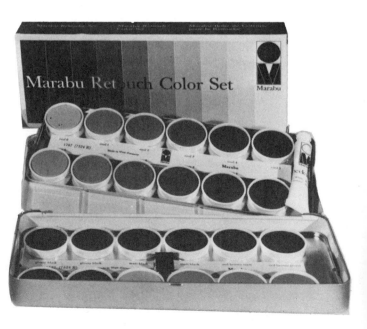

Cray-Pas Sticks

Round sticks of compound crayon and pastel that blend and mix rather like oil pastels, not waxy or chalky. The brilliantly pigmented colors are very clean to use. Available in sets of five sizes from twelve to fifty colors.

Cost: $6.50 (set of 50 sticks)

Charrette Corporation; A I Friedman

Metallic Opaque

An extremely dense, black graphite, water-based opaquing liquid for working on negatives, glass, or strip film. Non-crawling, flat, and smooth. Opaque can be removed by washing in water. (Speed-O-Paque is the red clay version for the same purpose.) 2 oz and 8 oz jars.

Cost: $2.25

M Grumbacher, Inc

Pelikan Graphic Black & White

Opaque, waterproof correction and retouch black and white that dry quickly with a matte finish, eliminating reflections for reproduction. Adhere firmly and will not dissolve or bleed when painted over, but may react with some ink formulations. Take all surfaces with excellent coverage. Black comes in 1 oz tubes, white in 2 oz glass jars.

Cost: $1.40 (black); $2.50 (white)

Koh-I-Noor Rapidograph, Inc

Snopake

The new formula Snopake requires no thinner and is non-flammable; available in either water-base or quick-drying spirit-base. The brush-in cap is convenient, but it is not designed for detail work. Excellent for most corrections; will not crack or peel even on acetate. Handy 1/2 oz spillproof bottles with brush, or 1 oz wide-top jars.

Cost: $1.00 (1/2 oz)

Charrette; Flax's; and most stationery stores

Color Compass

A comprehensive guide to the use of color, with text, diagrams, and illustrations discussing theory, color mixing, and values. Twenty pages, including charts on color mixing, color identification, value, color selection, double primaries, and color harmony, with a dial-a-color harmony wheel.

Cost: $3.50

M Grumbacher, Inc

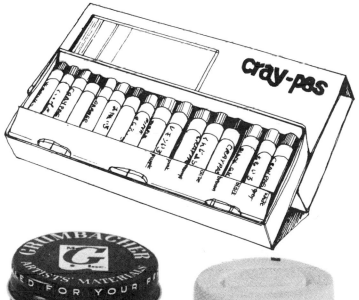

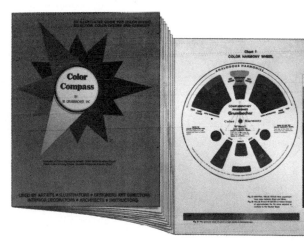

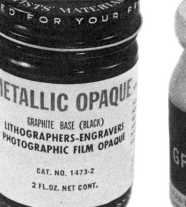

Palettes

Many things around the house will serve as a paint palette, including china saucers, enamelled trays, small shallow porcelain dishes, shallow square melamine trays, shallow glass jars with screw tops, etc.

But if you're not into so high-tech an approach, all art stores have a handy selection of palettes. An inexpensive favorite is the plastic slant type, made of opaque white stainproof plastic with eight deep wells and slants (No 985).
Cost: $3.25

Color Storage Box

It's handy to keep your color mediums in a portable box, most of which are made with the oil painter in mind. An excellent one is the stained maple type with five different-sized compartments and an outside bracket to hold the lid open. Comes with conventional flat, wooden palette; 12" x 16."
Cost: $18.00

Winsor & Newton, Inc

Blair Workable Fixative

Aerosol spray of clear, permanent waterproof protection with a matte finish, that can be worked on after drying. The no-odor version has, in fact, a light, pleasant scent—a deodorant for your artwork. 16 oz can.
Cost: $3.20

Blair Art Products

Art-Tec Clear Gloss Spray

A finishing fixative to protect artwork, drawings, documents, proofs, etc., that forms a non-yellowing, permanent acrylic shield. Prevents fading and is totally waterproof; dries in minutes. 16 oz cans.
Cost: $2.75

All Flax stores

Krylon Dulling Spray

A clear dulling spray that eliminates glare and reflection on any surface to be photographed or lighted. Easily removed with a wet cloth. 16 oz can.

  Cost: $3.00

  Borden Chemical Co

Pressure Graphic Protective Coating

A spray especially designed for most makes of pressure graphics, in either gloss or matte finish. Both are quick-drying and colorless. The matte type is reworkable; the gloss is a hard coating for pressure graphics applied to hard surfaces such as metal, glass, or painted panels, as well as artwork. 16 oz cans.

  Cost: $4.25

  Letraset USA, Inc

Graphic Aids

For our purposes a graphics aid is any special material or piece of equipment used in the preparation of graphic imagery for reproduction, and not covered elsewhere in this book. Such aids include pressure graphics, typographical devices, and production equipment.

Pressure Graphics

Self-adhesive transfer images designed for reproduction may simulate set type, hand lettering, and drawn images of all kinds; usually they include tinting mediums and collections of ruling tapes for all possible graphics needs. The major pressure graphics collections are manufactured by Letraset, Zipatone, Chartpak, Prestype, Mecanorma, Formatt, Instant-Type, C-Thru Graphics, Geotype, Tactype, and Alfac; in addition, a limited number of companies, including Bishop Graphics and Brady, produce specialist imagery such as computer circuitry.

In all cases of general imagery the collections are similar, and include extensive selections of alphabets, tints and screens, ornaments, symbols, and tapes; collections are expanded pretty much every year, and all the major manufacturers produce accessories and storage cabinets for their wares.

In the development of pressure graphics, both prices and quality have become fairly standardized; and so, for most of the more popular models, there is little difference between one set and another. What you will buy will depend largely on what is available at your local art supply store; no retailer will carry them all, and very few retailers will carry the complete range of any one collection. In the next few pages we highlight some of the best features from different collections, but we suggest you obtain complete catalogs from your art supply store or the manufacturers since our information is necessarily selective.

Instant Lettering

For most alphabet transfer needs we prefer Letraset Instant Lettering, which has been associated with quality from the beginning and was for a long time the standard for dry transfer sheets. With its sharp edges and crisp corners, a Letraset letter can be enlarged up to 30% and still maintain reproduction fidelity.

The letters consistently transfer smoothly and completely without breaking up, and letter adhesion is permanent once burnished. Little pressure is needed to transfer, and the whole letter need not be rubbed down. Instant Lettering is removed with adhesive tape or a soft eraser.

There is a letter spacing guide on each sheet, but letter spacing is a skill that has to be acquired with any of the pressure graphics. While it is the most expensive of the pressure graphics, Letraset is also the most reliable. Its collection includes over 390 typestyles (black or white) in either the standard range or the special Letragraphica series. Sheet size: 10" x 15".

Cost: $5.60 (standard); $5.95 (Letragraphica); $4.50 (Project-a-type); $2.25 (Body type)

Letraset USA, Inc

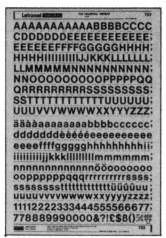

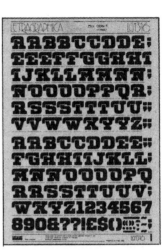

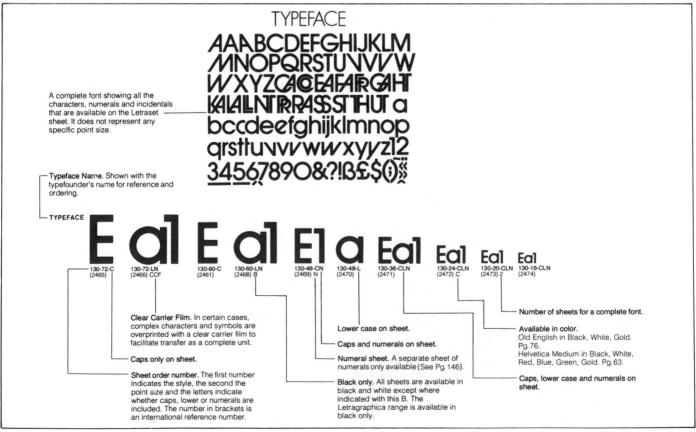

TYPEFACE

A complete font showing all the characters, numerals and incidentals that are available on the Letraset sheet. It does not represent any specific point size.

Typeface Name. Shown with the typefounder's name for reference and ordering.

TYPEFACE

130-72-C (2465)
130-72-LN (2466) CCF
130-60-C (2461)
130-60-LN (2468) B
130-48-CN (2469) N
130-48-L (2470)
130-36-CLN (2471)
130-24-CLN (2472) C
130-20-CLN (2473) 2
130-16-CLN (2474)

Clear Carrier Film. In certain cases, complex characters and symbols are overprinted with a clear carrier film to facilitate transfer as a complete unit.

Caps only on sheet.

Sheet order number. The first number indicates the style, the second the point size and the letters indicate whether caps, lower or numerals are included. The number in brackets is an international reference number.

Lower case on sheet.

Caps and numerals on sheet.

Numeral sheet. A separate sheet of numerals only available (See Pg. 146).

Black only. All sheets are available in black and white except where indicated with this B. The Letragraphica range is available in black only.

Number of sheets for a complete font.

Available in color.
Old English in Black, White, Gold. Pg. 76.
Helvetica Medium in Black, White, Red, Blue, Green, Gold. Pg. 63.

Caps, lower case and numerals on sheet.

Color Creation Lettering

Chartpak color creation materials are designed for use on the Xerox 6500 color copier; five of the most commonly used typefaces are available in six special colors: red, blue, green, yellow, cyan, and magenta. These colors also come as large sheets of opaque film, and match the matte acetate tapes available in seven widths.

Cost: $2.00 (film sheets); $3.00 (colored lettering); $1.20 to $2.90 (tapes)

Chartpak Graphic Products

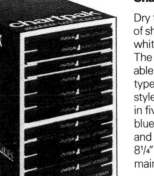

Chartpak Shadow Lettering

Dry transfer sheets in a series of shadow letter styles, black and white and with one color added. The two-color sheets are available in nine popular drop shadow type styles and one outline-only style. Each style can be obtained in five opaque colors: red, light blue, green, yellow, and white, and in a choice of three sizes. 8¼" x 11¼" sheets are intended mainly for layouts and visuals.

Cost: from $3.00 to $4.50

Chartpak Graphic Products

ABCDE abcde

X10018N

ABCDE abcde

X1018CL

ABCDE abcdef

X1418CL

𝕬𝕭𝕮𝕯 abcdefg

X2818CL

ABCDEF abccd

X11518CL

B

Zipatone Shading and Pattern Films

Originator of the preprinted method for applying pattern overlays (1913), Zipatone is still synonymous with these tinted and patterned sheets. The Zipatone line of self-adhesive shading films is a comprehensive series of over 340 patterns, top-printed on a clear, matte acetate which can be scratched for highlight and detail. The adhesive is "encapsulated" to reduce the surface tack to zero, allowing for the easy application of large areas without trapping air bubbles. Properly burnished, the adhesive adheres firmly and is completely heat resistant. All Zipatone sheets are 10" x 14" and are available in black — and, in some cases, white as well.

The Series 6500 are extra large screen tints for large areas, with a special wax adhesive to allow repositioning. 18" x 24", available in values from 10% to 60% with a standard 65 lines/inch in black only.

Cost: $1.85 to $3.90; $6.00 (Series 6500)

Zipatone, Inc

Instantex

A dry transfer system for adding texture to illustrations. The twenty patterns, used singly or in combination, give a wide variety of freehand drawing and shading effects in a line-conversion style perfect for reproduction. Transfer of the black textures is effected by drawing on the back of the face-down sheet; although the sheet itself is transparent, it's very hard to see what you are doing through the texture, and thus it is best used with a tracing of the master drawing on top as a guide. The finished results should be sprayed with a clear protective spray.

Cost: $3 (10" x 15" sheet)

Letraset USA, Inc

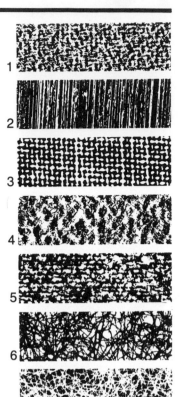

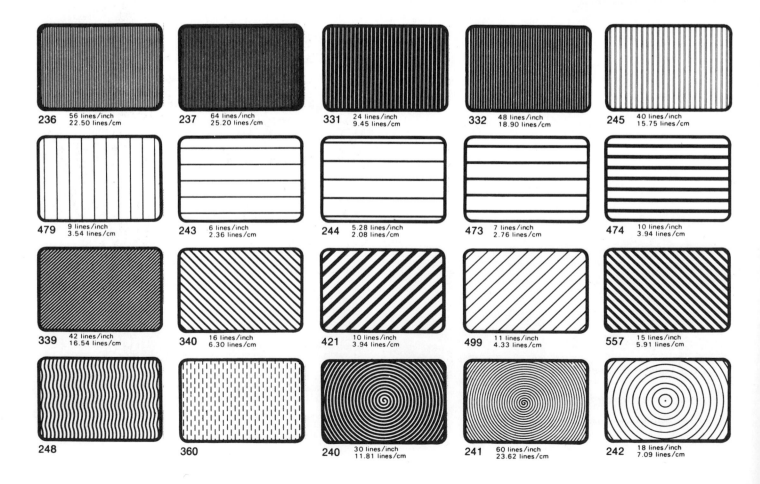

Chartpak Graphic Tapes

Chartpak was the originator of the tape method of charting, and has developed an extensive range of good-quality tapes of all types for every imaginable use. Using tapes eliminates hours of repetitive handwork with pen and ink, and the cost of numerous duplicate stats or color keys. Single color tapes are available in gloss finish for presentations, or matte finish for reproduction, in a range of sixteen colors of ten widths each. Transparent, projectable tapes come in seven colors and nine widths each. The extremely flexible crepe paper tapes that curve easily come in six colors (including black and white) and nineteen different widths. The striped pattern tapes — transparent or opaque gloss — are available in 221 patterns of six widths each, ten of which can be obtained in one of seven colors. Symbol tapes for all kinds of special uses are available in both gloss opaque and transparent base film; some are in

color as well as black. The 195 different patterns of decorative border tapes are printed on gloss transparent base only, except for the six Benday tints and 1 pt and hairline rules, which are also printed on opaque white base. There are also mechanical production tapes to match typography point sizes, fluorescent tapes, and metallic, gold, and chrome tapes. In addition, Chartpak will custom-make any tape rolls to your own design specifications, provided you order at least twenty rolls.

All of Chartpak's tapes come in rolls of either 324" or 648".
    Cost: $1.10 to $4.20 (per roll)

Chartpak Graphic Products

Letraset Rules & Borders

A very good quality range of border designs that is expanded from time to time. Black, 10" x 15" dry transfer sheets.
    Cost: $5.23

Letraset USA, Inc

C/B/F Border System

An extensive series of dry transfer border designs with interchangeable corner elements and decorative motifs that transfer very easily and must be carefully burnished. The unique design selection is expanded frequently; all designs are available in six colors plus black and white. 12¼" x 16" sheets supplied in a protective plastic sheath.
    Cost: $3.75

C-Thru Graphics

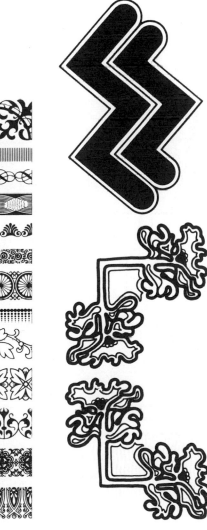

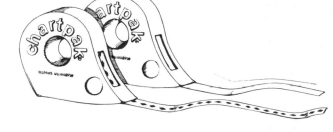

Formatt—Cut-out Acetate Aids

The Formatt graphics aids system is based on printed micro-thin, matte acetate film images which are cut out and lifted off a backing sheet. The main advantage of the low-tack, self-adhesive Formatt sheets is that they are *repositionable;* they are also crack-proof, scratchproof and heat-resistant. The Formatt catalog includes over 320 letter styles, a large collection of sheets of numbers, borders, symbols and ornaments, and a very useful series of sheets called the "library of shapes." All the standard dot screens, line shading tints, special effect and texture patterns, and cartographic patterns are included in the Formatt range. Like all the other major pressure graphics systems, Formatt produces a complete range of charting and graphic art tapes, storage cabinets for their sheets and tapes, and various items of equipment such as opaquing pens, artwork boards, knives, and burnishers.

In general, Formatt is one of the essential pressure graphics collections; although it is of good quality, it is still cheaper than other transfer graphics systems.
Cost: $2.25 (10" x 14" sheets)

Graphic Products Corporation

Pressure Graphic Burnishers

A well-balanced tool designed to make all dry transfer applications faster and more precise, this is far better than the stopgap ball-point pen or clay modeling tool. The spoon tip model is ideal for large areas, and the flexible smooth Teflon pointed tip model works best for fine, detailed work. Metal handles with black oxide coating.
Cost: $2.95

Letraset USA, Inc

Burnishing Roller

A useful burnishing roller should be about 3" wide and made of either hardwood, Teflon, or clear lucite. None of these will pick up wax or rubber cement, as the rubber brayer tends to do. We prefer the 3" lucite version.
Cost: $4.45

Portage

Another Burnisher

A Teflon tool pointed at one end and broad-chiseled on the other, with roller attachment on one side.
Cost: $3.50

Zipatone, Inc

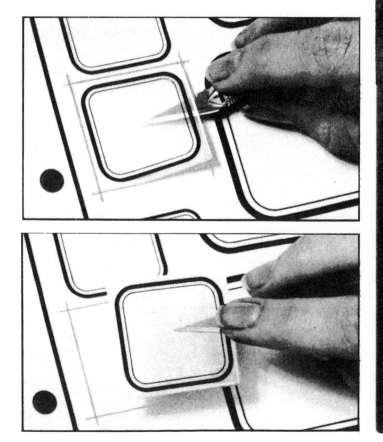

Letrasign

Large size letters (⁵/₈" to 6" characters) made of durable PVC with self-adhesive backing suitable for both indoor and outdoor use. These letters are the standard Helvetica Medium typeface only, in black or white, and are only supplied in packs of five. Sheets of the Letrasign self-adhesive vinyl, 9¹/₂" x 15", are also available for cutting out your own one-off designs.

Cost: 90¢ to $4.00 (per pack); $3.25 (vinyl sheets)

Letraset USA, Inc

The Letraset Catalog

The most impressive and informative of the pressure graphics catalogs, the casebound Letraset catalog is a well-arranged inventory of all the Letraset products and includes much informative data and advice on product use. It also includes the Technical Handbook material that demonstrates all the techniques for working with what has become a high-quality graphic arts system.

Cost: $2.95 (deluxe edition)

Letraset USA, Inc

ABCDEFGHIJKLMN
OPQRSTUVWXYZ
abcdefghijklmnop
qrstuvwxyz 1234
567890&?!£$ß
()⅞%

2" approx (50mm) ● ○

6" approx (150mm) ● ○

Letragraphix

This is a regular brochure put out by Letraset to promote new products and applications, and includes visual ideas and graphic techniques, and information about design competitions. A good example of creative product promotion that is, at the same time, informative and helpful.

Cost: free

Letraset USA, Inc

Type Sizes

Although typefaces may be identical from one brand to the next, and have the same weights and proportions, they may not be the same size overall. The comparison chart below was prepared by Mecanorma as a visual example of the discrepancies among type sizes from three major pressure graphics manufacturers; it indicates the importance of matching type size by actual measurement rather than by relying on indicated point sizes. The variety in the ways that type sizes may be described — Didot points, picas — is the result of a lack of standardization in the development of typography over the centuries. The point size of a letter is an ambiguous description of its actual height, and you should always check a manufacturer's size to see if it is what you require.

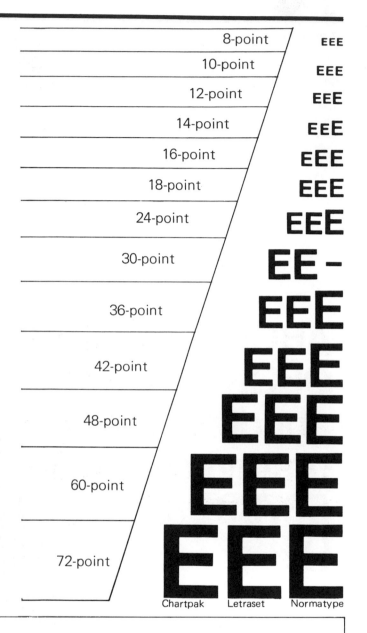

8-point	EEE	
10-point	EEE	
12-point	EEE	
14-point	EEE	
16-point	EEE	
18-point	EEE	
24-point	EEE	
30-point	EE –	
36-point	EEE	
42-point	EEE	
48-point	EEE	
60-point	EEE	
72-point	EEE	

Chartpak   Letraset   Normatype

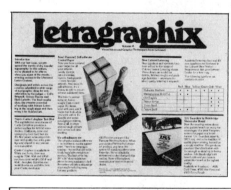

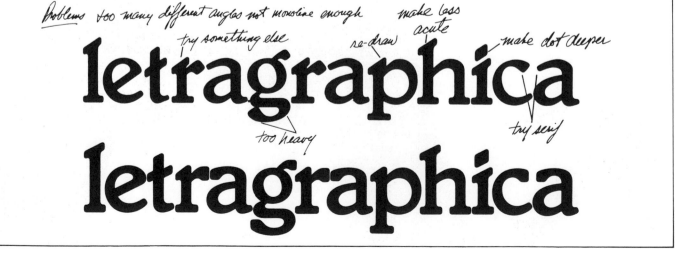

Make Your Own Dry Transfers

There are now several photo-chemical systems that allow you to make your own dry transfer sheets quickly and relatively simply. 3M's "Image 'n Transfer" is well known, but it requires specific chemicals to clear the sheet of unwanted non-exposed areas. The Autotype Artsystem uses the same ultra-violet expo-sure technique, but you need only water to wash away the non-image areas.

For black images your original must be in negative or positive film form; the Artfilm is exposed under ultra-violet light for two minutes, hung, washed —you can use a shampoo spray —and dried. Then it's ready to rub down.

You follow the same proce-dure for color dry transfer sheets as you do for black, but instead of water you wash with a dye stop, then immerse the film in a bath of the colored dye. (Colors can be mixed from the basic seven-color dye set.) Wash with water, dry, and rub down.

Once you have the exposure unit (actually, all you need is an ultra-violet light bulb), the black or color film, and the dyes and dye stop, you are set up to make any images you need into dry transfer quickly and cheaply.

Experimenting with double expo-sures, bleachouts, and multiple register lends an endless variety to the possible effects for presen-tation work, and a 7" x 11" sheet ends up costing only about $6.60, plus the cost of making your original film. The price shown below is for one five-sheet pack of black film and one five-sheet pack of color film; set of seven dyes (1 litre each); color match guide; dye tray; funnel; two measuring flasks; spray bot-tle; squeegee; dye stop; two transfer tools; a desk-top dropper pack; and the exposure unit. The film comes in 11" x 14" sheets or tubes containing 19½" x 23½" sheets.

Cost: $198 (Five-sheet pack of 11" x 14" film: $20.00)

Autotype USA, Inc

Velvet Touch Copy Film

A film that allows you to create your own custom dry transfer images quickly and econom-ically, using any office copying machine that produces solid black areas. The "original" image has to be in the form of negative film, which is used as the master to copy onto the self-adhesive copy film. The image is transferred by scoring around it lightly, positioning, and burnishing.

Each ten-sheet packet of 10 x 14" copy film includes two sheets of the negative film.

Cost: $1.50 per sheet

Chartpak Graphic Products

1 For black start with a negative or

2 Expose the film to Ultra Violet light through the

3 Spray with water until the image is sharp

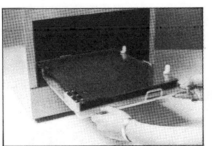

4 Dry it.

The Border Hoarder

Five volumes containing a total of 150 ready-to-use original border designs, many of them very elaborate. These are clip books; either clip and paste, or have them camera-copied to any size. A worthwhile library, which amounts to about 33¢ per border design, if you buy all five volumes at one time.

Cost: $15.00 (or $50.00 for all five)

Richard Sclatter Design

Perspective Plus/TI-59

A system of drawing photographically accurate perspectives from any viewpoint by use of a mini computer, the Texas Instruments TI-59 calculator. After you enter information about the observer's line-of-sight, and the location of points on the object, the *programmed* calculator displays the position of each point in the perspective. Plotting and connecting the points completes the drawing. The procedure is very straightforward, and the results free of noticeable distortion; with only an elementary knowledge of geometry and, perhaps, algebra, you can easily draw perspectives of any object, from any viewpoint, without concern for vanishing points or complex graphic constructions. The Perspective/TI-59 kit consists of special programs (*not* magnetic cards) for the calculator, operating instructions, sample perspectives, and examples. The TI-59 calculator is not included.

(Kits also available for other calculators.)

Cost: $29.95

Mobius Design

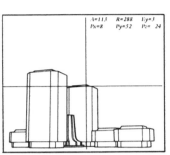

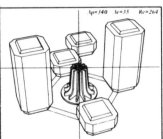

Design No. 185 Volume 3

Design No. 177 Volume 5

Design No. 114 Volume 1

Design No. 170 Volume 4

Slide Rule Copyfitter

A classic slide rule by which two known factors are adjusted to a third known, giving the answer. Quick and simple and cheap.

Cost: $5.00

Taylor Publishing Co

Character Counter

A transparent template that provides an instant character count of typewritten copy, and is absolutely accurate. An effective timesaver.

Cost: $4.50

The Type Aids Co

Type-Line Gauge

Ideal templates for quick ruling-off of any number of type lines in any point size from agate through 16 pt. The calibrated scales give width of line, number of lines, and inch measurements. These scales are useful for layouts, copy-fitting, and determining exact leading; they come in a set of five 8½" x 11" cards.

Cost: $3.95

The Type Aids Co

Haberule Copy Caster

A sixty-eight-page book designed to help you select type quickly, and count characters and fit copy accurately. Over 800 American and European typefaces from 4 to 48 pt are keyed to fifty-three character count scales in a range of 4,000 fonts. Plastic bound, 7¾" x 9", and includes a plastic 6" typescale with agate, 6, 7, 8, 9, 10, 11, and 12 pt calibrations plus elite, pica, and inch rules. Revised edition.

Cost: $14.95

Arthur Brown & Bro

Copi-Counter

Resembling a small, double-faced pocket watch with a wheel at the bottom, the Copi-Counter rolls over copy measuring the total length in agates, picas, and inches on its sweep hand dials. Used for calculating lines in typewritten copy, characters in a manuscript or typeset galleys, and distances on maps, and for editing and cutting copy. Complete with leather case.

Cost: $7.25

Arthur Brown & Bro

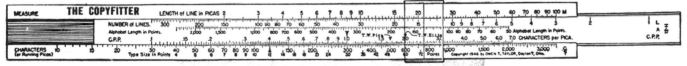

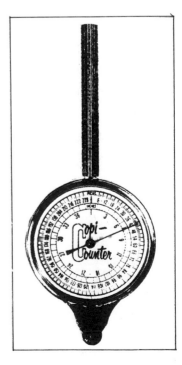

Haberule Type Gauge

Available separately from the *Copy Caster* manual; yellow plastic, 10" or 6", calibrated as described above.

    Cost: $3.75 (10")

Arthur Brown & Bro

Pre-screened Photographs

By inserting a Vari-Stat screen into a Polaroid camera when you load the film, you will have a half-tone screen photograph ready for pasteup in sixty seconds. Very simple, very quick. The quality is, of course, only as good as the Polaroid photo you take. Included in each kit are 65-, 85-, and 100-line screens, and a manual with suggestions for getting the best possible results from the Polaroid technique. The camera is not included.

    Cost: $19.50

Fototype, Inc

Emoscop Magnifier

The best of the magnifiers, the German Emoscop transforms from 3x telescope and telescope-loupe to 5x and 10x magnifiers, to 15x loupe and to 30x microscope. For most graphic applications the 10x magnifier is the most useful. Comes in leather case and includes a transparent "tripod" to give fixed focus at high magnifications.

    Cost: $41

Henniker's

Engraver's Magnifier

A fine, powerful folding magnifier designed for lithographers and "engravers" — a 12x or 20x magnification ideal for the graphic arts. Plastic and metal.

    Cost: $19.95 (12x)

Arthur H Gaebel, Inc

The Linen Tester

The most popular 5x, 7x, 10x, or 12x magnifier available in two qualities. Bausch & Lomb is the top-quality folding 5x magnifier with calibration scale in a 1" field ($32). There are others made to the same basic design with lower-grade lenses in 1/4", 1/2", 3/4", and 1" fields. Linen testers fold flat and when set up are always in focus.

    Cost: $7.50 (7x, 1" field)

Arthur H Gaebel, Inc

The Graham Pasteup System

A pin register system for preparing anything from simple pasteup work to complex mechanicals requiring many overlays. A system such as this is fast and easy to use, and ideal if you prepare a volume of work ready for printing. It consists of a plexiglass pasteup board with precision drilled holes, steel dowel pins, and a precision hole punch. The plexiglass board (13" x 19½" x ⅜") has holes along two sides to accommodate the ½" dowels, and is designed to be used on a light table if required. The hole punch machine is on a clear plastic base with a precision center line. The four heads will punch four holes with 2¾" and 7" centers into thin board, acetate sheets, or plastic grid sheets, providing a precise alignment and register system. The plexiglass board is thick enough for a T-square.

Cost: $320.00 (precision punch); $30.00 (plexiglass board with dowels)

Dot Pasteup Supply Co

Proportional Scale No PS79

The most readable 6" proportional scale for calculating enlargements and reductions of photographs, artwork, and layouts. Constructed of two circular discs of laminated vinyl that provide a scale from 10 to 1000%.

Cost: $3.00

C-Thru Graphics

Scaleograph

A precision mechanical device for scaling and cropping photographs and artwork without complicated calculations. Simple to use, scaled in picas and inches, the scaleograph is made of vinyl and aluminum, 11" x 12".

Cost: $18.00

All Flax stores; Charrette Corporation

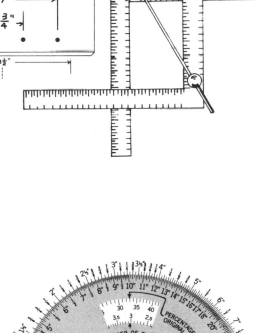

Halftone Screen Determiner 719A

An ingenious, wedge-line grid device that reveals the halftone screen count when placed over the printed halftone and moved slowly up and down — the transparent grid area forms a moire star pattern somewhere along the scale. The edges of the square plastic protractor are marked in picas and agate lines. The reverse side determines the angle of each color screen of a full-color printed halftone, clearly separating each color except the yellow.

Cost: $2.75

Arthur H Gaebel, Inc

Pica Grid

Another transparent template that has many uses as a time saving layout guide in preparing typography or photos for reproduction, squaring up, and aligning and centering. Called the Photoguide, it is also used to check engraver's proofs and layouts for accuracy.

Cost: $2.35 (8½" x 11"); $4.45 (15" x 19⅜")

The Type Aids Co

The House of Grids

This company produces transparent positive film grids of superb accuracy for all needs including layout, film make-up, and preparing artwork. They come in a variety of colors, and in 130 different sizes and scales including inch, pica, point, millimeter, computer, didot, and so on. House of Grids will also custom-make them to fit your special needs. Consult the catalog for details of the complete range of both transparent positive film and board grids.

Cost: from $12 to $124

The House of Grids

Pica Grid Boards

Plate Bristol boards (300 lb) printed with accurate non-repro blue grids available in eight or ten lines per inch, millimeter, 2 mm or pica rulings. All come in 22" x 28" single sheet size, or in packages of twelve 11" x 14" sheets. Ideal for pasteup, layouts and dry transfer lettering. (If you use a lot of boards, it may be cheaper to have them printed up in quantity by your local printer, on a board stock of your choice. The master grid can be obtained from The House of Grids — see above.)

Cost: $1.60 (22" x 28")

C-Thru Graphics

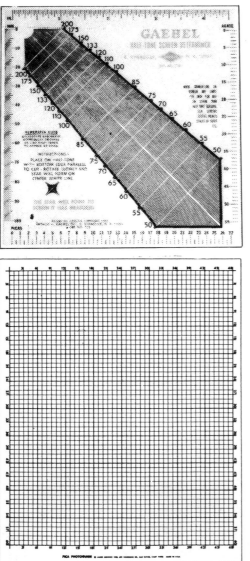

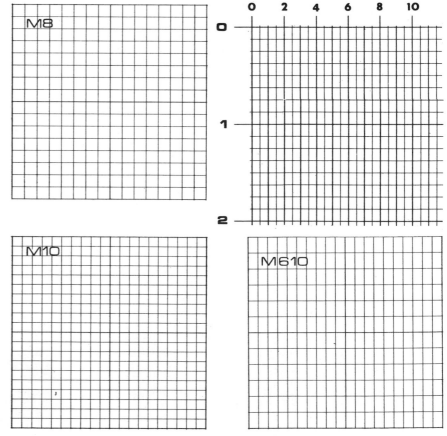

Planning and Pasteup Grids

The ideal graphic arts layout sheet is printed in a pica grid, and this Dot system has pica layout paper (50 lb) and matching pasteup/ruling paper (80 lb) designed for use on a light-table. Both are calibrated with zero center for accurate centering of all elements. Sheet sizes: 19" x 12½" or 9½" x 12½"; pads of 100 sheets.

Cost: $4.50 (19" x 12½", layout paper); $15.00 (19" x 12½", pasteup paper)

Dot Pasteup Supply Co

Alignment Ruler GA91

A laminated, tough, transparent 2" x 18" plastic rule with very clear red calibrations: pica scale with zero centering, inch scale in 16ths, plus alignment rules in 2-pica spacing. Useful for lineup, and for centering copy or art.

Cost: $1.75

C-Thru Graphics

Self-closing Tweezers

Handy tweezers for pasteup work: they open when squeezed and will grip firmly when pressure is released. Chrome finished steel.

Cost: $2.00

X-acto

Square Cutting Guide

A right-angled device in two parts that makes it quick and simple to cut everything to consistently accurate 90° angles. By using the transparent plastic angle A up against angle B, all four sides of a square can be cut without moving the art. Small slots in the angles make it possible to cut corner corner points cleanly. A 13" x 13" angle and an 11" x 11" angle, calibrated in inches.

Cost: $16.00

Dot Pasteup Supply Co

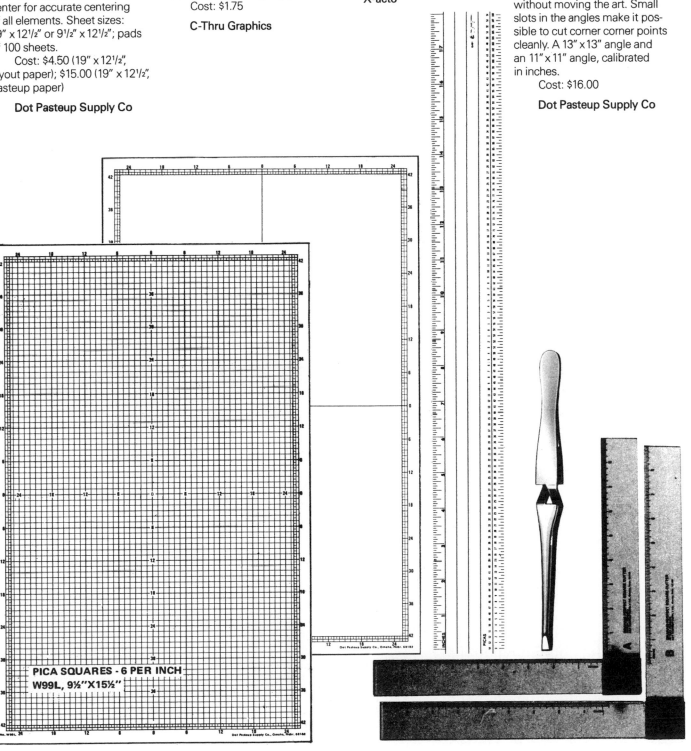

PICA SQUARES - 6 PER INCH
W99L, 9½"X15½"

Art Sharp Cutting Board

A special high molecular weight plastic sheet for cutting on, which will not blunt blades as fast as most do. The $^3/_8$"-thick plastic board has self-sealing characteristics for all but the deepest cuts, and can be "reconstituted" by cleaning with steel wool or emery paper. A very smooth, semi-soft, and long-lasting cutting surface; 12" x 18" x$^3/_8$".
   Cost: $18.95

   Portage

Larger Equipment

Seerite Opaque Projector

For copying and enlarging artwork, designs, or photographs. This inexpensive projector covers a 6" x 6" maximum area and will enlarge up to 84" x 84" at a 12-foot distance. Larger originals can be projected in sections. Optical system consists of two optically ground and polished 3$^1/_2$"-diameter lenses mounted in a 5$^1/_2$"-long barrel. Light source by ordinary incandescent bulbs up to 200 watts. Automatic fan cooling; slide platform with clips can be removed for copying from books. This unit cannot reverse or reduce an image.
   Cost: $99.95

   Testrite Instrument Co, Inc

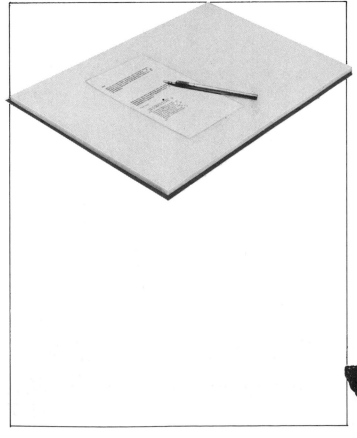

Camera Lucida

A prism-operated device for copying drawings or any artwork, or copying "from life," whether in the same size, smaller, or larger. A prism projects the image onto the paper while permitting your eye to see image, paper surface, and pencil at the same time. Comes in a case with twelve lenses of different focuses. A versatile and widely used instrument.

Cost: $195.00

Charrette Corporation; all Flax stores

Artograph DB-300

A direct opaque projector that weighs only thirty-five pounds, and clamps to any sturdy drawing table or other support. A relatively low-priced instrument, the new Artograph has a normal range of 300% enlargement or reduction, which can be extended to 600% by swiveling the housing 180° and projecting onto a

Desktop Light Box

The Portatrace light box is slimline, elegant, and inexpensive with cool, uniform fluorescent lighting and an opal plexiglass surface. Stainless steel and aluminum construction; 115 v; five models with two, three, or four lamps. Model 1824-4 is 18" x 24", four lamps.
    Cost: $123.00

A l Friedman; Sam Flax

Rabbit Light Boxes

Another handsome, well-designed light box with uniform lighting. Cabinet made of laminated birch plywood with metal edges on two sides; glass working surface with separate acrylic diffuser; two fluorescent bulbs plus a **V**-reflector that provides as much light as four-bulb models. Six sizes available.
    Cost: $130.00
(19½" x 25½")

Charrette Corporation

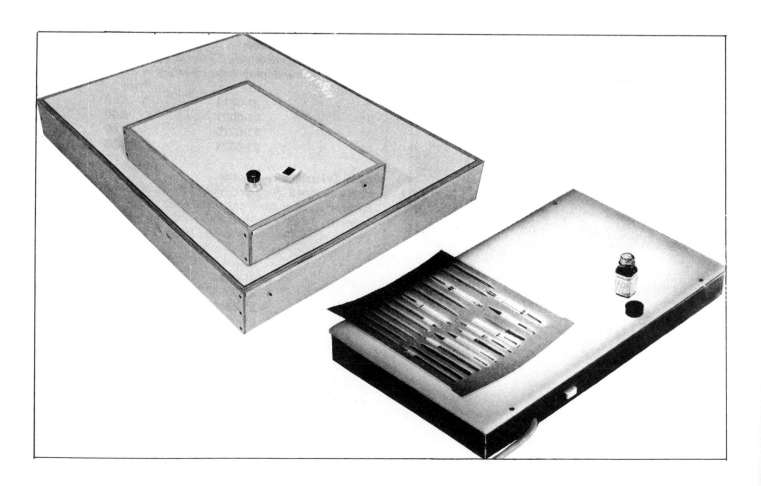

The Safe-Trim Junior

A fast and accurate paper trimmer that works with a push and spring-loaded action. Formica platform with silk-screened rulings in inches and picas to guarantee a perfect right-angle trim every time. Very quick and easy to use, the Safe-Trim has a thick plexiglass safety shield, thick aluminum side guards, and self-sharpening hi-carbon blades. 17" wide.
      Cost: $114.00

Portage

Nikor Safety Trimmer

Rigid, non-wraping aluminum, black anodized board with glass-smooth hard surface on rubber footrests. Permanently engraved guidelines to accurate 1/2" intervals and solid extrusion scale calibrated to 1/16" for precise positioning. Edge blade and cutter wheel of fine ground alloy steel with cutter wheel guard; lubrication-free nylon bearings. Optional extras include an edge-lite for absolute accuracy, a hold-down bar, and a guide bar. Four sizes: 12" x 12", 16" x 16", 20" x 20", and 24" x 24".
      Cost: $10.00 (20" x 20")

A l Friedman; Portage

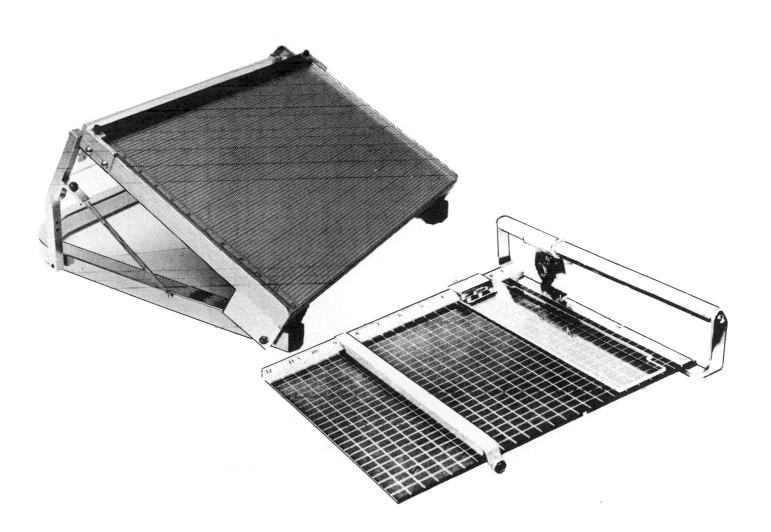

Dahle Lever Cutter No 567

A superb-quality guillotine with hollow, ground-steel blade that sharpens itself on the counter blade; completely protected in that the spiral safety shield automatically wraps itself around any exposed blade area. Automatic clamping bar accommodates up to fifty sheets of paper for one cut; adjustable alignment bar, back gauge on a calibrated metal scale, and extension tray. One version of the many Dahle lever cutters.

 Cost: $239.95 (21½" length of cut)

 Dahle USA, Inc

Dahle Rolling Trimmer

A beautifully made safety trimmer in five model sizes that will easily cut paper, cardboard, film, photopapers, and similar materials. Completely enclosed, self-sharpening steel cutting wheel and safety guard-rail/clamping bar, mounted on an all-metal frame with rubber feet. The board is unfortunately engraved with a cutting guide in the continental A series paper sizes, but attached to the clamping bar is a plexiglass scale calibrated in inches, and a metal right-angle ruler calibrated in inches and millimeters. Optional extras include a paper roll cradle and backstop.

 Cost: $131.95 (26³/₈" length of cut)

 Dahle USA, Inc

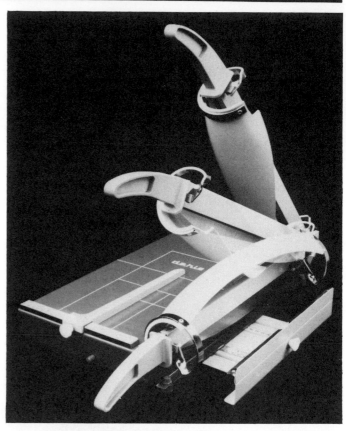

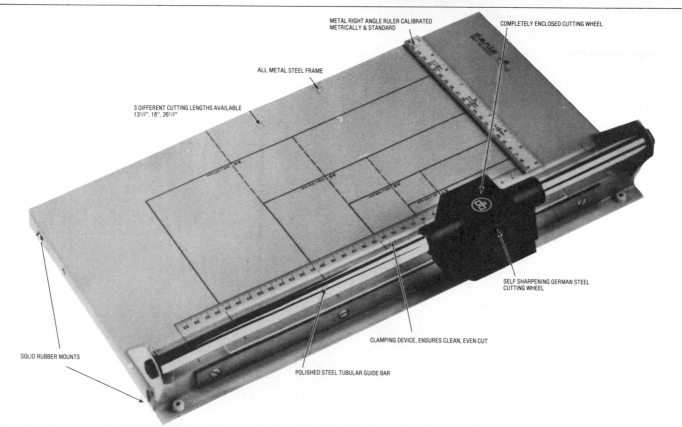

METAL RIGHT ANGLE RULER CALIBRATED METRICALLY & STANDARD

COMPLETELY ENCLOSED CUTTING WHEEL

ALL METAL STEEL FRAME

3 DIFFERENT CUTTING LENGTHS AVAILABLE 13½", 18", 26½"

SELF SHARPENING GERMAN STEEL CUTTING WHEEL

CLAMPING DEVICE, ENSURES CLEAN, EVEN CUT

SOLID RUBBER MOUNTS

POLISHED STEEL TUBULAR GUIDE BAR

C Support Systems

Editorial

Typesetting

Photo-Mechanical Supplies

Photography and Multi-Media

Printing

Paper

PHOTOMECHANICAL PLASTIC LINE CONVERSION BY ELSTAN STUDIO, NEW YORK

C

If man does not live by bread alone, neither does the graphic artist live by pen alone. And unless you want to take the enormously expensive and complicated steps of forming your own organization to handle all your basic service needs—an unlikely option at best—you're going to have to rely on others to provide you with information, materials, and services.

All the support systems discussed in this section are individually complex. Under ordinary circumstances, they are sufficiently large and/or specialized that they remain separate from one another in the professional world. It is not necessary that the designer or illustrator be intimate with *all* their technicalities, but it *is* necessary to be familiar with the ways in which they operate.

We have chosen to identify them, delineate their relevance to the graphic artist, and recommend some ways in which you can become more familiar with any or all, if you choose to do so. Bearing in mind that numerous volumes have been written about each subject area in this section, you might think of this chapter as a Gray Line bus tour of a new city: You will not get off this bus with a detailed knowledge of the metropolis, but you will have a good sense of what's important about it, and which sections of town you'd like to explore in greater depth later, on your own.

These are commonly called proofreader's marks. We prefer to call them designer's marks. Because designers commonly use them to mark up copy and proofs. These marks are your special alphabet.

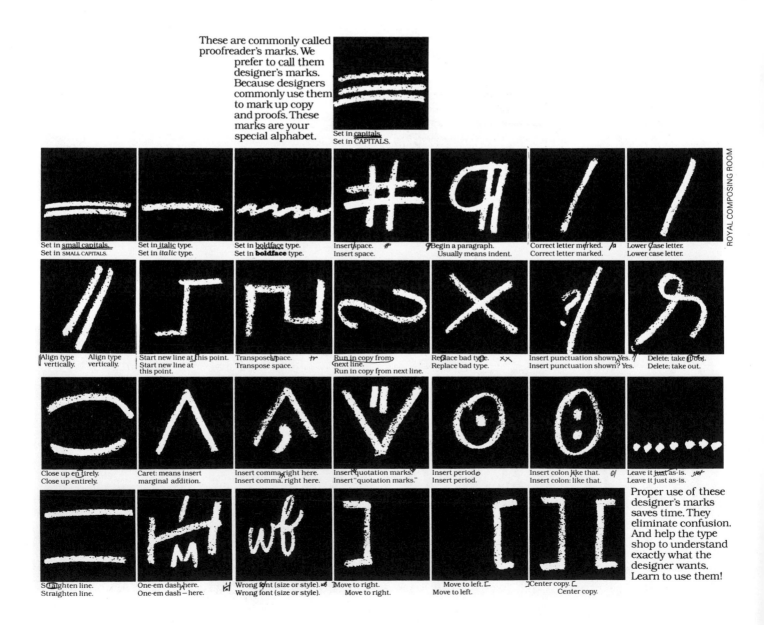

ROYAL COMPOSING ROOM

Set in capitals.
Set in CAPITALS.

Set in small capitals.
Set in SMALL CAPITALS.

Set in *italic* type.
Set in *italic* type.

Set in **boldface** type.
Set in **boldface** type.

Insert space.
Insert space.

Begin a paragraph.
Usually means indent.

Correct letter marked.
Correct letter marked.

Lower case letter.
Lower case letter.

Align type vertically.
Align type vertically.

Start new line at this point.
Start new line at this point.

Transpose space.
Transpose space.

Run in copy from next line.
Run in copy from next line.

Replace bad type.
Replace bad type.

Insert punctuation shown? Yes.
Insert punctuation shown? Yes.

Delete: take out.
Delete: take out.

Close up entirely.
Close up entirely.

Caret: means insert marginal addition.

Insert comma, right here.
Insert comma, right here.

Insert quotation marks.
Insert "quotation marks."

Insert period.
Insert period.

Insert colon: like that.
Insert colon: like that.

Leave it just as-is.
Leave it just as-is.

Straighten line.
Straighten line.

One-em dash, here.
One-em dash—here.

Wrong font (size or style).
Wrong font (size or style).

Move to right.
Move to right.

Move to left.
Move to left.

Center copy.
Center copy.

Proper use of these designer's marks saves time. They eliminate confusion. And help the type shop to understand exactly what the designer wants. Learn to use them!

Between the written word and the printed page, an enormous number of things happen. In a commercial venture, the client is bound to want to make some changes in the text. An editor will have at least a few teensy emendations, or may try to rewrite the entire piece. A copy editor will correct grammar and punctuation, and — in a large enterprise, such as book or magazine publishing — will style a manuscript according to house specifications. (Should a number be printed as *20* or *twenty?* Shall we use dashes, commas, parentheses — or a combination of all three?) Sometimes an ambitious proofreader will contribute stylistic notions of his own. And a good indexer may keep the author up nights tracing references through his text. For our purposes, all these steps are thought of as *editorial.*

Somewhere along the line, the designer will enter the picture as the interface between the words and their presentation. Since design may alter editorial concepts, and editing may change design concepts, it is easier on everyone if the designer steps in sooner rather than later. In fact, the ideal situation is one in which editing and design are seen as two aspects of a single process, and are executed simultaneously, or at least in tandem. Unfortunately, such is rarely the case.

Ordinarily, the differences between design and editorial functions are more apparent than the similarities. Even when the two are closely knit, as in the offices of a magazine, a schism seems to exist between them.

Because the designer *must* be conversant with the editorial process at least as far as knowing the necessary steps through preparation of concept and copy; and because an editor *may* know little more about production than how to manipulate words; and because there is a rather ingrained tendency to exclude the designer from the editorial end of things, it is the graphic artist's responsibility to insist on being part of the team that conceptualizes the presentation of a piece, rather than a lackey employed to make a job look pretty. When the designer — or illustrator, or photographer, as the case may be — takes this part of his role seriously, everyone involved can be confident that the problems of a job have been identified, and that effective communication by design, as well as by word, is taking place.

A Manual of Style

In addition to the essential knowledge of proofreader's marks, and the ability to specify, code, and correct manuscript and type galleys with clarity (see p.190), a designer must also understand *style:* the details of form concerning language and the written word.

For more than sixty years the University of Chicago Press has published *A Manual of Style,* and the book has been the standard reference tool for authors, editors, typographers, designers, printers, and proofreaders. It is constantly revised and updated — it is now in its 12th edition — with bookmaking in mind, so that it is likely to cover every problem you'll ever have in determining the correct forms for typesetting. Throughout, the manual provides clear and simple guidelines for preparing, editing, and correcting copy. The forms it suggests are both economical and easy to grasp. Although some publishers and clients have other preferences, this is the style manual most commonly used in the United States, and reflects the current common use of the American language. It is an essential reference book for the designer's library.

Cost: $13.95

University of Chicago Press

The Elements of Style

Anyone who deals with words in a serious or professional capacity should be familiar with this delightful little jewel of a book. Back in the 1910s, when William Strunk taught English at Cornell University, he put together a privately printed manual of style for his students. In 1957 the Macmillan Company asked E. B. White — a former student of Strunk's, and a leading writer in his own right — to revise that work for the trade. *The Elements of Style* — or "the little book," or Strunk & White, as it is known in some circles — covers *all* the fundamentals of plain English in a concise, emphatic, and utterly charming fashion. Moreover, as a style book, it contains lessons that even non-verbal people can use.

Cost: $1.65 (Second Edition)

The Macmillan Company

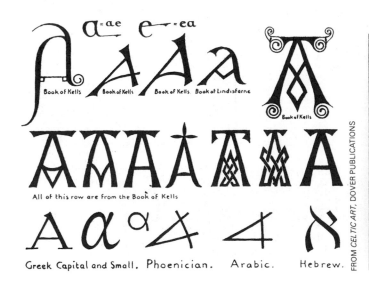

All of this row are from the Book of Kells

Greek Capital and Small. Phoenician. Arabic. Hebrew.

FROM *CELTIC ART,* DOVER PUBLICATIONS

Typesetting

Typography is the art of selecting typefaces and determining their sizes and spacing requirements for a design or layout. A typographer can be either the designer who specifies and arranges the type, or the person who operates the typesetting equipment.

Not long ago, typography was a craft that demanded a certain expertise, and commanded a commensurate respect in the graphics professions. But in the changeover from hot metal to phototype, it became something of a lost art. Currently, skilled typographers are engaged in a struggle to re-establish both the value and the status of their trade; and while a designer may not be expected to be an experienced type artist, he is certainly expected to have a solid grounding in the subject.

In our modern world, where efficiency is frequently measured in time and money, it is easy to lose sight of the purpose behind an art—and even of the art itself. Type is designed not only to communicate words, but to communicate sense and sensibility as well. As a communications skill, the art of typography is an art of aesthetics and meaning.

The printed page, for instance, can be an object of great grace and beauty, or a piece of expediency. The art of the typographer embraces the ability to know the difference, and to apply a solution to any piece of copy that is appropriate to its purpose.

Typographic characters may be assembled manually or mechanically. The most popular and inexpensive method in use today is phototypesetting. This recent innovation has been available commercially only for about twenty years, and despite the amazing advances in its technology—many of which are predicated on equally amazing advances in computer technology—its basic principles are largely carry-overs from a previous technology: casting type in hot metal.

Both major methods of hot metal composition, linotype and monotype, were invented during the nineteenth century, and are still very much in use. While more expensive, and sometimes harder to come by quickly than the more modern methods of setting type, both linotype and monotype have a quality of letterform and letterfit that phototype can rarely duplicate.

Metal Type

Although mechanization makes both metal type systems (Linotype and Monotype) faster and more efficient than those used since the fifteenth century, in theory they are not very different from the older period's system of single-unit handsetting. Single character metal type, which was the significant advance over the slow and exacting craft of carving entire pages in wood, remains essentially unchanged since its invention by Johann Gutenberg, and all contemporary typographic terminology derives from his system.

Monotype

Monotype is the process of casting individual metal letters in composed lines; it is also the registered trade name of the Monotype Corporation Limited. Long synonymous with quality type and typography, the Monotype system uses two machines: a keyboard perforator and a type caster. A paper ribbon is prepared at the keyboard with precise information concerning the job to be composed. The ribbon is then fed to the casting unit where rods controlled by the perforations position character matrices over a mold, through which the hot metal alloy is pumped.

Monotype was superseded by Linotype for most printing work, and with the advances and economies of phototypesetting and offset lithography, it has all but faded away. Recently, however, there has been a minor renaissance of hot metal typography, largely due to the fact that the costs of photosetting have risen, and because there is still nothing more pleasing typographically than well composed hot metal type printed on letterpress machines. Monotype is also still used for special repro and printed offset services, some magazines, and in the sort of standing job that needs minor corrections and changes from time to time. Even though most hot metal type shops have converted, or are converting, to phototypesetting, many hot metal typographers still refuse to make the change to computer technology.

Monotype jobbing case

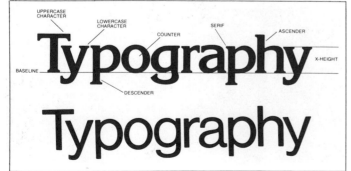

FROM *PHOTOTYPESETTING: A DESIGN MANUAL,* WATSON-GUPTILL PUBLICATIONS

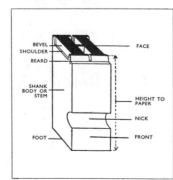

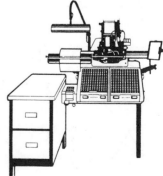

Monotype keyboard

The Monotype Recorder

During the 1950s and 60s, this regular publication of The Monotype Corporation was *the* typographic journal for designers, typographers, and printers. Its back issues are an invaluable collection of type history, lore, and information that even *U&lc,* the periodical of the International Typeface Corporation (see p.218), is hard put to emulate. If you can find them, copies of the *Recorder* make fascinating reading as classic examples of typography thinking of their era. The *Recorder* was set, of course, in hot metal printed letterpress.

The Monotype Corporation

Linotype

Linotype or Intertype machines combine keyboard and caster with no intervening punch betwen them. A matrix of each character is released from the top of the machine to assemble lines ("slugs") of type, into which the hot alloy is pumped. The matrices then return to their proper compartments. Linotype's advantages over monotype are that a solid line of type is easier to handle than a line of numerous letter-parts, it cannot be spilled or upset, and the comlete line is faster and cheaper to produce.

Basic Typography

If you want a solid background in typography, a lucid, well illustrated primer such as this one is invaluable — particularly in an age of computers, when basics such as those covered here are by-passed. *Basic Typography* is the best little book available on type, typography, and typesetting, including its succinct coverage of hot metal. The book divides typography into the three essential stages: principles, mechanics, and practice.

Cost: $10.95

Watson-Guptill Publications

Typologia

Frederic W. Goudy was a master type designer of the old school. He wrote this book as a personal reflection of his work in type design and type production, with comments on the history of typography, the earliest types, legibility, and fine printing. Reading *Typologia* is an involving way to acquire essential background information on the art, while reflecting on the conclusions drawn by a devoted craftsman intensely interested in every phase of designing with type. The handsome paperback edition is reproduced from the original.

Cost: $3.95

University of California Press

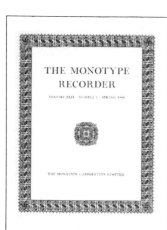

Linotype casting machine

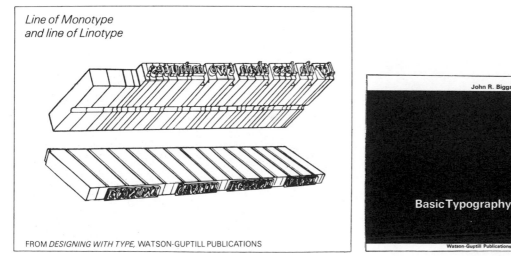

Line of Monotype and line of Linotype

FROM *DESIGNING WITH TYPE,* WATSON-GUPTILL PUBLICATIONS

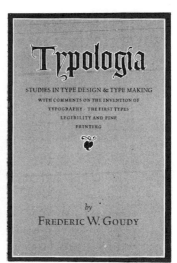

Book Types

Some major hot metal typesetting work is still being produced in England, particularly for books; and the firms that do it actively solicit jobs from the United States. One such company, William Clowes & Sons, publishes a lavish 458 page hot metal type specimen book expressly for bookmaking. Far more than a mere specimen catalogue, though, *Book Types* is an authoritative resume of contemporary hot metal typography that shows, on a variety of papers, every text face the company carries, in every combination of size, spacing, and page formats. It is the most instructive and easy reference book on its subject we've seen, though not simple to acquire unless you are a real potential client.

Cost: free

**William Clowes &
Sons Ltd**

Direct Impression Typesetting

A development of the use of a standard typewriter to produce copy for mimeograph, DIT composes reproduction quality type from a specialized electronic machine that resembles a typewriter, has the capacity to change typeface, type size, leading, letterspacing, and justification, and has certain memory functions. While strike-on typesetting does not really replace either hot metal or phototype, since the general appearance of its copy is somewhat inferior to that produced by the other methods, it does supply a quick, low-cost alternative that has allowed individuals and small businesses to own or lease their own typesetting equipment. Sophisticated machines that produce imitative hot metal settings are manufactured by IBM and Addressograph-Multigraph. But both machines have been eclipsed by the introduction of direct entry phototypesetting.

The IBM Electronic Composer

The most advanced strike-on equipment on the market, this is the typesetter for use in any small office. It is a relatively easy machine to learn to operate, will perform many of the functions of a low-cost direct entry phototypesetter, and plays out set type automatically in any combination of 130 golfball typefaces after copy has been typed and coded into the memory. The composer is also, of course, a very expensive "Selectric" typewriter.

Cost: $8,850.00; or $235 monthly lease; or $265 monthly rental.

IBM Office Products Division

Phototypesetting

The first mechanical phototypesetters, developed in the late 1940s, were Linofilm and Monophoto. In the mid-1950s electromechanical systems appeared, quickly followed by cathode ray tube machines (photo/scan systems) that could not only set type at high speed, but could also set line drawings, logotypes, halftones, and make up complete newspaper pages. The fourth generation phototypesetter, still in development, uses a high-precision laser to generate type and any other graphic required at exceptionally high speed. While this digital/scan system is in the works, the bulk of equipment in commercial use is electromechanical (photo/optic) systems.

Three basic components make up a phototypesetting system: a keyboard for input; a computer for making decisions; and a photo unit, or "typewriter," for output. The addition of an editing/correcting device, such as a video display terminal (VDT), yields a typical cold type system. Numerous manufacturers offer a large variety of this kind of phototypesetting equipment ranging from simple to complex, and sold, rented, or leased as separate components or complete units. Very briefly, the components function as follows:

Keyboard/Input: There are two kinds of keyboard: the counting kind, with which the operator makes decisions, and the non-counting kind, with which decisions are made by the computer. The former can bypass the computer, and the tape (or disc) can go directly to the photo unit. Such operator controlled keyboards are used for jobs with complex settings, such as tabular material, mathematical equations, formulas, and so on. The simpler, less expensive, non-counting keyboard produces an "idiot" tape from which the computer makes end-of-the-line decisions about justification, hyphenation, leading, etc. This system frees the operator to type continuous copy at maximum speed. Input information is stored on a perforated paper tape, the most widely used medium; or magnetic tape, which holds more information than the paper and can be re-used; or disc, usually a floppy disc, which is also re-useable, stores even more information than the magnetic tape, and offers "random access" for quick and easy corrections.

Computer: Computers vary tremendously in function, size, programming and memory capabilities, and location within the system. They may be part of the keyboard, part of the photo unit, or they may stand alone. How well a computer functions depends on its programming (known as "softwear"), but most of them make end-of-the-line decisions and control the output of the photo unit. There are five different kinds of programs that relate to resolving the problems of line breaks. They are: hyphenless; discretionary; logic; exception discretionary; and true dictionary. The first program depends entirely on the operator, while the last carries a 12,000 word program and requires no operator discretion whatsoever.

Photo unit/Output: The output unit sets type by a combination of photographic, electronic, and mechanical components. Some photo units are so fast it would take several input operators to utilize their capacity fully. Although units vary considerably one from another, all operate basically the same: a high-density light is flashed through the characters (which are carried as negative images on the type font) projecting them on to photosensitive paper or film. The carrying capacity of fonts (which come in disc, film strip, and grid forms) varies from system to system, as does the typesetting speed, which may range from 15 to 200 lines per minute.

Processing, or proofing, is done on a separate component which may or may not be part of the system. Normally, it uses a daylight-loading method whereby the cartridge is removed from the computer and fed through a processor unit. Copy proofs are made from the developed positive on high quality office copying machines such as those manufactured by Xerox, Cannon, or Kodak.

All the components mentioned above must be considered when selecting a phototypesetting system for any job. It is also necessary to take into account such facors as available typeface designs, photo reproduction quality, accuracy of character positioning, and, of course, calibre of operators from input through processing.

Editing/Correcting: It has been estimated that it takes thirty times longer to correct a typing error than it does to type something correctly. There are four increasingly costly stages in the typesetting process at which corrections can be made: before, during and after keyboarding, and after typesetting. During keyboarding the operator can see what corrections are necessary on a VDT screen or a paper play-out. After keyboarding corrections can be keyboarded in when the tape is played back through a VDT terminal. Alternatively, a line-for-line printout can be checked and corrections made on a separate keyboard.

After typesetting, the tape can be corrected on a keyboard that produces a second, corrected tape that is run through the photounit again (editing-and-merging). Otherwise, small patches of type can be reset separately, then stripped in on the original repro or film.

FROM *THE E B EDDY HANDBOOK*

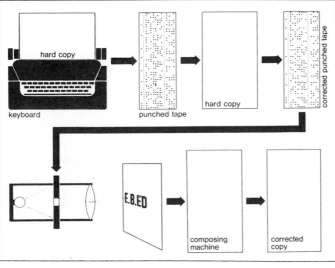

Editing and correcting sequence

Direct Entry Systems

Direct entry systems are basically self-contained facilities that combine input, computer, and output in the same units. Thus, as the operator types, the copy is set. Used for in-house typesetting in offices, agencies, and design studios, they are relatively inexpensive, simple to operate, and ideal for setting straight copy. They are the most widely used photo/optic systems, and range from low-cost, limited capacity machines with minimal flexibility, to expensive and sophisticated equipment whose abilities are similar to those of large commercial phototypesetting machines.

The CompuWriter II

A versatile, low-cost, direct entry machine that can be programmed to handle variations in composition for run-around copy and indents. It will set type from 6 to 24 pt to a maximum or 45 picas, and has all the requisite visual displays that allow the operator to keep track of all functions. The CompuWriter has become very common, and is a recommended system for beginners. Compugraphic offers 250 typefaces for this machine, at extra cost of course, and both a processor and proofer are necessary ancillary equipment.

Cost: $7,950.00

Compugraphic Corporation

Understanding Phototypesetting

A basic primer that starts with the fundamentals of typography and the printed page, this book makes all the technology of cold-type systems easy to understand. Chapters include typography, photolettering machines, phototypesetting machines, editing devices, processing equipment, pasteup, and more, all well illustrated. Apart from its technical clarity, however, the book is put together in a rather amateurish fashion, and is somewhat of a mess — an unfortunate dimension, considering its subject and high price.

Cost: $24.50

North American Publishing Company

The Photo Typositor

One of the first display typesetting units developed, this is still the best of its kind (other smaller, desk-top machines are described in Section C). It is sophisticated, compact, yet inexpensive, and sets display typography in daylight. There is no plumbing: the unit is entirely self-contained, and it features a precise viewing system for exact spacing, enlargement, reduction, and modification of the typeface. Reproduction quality is high, and the manufacturer supplies a film font library of some 2,400 types.

Cost: $3,250.00 (Model 3100)

Visual Graphics Corporation

Compuwriter II

Type Design

The environment of type design has been altered radically by contemporary technology, resulting in increased demand for new designs, and for modifications of old ones. The major typeface producing companies — ITC, Mergenthaler, Compugraphic, and Letraset — regularly add new designs to their catalogues that are free from the laborious and time-consuming restraints of the hot metal systems.

One result of computerized phototechnology is that type designers are able to achieve greater accuracy in shorter periods of time than heretofore. Phototype fonts are cheaper to produce than metal ones, and they are checked for accuracy far more frequently, partly because a finer grid is worked within—as many as fifty-four units in photosetting, compared with nine or eighteen in metal casting. Such increased flexibility allows greater design latitude with less character distortion.

Today, the major typeface design problem is creating optimum legibility and letterfit from a single design. to work throughout the point size range. (Text and display versions are still designed separately, as a rule.) In hot metal such conformity was not necessary, since each size of type design was likely to be proportionally different from the others. The photographic process also creates the whole new problem of smear and distortion, which must be compensated for.

As a result of combining CRT and laser with computer technology, a new generation of typefaces is now being developed. Known as optical character recognition (OCR) designs, it is type that can be read by machines, and it is revolutionizing our communications systems. Obviously, such a development opens a grand arena for type designers.

The challenges that the new technology pose for type designers are complicated by the engineering of new typesetting machinery, which often has little regard for the subtleties of type design. Therefore, a designer may be forced to redesign a true-cut italic or bold face to insure that it shares common character widths with its Roman counterpart—a monumental problem. But the challenges and complications themselves point up the fact that phototype design must be seen as an entirely new medium, as different from metal moveable type as metal was from the single, carved block of wood.

Jan Tschichold: Typographer
[Ruari McLean]

Jan Tschichold, who died in 1974, was the most lucid, intelligent, and influential of the first generation of professional European typographers. Since he wrote only in German, and very few of his books have been yet translated into English, his ideas have never been fully understood in the United States.

This profusely illustrated volume traces Tschichold's remarkable career, and includes the only translation of some of his most important essays. Its invaluable information is crucial to understanding the roots of contemporary typographic theory and practice.

Cost: $25.00

David R. Godine, Publisher

Manuale Typographicum
[Hermann Zapf]

Zapf is a contemporary master of the craft, and his exceptional book is a true manual of over 100 typographically designed pages, each containing a sample typeface and quotations on type and printing in eighteen different languages. Impeccably selected, beautifully designed, and superbly produced, this special book stimulates both the eye and the mind.

Cost: $75.00

Upper & Lower Case Bookshop

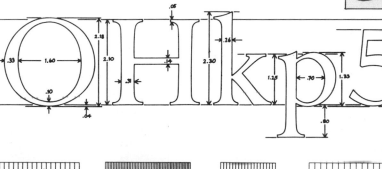

18-unit

54-unit

18-unit narrow

18-unit expanded

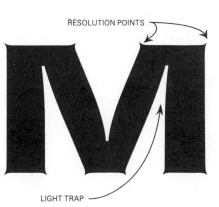

RESOLUTION POINTS

LIGHT TRAP

"Similar to" -ism

"Similar to" -ism is the copying and offering for sale of another person's creative work.

Current abuse of the words "similar to" informs you immediately that:

1) The typeface was not produced from the originator's art.
2) Use of it was not authorized or licensed by the designer.

Unauthorized copying of typefaces is widespread because a type design is easily camera-copied. We are all familiar with type-style catalogs where a face is identified, in small size, with an unfamiliar name and/or the telltale "similar to," followed by the type's original name in a larger size.

Today's typeface camera-copier are little different from the record pirates of a few years ago. They wait until a face becomes popular. They wait until the originator's promotion has created a demand—then come out with their copy, taking advantage of the market already established, assuring themselves of a substantial profit every time. They risk nothing. They do not copy a "dud" and never take a chance on a loss.

Type masters made from high-quality original art are sharp, consistent in size, true in every stroke, serif, and detail. Type masters made from any but original art are less sharp, are less true to the weight of strokes and the fine details that distinguish an original from a copy.

Here, for example, is an ITC Lubalin Graph letter enlarged from a grid made from original art. Compare it with the letter enlarged from a grid being offered for sale as "similar to" Lubalin Graph.

. . . But more is lost than meets the eye. When "similar to" typeface manufacturers bypass the original art, they also bypass the royalty payment to the designer. This practice is so common that some of the most creative type designers have been driven from the market. Their incentive to create new faces is stifled, fewer new top-quality designs are brought to market, and in the long run you are the loser. Some of them have gone to book designing and other forms of typographic art, rather than create, in effect, for the benefit of the copyist.

And that's just the tip of the iceberg illustrating how the quality of typefaces and the supply of new styles are being stifled . . . or how you are being ripped off by "Similar to" -ism.

Typeface designers receive royalties from phototype companies that supply typesetting, or from the type franchise itself. When typographers add a slight extra charge for each word typeset in an exclusively commissioned typeface, a portion of this extra charge is paid to the designer.

Alternatively, the company that produces and supplies the type fonts may charge its customers, the typesetters, a one time fee of about $30—a small amount that is *not* passed on to the purchaser of the typesetting. In this case, the designer receives his royalty out of that one time charge. This is the ethical system that ITC has promoted for some time, and enforced under its licensing agreements. It has played a major role in reducing instances of "similar to" -ism.

—adapted from *Upper & Lower Case,* March 1977 and September 1978

New type design suggesting the computer age

JON HENRY

Typeface Libraries

Most of the major typesetting companies have typeface catalogues of their own, and these books can be obained directly from Compugraphic, Mergenthaler, Visual Graphics, Monotype, and other corporations. The second major source of typeface collections and new type designs are the dry transfer type companies like Letraset, Zipatone, Chartpak, and Mecanorma, referred to in Section B (see pages 97–105).

Some manufacturers supply fonts only to the phototypesetting companies, and specialize in specific systems. Storch, for example, produces fonts only for the Alphatype and VIP (Mergenthaler) systems. Others, such as ITC, supply every system and the dry transfer companies as well. ITC reviews all its typefaces, and periodically features new additions to its range, in its own U & lc magazine (see p.218).

Mergenthaler produces a neat series of spiral bound, detailed reference volumes which show their types in all sizes and text settings. The Mergenthaler catalogue includes the Linotype collection, plus two European collections, Stempel and Haas, in nine volumes: General, Text, Display, ITC, News and Classified, Special, Non-Roman, 54-Unit Text, and 54-Unit Display.

Cost: $50.00 (complete set)

Mergenthaler Linotype Company

Mergenthaler Linotype Stempel Haas

General Typefaces

The VGC Library

This comprehensive catalogue of some 1,700 typefaces, many of which have never appeared as full alphabets before, is arranged alphabetically, and includes an introductory section that deals with unusual and creative uses of phototypography.

Cost: $13.00

Art Direction Book Company; Visual Graphics Corporation

Cathode Ray Tube designed letter

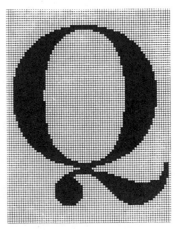

Dry Faces

Inevitably, there had to be a directory of types available from the many dry transfer companies. Happily, this one is an extremely handy research tool with type-faces grouped in three categories (serif, sans serif, and decorative), and arranged to include the illustrated font, name(s) of manufacturer(s), code numbers and sizes available.

Cost: $14.50

Art Direction Book Company

Cherokee Caslon Bold by VGC

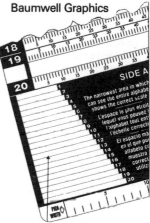

Going Metric

A 1977 Gallup Poll indicated that 45% of the American populace opposed conversion to the metric system, while only about 24% suported the concept. And in 1979, the *American Metric Journal* advised that any attempt to force metrics on an unwilling public would lead to chaos and significantly higher prices. Using the metric system selectively, however, may be of some use; and converting the rather arbitrary printer's points and picas to the arbitrary metric system *may* be practical for an era of photocomputers.

"Since the days of Fournier, beginning printers and fledgling artists and editors have memorized the number of points in a pica and the number of picas in an inch. Unfortunately Fournier's rule has not been a universal standard. Points and picas are used on the English side of the channel but not on the continent where type is calculated by the Didot system whose points are a hair larger than the English point.

"Now another measuring system is approaching — one which may solve the European problem of dual, non-compatible type measuring systems . . . . Already a few type manufacturers in the United States, particularly in the transfer type field, are measuring their type-faces in millimeters. Some newspapers have begun measuring column "inches" in centimeters.

"The printer's rule won't be calibrated overnight. Printers are seldom known to do anything hasty. But for the next decade or two we may find ourselves using both points and millimeters, picas and centimeters."

— *Sandra B. Ernst*

The table here shows a quick reference method of comparing picas to points, metrics and inches; it comes from Sandra B. Ernst's book *The ABC's of Typography.*

Cost: $8.95

Art Direction Book Company

Unitype Copyfitter

Here is a compact copyfitting tool that works for all typesetting systems; requires no books, charts, or formulas; and gives you a measureable alphabet to work with. It is a transparent gauge with pica, metric, and didot scales, and standard and elite typewriter character counters. All you need is a complete alphabet to calculate from.

Cost: $6.75

Baumwell Graphics

Points	Picas	MM	Inch
	1	.35052	.0138
	2	.70	.03
	3	1.05	.04
	4	1.40	.06
	5	1.75	.07
	6	2.10	.08
	7	2.45	.10
	8	2.80	.11
	9	3.15	.12
	10	3.51	.14
	11	3.86	.15
1	12	4.21	.17
	13	4.56	.18
	14	4.91	.19
	15	5.26	.21
	16	5.61	.22
	17	5.96	.24
	18	6.31	.25
	19	6.66	.26
	20	7.01	.28
	21	7.36	.29
	22	7.71	.30
	23	8.06	.32
2	24	8.41	.33
	25	8.76	.35
	26	9.11	.36
	27	9.46	.37
	28	9.81	.39
	29	10.17	.40

Points to metrics

Photo-Mechanical Supplies

A fundamental part of design for the graphic artist is the preparation of artwork for reproduction or for platemaking. This particular skill includes the process of making a *mechanical,* a board art that involves a large range of general background knowledge and specific acquired skills.

Preparing mechanicals — being a paste-up artist — is the first career step for many graphic designers or is, at least, an essential part of their graphics education and training (see Section E. p.176).

Without a thorough familiarity with this process, a designer in graphics communication has a severely limited creative capacity.

Since this is not a how-to book, it is not the place to outline the complexities of creating camera-ready material boards; rather, we will simply suggest some sources of guidance, information, and supplies.

Advertising Agency and Studio Skills
[Tom Cardamone]

One step up from van Uchelon's book, this is the guide to the preparation of art and mechanicals for production that includes all the complicated procedures used by most art and production departments in advertising agencies.
    Cost: $7.95

Watson-Guptill Publications

FROM *THE E B EDDY HANDBOOK*

The Lithographer

His title is something of a misnomer; actually, the photo-lithographer is the trade supplier of most of the components of the mechanical, other than type, to printers, studios, and designers. The lithography house will also make negatives for plate-making, and sometimes make the printing plates themselves. Lithographers' particular stock in trade is their intimate understanding of what is required to have everything ready for the press. A good relationship with a lithography house is crucial to a graphic artist.

Once you have been through the process of acquiring the illustrative material, retouching, cropping, scaling, and marking up for the camera, the lithographer will supply your screened or line copy — or combinations of the two — or your negative or positive film. These precise photo-mechanical skills greatly extend the range of graphic effects available to the designer, who should, in any case, be familiar with all the various screens and their possible combinations in both black & white and color.

The Screen

The ideal mechanical is one in which all the various elements intended for the printing plate are combined as one unit at the same size as the finished, printed sheet. This is the same-size, camera-ready copy that can then be photographed in a single shot and the film exposed onto a plate without further handling.

Most often, a halftone of an illustration or photograph is not actually pasted down on the mechanical, but stripped in separately to the final negative. This approach avoids the loss of detail that may occur when a paper halftone print is photographed as part of the complete line mechanical, which can occur particularly if the halftone is a fine screen.

A halftone is the conversion of a photograph, or any other illustration that includes a complete tonal range, into black and white dots. The original art is photographed through a screen — a precise criss-cross pattern of lines that break down the image into a pattern of varying sizes and dots.

Halftone screens range from 55 to 300 lines per inch; the quality of paper on which the art will be reproduced usually determines the grade of the screen. For instance, newsprint will accept up to 85 line screen, normal book papers will accept up to 120 line, and most coated papers will accept up to 150 line. Ordinarily the really fine screens are used only for very high quality duotone or color printing.

Screen Tints

Usually used for solid areas of color, these screens represent 10% increments of the grey scale from 10% to 90%, and can be combined with other screens in a variety of ways.

film

copy

developer

film

film

printing plate

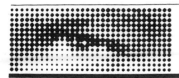

The plain halftone

Halftone silhouetted

Straight line screen

Concentric line screen

Cut line screen

Linen screen

Steel engraving screen

Steel etch screen

Fine grain screen

Fine mezzotint screen

Coarse mezzotint screen

Burlap screen

Coarse wood grain screen

Mesh screen

through textured glass

High-contrast line plate

FROM *FOLIO MAGAZINE;* "GRAPHIC IDEA NOTEBOOK" BY JAN V. WHITE, AUTHOR OF *EDITING BY DESIGN*

Tone-line conversion

Solid line silhouette

Bas-relief

Solarized image

Posterization

Xerographic distortion

xerographic Distortion

Distortion of textured original

Six of the halftone screen range

15

55

65

65 screen at 90°

100

120

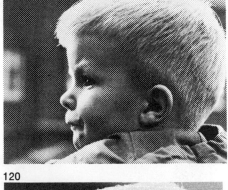

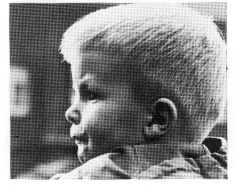

Line Screens

Most lithographers carry an array of special effect line screens which can be used separately or in carefully planned combinations. The basic range consists of: vertical or horizontal lined screen, mezzotint, etching screen, circle line screen, linen screen, and brushstroke screen. Utilizing these screen patterns with a selective masking process, halftones and tints, will yield a vast range of special effects. Creating line conversions in this way is a precise photomechanical craft that produces *posterization* and *solarization*.

Line conversion by Elstan Studio

"Real creative reproduction combines the abstract, artistic concept with the concrete, mechanical process, the whole time keeping in mind the final printing process. Most art directors and production managers don't always have an appreciation for the printer's problems. It's important to point them out, because it may alter their entire approach.

If an artist tells me the effect he wants, I can tell him what to do to get that effect. I take my thirty years of experience as an artist and special effects expert, and transform it into five minutes of advice on the phone. I have to educate myself before I can start a job. I have to know what kind of paper the job is being printed on, what type of press, and the type of plate. Those three factors influence the kind of effect I should use. And sometimes, I have to say to the art director, 'What you think is beautiful may not work when it comes to special effects.'

For some effects, you must do a tremendous amount of retouching beforehand. If I have to airbrush or retouch to help the photo, I do. If the artist would rather do the retouching, we can at least guide him to the areas that need it the most.

One of the problems that arises is holding fine lines. We can shoot old etchings and engravings and maintain an exceptionally high quality in line. Tone against tone with no seams is another art problem we have solved.

I'm constantly looking for ways to get everybody — artists, special effects experts, and printers — together, so that we can speak the same language and under- stand each other better."

—Ed Ferris, director of *Mask-O-Neg*, New York

The Halftone Reproduction Guide

A proven reference tool useful for making precise decisions when specifying tints, duotones or triple dot process. The same halftone is illustrated in single-dot, double-dot, flat color, duotone, and triple dot in two color printing. Each page shows color bars for black and the second color in solid tone and tints of 80%, 60%, 40%, and 20%, as well as reverses, surprints, and other comparative aids. Both coated and uncoated papers are used, and one hundred of the most widely used colors are demonstrated. This is exactly the type of reference you need to get the maximum effect from two color printing.
Cost: $29.95

Art Direction Book Company

An offshoot of photomechanical skills are these photo-lithographs by J. Seeley which were produced without the use of screens or process camera, but were inspired by the photomechanical process and end result. This inventive series was published in U&lc, March 1978.

© J SEELEY

The Office Repro Camera: Pos One

For a fairly low investment, you can have your own camera and processor that demands a minimum of technical knowledge, and will produce good quality line and screened prints with a minimum of fuss. These compact, daylight-operating units produce fast, economical stats, screened prints (veloxes), film negatives or positives, special effects, and even posterizations. Optional extra attachments will allow copying from books, making color cells, slide enlargements, and even offset plates. Once you get the hang of the process, the savings in time along make these machines well worth their price; and with some extra effort in developing your camera skills, you can duplicate most of the services provided by the lithographer. VGC's Series 316/320 unit is the most economical on the market, and their 516/520 unit has the added ability to process phototypesetting on resin-coated reproduction paper.

Cost: $3,495.00 (Autofocus model)

Visual Graphics Corporation

The Pantone Color System

All the screen possibilities provided by the lithographer apply to pre-press color proofing, and extend the line and tone combinations dramatically. Apart from Agfa-Geveart's system (Copychrome), the standard color-to-ink matching method is the Pantone system — a color-data system to standardize color and color matching throughout the printing and graphic arts industries. Ink manufacturers consult with Pantone, Inc. to maintain color control, and Pantone supplies custom color matches throughout a worldwide color communications network.

Not long ago, you had to match colors to the limited range available from an ink manufacturer, and each company's colors were different. It was a hit and miss method of mixing your own color swatch from gouache paint, and asking the printer to match and mix. If the color could be matched, often the density and texture could not, and the transparent printing ink created an entirely different visual effect from what you wanted. But with the Pantone system you have the basis of a color language for conversations betwen the designer, lithographer, printer, and ink manufacturer.

Designers and graphic artists plug into the Pantone color matching system through Pantone's ink sample books, matched papers, overlays, and felt tip pens available from art supply stores. Lithographers work with Pantone colors through "Color-Key" film which is unfortunately limited to forty-eight colors only.

There are many Pantone specification books, paper sample collections, color selectors, and guides, all using a standard numbering system. One of the most useful is the *Pantone Color Specifier, Designers Edition.* This is a dictionary of over 6,000 numbered tearout color chips containing all the 500 matched colors in the system.

Cost: $24.00

Pantone Inc

CA Color Guide

Another important tool for working with color is this guide that shows the printed results of combinations of printing ink colors. This is a tool that is hard to be without. The *CA Color Guide* lays down a full range of base colors, one to a page, in a full range of tints from 100% (solid) to 10%, and also shows the results of adding a range of black tints from 70% to 10%. Thus, each page shows forty different colors derived from black plus one other. Although the base colors are not matched to the Pantone system, they can be matched with reasonable accuracy to that or any other ink matching system.

The *CA Color Guide* includes a very useful section of fifteen charts on process colors and their combinations. For example, you can check the color produced by adding a 30% process blue to any of the forty combinations of process red and yellow, and so on through the entire range of possibilities. Further, there is a very informative section dealing with the proper way to specify duotones for maximum effect. It is available with coated or uncoated paper, spiral bound, and cloth-covered.

Cost: $32.50

Communication Arts

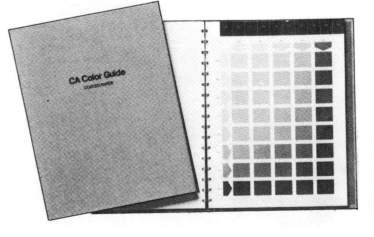

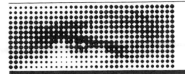

Dial-A-Color

A handy little tool to determine process color formulations. Four color wheels rotate over each other, allowing you to view any color mix. The standard process colors, calibrated in 10% gradations, will reveal up to 9,000 colors. It's simple, effective, and cheap.

Cost: $7.65

Dial-A-Color Company

Indenticolor

This unique pre-press color proofing system uses no screen or platemaking procedures, yet produces a facsimile of the final printed job that looks and feels as if it has been printed. You supply the mechanicals as you would to the lithographer or printer, and the Headliners franchise (in all major cities) will supply any number of highly accurate proofs using their 320 color range.

Headliners International Inc

Chromatec Imaging System

If you really want to get into producing your own color proofs, this is a fairly simple and inexpensive system that need not be messy, provided you are careful. It uses several inks including process color, and a photo-sensitive developing mechanism. The results are identical to press proofs, and images can be reproduced on virtually any material you choose. The machinery consists of a processor, a developer, and three coating rods which are operated by hand in a five-step process that takes about ten minutes. As with any such kit, you have to be diligent about keeping everything clean and tidy, or you end up with ink over everything.

Cost: $450.00 (standard basic kit)

Metro Supply Company

The PosColor Machine

This self-contained unit, designed for the studio, is an extension of Visual Graphics' compact camera/processor system that produces instant color copies from originals. Any color original, from a 35mm transparency to a 20" x 24" piece of opaque art, can be copied into color stats, full-color film transparencies, or black and white copies. The PosColor is the perfect machine for those who continually need color proofs for clients, and who would like to save substantial amounts of time and money. It will copy anything in color, from color layouts to product shots of three dimensional objects.

Cost: $9,995.00 (System 7000)

Visual Graphics Corporation

The world's most finished rough.

Chromatec

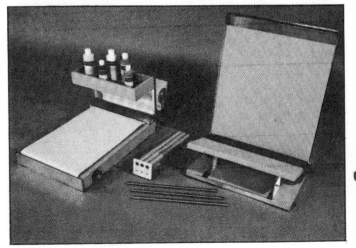

Photography and Multi-Media
Part I

Sooner or later, everyone involved with graphic communications makes use of photography in one form or another. Most photographic needs can be cared for by local professional photographers, or by stock agencies ranging from the National Archives, where you can buy prints for as little as $5.00, to Magnum and Black Star, which may charge thousands of dollars to assign one of their staff to do some special work for you.

The art of being a professional photographer is amply documented in several books, such as Robert Foothorap's *Independent Photography* (Fireside Books, Simon and Schuster, $7.95). Photographic hardware, which is beyhond the scope of this book, is covered in many readily available volumes.

Nonetheless, many graphic artists are competent photographers in their own right, and there are two cameras we should mention that are useful tools for the designer — not necessarily for producing final, finished photographs, but for preparing layouts and comps, and for communicating your requirements to the photographers you employ.

The Polaroid Reporter SE

Instant photography has come a long way since the first Polaroid camera (Model 95) was introduced in 1947. Today, Polaroids are a valued tool for professionals. The new Polacolor 20 x 24 format, for example, is used in fields as diverse as medicine and advertising. The SX-70 series is the top of Polaroid's line, but the Reporter SE is probably more useful in the context of graphic design.

Like the other Polaroids, the Reporter SE is a folding camera; but it accepts five different kinds of color and black and white film: Polacolor 2, Types 108 and 88; Types 87, 107, and 105 P/N black and white. It includes automatic exposure control and electronic shutter, and focuses from 3½" to infinity. Black and white film develops in fifteen seconds and color in one minute, which makes this camera the perfect tool for testing photographic concepts indoors and out.

The Reporter SE also comes with a No-Fault Photo Guarantee, which means that Polaroid will replace any film that doesn't develop as well as you think it should.
Cost: $72.50

Polaroid Corporation

Minolta 110 Zoom SLR

This little camera points the way to the future of the 110 film format, and may even be superseded by the time this book goes to press. Although not yet a professional instrument, it is the first 110 film camera that is a precision tool, with through-the-lens viewing. It's very light (less than one pound) and compact, and has a lens that zooms from 25mm to 50mm (the equivalent of 50mm to 100mm in a 35mm camera), and automatic metering. It's ideal for gathering quick photographic information and references, and professional labs now give one day service for 110 film.

The list price is still high, but discount camera stores make it available for as little as $160.
Cost: $292.00

Minolta Corporation

Photography and Multi-Media,
Part II

Your other principal photographic support system is the various photo labs that are in all major cities, and present in many smaller ones. They supply a large range of services to the graphic artist, including dye transfers, C prints, duplicate transparencies for reproduction, retouching, slides, copy work, black and white prints, color stats, custom developing, photo enlargement, and even plastic lamination.

Photo labs vary in the variety of services they provide, the quality of their work, and the prices they charge; many specialize in particular fields. You definitely want to establish good relations with as many such labs as necessary to fill your needs, and apart from your own experience, the best way to learn about them is to ask local art directors and other professional graphics people about their experiences with labs in your area.

Electronic Graphics

Electronics can produce the special effects demanded by designers a lot less painfully than lithographers can; subsequently, machines are taking over much of their work. Electronic graphic applications within the television/video medium became increasingly apparent during the 1970s (see Section E), and have provided the impetus to develop electronic graphic technology for other media as well, such as murals, projected images, film, and transparencies for offset lithography.

Any color or black and white image can be solarized, posterized, or colorized through the use of a color-coded computer and a video screen. The resulting, infinitely manipulatable image appears on the video monitor, providing instant feedback regarding suggested color changes. In a single hour it is possible to generate hundreds of color design variations, and reproduce as many as you wish onto slide film or video tape. The final results are taken from the video monitor, and while they do contain video screen lines, these are so small that they are virtually unnoticeable unless you make a substantial enlargement of your image.

This electronic graphics system can do all your color experimentation, create sepia tone, duotone, or tri-tone effects, dissolve sequences, and provide typographic enhancement, separations of color, patterned backgrounds, and posterization — all for a surprisingly low cost.

Average cost: $150.00 per hour

Metacolor, Inc

Camera Graphics

Effects similar to those created electronically can be achieved by conventional means as well. In this capacity, the camera is somewhat limited but its results can equal those produced by electronic means, if you know precisely what you want to accomplish. Transparencies made in this fashion need cost no more than electronic graphics.

The Incredible Slidemakers

Audio-Visual Computer Programming

The ultimate slide/sound presentation uses multiple carousel projectors and a tape deck linked and programmed through a computer unit to produce a variable speed presentation with dissolves, flash fades, freezes, and instant editing capacity. The effects possible through computer units go from movie and video simulation through multi-image effects that can be varied or changed constantly. These computer units are available from:

Audio Visual Laboratories, Inc; Clear Light Productions, Inc

Audio-Visual Presentation

The combination of slides and sound is an increasingly popular, economical alternative to both film and video. Playback operation is very easy, and programs can be designed to be used by virtually anyone without special training. Many photo labs now offer a-v services, and companies specializing in the medium have opened in many major metropolitan areas. The complete source of all necessary hardware is the *Audio-Visual Catalogue,* from the Photo & Sound Company.

Cost: free

Photo & Sound Company

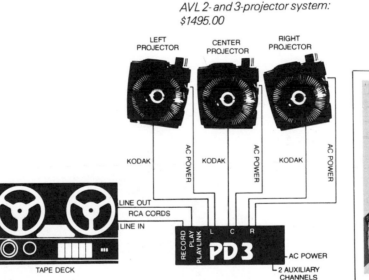

AVL 2- and 3-projector system: $1495.00

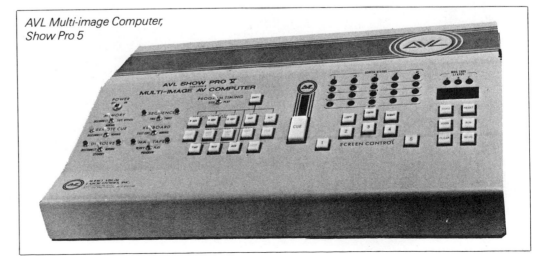

AVL Multi-image Computer, Show Pro 5

Editing and Viewing

When working with transparencies, film, and audio-visual graphics, it is important to use equipment designed for professional use. This is particularly true with regard to viewers, which must have balanced light dispersion delivering light at around 5000°K. The Matrix Model 2049A is a large capacity, portable viewer that rests in vertical or horizontal positions; its 17½" x 47½" surface accommodates 200 slides or ten 8 x 10 transparencies, and provides even lighting (with dimmer control) that has two 40W, full spectrum, fluorescent lamps. It can be used with two standard Editing/Retrieval overlays that contain 88 slides each.

Cost: see catalog

Matrix Division / Leedal Inc

Editing / Retrieval Overlays

To make editing much faster and easier when you are handling a volume of slides, each overlay holds 88 slides and fits Matrix Models 2049A and 1825A, as well as the large Console Editor II. Overlays are ideal for sequencing and storing slides for later use.

Made from extruded, black anodized aluminum, they are designed to fit a special retrieval/storage cabinet that holds fifteen overlays.

Cost: $12.00 each

Matrix Division / Leedal Inc

Sell-O-Vue

This is a system of instant visual aids that are effective and economical. It is based on a 35mm color mount containing 8 or 12 frames, combined with a unique, fully assembled precision viewer that slips on the mount and folds flat. From this basic concept, the Taylor Merchant company will make up quantities of any slide program combined with multi-media accessories to your own design, ranging from printed literature and brochures to cassettes, special letters, slide wallets, and so on.

The system allows for the presentation of your sample or portfolio in an attractive form that is cheap enough for you to leave behind with your client. The combination possibilities are highly variable; the price given here is for the Sell-O-Vue viewer with an 8-frame strip, in a quantity of 300 units.

Cost: $495.00 ($1.65 each)

The Merchant Taylor Corp

Printing

The five major systems of mass reproduction, or printing — relief, planographic, intaglio, stencil, and electrophotographic — cover the basic printing processes in common use: letterpress (relief), offset lithogrpahy (planographic), rotogravure (intaglio), silkscreen (stencil), and direct electrostatic (electrophotographic).

Offset lithography has enjoyed the greatest development of the five systems within the printing industry over the last fifteen years, and has almost entirely replaced letterpress. But direct electrostatic reproduction, which began with the Xerography process, is the wave of the future.

The combination of laser technology and upgraded Xerographic techniques places the printing industry on the threshold of a major revolution. By the mid-1980s, for example, computer terminals will facilitate the composition of a multi-page booklet within a matter of seconds; offset quality copies will be waiting minutes later on the other side of the plant, or even on the other side of the country. Everything will have been transmitted electronically, without the use of printing plates or presses.

Because of rapid technological advances such as this, it is crucial that designers keep abreast of new developments in the printing industry. Otherwise, all print design may end up in

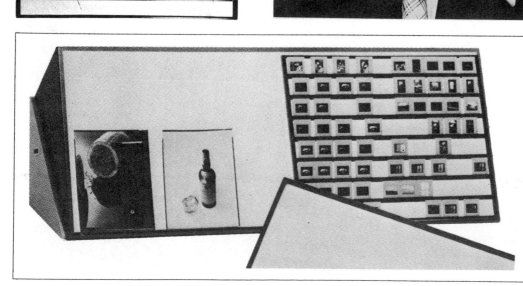

WARREN'S WALLER PRESS

the hands of computer operators at the print shops, and graphic designers will find themselves relegated to mere decorators once again, rather than responsible project directors.

Printers are moving into the future, and designers must face the future's implications. An immediate step is to become familiar with the data-processing presses themselves. In the longer term, education — stronger links between the printing industry and graphic design courses — will enable visually oriented graphic artists to grapple with tomorrow's technology.

Printing is a growth industry; except for the threat of a paper shortage (see below, p.141), it is estimated that there will be an annual increase in receipts of 3.5% between 1978 and 1982, allowing for inflation.

Relief Printing

Letterpress is the commercial application of relief printing. The material used to transfer the image onto paper can be metal, wood, linoleum, rubber or glass. In relief printing, ink is transferred to paper directly from the raised parts of the image or type.

Letterpress printing still gives the best quality reproduction, since no other process can duplicate the combination of handset type bit clean and strong into a sheet of well made paper, or the brilliant black of a well printed metal or wood engraving. But phototypesetting and offset lithography offer cheaper and faster commercial printing, and today letterpress is reserved for special work where quality is of the essence. Consequently, letterpress machinery has become quite cheap, and many designer/printers or beginning printers learn the craft of print on old letterpress equipment.

Printing It
[Clifford Burke]

This is an excellent little book on the *craft* of printing, written by a well known poet, master printer, and book designer. For years, Clifford Burke has been conducting a one man campaign to take the mystery out of printing and restore common sense and taste to the craft. His book, then, is oriented to those who want to do their own printing. *Printing It* is a standard guide for the novice, covering and comparing small scale letterpress and offset litho techniques and problems, and telling you all you need to know to reproduce anything — with style — yourself.

Cost: $3.00

Wingbow Press

Stamp It Out

Along with Polaroid film and the Xerox machine, the rubber stamp — a primary form of relief printing — has become an art and design medium. Stamps are cheap, instant printing; they are portable, giftable, adaptable, and artistic. The ultimate recognition has been bestowed on rubber stamp art by none other than the Museum of Modern Art, and there is a limited edition magazine devoted to the medium called *Once.* The use of stamps in correspondence art, collage, and printmaking has been growing fast. They are used in pamphlets, posters, company logos, magazine illustrations, and as personal signatures known as "chops," taking the place of the traditional wood block or signet ring. Apart from creating the original designs and their stamped combinations, the art of the rubber stamp lies in making the finest possible impression.

Rubber stamp makers exist everywhere nowadays, and all the hardware you need to make your own is easily available. The New York Yellow Pages, for example, has two-and-a-half pages devoted to rubber stamp related businesses and Workman Publishing has issued *The Rubber Stamp Album.*

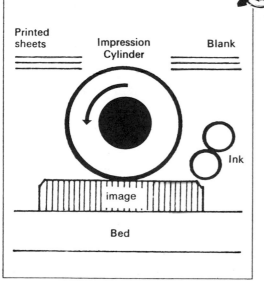

FROM *BASIC TYPOGRAPHY*, WATSON-GUPTILL PUBLICATIONS

Printed sheets

Impression Cylinder

Blank

Ink

image

Bed

DO NOT ABUSE, BEND, CLIP, DEFACE, ERASE, FOLD, GOUGE, HACK, IGNORE, JUNK, KERF, LOSE, MUTILATE, NEGLECT, OCCLUDE, PUNCTURE, QUARTER, ROLL, SPINDLE, TAINT, UGLIFY, VEX, WRINKLE, X-RAY, YERK OR ZAP THIS ARTWORK

RUBBER STAMP ART CONVENTION

typŏ graphics

Planographic Printing

Traditionally, offset lithography has been used, rather than letterpress, if a print run was to be large, and/or if it involved a lot of halftones. Today, however, technical improvements in phototypesetting, printing equipment, and photomechanical preparation of negatives and plates have made offset so universally popular that letterpress can no longer compete with it economically.

In offset lithography (as distinct from direct lithography, which is no longer commercially viable), ink is transferred from a flat plate, usually zinc, to a rubber blanket, and then to the paper. Those parts of the plate which are to print the image are greasy and attract the ink; the other parts of the plate are not greasy and attract water which repels the ink. Good offset lithography is frequently more attractive and effective in both color and black and white than average letterpress printing quality.

It is the small, sheet-fed offset press that has permitted the proliferation of "instant print" shops all over the country, bringing inexpensive printing within everybody's reach, and competing successfully — at least for the time being — with Xerographic copying.

Web-offset machinery has made printing large quantities of multi-page tabloids and periodicals economically feasible, and the recent trend toward narrow-web machines has made short-run work more economical than sheet-fed offset.

Finally, the recent perfection of continuous tone reproduction is a significant development in commercial lithography, since it creates the best possible image transfer quality available.

Manual of Advanced Lithography
[Richard Vicary]

Offset lithography is a skilled craft at its best; and since the 1950s, technical advances have also encouraged the *art* of lithography to produce very high quality prints. This book underscores the true potential of the lithographic printing process, and, as the title implies, it is intended for the graphic artist who wishes to make *quality* reproductions. Although Vicary's is an in depth study of lithography, and is somewhat removed from commercial practice, it provides excellent background information on the major printing system in use today.

Cost: $12.50

Charles Scribner's Sons

Intaglio Printing

The application of this system is known as gravure; both rotogravure and sheet-fed gravure are processes of intaglio printing from engraved cylinders on a fast-moving press. The cost of the cylinders places gravure printing far beyond the reach of most print media users, since a print run must reach hundreds of thousands of copies before the expense of the cylinder is justified. Still, many large, color-run magazines use rotogravure because, once on the press, it is

Manual of Advanced Lithography
Richard Vicary

easy and dependable printing, and there is no better process for reproducing art and photographs in quantity.

In gravure, ink is transferred to paper from wells sunk *in* the cylinder's surface (intaglio). A soft blade wipes all ink from the non-printing areas *on* the surface of the cylinder. The depth of each well determines the amount of ink transferred from it to the paper. The results of gravure printing are soft yet precise, blending all the tones in the original to resemble continuous tone prints.

Intaglio printing is also used whenever security is involved, or when quality embossed effects are desired. In both such instances, a steel or copper engraved plate is used to transfer the ink, under pressure, to the paper.

In the near future, computer and laser technologies may liberate gravure to compete in the shorter-run arena presently dominated by web-offset, by reducing the costs of cylinder engraving. Then we might expect to see the development of the small gravure press, and wrap-around plates for the cylinders.

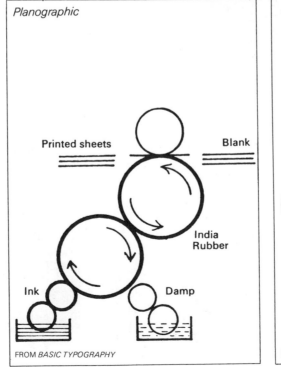

Planographic

Printed sheets   Blank

Ink   India Rubber   Damp

FROM *BASIC TYPOGRAPHY*

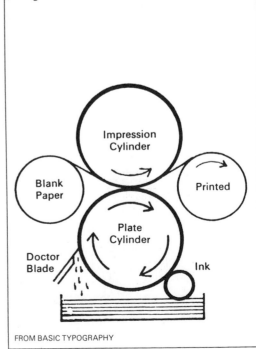

Intaglio

Impression Cylinder

Blank Paper   Printed

Plate Cylinder

Doctor Blade   Ink

FROM BASIC TYPOGRAPHY

Stencil Printing

Best known in its application as silkscreening, or serigraphy, stencil printing is best suited to line work and large areas of solid color, although coarse screened halftones can also be printed in this fashion. No other printing process can lay down so large a quantity of ink while making so little mess as silkscreen, and the rich color that results is both the hallmark of the process and the reason it is widely used for printing fabrics.

Stencil printing is usually used for short-run printing, where the large plates and high press costs of other processes cannot be justified. In silkscreen, ink is squeezed through the open parts of the screen onto paper or other material. Non-printing areas of the screen are hardened chemically to solidify the mesh and prevent the ink from coming through. The screen itself may be made of silk, nyon, or fine wire.

Stencil duplicating, known as mimeography, is another common stencil printing application, really of use only for the cheap reproduction of items such as internal literature. The large range of compact office printing equipment available nowadays that utilize a combination of stencil and offset processes still compete well with office copying machines in terms of cost per printed sheet, and some of them — offset duplicators — can even match the quality of offset lithography for simple jobs.

Electrophotographic Printing

Up until now, direct electrostatic transfer has not been thought of as printing; rather, it has been referred to as "copying," since the surface to be printed never actually touches the "forms." But by any name it is a rapidly developing system of reproduction that promises to shake up both the printing and the communications industries.

In this form of impactless printing, an image is projected onto a positively charged surface, and light erases the charge from areas that are to remain clear. A negatively charged dry pigment is spread over the entire printing surface, and a new charge transfers the image to the paper. Heat then fixes the image on the sheet.

The basic electrophotographic process was developed by the Xerox company, and now over a dozen other companies have developed or are developing their own printing/copying machines for all manner of specific needs. The current objective is to produce four-color process effects from a single image transfer; the perfection of that technology will signal the demise of offset lithography. The companies pouring time, talent, and money into the development of electrophotographic processes include Xerox, Minolta, 3M, Gestetner, Canon, AB Dick, Mita Copystar, Savin, Pitney Bowes, SCM, and Oce Industries — to name a few. Some of their work involves combining electrostatic transfer with photographics, laser, and jet-ink transfer.

Nearly all copying machines now on the market are capable of achieving crisp, detailed images with large areas of solid black, and some can reproduce color fairly well. While transfer fidelity is still being perfected, all other aspects of reprographic machinery, such as computer controls and memory, high-speed operation, folding, collating, reduction and enlargement, microfilming, and transcontinental electronic transmission have all been sufficiently perfected to create remote-controlled *printing* systems.

The Xerox 3107 Copier

By now, reprographic machines are the common way to make copies of art and design, including layouts and dummies, by graphic artists in all fields. Of all the copiers on the market, the Xerox 3107 copier is probably the most useful. It reproduces crisply, the black is dense, it will take paper as large as 14"x 25", and it offers a reduction mode. While it cannot yet qualify as an essential part of a design studio, access to a 3107 is a significant convenience when proofing and checking any graphic work.

Cost: $5,600.00

Xerox Corporation

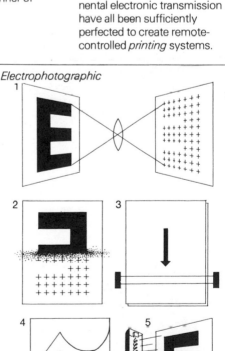

Electrophotographic

FROM *THE E B EDDY HANDBOOK*

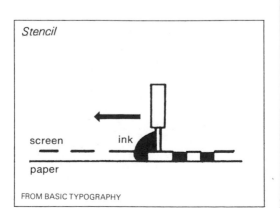

Stencil

screen   ink

paper

FROM BASIC TYPOGRAPHY

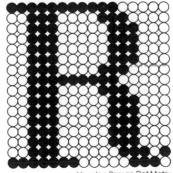

Versatec dot matrix for electrostatic writing machines

Versatec Roman Dot Matrix

Copyart: The First Complete Guide to the Copy Machine
[Patrick Firpo, Lester Alexander, Claudia Katayanagi, Steve Ditlea]

Without a doubt the most unusual and innovative book of graphic arts techniques around is this fully illustrated volume that shows how copying machines are being used imaginatively and creatively. *Copyart* signals the advent of a new art form, and announces copiers (particularly the Xerox 6500) as a means of self-expression. Copyart has been around for at least ten years, but the form really blossomed in the late 1970s. This book traces its short history, and compares the merits and shortcomings of the various copying processes. The copier is clearly an important new tool for artists and designers and illustrators, designers, and art directors who have access to any good reprographic machinery, especially color copiers, should have a field day with this book. It includes most of the copy crafts using slides, overlays, collages, "limited edition" printing, paper murals, light paintings, photographic distortion, "visual diaries," animation, blueprints, body art, masks, and so on.

    Cost: $7.95

Richard Marek Publishers

DIABLO AFTER DARK JULY 4 1979.

Handbook of Printing Production
[Paul Arthur]

A superb review of the entire printing process from the point of view of a client or designer who has to make a series of specific decisions. This book was planned and produced by the E B Eddy Company, printers, to provide simple, clear planning and production techniques essential to "... effective communications in print." It is beautifully prepared, with many diagrams, charts, tables, and photographs (shown in this section) that do more than just supplement the simple text. The table of contents — a fold out planning sheet — accurately outlines an eleven-stage print preparation plan that takes you from determining functions to evaluating the results.

Not for sale

E B Eddy Forest Products Ltd

Graphic Design and Reproduction
[Peter Croy]

A complete working handbook for everyone concerned with the graphic arts that provides a comprehensive reference to all stages of the transformation of design to the printed page. It is written by a German designer, and it is the designer's point of view that makes the book so valuable, particularly in the detils of the various printing processes and their uses. This well illustrated, lucid book that covers everything related to print, suffers, however, from being somewhat out of date — nothing that a badly needed revision could not clear up.

Cost: $15.95

Hastings House, Publishers

Paper

As far as paper is concerned, the outlook for the future is bleak, or uncertain at best. In 1978 the demand for paper in the United States was approximately 2,700,000 tons, but we produced only 2,300,000 tons domestically. We imported about 160,000 tons, leaving us with a gross shortage of some 240,000 tons. According to the American Paper Institute, the printing industry alone will require 3,780,000 tons of paper in 1980, and no one knows where it will all come from.

Besides the quantity, the quality of paper is a real problem for the immediate future. According to Brett Rutherford of the National Association of Printers and Lithographers, "the state of our printing heritage is a national disgrace and an impending world disaster." There is not enough paper, and what there is has become very expensive, and what you can buy is of such poor quality that books made from it fall apart after only thirty or forty years.

So far, all our paper is made from trees, and few people have gotten around to questioning the wisdom of this course. Trees are in short supply. All the easily cleared forests are gone, and building construction takes a great deal of what forest is still accessible. An increasing awareness of our environment's limits has resulted in considerable pressure to oppose destruction of our few remaining forests, and also to oppose destructive, high tech logging methods that include the use of defoliants and herbicides. The pollution controls and environmental protection conditions imposed by regulatory agencies such as OSHA and the EPA on the logging industry are surely to be applauded; but, when combined with the escalating costs of essential industrial energies, they have contributed to the expensive paper shortage. Although monocultural forestry management programs are designed to grow more trees faster than in the past, there still

are not — and will not be, in the foreseeable future — enough trees to supply our insatiable demands for paper.

Despite advertisements and promotions from the paper companies and the American Forest Institute, which claim there is plenty of "unmanaged" forest land and that the American forest is only half as productive as it could be, the fact remains that prior to the timber glut caused by large scale logging in the nineteenth century, paper was made largely from plants and recycled rags. That paper was superior to ours, since it was not rich in the acids and chemicals of treated wood pulp. In fact, the use of wood for papermaking did not even begin in the west until 1806. Before that time, hemp fibre was the main ingredient in paper, and flax and linen rag the principal alternatives.

By any rational criterion there should be an immediate moratorium on the destruction of our few remaining forests. When we kill off our trees and cut them up for paper pulp we are not only using a less than perfect raw material for our purposes; we are also shortening our own days on this planet.

When we consider our rapidly diminishing timber supply, the ecological disasters that result from lost watersheds and oxygen sources when we log too extensively, the deteriorating books in our libraries (see below), and the high cost of paper imports, it would seem a prudent — and commercially viable — move to repeal anti-hemp legislation and initiate a crash program to raise hemp, flax, kenaf, a newly discovered stalky relative of hemp, and leucaena, a sort of tropical alfalfa that can grow twelve feet in six months. All these sources could provide the paper we need without killing our environment. The time to do it is now. Along with a few other enlightened steps, such a program might also help, in Sir Albert Howard's words, "to put an end automatically to the remnants of this age of banditry now coming to a disastrous close."

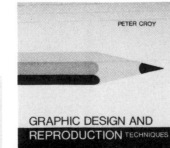

Our Books Are Dying

" The Library of Congress estimates that as many as one third of its eighteen million books are so badly deteriorated that they would be irreparably damaged if used because of their brittle and crumbling paper.

At Harvard University Library, more than 30,000 volumes are in a state of advanced decay.

Nearly half of the New York Public Library's five million volumes are in advanced state of disintegration.

Members of the Association of Research Librarians report that "a large number" of their 220 million books are similarly endangered.

The villains are neglect, shoddy materials including poor paper, and today's slice-it-with-a-knife polluted air. An arsonist could hardly do as much damage as is being done today under the noses of librarians and book collectors. *"*

—Brett Rutherford,
Book Production Industry,
June, 1979

Making Paper From Hemp
[Jack Frazier]

The fibrous hemp plant is an incredibly prolific and useful annual crop which has achieved a bad reputation in certain circles because a vicious nitwit named Henry J. Anslinger, Commissioner of the Federal Bureau of Narcotics in the 1930s, chose it as an issue on which to build his power. (The story of Anslinger's very nasty, racist demagoguery is lovingly outlined in Albert Goldman's *Grass Roots,* published by Harper and Row, 1979; $12.95.)

Jack Frazier traces the use of hemp throughout history, including its cultivation in eighteenth and nineteenth century America as a lucrative, large-scale business, and the revival of hemp husbandry in this country in the 1940s, when the Japanese cut off our supply of Manila rope and twine from the Philippines. Although the '40s experiment with hemp was astonishingly successful, the last government publication to extol the virtues of

hemp agriculture was *The Farmer's Bulletin No. 1935,* reprinted in 1952. Frazier's more recent book is a mine of carefully researched information about a plant we sorely need once more in order to produce decent quality paper.

"Every tract of 10,000 acres which is devoted to hemp raising year by year is equivalent to a sustained pulp-producing capacity of 40,500 acres of average pulp-wood lands," according to the 1916 Dewey/ Merrill report, *Bulletin No. 404,* U S Department of Agriculture.
Cost: $4.95

Solar Age Press

Papermaking
[Jules Heller]

In our society, and especially in our profession, paper is often taken for granted. An awareness of how this precious and significant material is made, then, is of particular interest to artists, printers, designers, and anyone else involved in print production. Heller's book combines an informal history of the subject with information about the many stages of making paper; his text is liberally sprinkled with anecdotes and quotations revealing many attitudes about paper. Heller discusses paper types, their properties, the practice and theory of papermaking, and how to make paper at home. The book is well illustrated throughout, and includes artwork by artists using their homemade paper.
Cost: $22.50

Watson-Guptill Publications

Advertising the managed forest, American Forestry Institute

—1950

—1940

—1930
This is the year the surrounding trees were harvested.
—1920

—1910

—1890

—1840

—156 years ———— 20 years —

PAPER MAKING

BY JULES HELLER   HOW TO MAKE HANDMADE PAPER FOR PRINTMAKING, DRAWING, PAINTING, RELIEF AND CAST FORMS. BOOK ARTS, AND MIXED MEDIA

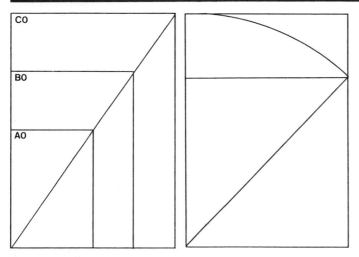

International ABC

An internationally standardized system of sizes for printing and writing papers has been in operation on the continent for over thirty years and has been adopted elsewhere throughout the world. The basis of the standard series is a sheet of paper whose sides are in ratio $1:\sqrt{2}$. However many times the sheet is folded in halves, the subdivisions always remain in the same proportion. There are three basic sheets, A B and C, which are related by a common dimensional ratio. Sizes obtained from subdividing these sheets are designated by numerals, thus: A4, B6 or CO.

US Standard Sizes

Paper comes in all sorts of sizes in the United States, and there are recognized paper sizes that are associated with different paper grades or types. For example, the basic size of a bond paper is 17 x 22, and although a basic sheet size is a standard size, bond paper may also be cut to sizes of 17 x 28, 19 x 24, 22 x 34, etc. and all are considered standard or regular sizes. In other words, it's a mess.

The diagram shows five of the basic sheet sizes from which the more commonly used sizes are derived, and the "standard" sizes usually refer to the size from which the 'basis weight' of the paper stock is obtained.

The DIN paper size system:
1:1.414 ratio

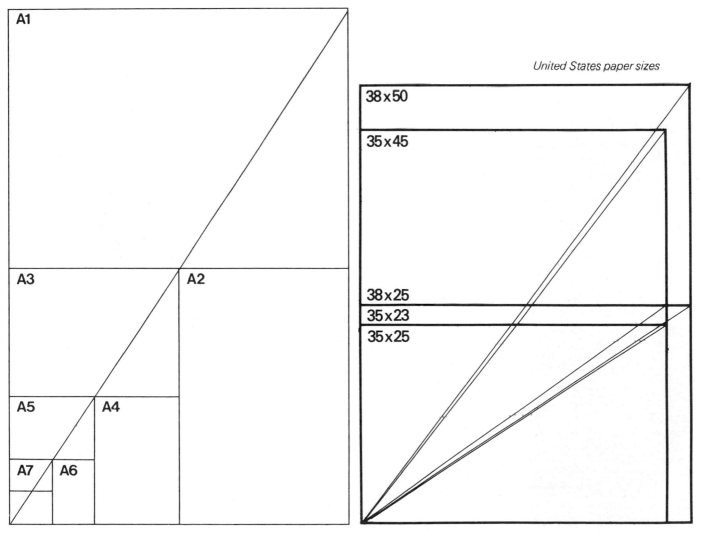

United States paper sizes

Resource
[San Francisco]

Resource is essentially a propaganda magazine published by a major paper manufacturer, Crown Zellerbach. Its concerns are paper and the paper business, paper problems, paper and pollution, paper and watersheds, paper and tree harvesting, paper as a renewable resource, and paper and politics. The magazine is beautifully designed and produced, and despite its obvious biases, very informative. It is a free quarterly for Crown Zellerbach employees and friends, and you'll have to convince them to put you on their mailing list.

Corporate Communications Department, Crown Zellerbach

The Printing Salesman's Herald

Every so often Champion Paper publishes a very good thematic journal on a particular aspect of paper. It is usually extremely well conceived, designed, and produced, and is always of considerable interest, even though its purpose is to help the print salesman sell Champion Papers.
    Cost: free

Champion Papers, Marketing Services

The Competitive Grade Finder

This is the annually revised catalog of available papers, compared and cross indexed. It lists all the manufacturers and distributors, and their brands and grades of paper, with brightness and opacity charts and prices. If you specify or buy paper, this is an invaluable aid in finding the stock you want, ascertaining its availability and price, and determining the alternatives that exist.
    Cost: $15.00

Grade Finders, Inc

Imposition Manual

One of the most confusing aspects of print is knowing how the final product is to be folded, and how one page is to be imposed relative to another for the printing press. Imposition is determined by the type of press and folding equipment to be used. This manual diagrams 151 imposition possibilities, which depend on the nature of the job and is a very handy reference tool.
    Cost: $2.50

Baumfolder Corporation

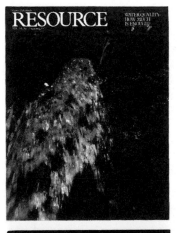

DOUGLAS FIR
Its symmetry and soft, flat needles growing completely around the twig make young Douglas fir popular Christmas trees. When mature, Douglas fir is the strongest of all American woods and so is widely used in construction, as railroad ties and for poles and piling.
Douglas fir grows from the eastern base of the Rockies to the Pacific Coast and is one of the main species grown in the commercial forests of Oregon and Washington. Its reddish brown bark grows in irregular oblong plates that may reach a thickness of up to 12 inches. The wood is yellowish to light red and fairly lightweight. Needles are ½ to 1 ½ inches long, and cones are 1 ½ to 4 ½ inches long.

Douglas Fir
Pseudotsuga taxifolia

The Design Crafts

Magazine Design

Newspaper Design

Book Design

Advertising Design

Packaging Design

Hand Lettering

Calligraphy

Cartography

"Logoptics"

D

Within the graphics profession there are numerous specialist disciplines, each demanding its own particular knowledge and skill. In this chapter, we've chosen to restrict ourselves to those specialist areas that are adjuncts to graphic design, and with which the graphic designer *must* be conversant.

Although there are surely relationships among them that will be clear to any graphics professional, this section speaks only indirectly about designing for the electronic media; about display and exhibition design; and about environmental design, which is more appropriately associated with the planning and architecture professions than with graphics. This chapter is about *information design,* covering the broad area of design and design-related crafts used traditionally in the print formats.

Magazine Design

The journalistic relationship between words and pictures is one of the most ephemeral, yet stimulating, areas for graphic design. It is ephemeral, of course, because what is news one week is old history the next, and stimulating because deadlines and other pressures demand that editorial and visual thinking be flexible enough to respond to reader needs and expectations.

The magazine designer/ art director of today may also be expected to continually revise his procedures to accommodate new production methods brought about either by economic necessity or by technical innovation. Moreover, in an operation where many people, with diverse talents and responsibilities, have to accomplish specific tasks in a fairly rigid order of temporal priorities, design systems and procedures must be established and adhered to, even as they undergo constant re-examination.

Publication design is related to the nuts and bolts of production problems and every magazine has its own production methodology. While the trend from hot metal to phototypesetting continues, a new breed of computer-directed machines that deliver completely assembled page layouts is in development. Some magazines are already exploring the problems of going directly from layout to film assembly.

For a new magazine starting off, as *New Times* did, with such updated procedures as combining layout and film assembly into a single operation; or for a magazine changing production procedures to cope with a two-week schedule rather than a monthly one as *Esquire* did for a while under Clay Felker's direction, the problems are not so overwhelming. But for an established magazine with ingrained working methods, completely abandoning old, familiar techniques can be an enormously disturbing business.

Even such standard furnishings as drawing stands are being replaced these days by light tables. Light tables, in turn, will soon be superseded by computer terminals that combine and manipulate text, headline, and image within a given area. Some versions of these terminals provide for the control of layouts on a viewing screen, but most depend on predetermined layout grids drawn from a "menu" of encoded grid structures and variations built into the system.

In the future the controlled area composition of a magazine's front and back matter, which usually remains consistent from issue to issue, will free the designer to devote more time to the creative challenges of page design.

Understandably, computer-aided design still makes graphic artists anxious. When all their design training and most of their experience favors innovation and the unexpected, it is disconcerting to be faced with batteries of machines with appetites for structured form and repeatable patterns.

"As magazines have become more specialized so have their problems. This makes it hard to generalize about the effects of the technical revolution on their design. But it is now clear that film is becoming the dominant material in publication production. It provides the designer with a new typographic freedom in the development of his layouts. It has expanded the range of selection and added greatly increased flexibility. Together with these gains, however, there has been a corresponding loss in the imposed discipline of the metal form. The designer has also discovered that filmsetting lacks the predictable standardization he has come to expect from hot metal. The publication designer will have to rely more heavily in the future on the self-discipline offered by carefully planned grids and design systems. This will mean a trend toward tighter organization in layouts and a greater reliance on imagination in images and illustrations and in display typography for graphic excitement. There is already strong evidence of a return to symmetrical form in magazine layouts."

—Allen Hurlburt, "Magazine Design in the Seventies," *Penrose Annual,* 1977-1978.

Six of the visual magazines of the seventies: the late New Times, *the revived* Esquire, Omni *with its emphasis on illustration,* Geo *and its excellent photographic presentation, a revitalized* Time *with more color, and the tabloid* Wet, *reflecting a preoccupation with style.*

Far left: representative layouts from Geo, Omni, Wet *and* Time.

Editing By Design
[Jan V. White]

This book is designed as a primer that explores the basic conceptual definitions of *magazine,* and explains how to use those concepts to enhance the product — in other words, to make a better magazine. White does not deal with the crucial area of production procedures which affect design, nor with the problems of new computer technology, but he does cover the visual aspects of publication. The book's principal focus is on the enormously problematic inter-relationship between editing and design — two functions that are normally thought of as separate. Confronting this issue, *Editing By Design* is highly informative, supporting each of its positions with detailed illustrations. All in all, it is the best book on publication design available, covering all the fine points of visual technique without ever advocating any sort of stylistic preference.

Cost: $18.50

R R Bowker Co

[Note: paperback edition published by Watson-Guptill, along with the companion volume, *Designing... For Magazines.]*

BILL SANDERSON

Top: ideal illustration techniques for newsprint — scratchboard.

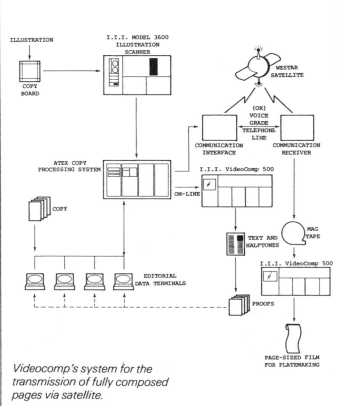

Videocomp's system for the transmission of fully composed pages via satellite.

Newspaper Design

It is still unusual for a newspaper to consider design to be part of its production system particularly in the United States. But it appears that conditions are changing. In the 1970s, for instance, traditional forms of presentation have been altered by technological advances that require changes in attitude and habit. The shift from hot metal to phototypesetting, as well as the introduction of computer page makeup and facsimile transmission equipment, has introduced the virtually new field of newspaper design, and subsequently the requisite newspaper design department.

Newspaper *design* is usually considered to have begun in fact in 1958, at the London *Daily Express.* That paper introduced to the traditional repertoire of newspaper presentation techniques "a spectacular new trick" — graphic design. Its purpose then was to introduce a feeling of modernity into the paper, while retaining the robust qualities of traditional newspaper presentation. A host of British papers, including the *Sunday Times, Daily Mirror,* and *The Observer,* followed the *Daily Express'* lead. The power and effect of the art directed broadsheet was quickly realized.

In the United States, broadsheet newspapers have not been noted for their journalistic design. The broadsheet is an unwieldy anachronism from the reader's point of view, and its potential — providing, as it does, a nice big piece of paper over which the designer may let his or her ideas flow — has been explored by only a handful of dailies in this country, notably the *Chicago Daily News,* the *San Francisco Examiner,* and the *Minneapolis Herald Tribune.*

Perhaps resistance to the designed broadsheet has resulted from the fact that it demands a complete re-evaluation of the journalist's process, as well as a modernization of the production and printing department's equipment. Neither the large newspapers nor the trades unions have been eager to face the implications of such vast upheavals.

But the form and the content of a newspaper are so closely linked that they can rarely be separated. As a result, they have usually been laid out by journalists who happen to be somewhat adept at design, rather than by designers who happen to be adept at journalism. As the *San Francisco Examiner* has shown, intelligent newspaper design can create a feeling of bigness and a sense of occasion with a subtlety of expression that has not been utilized in the past.

"The newspaper graphic designer has to be able to understand and respect the essential journalistic function of what he is asked to do—whether it is to design a diagram explaining how a bank was robbed or a heading block for a book which is being serialized. He has to be able to think on his feet at all times, for he will frequently be asked to give substance to impossible concepts.

The challenge in such a situation is to understand what lies behind the concept, and to produce an acceptable, workable alternative, not in ten minutes' time but immediately. The newspaper graphic designer has to be able to start a job before all the facts are available and change it radically, if necessary, when they become available. He has to be able to tolerate having a job rejected at the last minute because the story it was to accompany has either been supplanted by another, or drastically reduced in status—even though that job may have stretched his ingenuity, technical resources, and nerves to near breaking point."

— from Raymond Hawkey, "Graphic Design in Newspapers," *Penrose Annual,* 1973.

It is also essential that a newspaper designer be on top of the new computerized layout systems looming on the horizon, not excluding those that allow typesetting to be done directly from the journalist's typewriter. He or she must be able to deal

with the sometimes bizarre restrictions of the newspaper unions. And finally, the newspaper designer must be able to live with the knowledge that his work will not be enshrined on coffee tables throughout the land—that at the end of his work, his product will appear on poor quality paper, under-inked at times, scummed at others, and end up twelve hours later as the trash can lining.

Still and all, it is exhilarating to be involved in so immediate and spontaneous an area of information design, where ideas reach fruition instantly or not at all, and where the success or failure of a concept can be assessed within hours rather than months. It was the alternative, or "underground," press of the 1960s and early 70s that most fully exploited this immediacy and played with the design possibilities of the newspaper format, pointing to the layout potentials inherent in the medium. Unfortunately, most established newspapers never really noticed the graphic wizardry of tabloids such as the *San Francisco Oracle, Rolling Stone, Organ, Oz,* and *Ink.* They still don't.

San Francisco Examiner's *redesign dummy, 1973 (top), and the 1979 compromise version.*

D

Editing and Design
[Harold Evans]

This is a remarkable series of five volumes by the master technician and theorist who directed the redesign of London's *Sunday Times.* Of particular note are volumes four, *Pictures on a Page* (quoted below), and five, *Newspaper Design.*

Volume five has great value both as a textbook for beginners and as a source of new ideas for the most hardened of night editors. It is especially up-to-date and thought provoking concerning editing and design, even though it does not go as far as it might when considering future printing and production methods for a business that has clung to its old habits and techniques with tenacity. Neither does Evans really ever address the critical relationship between editors and designers. But, useful as the book is, the worst thing about it is that it may not be easy to find in the United States

Cost: $10.00

Heinemann, Ltd

If Reporters Could Draw...

Every day there is news that cannot be properly communicated with words, notably news whose essence lies in visual and spatial relationships. If that sounds a mouthful, consider the headline: RESCUERS DIG FOR MINERS TRAPPED BY RISING WATER.

Spatial relationships are the heart of that drama, and the outsider cannot fully comprehend it without graphics—a diagram of the underground workings locating men, flood water, and rescuers, an indication of the scale of distances between them, and the rate of the rescuers' progress. A straightforward photograph cannot do this.

The same is true of drawing. That it may be more than decorative or that graphic art can create an entirely new dimension to communication, is appreciated by only a handful of publications in the world.... A single drawing illustrating a feature is not graphics. It is an illustration. So is a single photograph in a news story. But both become graphics if sign systems or words or symbols are made an integral part of the drawing or photograph....

But there are much more sophisticated possibilities for information graphics where symbols and art together diagnose a complicated issue more succinctly than is possible in words alone. And there is a second area where display type and drawing provide a more economical but more evocative display unit.... Flavor graphics are essentially decorative; fact graphics are concerned not with images but with information.

—from Harold Evans,
Editing and Design.
Four: *Pictures on a Page.*

Replacing the News Photograph: The storming of the American Embassy in Nicosia as told by a Newsweek *fact graphic, and accompanied by photographs.*

Book Design

Except for the rare ones with a penchant for examining the fine print on the verso of the title page, most readers do not notice that books are designed at all. Yet, it is often through design that the book buyer is able to have the best possible presentation of his purchase's contents.

Book design requires a discriminating use of many complex manufacturing choices, as well as the cooperation of author, publisher, editor, production manager, copy editor, typesetter, illustrators, and printing craftspeople. Thus, in addition to his knowledge and imagination, a book designer must be able to coordinate many people and many areas of expertise.

Even so, design is seen as incidental to many books, and some publishers still regard it as an unnecessary expense—something that could easily be handled

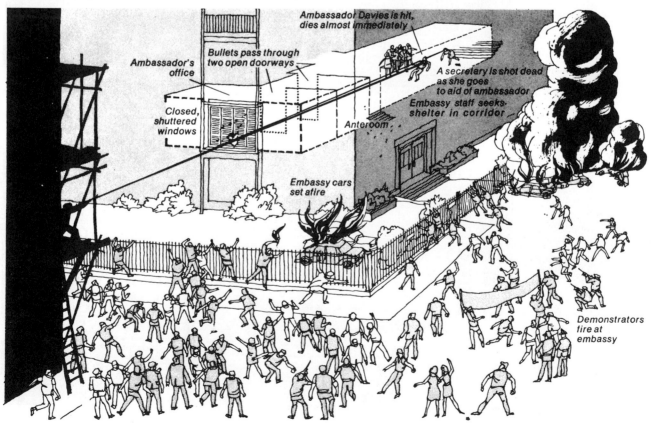

Ambassador Davies is hit, dies almost immediately

Bullets pass through two open doorways

Ambassador's office

Closed, shuttered windows

Anteroom

A secretary is shot dead as she goes to aid of ambassador

Embassy staff seeks shelter in corridor

Embassy cars set afire

Demonstrators fire at embassy

DON MCKAY

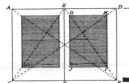

by a production department or typesetter. For such publishers a book designer needs not only his special, saleable skills; he or she must, in addition, be prepared to fight for what can easily be seen as a niggardly fee.

As book publishing has expanded into a five billion dollar per year industry under the conglomerate ownership of companies such as Gulf + Western, RCA, and CBS, books themselves have begun to be an indistinguishable part of the amorphous business known as "the media." In the corporate efforts to save dollars, design has often gone by the boards. In fact, the judges for the 1978 AIGA book show lamented the poor quality of the entries, and grieved over the disappearance of traditional standards for book design and production. It seems that the new publishing technologies discussed elsewhere in this volume are encouraging a sloppy, uninformed approach to the very old discipline of making a fine book.

As book publishing moves into its computer-based future, it is more important than ever that book designers become familiar with the traditional standards of design excellence, and adapt both new strictures and new freedoms to their arcane craft.

Otherwise books will become simply another way in which data, instruction, and entertainment are mere computer output.

Despite the technological advances of the electronic media, books are not likely to disappear. As Erwin Glikes, publisher of Harper & Row's adult books division, observes, "Television is not satisfying to many Americans. It cannot feed that part of their spirit that searches for meaning. Good books can do this, and the challenges for publishers is to find and encourage good writing and good thinking." And, we might add, good presentation.

The Design of Books
[Adrian Wilson]

Although a little outdated now, this is generally the best work on book design. It is written by a well known book designer and small press craftsman. Wilson's conscientious approach to book design is delightful and concise, both in the writing and in the wealth of carefully chosen illustrations. *The Design of Books* covers all aspects of bookmaking, from layout to the creation of limited editions and everything is presented with a sense of historical perspective, enthusiasm, and total enjoyment.
Cost: $7.95

Peregrine Smith Publications

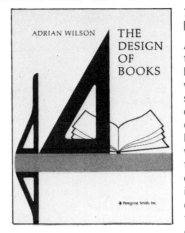

Above: Martin Dominique Fertel's ideal of the proper ordering of a title page (1723), and below, a William Morris title page (1893).

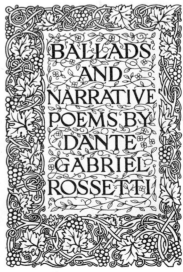

The Small Press Movement

In the past decade and a half the publishing industry has gone through some major changes that have affected what is published commercially, as well as how it is published. Size, standardization, and the search for enormous profits from blockbuster best sellers have become the rule in the most visible parts of the business.

As a consequence, some exceptionally fine writers, designers, and illustrators have quit the industry in disgust, or avoided entering through its portals at all. But they did not quit making their books; they simply make them in a different arena.

A proliferation of artists and craftsmen have been reviving the art of fine printing and bookmaking. Some of their volumes, produced by small private presses all around the nation, are breaking new typographic and visual ground, and adding new dimensions to the book format; some use the challenges of technology to expand the traditional notions of design and bookmaking. The real innovations taking place in the work of the best dedicated small presses will, in time, filter up to larger, more commercially oriented publishers. But you needn't wait until the big guys get in on the act to see this work. The fine printing and bookmaking contributions of the small presses can be seen in the annual AIGA Books show, in the category devoted to limited editions and fine press books.

Fine Print

This magazine, devoted to the art of the book, is in itself an example of classical modern design and print, book style. Generally, *Fine Print* is an entertaining, worldwide excursion into the various aspects of book craft: calligraphy, typography, printing, design, bookbinding, papermaking, and illustration. With sensitivity for the history of the craft, it is also a showcase for a different designer/printer each issue. It reviews finely printed and limited edition books with a critical eye, and also reviews current books about books and related arts. A magazine for bibliophiles of all sorts, *Fine Print* presents — in color and black and white — examples of fine book design and calligraphy in each of its quarterly issues.

Cost: $12 per year

Fine Print

Copyright for Book Designers

The right of a graphic artist to retain control of his or her work after its initial use, and to sell subsequent onetime rights to it, is known as a "graphic right." It is a cause that has recently been taken up by a book designer.

In 1977 Jean Stoliar, a leading freelance designer, pursued copyright to her design for a book after the publisher used some of her work on a billboard without paying her any fee for that usage (she won a settlement), and after a paperback publisher changed her design for its edition of the book. Although the Copyright Office did not understand what was so unique about a book design, nonetheless her design was registered by the publisher, and when rights were offered for sale, her design was made available separately, so that a subsidiary publisher might purchase the book with her design, or without if it chose to create a new design.

"The significance of copyright for works of art and design lies in the fact that, once granted, the artist's inherent rights are established with the same force of law as they are for written works. The real problem is defining what is a unique work, something that has identifiably unique characteristics which, if copied, would constitute a violation.

"A design is an arrangement of other elements, and the notion of an arrangement as a unique artistic creation is in itself beyond the comprehension of most people today.... Stoliar believes that even though it may be possible to copyright designs, it will take a long time and much education to achieve a widespread understanding of what design really is and what is not permissible under a design copyright."

—Paul Dobler, *Publishers Weekly,* July 4, 1977

An example of what can happen to *you* without Copyright. A stunning non-fiction trade book, lavishly designed and illustrated.			
	Designer	Publisher	Author
First printing	1,200.00	180,000.00	45,000.00
Twelfth printing	—	990,000.00	247,500.00
Paperback sale	—	250,000.00	250,000.00
Movie Sale	—	500,000.00	500,000.00
Total*	$1,200.00	$1,920,000.00	$1,042,500.00

*The above figures represent gross income and are purely hypothetical. Actual figures will vary widely depending on each publisher's business practices and on the author's and designer's professional standing.

AIGA Book Show award winner, 1975; Sailing to Cythera.

JAY KEE

The Literary Market Place

The *LMP* is an indispensable tool of the publishing industry. Revised annually, it is a catalog of all data that pertains to publishing: book and magazine publishers, calendar of trade events, editorial services, artists and art services, paper mills and suppliers, photographers, agents, associations, etc. If you want to know who to contact, their correct address, phone number, and the name of their assistant — it's all in the *LMP*.

Cost: $27.50

R R Bowker

Advertising

One of the peculiar problems of advertising is that it is executed by a very large team of specialists in all areas of communications, and as part of that team you have to cope with a high level of internal politics. Advertising is now an extremely refined "science," and the creative department of any agency takes only a small part in the whole procedure. Advertising art direction, for example, has become intricately involved with marketing considerations and market research analysis.

In advertising, two levels of creativity operate. The first is strategy — defining the problem up front — and involves a close relationship between client, market researchers, and design-ers. Art directors are necessarily involved in strategy through briefings. Once strategy has been resolved, the second level of creativity — developing the concept, or working out visual ways in which the strategy can be presented — is the creative department's bailiwick.

An advertising art director must be able to conceptualize succinctly. In addition to being adept at the execution of ideas, he or she must be able to originate them, and express them on paper. As with all the specialist skills employed in advertising, it is divergent, rather than linear, thinking that is the ideal.

Advertising art directors must be sufficiently curious people to understand and relate to others who may be quite different from themselves. It is essential that they be able to deal with attitudes outside their own experience. In an agency, research personnel may be relied upon to provide frames of reference, as well as the data necessary to support a given strategy. Some experts claim that the close relationship between the creative and research departments of agencies — a relatively recent phenomenon — is what provides the real validity to the value of market research.

Working in advertising invariably raises the question of advertising's overall value. More than most fields of endeavor, advertising makes clear that human commerce is largely predicated on one form or another of manipulation.

Advertising is a very bald form of manipulation. The issue that arises for many people working in advertising really comes down to a question of ethics — whether or not it is right to be so consciously and intentionally persuasive. The question becomes whether a given adver-

Participatory advertising: the unfinished copy line was an open invitation to hit-and-run grafitti guerillas. Messrs. Heinz were not amused.

tising campaign is misleading or not; or, in some cases, whether the advertising encourages people to do what is clearly *not* in their own best interests.

As you might imagine, there are no written rules for ethical conduct in advertising. Yet, agencies are on record as refusing certain clients out of their moral and common sense, when they perceive a product to be harmful, or even simply unnecessary in the marketplace. Ethical considerations, then, can play a surprisingly large part in formulating advertising strategy — popular impressions to the contrary.

Advertising design covers the whole range of the media, with each medium requiring its own sorts of strategy criteria. According to Malcolm Baker, Market Research Director at the McCann Erickson advertising agency:

"Magazine advertising lends itself to a more contemplative approach, and is the least stilted of all mediums. The poor quality of advertising in the television medium seems to have something to do with the innate conservatism of the clients, particularly the more successful clients. The belief appears to have grown up that in order to be noticed you have to shout very loud. I have found that whispering can be just as noticeable because any media system functions on the basis of

contrasts, especially nowadays. Besides, people are quite sophisticated in their understanding of what advertising is — or isn't."

Whether the public is sophisticated or not with regard to advertising, it is certainly becoming discerning in its appreciation of advertising's power, and the ways in which it *can be* abused. Coupled with a sort of general public distrust of powerful entities over the past decade, this appreciation may even be capable of diminishing advertising's impact. According to a *Dun's Review* report, in 1978 their survey of public issue (advocacy) advertising found that only 6% of the people questioned considered such advertisements "very credible," while as many as 53% found them "not credible." Since corporations use advocacy ads to promote certain positions on issues of public importance (consumerism, government regulations, pollution control and conservation, etc.) — usually in order to justify their own activities — the public's reaction to even the relatively high quality advocacy advertising suggests a growing cynicism toward advertising in general.

Malcom Baker again:

"In defining the criteria for the marketing strategy, you have to have research that is *actionable.* I get asked to do research all the time that no one's going to be able to act on, it's just gratuitous. I worked on a research project once involving children and ice cream in which we came up with some information that the creative people could not act upon. The results were all soft, qualitative data, and we had several hypotheses that we felt might be true as a result of talking to all those kids. It was all relevant to products that the manufacturer might produce and advertise. One hypothesis was that boys would bite ice lollies and girls would suck them. I forget the reasoning for that conclusion now, but it was obviously Freudian and, I think, quite respectable. We gave ice lollies to a lot of children and watched, and it was true, we proved our hypothesis. It was statistically significant, but there was nothing we could do with the information, nothing the manufacturer could do with it, short of producing penis-shaped lollies."

Packaging

Overall, the graphics of packaging are caught in a dreary cycle that reflects what has been called the "herd instinct and well worn cliches," a phrase that describes both current packaging construction and its surface graphics. There is also a widely held view that packaging should be minimized because it creates so much excess garbage — that perhaps, to paraphrase Thoreau, the best packaging is no packaging at all.

At some time or other, most of us have been conned by packaging; and as a result we might argue that packaging is fundamentally anti-social. However, it is a superficial solution to demand brown paper bags for everything. For packaging actually performs a number of complex roles for which the plain brown wrapper simply won't suffice.

All packaging is a compromise among three often conflicting design factors: the cost of the packaging, its efficiency in protecting the product, and its

Identity Advertising: promotion of Durex, *a European contraceptive brand name. Benton & Bowles agency.*

effectiveness as a display or advertising medium. There is also the not insignificant ritual to be considered of unpacking products. This ritual marketing people call "added value." A good example of added value is the ritual of opening a cigar pack, removing the translucent paper, sliding the knife in under the lid, opening the box, removing the thin wooden overlay, pulling out the cigar and removing its band, then carefully snipping the end of the cigar. Compared with merely stuffing a stogie in your maw, all of that can be seen as a significant part of the pleasure of smoking a cigar. This is to illustrate that a lot of things seem to be worth more if you wrap them up right.

The fundamental problems of packaging do not lie in creating the graphically alluring outer wrap, but rather in packaging technology, the aspect treated with ignorance by many designers and most packaging companies reluctant to change because of the high tooling costs. The trend in packaging is toward a lot more of the same old stuff, with more and more things put into more and more packages, largely due to the influence of mass marketing systems used by supermarket and fast-food chains. As packaging becomes increasingly expensive, complicated and wasteful, far from entering a brown bag era, we seem to be moving rapidly in the opposite direction.

Imaginative packaging is not to be found on the supermarket counters, although there is no reason why it should not be there. The packaging field that has supported the most exciting and original surface designs of all is record album covers. These have anticipated virtually every major graphic design move over the past fifteen years. Elsewhere there has been one very tempting response to all the clutter in mass market packaging: the "plain and simple" response, which has come on with a vengeance as in the European design shown below, from *International Stores*. But these solutions succeed largely by contrast with the visual confusion of the competition.

"In packaging, as in so many other fields, most designers think in cliches; and that is what most manufacturers want. Major opportunities for packaging occur all the time but they demand that the designer should understand packaging technology and that he should appreciate the overall marketing requirements of the job including advertising and other forms of promotion. They demand from the client that he should be genuinely prepared to make major technical changes, as big in their way as the changes from the battleship to the aircraft carrier.

Most companies, whatever they may say, won't take the risk. They talk big but they act small."

— Wally Olins, from *Design,* December, 1977

Hand Lettering

Ever since graphic artists perceived the need to make type and lettering suit their fantasies, they have searched for ways to manipulate the letter form and make it an integral part of the design concept. Unlike typography, which focuses on individual letters, hand lettering focuses on the word or phrase. Word patterns, then, help to determine the form or natural rhythm of the finished hand-lettered design. An almost limitlessly malleable amalgam of illustration, calligraphy, and type design, hand lettering offers a unique solution to all sorts of display lettering problems.

In its present form — today a full-blown revival, resulting indirectly from the cultural and media explosions of the 1960s — hand lettering revives something of the engraver's art from the nineteenth century, poster lettering from the early 1920s, advertising letterforms from the 1930s, traditional "studio" art from the 1940s and 1950s, and the psychedelic montages of the 1960s.

In this eclectic contemporary atmosphere, designers can draw freely on all the roots of hand lettering to construct letterforms for titles, labels, and packaging and logo design. The only two major requirements for letter designing are love of alphabets and lettering and a mastery of the precise drawing skills of the technical illustrator. Beyond these, letter design wants only pen, ink, paper, white-out, and imagination.

CONRAN ASSOCIATES/INTERNATIONAL STORES

BECKY WILSON

Calligraphy

The ancient art of the scribes, the art of elegant and beautiful handwriting, is experiencing a resurgence of interest unsurpassed in the United States in this century, and it is finding a place in the world of commerce on a larger scale than ever.

The full potential of penmanship is better expressed by example than by verbal description, and we include, therefore, a selection from many sources to illustrate one of the goals of fine calligraphy: to make the reader/viewer forget the letters. Perfection is not the goal, but rather the inspiration into the letterforms of a life, a mood, a rhythm, a freedom that, while hard to achieve, is the hallmark of a fine hand.

The second major objective of calligraphy is to communicate to the imagination, without loss, the thought or imagery intended by the author. In this sense calligraphy expresses its relationship with type. A master calligrapher, Edward Johnston, wrote in 1902:

"And the whole duty of beautiful typography is not to substitute for the beauty or interest of of the thing thought and intended to be conveyed by a symbol, a beauty or interest of its own but, on the one hand, to win access for that communication by the clearness and beauty of the vehicle and, on the other hand, to take advantage of every pause or stage in that communication to interpose some characteristic and restful beauty in its own art."

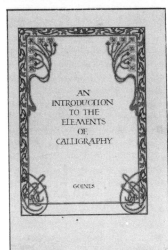

RAPHAEL BUGOSLAV

An Introduction to the Elements of Calligraphy
[David Lance Goines]

"Why write what cannot be read or that which assaults the eye? The typewriter is fast, uniform and legible and answers most commercial and academic requirements. The small amount of writing left over, such as personal letters, must be handwritten, and should be beautiful."

David Lance Goines is an increasingly well known designer and fine printer. His instruction book on the rudiments of calligraphy — which he designed and printed himself — is the most concise, lucid primer in the field, and an excellent place to take one's calligraphic grounding. The very large format paperback is hand scribed throughout, and is, itself, a lovely example of calligraphy.

Cost: $8.00

Saint Heironymous Press

TSGIRWIN

Learning Calligraphy
[Margaret Sheppard]

Most of the many instructional books on the art, craft, and skills of calligraphy are unnecessary. Initially you need some guide to introduce you to a proper grounding in the subject; after that you need a skilled and experienced instructor to encourage your ability to see and understand letterform. From then on, references come from all sources in your daily life.

Learning Calligraphy takes the student a few steps further than Goines' *Introduction;* it explores visual design with the pen, offers a historical background on the art, and provides some very detailed technical advice. Each chapter includes historical and contemporary examples that are especially well suited to the alphabet style under discussion, and warns you of its pitfalls as well. Calligraphy is mind training, as many practitioners will point out. It is a way to discover yourself through letters; and this book is an excellent primer for that training.
Cost: $7.95

Collier Books

The Calligraphers' Engagement Calendar

Add this 8¹/₂" x 8¹/₂", two-color spiral-bound book to the fall list of fine desk calendars, marking it as something especially calculated to please the eye that enjoys graphic art and lettering. More than sixty contemporary calligraphers have supplied pages employing selected verses from the Old Testament, including Proverbs. One of the most interesting things about the little volume is the variety of styles that it represents, and nearly all of them represent an excellence in calligraphic design.
Cost: $8.95

Society of Scribes; Taplinger

Two Other Sources

Among the many reference books on alphabets, letters, type, and calligraphy (see Sections C and H), those titles published by Dover Books and those from the Art Direcdon Book Company are, in general, especially worth noting. A few books from each publisher are reviewed in Section H of this volume, "Magazines, Journals, and Books."

Pentalic

The Pentalic Corporation manufactures a complete line of calligraphic supplies, as well as literature on the use of its equipment and on calligraphy. They are perhaps best known for their universally available fountain pens and nibs. Pentalic's widely distributed *Instruction Copy Books,* detailing basic practices of movement and style in simple step-by-step procedures, are designed to introduce people gently to calligraphy. Their complete catalog is free.
Cost: 20¢ (Instruction Copy Books)

Pentalic Corporation

Friends of Calligraphy

The Friends is neither a guild nor a professional group, and you can sign your cat up as long as you pay its dues; but they do hold workshops, lectures, and get-togethers to promote calligraphy and a network of instructional courses. Friends is a dedicated organization with high standards. Their particularly valuable newsletter is well worth the $10 membership fee and contains fine examples of the work of members. The group organizes study trips abroad, and in the United States presents calligraphy and type workshops, a Calligraphers' Fair, and various exhibits, in conjunction with other organizations.
Cost of membership: $10.00 per year.

Friends of Calligraphy

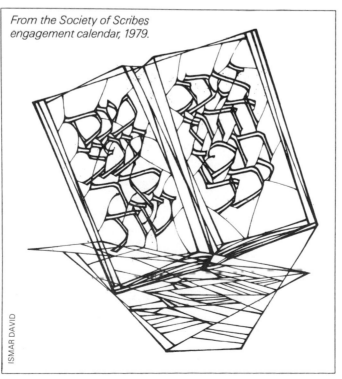

From the Society of Scribes engagement calendar, 1979.

ISMAR DAVID

D

Cartography

Explorations have always been major preoccupations of mankind, and throughout the centuries map making has become more and more a specialist graphic skill, requiring increasingly technical expertise. At its simplest level mapping is the basic art of symbolizing or diagramming complex concepts in two dimensions; and at its most complex it involves all the elecronic and computer sciences that organizations such as NASA can bring to bear.

Cartography is often limited by a lack of flexibility in the modes of presentation of maps, particularly because of the problem of projecting the spherical earth onto a flat plane. It is a basic discipline of cartographic design that the visual considerations of projection nearly always take second place to functional requirements, although computer graphics have expanded the range of what is visually acceptable. Good design in map making is related to the specific function of the mapping, requiring variable degrees of accuracy, selectivity, and comparative relationships. Typography is the major problem — how to fit on the map all the necessary typographical information without disturbing the elements of the landscape. The special problems of color coding, symbol shorthand, and contouring all have to be designed to translate quickly and comprehensibly.

The design of maps is a most complex subject that has only recently broken out of stifling conventions, and bigger strides have been taken in experimenting with map design in the last decade than in all the previous five put together. The U S Geological Survey is now developing laser mapping from aircraft that records profiles in minute detail. Demographic mapping is done with the aid of CRT (cathode ray tube) computers which visually plot the input data and photograph the results. Both these technologies have already radically changed our concept of what maps should look like, and NASA's space mapping is pushing the conceptual boundaries even further.

Principles of Cartography
[Erwin Raisz]

Good books on the subject of cartography are hard to come by, but this volume is an exception. Raisz, a long time lecturer on the subject, offers a very good primer for understanding the language of maps, and the foundation of the systems and techniques involved. However, although thorough in its discussion of translating the relationship of earth and land features to a map, the book does not adequately cover graphic style, which is the creative form of the end result, and is crucial to our reader. Neither does the book, written in 1962, cover the effects and changes in concept brought about by recent technologies. While one can hardly fault the volume for a lack of prescience, one can look forward to a revised and updated edition.

Cost: $11.95

McGraw-Hill Book Co

"Logoptics"

This is both the description and trade name for a company that develops graphics as a self-sufficient language. As it relates to packaging, the process is an attempt to get away from merely dealing with minor, cosmetic, and decorative solutions, and introduce instead a thoughtful picture language as a communications strategy. All designers work this way at some time or other, but *Logoptics* is a concerted, coherent attempt to combine packaging with visual psychology, marketing, and product management. The approach becomes particularly appropriate in devising packaging or labeling in a multilingual context — the old concern of international symbolism — or where adult illiteracy is severe. *Logoptics'* basic purpose is to *inform,* accurately and precisely, about what a product is for, how it is used, or exactly what it is; drug labeling is one obvious application.

All designers use graphics with some kind of logoptic content; used as the primary device with strict graphic priority, it provides both client and designer with a new starting point from which a more effective and creative result can spring. It may well be the most valuable new influence on packaging in — and for — years.

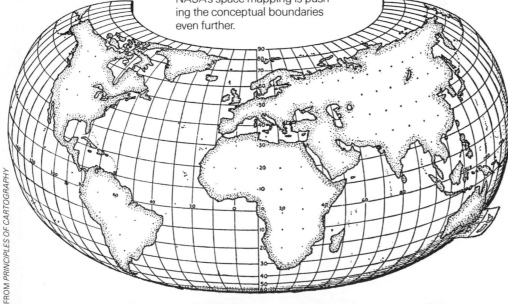

FROM *PRINCIPLES OF CARTOGRAPHY*

Education, or the Lack of It

ART CENTER, COLLEGE OF DESIGN

E

Measured by payroll or by total number of employees, the rapidly expanding graphics communication field is already one of the top ten industries in the nation. Yet, jobs do not go begging: The best positions are available only to the most highly and appropriately trained people. Where those successful candidates come from, however, remains an open question.

In *Communication Arts* (January/February, 1978), Rita Sue Siegel, owner of Rita Sue Siegel Agency, a design placement firm, related that, "This year Chermayeff and Geismar wanted to take a beginner from the pool of new graduates. They interviewed fifty. They were totally disgusted and ended up hiring someone who had two years experience at another design office. There wasn't one student they wanted to hire."

In other professional disciplines—law, medicine, engineering—this situation would be inconceivable. But within the graphics community it is common knowledge that most people fresh out of school are ill-prepared to practice their trade. Seymour Chwast, co-founder of New York's legendary Push Pin Studio, notes, "So many schools are doing such a bad job that many students may actually be wasting their time."

Professionals in different areas of graphics communication perceive the situation in much the same light: One way or another, graphic education is not getting its job done.

"I don't think schools have understood the creative ad-making process," says Sam Scali, Partner and Creative Director at Scali, McCabe, Sloves. "If you don't know how to do basic steps involved in approaching any solution, you can't even begin. Who's teaching this?"

Who, indeed? Education is defined as "the process of training and developing the knowledge, skill, mind, character, etc, especially by formal schooling..." And while such a definition may conjure up ideal images of Socrates interrogating his students beneath the spreading chestnut tree, in reality a school can do little more than provide a student with the fundamental abc's of his or her trade, advise students of those areas they need to develop in order to become professionally competent, and offer elementary guidance in one or more specific directions. Beyond this, your education will be up to you.

Strictly speaking, you cannot be taught good taste, esthetic judgment, or artistic talent. You can be encouraged to develop these skills in yourself—or discouraged from doing so—and you can be shown some methods by which you can effect that develop-

ment. But your native skills cannot be handed to you in a classroom, and no teacher can determine the quantity or quality of effort you need to expand them.

A successful education will be a process of self-discovery, and a successful teacher will be, most often, a guru-like mentor who takes you along on a few exploratory journeys toward his own interior, to show you how to recognize signposts, and then lets you take your own path to the center of yourself.

In order to be a mathematician, it is essential to know that $2 + 2 = 4$: that is elementary grounding. But at greater levels of sophistication, it is more important to know *how to add* than to know the specific answer to an addition problem. The eminent American novelist, Wallace Stegner, makes a critical distinction between tricks, which he does not like—"A trick is a gimmick"—and skills: "Skills are something else. Skills won't result in formulas, they will result in a capacity to deal with any lump of material, no matter what shape it comes at you in. I don't really like tricks, and half my teaching time I think I spend trying to knock ill-considered, and always borrowed, tricks out of young writers."

You may substitute "young designer" or "young illustrator" in the sentence above, and see if it applies to your idea of a graphics education.

For a long time, *graphic communication* and *fine arts* have been mixed and muddled into a single generic course of study in the United States, to the detriment of both fields. While fine artists have had to struggle with the problems of finding "commercial" acceptance, graphic artists have been *associated* with commercialism, and in the eyes of the fine arts-trained educators, have been engaged in hack work without artistic merit.

Influenced by William Morris and the crafts renaissance in turn-of-the-century England, and by Walter Gropius and the Bauhaus movement in Germany during the 1920s and 1930s, European graphic artists resolved their version of the education problem during the 1950s and 1960s.

The change, that is still being effected in Europe,

4000 BC   1000 BC

was coming down from the top shortly after World War II; but students, impatient for attention to their major and critical dilemma, hurried that change along with college strikes and boycotts of specific lecturers (and curricula) who were unable or unwilling to appreciate that their concerns were important and real. Ultimately, as the insistent graphic arts students began to formulate their own curricula, the validity of the applied visual arts received official sanction.

Although the battle waged by the students and professional designers was hard won, nonetheless it *was* won. They succeeded in getting design schools set up that were separate and distinct from the fine arts departments. They had schools they could attend where their needs were met; where they could learn the skills essential to their chosen profession; where they could find out about relevant areas of industry and technology; where they could discover areas of expertise that would support them in becoming practicing professionals; and where, through contact with established graphic artists, they could learn how the professional world they were preparing to enter really functioned.

With this art college structure established, European industry began to play a substantial role in graphic arts education. Perceiving that it was in their own best interests to become involved in design and aesthetics, businesses provided grants and scholarships, and in a variety of ways set out to insure the development of the graphic artists they knew their industries would need in the future. As a nearly inevitable result, European businessmen became involved in the graphics courses themselves, and it was quickly apparent that the exchange was beneficial to industry, the schools and their students.

Alas, while this cross-pollination of industrial and graphic education is becoming an established way of doing business in many parts of Europe, the battle is still being fought in the United States. Here, much design education suffers from the fine arts stigma attached to commercial practice. And as a direct result,

American industry remains largely divorced from the graphic arts. Indeed, even the graphic arts industry is still trying to convince itself to be responsible for graphic education in some way.

Walter Kaprielian, Senior Vice-President and Creative Director of Ketchum, Macleod & Grove, observes, ''The quality of art education has to be considered an industry problem. At every stage we complain about what the new source coming out of school is like. We forget a graduate moves from student to professional in a single day. It's been an inherent part of the business to voice our opinions—to say the kids aren't good enough, that they aren't getting the right education. But if this is so, we can't be critical without being prepared to help make it better.''

From inside as well as outside the graphics community, it is high time American commerce took the trouble to edify itself with regard to graphic communications. There is no excuse for inviting a client into a business office that is ugly, dysfunctional, or even downright repellent. There is nothing to be gained by sending letters or statements on stationery that was designed by accident, brochures and catalogs that were thrown together at the local printers round the corner. When one study after another demonstrates that people are deeply and strongly affected by the graphics surrounding them, it is merely stupid to refuse to learn and practice the lessons they teach.

It is still true in a large segment of American business and industry that the people responsible for buying or hiring graphic communications are utterly untutored in the area, and make arbitrary decisions more likely to discourage sales than encourage them. For their companies' sakes, for the good of the general culture, and for the individuals themselves, it is time for business to really look at what it sees every day.

However the American graphics dilemma is to be approached, its solution must include the schools. Three intriguing—and often opposed—viewpoints are expressed in the trio of excerpts reprinted below, pp. 164, 166, 168, 170, and 175.

700 BC

114 AD

3RD-4TH C.

4TH-5TH C.

Education Sources

In 1976 the Art Directors Club of New York sponsored an Educators Conference at the Parsons School of Design. The purpose of the Conference was to explore the reasons that design *education* seems to have so little to do with the realities of the design *profession.* The Conference posed two central questions: (1) How does the professional view the process of education? and (2) What are the best approaches to opening the way for students to get jobs? The dialogue initiated at the Conference continues to this day — as do the problems of design education.

The overall quality of graphic communications education in the United States has improved markedly over the past few years, but the better university level courses remain relatively few and far between. It is still difficult to choose a school intelligently; there is no definitive list that will lead the hopeful student to the "best" school in any particular graphics area. Much like wines, schools have vintage years; courses are only as good as the teachers; and the principal source of information for a prospective student, apart from personal acquaintances in the field, remains the school catalogs.

There are five basic graphics programs to be found in the technical schools, colleges, and universities that cover the subject at all.

Technical programs emphasize the production processes, and prepare students for entry level jobs in the graphic arts industry;

Management programs are business-oriented, and train students for supervisory positions within such graphic arts trades as printing;

Education programs offer courses in graphic communications along with teacher certification, qualifying students to teach vocational courses;

Industrial/ Technology programs offer industrial arts education as well as teaching credentials, providing students with the option to enter a graphics profession from either the industrial or academic side;

Design programs concentrate on courses in the arts related to printing and other communications media.

These five programs overlap at times; a school may offer any one or all five. The courses that follow have been selected for their excellence in *design education,* and are among those that have been most frequently recommended in recent years. There certainly are other excellent programs not mentioned here, and this list should be taken as a guide, rather than as an exhaustive or definitive statement.

All design curricula named here are four-year courses unless otherwise noted, and all the schools have graduate programs.

In reviewing the design courses offered by various schools, it is well to be wary of those which are an integral part of a Fine Arts program. The fine arts approach to design communications education tends to be quite divorced from the real world of the professional designer.

Schools of Art Directory

Annually revised, this is the directory of all schools of art that belong to the National Association of Schools of Art, an association that strives to promote and encourage high quality education in the visual arts. All the schools listed are either accredited by the Association, or are schools that are candidates for accreditation, or are schools that have standards consistent with those of the Association but wish to retain the option of seeking accreditation at a later date. Thus, to some degree, the schools listed in this directory are guaranteed to have sound curricula and a high standard of instruction and facilities.

The directory is only a listing, by state, of the school, its courses and the degrees it offers, and no more than that. Narrowing down the choice of school further requires checking with the institutions themselves.
Cost: free

National Association of Schools of Art

5TH–6TH C.

6TH–8TH C.

789 AD

13TH C.

Directory of Schools & Workshops

The dense, forty-page directory of schools and colleges published by *American Artist* since 1963 is the most comprehensive listing of *all* courses in design, fine arts, and crafts. If you are not absolutely certain what you're looking for, the wealth of information could create more problems for you than it solves. Then, its advertisements become a clarifying factor. But the Directory is always a good place to start a course search. Each college is listed alphabetically by state. The information is updated every year, and includes all courses offered, types of degrees available, number of students working toward a degree or certification, number of faculty members, and each school's accreditation.
Cost: $1.50

American Artist

Art Center, College of Design

This school offers professional design education. Totally committed to design and design only, it is widely known for its high standards, and practices a rigorously selective admissions policy. A potential student must have a good academic record in high school and college, and—not least— a strong portfolio. The Art Center grants a BFA in the departments of Communication, Design, Film, Illustration, and Photography; and a BS in Industrial Design.
Tuition: $1400 (basic) per trimester

Art Center, Pasadena, California

California College of Arts and Crafts

This small, independent, degree-granting college is a garden campus situated in the foothills between Berkeley and Oakland, across the Bay from San Francisco. Its Division of Design is a professionally oriented school offering majors in General Design, Graphic Design & Illustration, and Environmental Design. The extensive facilities of the Media Center are available. The college places emphasis on a broad, liberal arts education.
Tuition: $1425 (basic) per trimester

California College of Arts & Crafts, Oakland, California

California Polytechnic State University

Cal Poly's department of graphic communications offers a highly technical curriculum with a strong management orientation. The school is well known for its course work in printing technology and science, which is fully supported by a complete design curriculum and the extensive facilities of the university. It maintains a full-service printing operation run by a student production team, and produces a daily newspaper.
Tuition: $1600 (basic) per trimester

California Polytechnic, San Luis Obispo, California

EDWIN LOVE

VALERIE WINSLOW

FRAN ALVIN/CONNIE GRABOWSKI

ANNE THURLOW

EUGENIA QUAN

The Responsibility of Education

"The schools are not helping me do my job. I protest as a citizen and taxpayer. I also protest as a member of the design community, because the credibility of design as a constructive tool is being jeopardized.

The students are being handicapped by faulty education on the basic educational level as well as the professional skill level. They can't spell. They can't write grammatical sentences. Many of the letters and resumes that I get are really from illiterates.

They are blind to the requirements, the realities, the opportunities and the alternatives in the field. They have no idea of the state of the art and they don't even know who the best people are.

The chief evidence of the faculty deficiencies and lack of information is, of course, the portfolio. Graduates have no idea what a portfolio is, what it is to show or how it should be organized. If faculty members do try to be helpful, they usually give wrong, and in many cases harmful, information. When we ask why there are no sketches in a portfolio, students tell us, "Well, the teachers told us not to put any sketches in our portfolio, only finished work."

Too many graphic graduates I see are the result of very sterile situations. They're given sterile problems to solve and, of course, come up with sterile solutions. Their portfolios are over-edited and all the good stuff, the guts, taken out. There's no spontaneity. There's no emotional contact. No content, no humor, no wit,

no in-depth knowledge of typography, no experimentation with color, no warmth and richness. It's as if design can't be fun or enjoyable. Somehow, the attitude is that if you love what you do you're unsophisticated. It's uncool to be excited about design.

The so-called "better" graphic design schools are the most sterilized, in my opinion. They're admirers of the Basel method of education, which in its own context is a very sound education, but they show a lack of understanding of what it's about. Consequently, everybody is reduced to learning the same systems, the same grids. Instead of that being a basis, a springboard into some personal expression of design, it's the end. That's it. That's how every problem is solved.

Faculties underestimate the visual sophistication of employers. They underestimate the opportunities for talent. They do not know the kind of problems to give as vehicles for expression and development of talent. Chermayeff and many other practitioners we can admire are looking for new people to train. They only want to train the most talented people, the kind of people they can exchange ideas with, who, in the long run, will help them build their company. Since Chermayeff doesn't work with a 3M machine, but with a pen, a pencil, or a Pentel and paper, the least he can expect is that same ability from the new graduates that he interviews, the capability of showing how you put an idea on paper. They don't teach these techniques in school, they don't develop craftsmanship.

Industrial design graduates are lacking the most simple presentation skills which are very easy to learn by programmed exercises. Cooper Woodring, assistant manager of design at J C Penney, said this about the subject: "You can sell a bad idea with a good drawing, but you can't sell a good idea with a bad drawing."

There's no quality control mechanism on tenured teachers. There's no quality control on curriculum or on graduates. From the portfolios I see and the feedback I'm getting from clients, the schools and the teachers have misused our trust and they no longer deserve it.

There are people out there who have been well prepared over the past five years, but most of them have gotten this good preparation by accident rather than by good planning. They have been exposed to one or two dedicated, caring, knowledgeable, inspiring teachers, or a family friend, or were fortunate enough to have been apprenticed to a really top notch person who took the time to fill in all the gaps.

I think the practicing professionals have no choice but to get involved and take action. They should be involved in the selection of faculty and in the formulation of balanced curriculum. They should have something to do with the selection of students and the constant monitoring and evaluation of new graduates. Since institutions, such as schools, will only recognize other institutions, the only way I think this can be done is by strengthening the professional society accreditation committees.

You've got to demand accountability from these programs. You've got to do it through state-funded career education programs, asking them to qualify why they're giving money to certain schools. You've got to help unprepared undergraduates and their parents prepare civil suits against the schools that are stealing the money from the students and leaving them unprepared.

Most of the good teachers are in agreement with the following ideas that we have: On a conceptual level, design is a problem solving activity whose solutions happen to be visual. People are born with varying amounts of talent for visual literacy, and that talent needs nurturing. Visual organization is a discipline in itself that can be developed. Designers are people skilled in visual language; they create images, families of images, forms and families of forms.

They have to function and be credible in a world of visual illiterates. The only way for them to do that is to have the means of expression and communication that the visual illiterates have, the ability to verbalize and to write. They must be educated in all the disciplines that the visual illiterates are educated in: literature, history, psychology, sociology, science and technology, marketing and management. This, in addition to the skills of their own field, is a very big undertaking.

The best faculties are mixtures of people, but they have a common denominator. They're specialists in nurturing and guid-

continued on page 166

1450

1470

1506

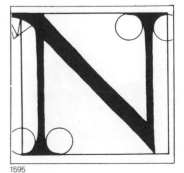

1595

The Design Schools

Comprised of the Colorado Institute of Art and the Art Institutes of Atlanta, Fort Lauderdale and Pittsburgh, The Design Schools offer first-class professional training in Communications Design, and claim to graduate more employable art talent than any other single source in the U.S. Courses of study are directed exclusively toward career objectives, with majors in Visual Communications, Photography, Graphic Design & Illustration, and Multi-Media. These colleges also work with local art directors clubs to sponsor seminars in a number of key cities. Jointly, they maintain an office in New York to promote the colleges and their graduates.

Tuition: varies, check with *The Design Schools* office.

The Design Schools

Drake University

Drake's College of Fine Arts offers a classical, university-style curriculum in communications design, with an emphasis on a broad education in the arts, and in form, vision, and values. The relevant major is Graphic Design/Commercial Art. With its excellent technical support facilities, this is still a traditional "art" college.

Tuition: $1575 (basic) per semester

Drake University, Des Moines, Iowa

Kansas City Art Institute

This small college is dedicated to providing a total environment for the designer, artist, and craftsperson. The department of design has an excellent faculty that offers fully professional programs and emphasizes the need for designers to be synthesists rather than specialists. The degree program for design students presents four options in course "clusters," of which Graphics and Communications Design is one.

Tuition: $3400 (basic) per trimester

Kansas City Art Institute, Kansas City, Missouri

Kent State University

Kent's new School of Art campus houses a progressive and extremely professionally oriented Division of Graphic Design & Illustration. The curriculum is an aggressive intellectual and analytical problem-study program emphasizing technological developments in the graphic arts industry. The basic course structure is augmented with field trips, special summer courses in Europe, and—in particular—a course called Glyphix. Glyphix functions as a professional studio providing design services to off-campus, non-profit organizations, and serves as an internship or apprentice program for design students.

Tuition: $1500 (basic) per trimester

Kent State University, Kent, Ohio

ing talent, conceptually and technically. The faculty should be a mixture of full-time and part-time teachers, the part-time teachers being practitioners as well. Retired practitioners often make excellent teachers. There should be crafts people, specialists in certain areas and generalists, people of many different points of view. They should have a history of preparing successful practitioners, and for helping people develop their own guidelines for continuing their learning after they get out of school. That's really the measure of the best education, that you are prepared to then go out and educate yourself.

In most of the better schools, the faculty takes part in the selection of the students; it's not left to the admissions people. There's also a portfolio review which shows talent level, design aptitude and the motivation of the person coming into the program.

Schools should not be supermarkets of academic services. Design schools should be elitist and *very* selective. An ordinary designer really can't make it out there, and there's no point in allowing these people to go through a program. There should be a tight sequence of required courses, a core curriculum as it's sometimes called. There should be a concentration on all of the essential skill areas. A student should not be able to take backpacking in place of structural representation. We've got to end the doctrine of permissiveness in intellectual matters. Seventeen to twenty-year olds don't know what's good for them. A balance can

be created between tangible and intangible, qualitative courses. It's been done in certain places and there's no reason why it can't be done in all of them. As Neils Diffrient said, "Having all the skills does not affect the ability to think, to develop a sense of judgment and a set of values."

Schools must be honest with the people coming into them as freshmen. They should tell the truth about the quality of the various departments. They should be able to tell prospective students, and their parents, about the dropout rate and the transfer rate. They should be prepared to give information on graduate job placement. The catalogs, instead of being pieces of sales promotion with fancy photographs, should be truthful and analytical and informative.

Again, the plan of action should be, for you as professionals, to strengthen your local chapters of professional societies and create or join educational committees. You should be able, as committees, to verbalize the criteria for well-prepared designers and what the functioning curriculum should contain. You've got to set up relationships with schools and encourage student membership in the societies. You should regularly review student work and, if necessary, set up remedial skill area classes. Because a lot of people who are running offices or have big jobs just don't have time to participate that much, you can rotate and share responsibility. You should interview graduates and help them with their portfolios, and you should set up co-op and apprenticeship programs.

If you care about your profession and your culture, take a stand and take action. History does not wait. The future is now.

—Excerpted from an address by RitaSue Siegel to the design conference at Stanford University, 1978

The Mystery of the Graphic Artist, or, Why 200,000,000 People Need an Art Education

Like it or not, there are some 200,000,000 people out there who don't know what a graphic artist is. And this is true from the top level level in government and industry, throughout our entire educational system, and right smack into our own field of graphic art and design where all too many of us are sorely in need of an education on the scope and requirements of our own profession.

Yet, the truth of the matter is that our industry—the communications industry, of which graphic art and design is an essential part—is one that is growing by leaps and bounds. It is an industry that encompasses such monied categories as design (corporate, architectural, packaging, editorial, film), art direction (advertising print, TV), typographics (type design and hand lettering), photography, illustration, printing and engraving, publishing (books, magazines, newspapers)—to name just a few. An industry that makes a vast cultural contribution to society. An industry with a responsibility to create better understanding throughout the world.

continued on page 168

1630

1720

1757

1788

Maryland College of Art & Design

An intensive short-course (2-year) in Visual Communications is designed to provide a student with the basic skills and background for a professional role in the applied arts, or for further specialist study. The curriculum is a balanced art/technical course, oriented toward the fine arts, offering an Associate in Arts Degree.

Tuition: $3120 (basic) full year

Maryland College of Art & Design, Silver Springs, Maryland

New York State University

At present, the communication design course is an option of the Art & Art History Department; but it is fast becoming a legitimate entity in its own right within the New York State University system. Although the course is still Fine Arts oriented, offering a major in Communications Design, the Art Department is planning a major overhaul to improve the relevance and effectiveness of its entire Communications Design program. The principal benefit of this or any design education at a major university is the campus atmosphere and the wide range of facilities and optional, elective courses available.

Tuition: $900 (basic) full year; $1500 for out-of-state residents

State University of New York at Buffalo, New York

Parsons School of Design

One of the oldest schools devoted to blending art and industry, this Greenwich Village campus recently joined with The New School for Social Research to expand its liberal arts program. The independent school offers extremely professional courses in all aspects of design and the environment, with an avowed purpose of preparing students for their role as designers in the business world. Its location in the center of the nation's traditional artistic and intellectual hub is a major asset.

Tuition: $3350 (basic) full year

Parsons School of Design, New York, New York

Pratt Institute

A uniquely comprehensive design college, the well-known Pratt Institute schools prepare young professionals for productive careers, and tend to accept applicants who already have defined career objectives. Its largest school, Art and Design, provides a thorough, detailed curriculum for Communications Design. Pratt's courses are continually modified to reflect the latest concepts and technological advances, and the vast majority of its faculty are practicing professionals. Admission to Pratt is rigorously selective.

Tuition: $3200 (basic, approx) full year

Pratt Institute, Brooklyn, New York

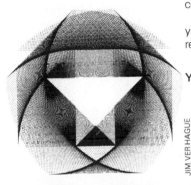

JIM VER HAGUE

LAWRENCE NEWTON

Master of Fine Arts in Communications Design

State University of New York University Center at Buffalo

PRATT INSTITUTE BULLETIN

1977-78

Nonetheless, the graphic arts is still considered an elusive profession, at best, at every level of society.

Trouble with the communications industry, it would seem, is lack of communication. An effective graphic artist is a communicator who, essentially, thinks visually. Conversely, a writer thinks verbally, but a good one also has the ability to visualize. The two together are largely responsible for promoting universal understanding. This being so, why then is the visual aspect of communications—the graphic arts—so totally and irresponsibly neglected at every level.

Look at it this way.

A guy picks up a book of matches in the street. He knows what to do with the matches all right, but does he for one moment ever contemplate how the message or illustration on the cover got there?

When directed through the maze of complicated architectural structure by means of informative signage, does it ever cross his mind who it was who figured out the letterforms and symbols? When he thumbs through books, newspapers, magazines, ads—when he looks at TV spots—does it once occur to him that the messages within required the astute involvement of an artist or a writer or both?

In short, nobody knows the business we're in. And society obviously needs education on the subject.

The general public needs education that must begin at the government level.

Educators need education from the professionals to inform them of the scope of an industry that offers great opportunities to creative students (the industry's quest for new talent is insatiable and the need for people willing to work is continuous) and let them know that art is no longer confined to painting and sculpture and that this is indeed a viable, highly paid profession. Graphic designers need to know the scope of the industry as a whole—to see beyond their individual specialties and be aware of the variety of areas beyond.

—Editorial in *Upper & Lower Case*, March, 1976

How wide is a degree?

In September, Professor Brian Smith, first incumbent of the Royal College of Art's Wolfson Chair in Design Management, introduced himself to the Association of Art Institutions with an account of attitudes and issues which will bear on his work in the future. One isolated comment seemed to have a more general significance than perhaps Smith intended.

Commenting on graduates from the "craft-based" design disciplines, Smith observed that "if the student is to work in industry, then a different kind of course is required to justify the breadth of education which a degree implies."

He is surely right to say that a degree implies a certain breadth of education. And we could go on to say that "broad," in the context of design, means much more than a "literary" veneer of Art History.

Design is occasionally described as "the skill of managing skills," a definition which expresses one vital quality among the so-hard-to-define attributes of the "professional designer." Though he may be a graphicist, photographer, modelmaker or silversmith, his foremost quality is the ability to think strategically and manage any combination of those precise skills in the execution of his strategy. It matters not whether he possesses those skills personally; it is sufficient that he understands their usefulness. Logically, he may possess no precise skills whatsoever; however unlikely that may be in practice, it should in no way interfere with his quintessential designing role.

It is surely the development of this primary attribute which a "broad" design training should aim for—the more so, since an honors degree in design must distinguish itself from a vocational diploma which is properly identified with precise skills.

But can "breadth" ever be maintained while the status quo compels staff and students to place so much emphasis on finished work? The graphic design student who picks film as his final-year specialization needs all that time just to learn *how* to make a film, never mind the broader aspects (*when* to make a film or *what* film to make). This extreme case illustrates a predicament which to some extent infects even the most industrial-looking finished student work: precise skills of implementation are developed at the expense of a broader strategic understanding. The case may also illuminate another, very ancient problem which Smith discusses: the confused distinction between art and design. If we come to recognize that the difference lies not in the *type* of finished work which the student chooses to offer up but in the degree of importance attached to finished work per se, then we may at last come to terms with the precious common spirit which does exist between artists and designers.

—Mark Brutton, *Design*, December, 1977

1816

LE TASSE

1820

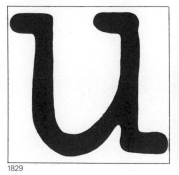

1829

1891

Rhode Island School of Design

This broad-based, liberal arts college has a comprehensive Division of Design, combining graphic design, photography, film, illustration, television, and printing, with superbly well-equipped physical plants and an increasing emphasis on job placement. In its predominantly academic environment, the design student is prepared as a futurist and innovator.

Tuition: $3775 (basic) full year

Rhode Island School of Design, Providence, Rhode Island

Rochester Institute of Technology

One of the "Big 3" schools for design and print education (the others are Carnegie-Mellon and Arizona State), RIT trains designers as technological experts and managers, and is one of the few colleges anywhere with a Printing Division and a Graphic Arts Research Center. The College of Fine and Applied Arts has programs in Communication Design and Design Applications; the College of Graphic Arts and Photography specializes in all the technical aspects of print production; the Institute College provides Audiovisual Communications programs and comprehensive courses in all the management sciences. As a whole, this is a unique private college dedicated to design and the graphic arts industry—a skillful blend of education and the "real world." The College of Fine and Applied Arts is guided by the conviction that technical competence provides the most satisfactory foundation for creative expression. Applicants are required to have a basic background in mathematics.

Tuition: $3096 (basic) per semester

Rochester Institute of Technology, Rochester, New York

School of Visual Arts

The Media Arts Department of this reputable Manhattan school structures its curriculum on the open elective system. Therefore, it is possible for a fine arts major to choose a course in basic photography or graphic design without the problems that ordinarily attend crossing departmental lines. Each student is encouraged to evolve in his or her own direction. The School of Visual Arts provides a balanced blend of fine arts and technical courses taught by a wholly professional faculty. Its location in central New York City makes available an impressive collection of the best art and design facilities available anywhere. A full-time placement center is maintained, as well as a Public Advertising System designed to provide students with practical work experience. Visual Arts also runs its own printing and publishing operation, the Visual Arts Press.

Tuition: $2800 (basic) full year

School of Visual Arts, New York, New York

Virginia Commonwealth University

Within the School of the Arts at VCU is a distinctly professional unit with a solid reputation: the Department of Communication Arts & Design. Like many other new communication design courses at universities, the scope and facilities of this department are expanding rapidly under the direction of an excellent faculty. An important concept added to the curriculum is Visual Research, encouraging the student to operate on the "frontiers of knowledge" and to identify the need for design in society. Facilities include a fully equipped graphics lab, typesetting, printing, video lab, animation equipment, and a resource center.

Tuition: $730 (basic) full year; $1460 out-of-state residents

Virginia Commonwealth University, Richmond, Virginia

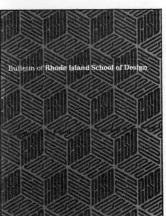

Bulletin of Rhode Island School of Design

CAROLYN VIBBERT

Dreaming of a Humane and Business-like Design School

"Young people seeking a first degree in design are seldom aware of the unique bias of a particular school until they are too deep into their courses to make a change. One of the tragedies of American design schools is the number of young graduates who have been insularized by their education then let loose to float about looking for a position.

There seems to be a strong undercurrent of discontent among designers and others with the present state of design education in the United States. With rare exceptions, however, their discomfort is not based upon a deep conviction about the quality of education and its obligations to prepare students to take their place in the next generation of designers.

Rather, they are concerned that the graduate should be immediately useful to them. Very few design offices will accept interns, nor are they likely to offer work to a young designer unless he already has two or three years' experience. That is not so much because they are generally dissatisfied with design education, but more because they would prefer another designer to pay the price of the graduate's transitional education.

Let us hope that, one of these days, designers will concede that an intern program would not only improve the quality of young graduates but would also draw the designer and teacher into a common cause. It is comforting to notice the rekindled interest in both formal academic accreditation and also the possibility of legal registration or licensing of designers . . . .

Though some designers at the meeting [ISDA, October, 1977] still referred to themselves as Renaissance Men (that tired old presumption) the summary of course preferences revealed a distinct myopia about the value of language, literature, philosophy and other cultural studies. National design boundaries are disappearing, but virtually no one believed that such courses were worthwhile.

Designers said it was the teacher's fault that students are not sufficiently articulate when they graduate, but the summary showed a lack of interest in oral and written communication. The tragic fact is that the design profession, however articulate it may be in client presentation, lacks the intellectual voice it needs to sustain its own validity with the public. As might have been expected, the meeting placed most emphasis on a presumed need for more courses in industrial design methodology and techniques . . . .

There are, however, signs that design is becoming more mature—less obsessed with the elitist notion of good design and more interested in the concept of design for people. This is bringing a new sense of pride into a field that has been sadly tarnished in the public mind by the extravagant formalism and irrelevant ornament of the past. The shift is evident in the pressure to redirect design education away from art and toward the social and behavioral sciences . . . .

This emerging awareness of design as an instrument of public service poses a complicated question for teachers and designers in the United States. If we believe in a more humane approach to design, as evidenced by our increasing preoccupation with the problems of the environment in its broadest sense, are we not caught up in a dichotomous design philosophy? One view of design holds that economic survival depends upon the ability to provide products that will be found desirable by others; success is measured in terms of the profits that can be earned by design initiatives. But another view holds that no one has the right to survive at the expense of others; and if you take a profit, you cannot help but diminish the quality of the profit or the service that is being offered.

Thus, design may be polarizing into two conflicting attitudes—one "social" and the other "imperial," though I do not in any way relate those terms to the political concepts . . . .

One would hope that the design academicians will strive for a better understanding of the current drive toward "social" design. Inevitably, some will view it as a dark threat to independent action and unbridled creativity; yet, while its rise may not auger well for the near future, others see in it a future for design that is more sensible and humane.

Philosophically, industrial design education in the United States is allied with "social" design; but design practice is primarily "imperial." That is the curious dilemma which faces industrial design in America. "

—Arthur Pulos, Pulos Design Associates and Chairman of the Department of Design at Syracuse University. Extracted from "Dreaming of a Humane and Business-like Design School," *Design,* February 1978.

Chronological alphabet letter series from Upper & Lower Case, *September, 1978*

1910

1957

1960

1977

Additional Listing

Other highly recommended schools are:

Carnegie-Mellon University — Strong technical/management orientation to the graphic arts industry.

Arizona State University — Highly technical course in graphic communications within the Technology Department.

Cooper Union School of Art and Architecture — Comprehensive printing-related courses in graphic design.

Boston University — Printing-related communication design course as an option within the School of Visual Arts.

Western Michigan University — Strong technical/management design and graphic arts courses.

Academy of Art, San Francisco — very broad based curriculum of courses in all graphic arts and related disciplines.

Vocational Education

All the schools mentioned above offer vocational courses in communications and media design. For details on part-time day or evening study programs, consult the special college catalogs. Some schools also offer intensive summer workshops and comprehensive University Extension programs.

The increasing public awareness of design and the media has also spawned a wide variety of communication design courses in community colleges throughout the country, and many special seminars on the subject as part of "lifelong learning" programs at the universities.

Museums often have art schools which list courses in design and the media; and in many cities a Center for Alternative Education features sporadic, sometimes interesting, esoteric, courses in the graphic arts.

For other forms of ongoing education, see Section F.

Financial Aid for Education

All costs shown above represent tuition *only*. It is imperative that you obtain specific information about the total cost of attending any school, including all the "extras" and living expenses, which vary drastically from one geographic region to another.

Bear in mind that at some colleges as many as 80% of enrolled students receive some form of financial aid. In 1977 students from families with incomes as high as $30,000 were eligible for assistance, but did not even apply for it; and in 1978, financial aid funds from all sources reached an unprecedented $12 billion. Also, since the income requirements for the Guaranteed Student Loan Program have been removed, any family, regardless of income, can qualify for a low-interest, special repayment loan. The college's official pricetag is not always what you have to pay! *Always* obtain a Financial Aid Form (FAF) from the college of your choice, and begin the application process. Administrators in both high schools and colleges will assist you with the necessary paperwork.

The earlier you plan for your design education, the better your chances are of attending your preferred design school. You and your family can gain a rough idea of your chances for financial aid by using the Early Financial Aid Planning Service. The service can also be used to apply for Basic Education Opportunity Grants.
Cost: $3.50

Early Financial Aid Planning Service

Meeting College Costs

Get a copy of this booklet from your high school counselor, and follow the instructions, worksheets, and tables that help you do your own eligibility estimate.

Student Expenses

"Student Expenses at Post-Secondary Institutions" itemizes costs at some 2,700 colleges. The directory will give you some idea of the amount you will have to spend to attend each college that interests you.
Cost: $4.00

College Board Publication Orders

Gaining Experience

There is no reliable, set way to obtain background experience in the creative disciplines of the graphic arts. There is no system of apprenticeship that can be counted on to provide solid training. Really useful education outside the two- or four-year college courses is very difficult to come by in many areas of the country.

For those who have passed through a good college course, securing work in order to gain the necessary experience is a relatively straightforward affair.

For those who enter the graphic arts profession more by accident than by design, and who cannot afford the time or cost of a full-time communications design education, vocational courses of variable quality exist almost everywhere. In order to find out which of these programs are worthwhile, you may have to undertake some thorough research.

Check the following sources in your area:

University extension centers
Graphic arts guilds
Community colleges
Private art schools
Local museums
Art directors clubs or illustrators societies
Local design studios
Local typesetting or printing companies, publishers, or advertising agencies.

Somebody at one of these places is bound to know which available courses are the most reliable, and it's probable that if there is a guild in your area they will have the best one. Check carefully: like standard university courses, these classes will be only as good as the teachers who create them. Many are not worth your time or money.

Courses will vary from fifteen-week workshops offered by guilds for about $250 (including membership), or private six-week courses costing about $100, to intensive one-day basic courses for approximately $45. These last are usually designed for corporate in-house production people. The university extension courses are also often one-day workshop/seminars more devoted to theory and philosophy than pragmatics.

Some designers, advertising agencies, publishing companies, or large corporations with their own art departments may take on inexperienced beginners occasionally, but usually they prefer someone who has at least a little real experience. Ideally, you should apprentice yourself to a designer—a practice the guilds are struggling to establish, in the true guild tradition. The benefits that fall to you from apprenticing are, of course, interesting real work and personal guidance at no cost to yourself. You should not expect payment for your time, however: in the apprentice arrangement, you trade off your time for supervised education and practical experience.

If there is a graphics guild in your area, join it as a first step.

Production and Paste-up Clinics

Look for announcements of the Walter B. Graham clinics and seminars. These are intensely practical one-day courses conducted throughout the country for beginners and those within the graphic arts trades who need to acquire board skills. Graham, president of Modern Litho of Omaha, has pioneered many of the most effective techniques for systematic production paste-up, and offers excellent advice and information on getting work camera ready to save time and money.

Graham's workshops are designed to familiarize production people and designers with all the latest techniques and tricks. Sessions involve a specific paste-up exercise, layout ideas and repro proofing. Participants receive tools, materials, instructions and a special equipment kit, and are invited to bring their own problems for discussion and advice.

Cost: $80.00

Idea Seminars

Complete Guide To Paste-up
[Walter Graham]

Of the numerous books available on design and preparation for printing, Graham's is the most valuable and unique, useful to both the beginner and the seasoned professional. It's full of sound, practical ideas, some very familiar, some unusual. The purpose of this manual is to promote systems that are as simple as possible. The text, designed for use in schools, business, and industry, is revised and updated periodically.

Cost: $19.50

North American Publishing Co

STANFORD CONFERENCE ON DESIGN

PICA Foundation

This is an extensive and complete graphic communications education program developed after years of research in the two Carolinas and Georgia, and is used extensively throughout the US. The PICA system is an audio-visual series of 58 self-instructional programs, designed for high school or vocational school students with particular interests or aptitudes within the graphic arts. Each of the programs are specific, and highly pragmatic, designed to teach precise skills, and are not concerned with design *per se*. The programs consist of "orientation" type and "performance" type courses and include step-by-step instruction programs such as "How to Make a Duotone," "Typestyles and Their Uses," "Orientation to Offset Lithography," and "Color Separations Made Simple." A carefully planned graphics instructional course for beginners, available through your local school or college.

The Printing Industry of the Carolinas Foundation (PICA)

Versatility in Reprographics

Although books are no substitute for practical experience, they are often essential to give the whole picture of a particular area and keep you up-to-date. This practical handbook from Kodak provides some very clear, technical information on the art of preparation for printing. Although it is primarily intended as a guide for engineers and architects who have their own drafting rooms, this booklet is a neat collection of short-cut techniques of the trade. (Kodak produces a vast array of educational publications, with a series designed for high-school and college level students on the basics of graphic design and printing. Send for their book catalog.)

Cost: Free

Kodak Publications

The New Graphics Master
[Dean Phillip Lem]

Many other useful technical and practical instruction books are included in Chapter O, but the *Graphics Master* belongs here, for it is the best single print production workbook published to date. Here, in one compact volume, are all the essential guidelines and technical data for the newest methods, processes, and techniques used in graphic arts production. *Graphics Master 2* brings them all together in complete, comprehensive, yet concise, easy-to-find-and-use indexed sections that provide instant solutions for your questions.

One of the finest features of this book is the graphic guides and tools included with each copy. Each book contains a process-color selector guide with more than 2,800 different colors in two twenty-four-page sections printed on coated and uncoated stock. There's a type face selector guide with 832 typefaces, a built-In copy-fitting scale, a ten-inch plastic laminated line gauge and pica rule, and a proportional scale.

This book is the perfect tool for anyone who creates, designs, plans, estimates, produces, buys or sells printing.

Cost: $37.50

Art Direction Book Co

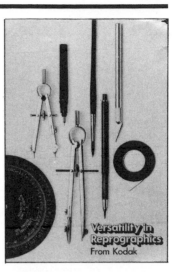

E

Education, or the Lack of It

Gaining Experience

A National Guild Structure

The National and Eastern headquarters of the Graphic Artists Guild are in New York City, the Western headquarters in San Francisco.

There are locals in various stages of development in many metropolitan areas of the country. The locals speak to the specific markets and needs of each individual area, supported by funds from the national, and energy from the regional, offices. Each local membership elects its own board, and its own representative to the regional and national boards.

The regional headquarters' function is to support the locals in their efforts to grow. It supplies literature, information and other benefits for their membership. Each local acts autonomously within the mandates of the Guild bylaws and is otherwise free to develop its own character, define its own needs and priorities as determined by its local membership.

The benefits that can be derived from the locals are
- a local newsletter
- a job referral system
- seminars on professional matters
- class actions and other legal matters such as grievances
- state legislation
- art material and travel discounts
- publications dealing with local issues, problems or information
- and most important, support to the membership in creating a more professional environment in which to work.

All the locals have many goals in common and can offer together some important national benefits such as
- a national magazine to contain news from each local and regional office
- brochures on specific areas of concern to the graphic artist
- a complete health plan
- a credit union
- a law firm on retainer on both coasts, well acquainted with those matters and issues that pertain to the graphic artist. Low cost legal advice is available through these firms to members as is the Guild's free grievance procedure.

- promoting contractual terms for the sale of limited reproduction rights only with any additional rights receiving further compensation.
- *Pricing and Ethical Guidelines, The Legal Guide for the Visual Artist,* and *The Visual Artists Guide to the New Copyright Law,* are definitive guidebooks offered free to all members.
- the Guild is initiating a major drive to inform buyers of the unacceptability of the "work for hire" clause and possible legal violations they risk.
- establishing the principle that artists and designers normally sell reproduction rights only and retain ownership of the original artwork. Due to Guild pressure this is becoming a standard in the industry.

It is not the Guild's aim to force acceptance of its standards by strikes, boycotts or membership discipline. Rather, the Guild's aim is to provide the collective and organizational support necessary for individual artists to achieve such standards in their dealings with buyers.

The Graphic Artists' Guild

Monday
Nov. 20

GRAPHIC ARTIST,

Admission Free

THE GUILD BUYS YOU CLOUT SF

Meeting
7:30-10pm

Wine
Reception
6:30 pm

UC Auditorium
Market
and Laguna

THE GRAPHIC ARTISTS GUILD PRESENTS

A PROFESSIONAL WORKSHOP: BUSINESS GUIDE FOR THE VISUAL ARTIST for Illustrators Photographers Graphic Designers

WEDNESDAY OCT. 4

THE GREAT DEBATE:
PROFESSIONALISM AND CREATIVITY IN THE GRAPHIC ARTS

GRAPHIC ARTISTS DEBATE

GRAPHIC ARTISTS GUILD NEWSLETTER

A NATIONAL VOICE FOR GRAPHIC ARTISTS

APRIL 1979

Business Seminar
a Graphic Artists Guild Success

by Sam Visiano

Guild Announces Programs on Pricing

GRAPHIC ARTISTS GUILD NEWSLETTER UPDATE

Box 783
Bolinas CA 94924

The Polluted Sea of Information

We know that graphics is capable of expressing visually physical processes. Is it within its scope to convey political or philosophical concepts? Unique to early picture-writing by the Chinese was their use of amalgamated pictures to express abstract ideas. All civilizations and cultures inevitably and unconsciously express their ideology and philosophy in their architecture, symbols and artifacts. But is it possible to reverse the process and consciously manipulate graphic forms to express or convey abstract concepts? Probably not in our current stage of development. At present the graphic armory only contains the techniques to express mechanical and organic processes, comparisons, locations in time and space, some non-geographical information by use of distorted maps, sequences of events, relationships, hierarchies and the like.

As to drawing, there are systems: linear perspective (which gives an *illusion* of perceptual volume and space); orthographic projections; plans and elevations (which give information as it is *known* to exist), as well as diagram conventions. It is also possible to use a combination of systems to present information in its most characteristic and accessible form. This alone is a formidable amount of knowledge and skill to acquire and handle efficiently and at present art schools hardly begin to come to terms with it. Hell-bent on academic respectability they substitute "liberal arts" for a proper and relevant study of graphic design.

It might be thought axiomatic that all people who aspire to art school have primarily a gift for drawing. This may be so, but sadly the person who solves problems visually and uses his pencil fluently as an analytical tool is a rare bird and not much found in art schools. The present educational system manages to suppress or divert the talents of the natural embryo designer.

Personality plays a strong part in the direction in which a

continued next page

The Mitchell Beazley Atlas of Body and Mind has outstanding illustrations which are the result of a cooperative effort between researchers, medical consultants, the "visualizer" and artist.

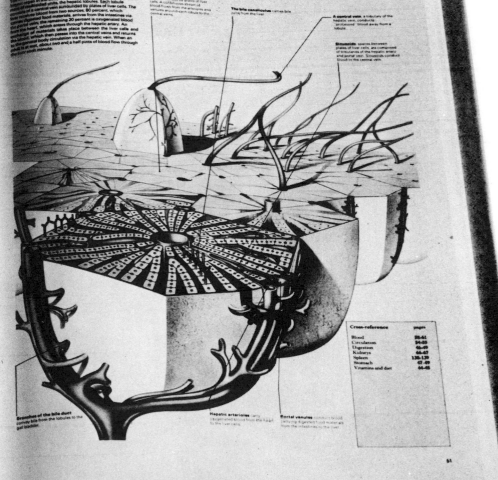

E

young art student may turn his talents. Outgoing, socially at ease people may aspire to the vague positions of "visualizer" or assistant art director in an advertising agency where the ability to organize other people's talents comes easily to them. Their vestigial gift for "drawing" will not go amiss but their position and career pattern will probably depend more on the image they have of themselves as a thrusting personality than on any deeply committed artistic sensibility.

The person who perhaps unexpectedly discovers that he or she has a gift for typography might take work in a minor publishing house to beaver away, increasing daily in confidence and ability.

The free-lance illustrator who can keep himself solely on his illustration is a fairly unusual person. Quite often he needs to make a relatively "quick killing" while his style is in vogue and his stamina is at its peak. All this is necessarily an over-simplification; human beings do not classify so easily. Expediency and opportunity play their part in the development of their roles.

There is however a rather typical kind of person who becomes a finished artwork specialist. Invariably he will be craft-oriented. This tends to go with a personality that is introverted, self-effacing. A solitary, maybe a country dweller, one who avoids the metropolitan social scene.

Reliable to a fault, there is a hint of the monastic in his approach to life. The danger is that this person is so enamored of his craft that he may be ill-directed to virtuosity over and above necessity. Artworkers may come through the BA degree system — sheer craftsmanship finally getting the upper hand — or they may have worked through the art studio system, perhaps finally to become free-lance specialists. At the least inspiring end of this spectrum is the man who bestows on the ill-considered ideas of others the fruits of his airbrush and scalpel. This is generally known as a "tarting up" operation. Ideally he should be genuinely creative and contribute his own powers of analysis to the problem, revealing truths about the machine or process he is visually describing that illuminate it for the first time.

Apart from the need (quite inappropriate) to get a degree in three or four years there are many pressures on the young

student designer. Some of these are simply economic, some are parental, some stem from the need for instant approval from their peers. Further pressures, real or imagined, loom large as the real world encroaches. As a rule people who commission art and design have a pigeon-hole mentality and tend to equate versatility with unreliability. Deadlines and tight budgets do not require them to be shocked or surprised too often. The dice are loaded in favor of the man who does one thing; consistently even if predictably. The word designer used to imply a non-specialist, someone who had a synoptic, total view of the world. Increasingly it has come to mean a specialist of some kind in the complex business of design.

It would be nice to think that a right political decision was taken because of a diagram made by a designer, probing like a surgeon's knife, revealing layers of truth. There *are* a great many talented designers; there *is* a wealth of artwork of high social and educational value. Unfortunately it has no easy passport to anybody's attention; it has to sink or swim in the polluted sea of information that is our daily environment.

—Philip Thompson, graphic designer. From *Design,* November 1977.

The Information Business

Within the three major design categories — Product Design, Environmental Design, and Graphic Design — the term "graphic" can be broken down further into two major areas: Information Design and Identity Design. This distinction is essentially a user classification; not entirely perfect, perhaps, but practical.

Peter Gorb, in *Living by Design,* suggests that *identity design* provokes the first awareness of graphic design, either from a corporate body and its advertising and publicity departments, or from an individual. As that awareness deepens through contact, *information design* leads to familiarity with the *environments* in which design operates, and finally to a knowledge of its *products.*

Information and *identity* constitute the business of graphic design. The importance of professional design does not reside in the visible qualities of the finished work; that visible treatment is subordinate, a literate expression of the designer's influence over the strategy that lies behind the work, or at least the designer's creative response to imposed limitations.

Unfortunately, graphic designers' achievements are measured instinctively by the amount of "graphic handwriting" present in the finished artwork; if the designer's contribution is not seen, then neither is it understood; and, consequently, neither is it felt to be necessary.

Neither "uncolored" information design nor information design "colored" by propaganda and ambition are seen to be inappropriate, and in both cases the graphic designer is able to make a valued contribution

The Business of Design

PENTAGRAM STUDIO, FROM *LIVING BY DESIGN*

"The journey of a thousand miles begins with a single step," said Lao Tzu. And for the sake of covering all the business pitfalls that confront people in the graphic communications field, we assume, for this chapter, that you are about to begin the thousand mile journey of the free-lance graphic artist.

Many of you will never take this step. The known securities of a regular job are not to be sneezed at, and are easily preferred to the hazards and singular responsibilities of self-employment. Yet, even if corporate life fulfills you utterly, you may find it useful to know something about the operation of a small design business, whose problems—and rewards—may not be so different from those your present clients faced in their own fields. And if the day ever *should* arrive when you can't stand one more minute of the boss, or the rush hour commute, or the smug, self-satisfied gleam in the eye of your friend who *did* go out on his own, you ought to be prepared.

The single step at the beginning of your journey is to provide yourself with some essential data that will demystify what may otherwise seem to be a forbidding facade of specialist demands that require careful training and experience. You may ease your mind. Most people who go into business on their own do so with no formal business education, little or no experience, and often without significant capital of their own. Should you take the first step, momentum will carry you forward and it's unlikely you'll ever look back.

As for the series of first moves, that's what this chapter is all about. There are certain things you must do to save yourself from disaster at the hands of the IRS or the state sales tax bureaucracy. You will have to deal with many different people, keep schedules, meet deadlines, organize paperwork, pay bills, and so on. The procedures are rarely very complicated, but it all has to be done at the same time, and done on time —even though you will surely run short of that last commodity.

Financing: How Much Do You Need?

Some graphic artists set out to be free lancers, while many others drift into self-employment after quitting some tedious or frustrating full-time job, vowing never to work in a similar situation again. Suddenly they are on their own with some equipment, perhaps a little money, and living quarters that will have to double as a studio, for a while, at least. Many design practices can be built from there.

It is possible to start a successful design business with little or no capital, particularly if you already have a few years of work experience behind you and have established potential clients and trade contacts. As a service business, communications design requires minimal operating overhead, and no significant stock inventory of any sort. Most service businesses can begin on very little initial investment.

Starting on a shoestring is entirely viable. It's even possible to start with nothing, if you're willing to make some sacrifices at the outset. For many people making such sacrifices is preferable to borrowing money from friends or relatives. However, it's a financial fact of life that business in general revolves around borrowing, investing, credit, interest rates, and so forth, and a bit of borrowing at the start is often the best way to get things rolling.

Other than borrowing from rich relatives and friends, early loans are hard to get. Banks are reluctant to take chances on new, untried ventures with inexperienced entrepreneurs. If you already have established a good relationship with your bank, you might be able to get a small business loan—up to 50% of your required start up capital. You are more likely to receive a *personal* loan, regardless of your business, particularly if the bank knows and trusts you, and you can put up some form of collateral. But a bank will usually require that you take out liability insurance or life insurance, naming it as beneficiary, before it will approve a loan without collateral. Be careful not to get in over your head.

The Small Business Administration (SBA) is a government loan agency that is even more frustrating to deal with than banks. The SBA is dependent on politics, and therefore on the whims of whoever is in power at the moment. To get an SBA loan you will have to obtain some private financing first; and you will have to go to great lengths to convince the agency that you have the ability to operate your business successfully, and that the loan can be repaid from business earnings. SBA can loan up to 80% of what you need, up to $50,000, with a five-to-eight year payback plan at an interest rate slightly better than the bank's. The SBA attaches a lot of strings to its loans, and many people have found them to be more trouble than the money is worth.

The SBA also offers a "Loan Guarantee Plan" under which the SBA "guarantees" 90% of what a bank may loan you. Such a guarantee, or collateral, is subject to the prevailing bank interest rates—which are very high these days.

Private financiers and silent partners, whose sole contribution is money, are worth looking into; but often they require you to give up such a large portion of the business that you may quickly find yourself feeling like an employee all over again—and unable to quit because of contracts and debts. Of course, if you're a new and shoestring operation, this expensive form of money is unlikely to make itself available to you in the first place.

Small Time Operator: How to Start your Own Small Business, Keep Books, Pay your Taxes, and Stay Out of Trouble
[Bernard Kamoroff, CPA]

An extremely useful manual for anyone about to start an independent business, or for anyone who has just begun that adventure. *Small Time Operator* discusses common types of laws and regulations, federal income tax law, and all those irritating little procedures you may not be aware of until you've already made the mistake of having ignored them. Its step-by-step instructions cover how to get yourself set up; how to keep books; how to expand into a corporation; how to deal with the various taxes you are liable for; and the areas of professional business help you may need. The book also contains all the ledger blanks for your first year. It is written by an accountant, not for the graphics profession specifically, and has the kind of financial overview essential for people who have little experience or aptitude in money matters.

Cost: $5.95

Bell Springs Publishing

A Guide to Business Principles and Practice for Interior Designers
[Harry Siegel, CPA]

Although it is written with the interior designer in mind, this guide explains how to run a design practice in general. Part Two is particularly good; it deals with obtaining work, carrying it out, and charging for it—the whole area of handling the client/designer relationship in a professional manner. Harry Siegel also pays special attention to the importance of careful paperwork and the procedures he considers mandatory for your own good management. The book would be even more useful in paperback, since the hardbound edition is unnecessarily expensive.

Cost: $16.50

Whitney Library of Design, Watson-Guptill Publications

The Incredible Secret Money Machine
[Don Lancaster]

One of the best books around on small business practices, *The Incredible Secret Money Machine,* is full of wisdom, wit, and informative experience. It's really exciting to read. The book is dedicated to those who are in business for themselves "on a total lifestyle basis." It advises the reader how to stay in control of a business in order to continue doing what he or she likes.

The excellent financial advice accurately points out that having enough capitalization is about the worst possible thing an independent can do, and will almost certainly scuttle "the whole machine." If you have the money you are only going to spend it. Avoiding excess money at the outset encourages good business habits and prevents you from making unnecessary expenditures that will commit you to even higher future costs. "It's real difficult for any beginner to increase the amount of money he is handling by more than 20% or so a year without starting to do stupid things with it or worrying too much about it."

Cost: $5.95

Howard W Sams & Co Inc

Four Ways to Organize Your Business

As a new independent business man or woman the four principal business formations you are likely to enter into require adherence to an increasingly complex set of regulations. Initially, you will probably do best to start with the one-person arrangement known as *sole proprietorship.* If and when it is time to expand your business you will have the choice of forming an associate relationship, a partnership, or a corporation.

Sole Proprietorship

The simplest and least expensive business formation is one in which the business itself has no legal existence apart from the owner, who receives all the profits and is personally responsible for all the losses. No licenses or permits are required to form a sole proprietorship. However, you *will* need certain licenses or permits to operate as a business. You may have to have a "fictitious name statement" if you want to operate under a name other than your own, in which case you may become John Doe, dba (doing business as) D. Sign Graphics. A fictitious name statement requires payment of a filing fee and payment of fees to one or more local newspaper(s) in which you must publish such a statement.

You will need a local business license from either the municipal or county authority which must be renewed annually. The cost varies from $10 to $100 each renewal. Within a city you may also be required to conform with local zoning and building regulations, which can be very costly. Be sure to find out what requirements pertain to your situation.

Then there is the seller's permit under which the State collects its sales and use taxes. Many practicing designers are not aware that this permit is mandatory; yet if you fail to acquire it, you could be in big financial trouble down the line. More material on this subject will be found in "Keeping Track for the Taxman," p.183 .

Associate Status

This is an arrangement whereby you retain your business as a sole proprietor, and simultaneously you "associate" with an established design company without becoming an employee. For example, you might become the graphics associate to an architecture/interior design group because you have something to offer the existing firm, such as potential clients, an outstanding skill, or some other expertise the larger company needs.

Associate status requires virtually no capital expenditure, entails no real risk, and allows as much aesthetic freedom as you might expect to have as the designer/owner of your own business. Frequently, it also provides the opportunity to work on challenging projects with an experienced group of people who already have the facilities you need. An ideal way to get established.

The Partnership

If you can't work out an associate status — and many excellent designers simply do not have the particular requirements an established company may need — a partnership is often a convenient way to establish your business, providing you and another one or two people are compatible enough to make to make a good team. Partnership allows you to share the burdens of responsibility, risk, and costs, and offers at least the possibility of some relief when jobs come in all at once. Besides, there are hidden advantages in the exchange of ideas, where two heads are better than one.

A partnership needs all the same licenses and permits the sole proprietorship needs; in addition, if the partnership employs personnel — such as a secretary or bookkeeper — you will need to apply for a Federal Employer Identification Number so you can pay a payroll tax. Yes, folks, another tax. You should also be sure to have appropriate insurance coverage: fire and theft at least, and, possibly, even liability insurance.

A Design Partnership

"We all begun with much the same background: low living standards, not much to lose, odd free-lance jobs, a little part-time teaching. By the time we joined Pentagram we had individual free-lance practice in common. Gradually we had each built our own reputations; generating work by our own efforts, then implementing it to a standard that at least led to another job. With any luck, we finished each year solvent. These are the necessary skills that make for being a good partner. The advantage that has arisen from the partnership is the freedom of owning one's own business combined with the security of belonging to a stronger unit.

Among design consultancy offices, the mixture of activities is never exactly the same. Some include market research, others public relations and there are those that act as print buyers or have large artwork studios. Pentagram knows its business is solely design. This is not perhaps as limiting as it seems. For one thing it embraces most kinds of design activity in which its customers are likely to be involved: their products, their environments, their information systems, their communication needs and their corporate identities. For another, the design activity—its creative solution and its effective interpretation—is founded on a depth and range of work which is not commonly offered to a designer . . . .

Fletcher Forbes Gill was a graphics group formed with the idea of dealing direct with industrial and commercial companies. After the first two years we faced the fact that half our work was graphics trouble-shooting for advertising agencies. We discussed the possibility of becoming an advertising agency, but discarded it in favor of developing a partnership that could cover a company's entire design requirements. To broaden our base, we then invited Theo Crosby to join us. Theo, an architect who was best known for his exhibition work, wanted to escape from running a team of forty other architects.

The success of our platform was symbolically confirmed when we were appointed design consultants on an international basis to British Petroleum, Britain's largest company. In 1969, we undertook a study of the European self-service station of the seventies. We could cope with the structure and the graphics but the equipment on the forecourt was beyond us. This need for expertise in industrial design led to collaboration with Kenneth Grange.

Early failures

Ralph Eckerstrom, the mastermind of Unimark, once described to me a conversation he had had with the senior vice president of the Ford Motor Company after a successful presentation in the boardroom in Detroit. Eckerstrom had said: "It is not a question of whether you and I communicate with each other but whether our middle management communicates with your middle management." The remark symbolized the difference in attitude between Unimark and the creative graphics "hotshop" of Fletcher Forbes Gill. I did not realize then that I would learn what he meant the hard way. In our four-year period as consultants to BP we made every mistake in the book. . . .

continued next page

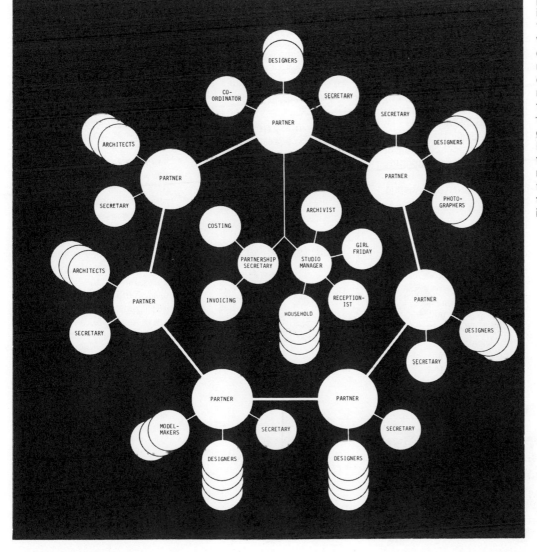

F

It has taken the experience of running a business that needs its own consultants, accountants, lawyers or management consultants to understand the experience that one of our own clients goes through when appointing us: the number of interviews, cross-checks and internal discussions that are necessary before a decision is reached. But at least when the consultant is eventually appointed the client really does want him to succeed. He will try to forgive errors and misjudgements as part of the learning process, desperately hoping he has not made a mistake because he cannot bear the thought of starting the procedure again. A consultant starts with a bank of goodwill that is all too easily squandered.

Multi-discipline buzz buzz

Like all designers, each of us was a prisoner of the specialization in which he trained. Our body of knowledge was small and our awareness of what else there was to know was correspondingly small. Luckily we were the kind of people who wanted to learn so it was inevitable that each of us should begin to dabble in design areas for which we were certainly not trained. We did learn a little more; but more important, we became very aware of how much more there was to learn. As a result, we were more than usually receptive to the multi-disciplinary concept and it made it very easy for people from different disciplines to agree to get together.

Nowaways "multi-discipline" is a buzz word. But the proposition to the client is that Pentagram is different from a consortium or loosely knit association of different skills put together to solve a single problem; that doesn't work because professional egos prevent constructive collaboration.

Pentagram was formed to solve such problems. In our first five years we have learned a good deal about working together and in retrospect what has happened appears very obvious. A multi-disciplinary approach is a reality at policy level but not at operational level: multi-disciplinary discussions, briefings and reviews are productive and fruitful but the business of getting the job done is so technically specialized that the work must be managed by a person skilled in that particular discipline. Designers write to Pentagram for employment "because I want to work in a multi-disciplinary office." However, as far as the operation of the project goes, the jobs are watertight. An architectural drafts-person cannot be exchanged for an engineering draftsperson, let alone for a typographer. There the dream turns to disillusion for the student aspiring to be a "Renaissance Man." But the proposition to the potential client is true, even though we are not immune from the occasional collision of oversized egos.

A good client relationship is one where an individual in the client organization develops confidence in the partner he deals with and considers the other as "also rans." Prospective clients often come to Pentagram to a particular partner because of a previous association, and we often benefit from the progress they have made in their own careers. Sometimes the enquiry is impersonal but after a meeting with more than one of us it is usually obvious where the rapport lies and we leave it that way. There is also a certain amount of natural selection. If a partner is really over-burdened, he won't be around to talk about prospective business.

If something goes wrong it has to be somebody's fault

We have in our time tried and discarded various methods of working. We have eschewed

Pentagram design: for Zinc Development Assoc. die casting conference of 66; Heinemann Brothers; Pirelli tires

teams that are put together to work on a specific project but include some members working on other projects at the same time. The failure here was always one of accountability. We eventually developed a system where each person in the office is responsible to only one of the partners and that partner is responsible for the job. The principle is simple—if something goes wrong it has to be somebody's fault. It ensures that we meet our promises and our deadlines.

However it is not the way we determine policy. Nor is it the way we reinforce our creativity. That is done by consensus—not easy to do amongst a group of equals. Lots of the consensus meetings are informal, but we do hold regular policy meetings, usually out of the office. Twice a year we disappear off into the country for a long weekend.

Two main things happen on these occasions. We raise our eyes to the blue skies for a long look at the future, and we cast them down for a good long session of introspective self-indulgence. Oddly enough, the mixture is a help. For one thing it enables us to deal with day-to-day operational problems in a new light. It also satisfies our need for consensus, without which we would no longer be a partnership. Votes are anathema to us. We would rather drift together than set course with a minority voice. Everything is easy if you are always rational, adult and intelligent. Except, like all creative people, we are often irrational and childlike with only occasional flashes of insight or inspiration.

So far our *modus operandi* has worked as a planning mechanism. We are roughly what we wanted to be when we started.

—Colin Forbes, *Pentagram* partner. From *Design,* January 1978

Incorporation

It is always wise to give corporate status serious consideration. Even if you feel it to be initially inappropriate, review the choice regularly. At some point it may become necessary. A legal corporation can be one individual as easily as two or more. But a corporation is a *separate entity* from the individuals who own it, both legally and financially. Forming a corporation requires a certain amount of legal work and, therefore, an attorney. Set up costs can easily amount to $1000 or more.

The major advantage to incorporation is limited liability of the stockholders — the debts of the corporation are not the debts of the designer/owner(s). There are also considerable income tax benefits, which a creative accountant can maximize to the fullest. Third, it is much easier for a corporation to obtain financing (or investment) capital than it is for any other legal business entity. Finally, a corporation offers the options of profit-sharing plans and pension benefits not ordinarily enjoyed in a freelance enterprise.

The disadvantages of incorporation lie in the morass of technicalities and prescribed formalities that corporations must adhere to that demand expenditures and raise overhead; and the additional state franchise and stock taxes that pertain to corporations.

Advantages and Disadvantages

In general, there are distinct advantages and disadvantages to whichever style of business organization you select. The disadvantages of sole proprietorship, associate status, or partnership are, first, that your business income is taxed as personal income — the more your business nets, the more tax you pay personally. This is particularly important if you have additional sources of income, or if you are married, filing a joint return, and your spouse has an income of his or her own. In such a situation incorporation could save you money.

Secondly, if you are unincorporated you are subject to unlimited liability for all debts, losses, and adverse effects of your operation. In a partnership, the personal assets of each and every partner are legally liable to attachments by creditors, which can place your enterprise in serious jeopardy. Covering yourself with insurance is the only way to protect yourself under these circumstances, and that may entail more expense than you are ready to bear.

Finally, if you want to name your business — incorporated or not — you will have to investigate the legal requirements regarding fictitious name usage in your locale. Using anything other than your own name may be subject to a variety of restrictions.

Keeping Track for the Taxman

The first element of good bookkeeping is to establish and maintain a comprehensive record of all deposits made into your business banking account. It goes without saying that you should keep separate personal and business bank accounts, and know the difference between income and capital. There is no sense paying taxes on a loan from your friend or the transfer of funds from your savings account, since neither is income. But unless you keep track of your records, those unexplained deposits may draw fire from the IRS.

Secondly, record all your business expenses, and pay by check whenever possible to provide an accurate ledger of expenses for the IRS. Credit card receipts are almost as good as cancelled checks, but for some auditors they don't quite measure up. There are credit card cases of designers taking clients to lunch in Los Angeles on the same day the same client took some other designer to lunch in New York....

If you can show comprehensive records of deposits and expenses largely in the form of cancelled checks to an auditor, you are almost free from the hot breath of the taxman. The last two elements are easy. Too easy. So easy, in fact, that many — especially inexperienced — business people neglect them, to their sorrow. They are: Keep a daily diary of incidental expenses such as parking meters, pay phones, pens bought at the airport and so forth. As often as possible, add a receipt to your log for each expense. And: Keep your invoices up to date, noting when you have been paid for each — or if you have not been paid.

Bookkeeping and Taxes

Bookkeeping is an integral part of your business, not something that has to be done just because of the IRS and state franchise tax laws. You *need* the information generated and organized by this process to run your business intelligently. Many businesses fail because they lack any system that provides essential information and accurate financial records for business management.

None of your bookkeeping records need be complicated. You can keep them simple, without expensive accountants or computers, especially if you run a sole proprietorship. But by all means, keep them. If you hate keeping records, pay someone else to do it for you.

From tax deductions to major expansion, the principles of a simple system are very well described in *Small Time Operator* (see above, p.179). If it's well set up to begin with, you can elaborate on any system to suit your growing demands.

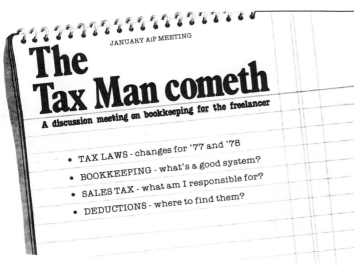

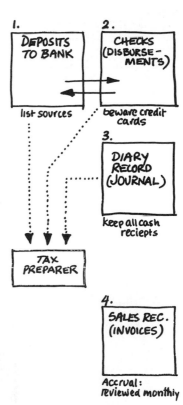

Taxes

The taxes that apply to an unincorporated graphics business are income tax, self-employment tax, sales tax, and the local business tax that buys your permit to operate as a business.

Income tax is to be filed if your gross income is $2450 or more ($3600 or more for joint returns), or if your net earnings from self-employment is $400 or more. All true business expenses are deductible, including overhead, transportation, bad debts, education, entertainment, insurance, moving, and travel. There is also an investment tax credit allowed on fixed assets such as tools, equipment, and furniture that is applied for the year of purchase, or may be amortized over a period of several years.

The self-employment tax is actually the independent agent's Social Security tax. For free lancers it is figured at the highest rate of all, approaching 9% on net business profits with a set maximum. You may owe no income tax and still be liable for a horrendous self-employment bite.

The penalty for failure to file an income tax return is 5% per month of the unpaid tax, unless you can show that your failure to file was not willfull neglect. Unless the IRS has received a W-2 or 1099 form from whoever has paid you money (you should also receive copies of these forms), they probably won't know you have earned the money unless they do an audit. But if you don't file, you are breaking the law, and there is no statute of limitations on how many years later they can come after you.

State Income or Franchise Tax

Not every state has some form of income tax on resident business yet, but most do, and their procedures are similar to those of the Federal government. Although specific rules vary from state to state, generally they allow businesses the same deductions as do the Feds.

Other State Taxes

Some states have a "Gross Receipts Tax" that may be levied in addition to their income tax. This is a tax on your total business receipts. It varies from a fraction of a percent to as much as 4%.

Other states have an "Unincorporated Business Tax" which can be as high as 5½% of net business income, or a "Business Privilege Tax" or "Single Business Tax" of up to 2.35% of net. The numbers and regulations concerning all this bureaucratic bother tends to change frequently, so contact your state government for current information. You don't get told things like this unless you ask, and ignorance of the tax laws is never any excuse for failure to support your government.

Sales or Use Tax

Several states slap a tax on all "non-essential" items, and this tax applies to the graphics profession in the same way it applies to a retail store. Exactly how it applies to art and design is sometimes surprising and controversial, so be careful to understand what is expected of you. In California, for example, sales tax applies to any sale or transfer of title or possession of a tangible nature, unless it is for resale. There are certain allowances and exemptions, but the State of California can, during an audit, claim 6½% of your *gross* income unless you can prove the exemptions. Another reason to keep careful records.

Beat Taxes!

Some excellent fellows of infinite jest hold the opinion that taxes have become the nation's major ripoff. One fascinating and somewhat radical publication advises you of your rights to avoid taxation, and tells you some of the tricks through which you may accomplish that nefarious end. The book, based on the precepts that relief from burdensome taxes will never come from government, and that only individuals can reduce taxes, covers ways to become exempt from witholding, beat social security taxes, fight the 1040 form to a halt, and use the "fiat money" attack. Although it probably goes too far for most people's nerves, it contains some enlightening information. It is entitled *Tax Wars*.

Cost: $7.95

Eden Press

Bill Collecting

Collecting on your bills is part of a good bookkeeping program, but doing so effectively can become an unpleasant problem. If the amount is fairly small, the small claims courts are a reasonable, quick way of pursuing your money. Provided you know how to use the courts.

Medicon, a seminar organization that offers business education classes around the country, has an excellent course on bill collecting. It includes instruction in cutting down on your number of unpaid bills in the first place. Then it covers when and how to sue, how to win your case, techniques to avoid unpaid bills, and how to deal with debtors who lie, evade, stall, frustrate, and just don't pay. An essential course for beginners in business.

Cost: $35.00

Medicon Corporation

Bankruptcy

Now that the bankruptcy stigma is no longer a heavy social taboo, this has become a popular way to straighten out personal and business affairs. Bankruptcies are at an all time high, especially among wage earners, who comprise 85% of all bankruptcy filings. Generally speaking, bankruptcy is a reflection of the state of the national economy and the growth of credit institutions. But if, for some reason, you have gotten so far into debt that you cannot see your way out of it, file. It's better than suicide, which is the route some people choose. It has been said to be the best consumer protection law around, and yet comparatively few people take advantage of it. It is not difficult to reestablish credit after filing for bankruptcy, and the American Bankruptcy Council will even advise you how to proceed. They also publish a couple of books on the subject of bankruptcy and sell a do-it-yourself bankruptcy kit.

Cost: $60.00 per kit

American Bankruptcy Council

Business Equipment and Services

Obviously, there are some essential items of non-graphic equipment you will need for your own business efficiency. You need a telephone right from the start, and, if you can afford it, an answering service or machine. You need a typewriter and a calculator. Beyond that, you will acquire office machinery when your finances allow or as you discover the need.

The telephone

There is little to say about the telephone itself that you do not already know, but the service is a variable which should be explored carefully and be matched to your needs. For instance, residence service is cheaper than business service; if you work from home there is no need to have the more expensive one. The variables themselves vary from one locale to another, and you should learn your options from your local telephone service representative before starting business.

When you order new phone service, or request changes in your existing service, make sure you understand all the costs involved. New service installation costs around $16, and any changes in existing service could cost as much. A connection charge is about $5, and interior wiring work is charged at $7-10 per outlet, jacks at some $2 each. Extra phones increase the monthly service cost, as does any telephone other than the basic unit we are all familiar with. Finally, if you are an unknown quantity to your local phone company, they may insist on a deposit ranging as high as $100 to plug you in. Our own preference is for the traditional looking telephone with touch-tone buttons, a standard item in many localities, quicker and more efficient than the conventional dial.

**The Pacific Telephone Catalog.
(A different kind of phone book.)**

The answering service

Since many people are still afraid that machines are here to stay, and refuse to communicate with them, the best answering service is definitely the personal one, where calls are taken by live people. These services are readily available in all urban areas at a reasonable cost, and are well worth the expense. Outside metropolitan areas, human answering service comes at a premium since the interconnection system gets to be expensive. A machine then becomes the practical way to go. The major advantages of the machine are that it represents a one-time cost only, and it does not misspell names. But which machine for you? We've selected two low-cost, reliable brands.

The Call Jotter

The basic requirements of a telephone answering machine are answer/record facility, voice activation, and remote message review. Anything less is inconvenient, anything more gets very expensive. Record-O-Phone's Call Jotter 10 has these features. Call Jotter 5 costs almost $100 less, but has no remote message review, a facility that allows you to listen to your messages over the phone from wherever you may be. Voice activation is also important, since it allows the caller to speak as long as he wishes instead of being cut off after 20 or 30 seconds.
Cost: $250.00

Record-O-Phone, Quasar Microsystems Inc

Call Jotter 10

Code-A-Phone

The Ford Industries' range of answering machines varies from a complete message center including a telephone, to an answer-only system. Model 222 is probably the most suitable, with variable announcement answer/record, voice activation, remote message review, and a call monitor control.
Cost: $395.00

Ford Industries, Inc

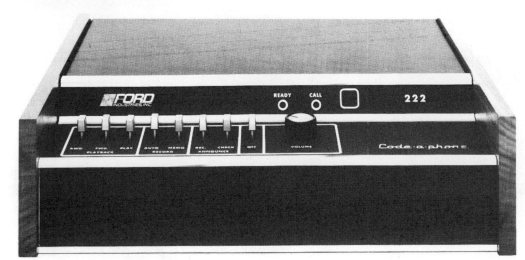

Code-A-Phone 222

Dictaphone

Both the above machines can be used as recorders for dictation and internal messages, but Dictaphone makes a useful little tool expressly for this purpose that you can carry in your pocket. Once you get used to using a pocket recorder, you'll find it as good as, or better than, pen and notebook for most things. The Travel Master 220 is one of the smallest standard cassette units on the market, and uses either batteries or a rechargeable pack. It also has electronic indexing to clearly identify different notations on transcribing equipment.

Cost:

Dictaphone Corporation

Typewriters

A typewriter is an essential piece of business equipment, and it is not wise to invest in cheap, portable models or unknown brands. You don't have to spend hundreds of dollars — reliable, reconditioned machines of all the better makes are available in major cities. Purchase a sturdy, well-made model that you know can be serviced easily and repaired whenever necessary. *Keep* your typewriter serviced — treat it like your car — and it will last a long time. If you can afford to go for the brand new jobs, consider the three following options. All can be leased on a monthly basis, and lease/purchase arrangements can usually be made.

Selectric 725

One of the best known and proven electric typewriters is the "Selectric." Its main feature, of course, is the interchangeable golf-ball type head. A versatile and durable machine, it is built to last for years. It is a fast machine, and incorporates many of the features that are now standard on other typewriters of similar calibre. Selectrics are also available from dealers in factory-reconditioned order — a somewhat less expensive, but not appreciably less good, option.

Model 725 is the medium-expensive, fabric ribbon model with the largest of the three carriage lengths to accommodate paper up to 15" wide. Choice of typestyles, 10 or 12 pitch spacing, and a selection of keyboard arrangements. 37 lbs., and widely available.

Cost: $675.00

IBM Corporation

Vantage

This new design response to the Selectric is a compact portable electric golfball typewriter designed by Olivetti. Only three companies produce golfball machines — IBM, Remington, and Smith-Corona, who owns the US rights to this Olivetti model. Vantage's golfball is mounted like the IBM's, but with a moving carriage rather than a moving ball. Otherwise it offers essentially the same features as the Selectric, but weighs less, is less expensive, and more gracefully designed. 24½ lb. Widely available.

Cost: $350.00

SCM Corporation

QYX

QYX is a very sophisticated office machine similar in some ways to IBM's memory typewriter. The significant difference is that its modular design allows features such as memory, text editing, storage diskettes, electronic display, and coupling units to computers to be "added" at a later date. If your business is likely to expand fast, and you want to make sure you have word processing equipment when the time comes, the basic QYX, level 1, includes all the conventional features plus push-button typestyle change, proportional spacing, and automatic recall of frequently used formats. It is an electronic machine with an electromagnetic print wheel that floats on a magnetic force field.

Cost: $1390.00

Qyx Systems

IBM Selectric

Qyx

SCM Vantage

The Electronic Calculator

It used to be that even if you weren't good at math, you would at least have to master a slide rule of some sort. But today the venerable slide rule has become a scientific relic in the electronic era that has produced its successor, the calculator. The electronic calculating machine can do everything the slide rule can do and more. Even matheatics can be found to be a creative experience once you've learned to really play with these classic examples of micro-circuitry. They have become so inexpensive nowadays that it is foolish to be without one, even if you have no use for it! At least ten companies manufacture large ranges of electronic calculators, so there is an impressive variety of the little beasts available at all prices.

Divisumma

A masterfully designed electronic calculating machine from Olivetti with print-out, available in a mains or battery-operated version. The keyboard is made of flexible plastic and is totally dust and water proof. Results are printed on special metal-finished paper by means of a nonimpact mechanism which runs at high speed with no noise.
Cost: $72.00

Olivetti of America

Canon Calculators

Canon has a particularly well-designed series of calculators, and we've selected four of their less specialized units, ranging from a low-cost print-out machine (it always helps to have a print-out, especially with typographic calculations) to a handy pocket-size version.
Costs: P10D, with print-out: $92.92
Canola L813, desk type: $34.00
Multi 8, with visible memory: $30.00
Palmtronic LD-10M2: $25.00

Canon Electronics

Sharp Calculators

All of Sharp's well-designed popular calculators come with LCD display, rather than LED, which makes their read-outs easier on your eyes.
Costs: EL-1163, mini-desk type with print-out: $60.00
EL-8128, slim, pocket-type: $19.00
EL-8130, super-thin, touch-tone, pocket-type: $21.00

Sharp Electronics Corporation

Electronics Supermarket

All of the above calculators, and many more, are available at discounted prices through the Markline mail-order catalog, which also offers some interesting literature on using electronic calculators and understanding solid-state electronics in general.
Cost: Free

Markline Co Inc

Sharp EL 1163

Canon Multi 8

Divisumma

A Telephone Timer

Time spent on the phone
is sometimes a billable item,
although it is not so important in
this regard to the graphics artist
as it is to the attorney or accountant. Consultancy work, however,
is often charged on a time basis;
and a lot of consulting can involve a great deal of time on the
telephone. This little instrument
attaches to the phone and turns
on and off manually, recording
elapsed time in tenths of a
minute up to 100 minutes.
Very useful, especially for
long distance calls.
Cost: $30.00

GRS Instruments Inc

Computer Phobia

In the very near future, small
computers for the office, business, and home will be as common as electronic calculators are
today. The uses of a small computer are limited only by your
imagination. But since this is not
the place to discuss computer
technology in any detail, we will
merely introduce you to the
concept and possibilities.

With the new, compact,
total systems available, there are
no surprises. In fact, you can
operate one efficiently without
any prior computer experience.
A good system never "grows
old," as new modules can be
added to update and expand your
equipment usage and power.
They operate like typewriters
and many programs require
no special programming.

You can use a computer for
all manner of business functions:
composing and editing letters,
storing data and information,
estimating production costs,
maintaining your financial journals and ledgers, producing
invoices and statements, com-
puting typographical specifications, regulating heat and light,
and figuring taxes. In between
jobs you can play a variety of
complex and sophisticated
games such as TREK-80, where
your starship takes on a whole
fleet of Klingons.

Computers are getting
cheaper all the time, and it's
worthwhile learning just how
useful one could be in your
work. There are Computer Educational Centers springing up all
over the place, and special retail
shops, or Byte Shops, which will
also help you find out how to
live with computers.

Among others, we rec-
ommend the popular and eco-
monic TRS 80 computer — four
systems that begin with the
basic Level I 4K unit ($499.00).
All systems are infinitely expand-
able, and Level II 16K is an ideal,
low-cost system to start off with.
Cost: $849.00

Radio Shack

Getting Involved With Your Own Computer: A Guide for Beginners
[Leslie Solomon and
Stanley Veit]

If you are nervous about all
this technology, as many people
are, read this book before going
further in exploring computers.
It is written in an easily understood style and presupposes little
knowledge of real mathematics,
logic, or electronics on the
reader's part. The book begins
with an introduction to data
processing and concludes with
a list of suggestions for using
and enjoying your own personal
machine. It effectively demysti-
fies computer systems, principles, and software, and most
of the small computer systems
are described in sufficient depth
so that a beginner can narrow
his or her search to an appropriate range of equipment.
Cost: $9.95

Ridley Enslow Publishers

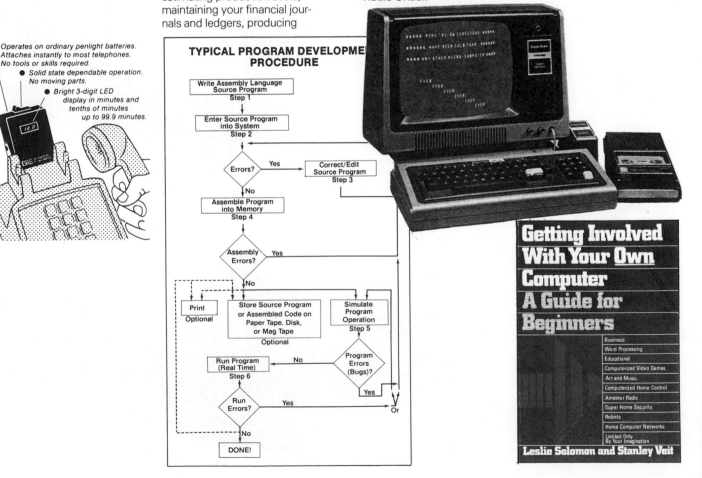

- Operates on ordinary penlight batteries.
  Attaches instantly to most telephones.
  No tools or skills required.
- Solid state dependable operation.
  No moving parts.
- Bright 3-digit LED
  display in minutes and
  tenths of minutes
  up to 99.9 minutes.

TYPICAL PROGRAM DEVELOPMENT PROCEDURE

Write Assembly Language
Source Program
Step 1

Enter Source Program
into System
Step 2

Errors? — Yes → Correct/Edit
Source Program
Step 3

No

Assemble Program
into Memory
Step 4

Assembly
Errors? — Yes

No

Print
Optional

Store Source Program
or Assembled Code on
Paper Tape, Disk,
or Mag Tape
Optional

Simulate
Program
Operation
Step 5

Program
Errors
(Bugs)?

Run Program
(Real Time)
Step 6 — No

Yes

Run
Errors? — Yes

No

Or

DONE!

**Getting Involved
With Your Own
Computer
A Guide for
Beginners**

Business
Word Processing
Educational
Computerized Video Games
Art and Music
Computerized Home Control
Amateur Radio
Super Home Security
Robots
Home Computer Networks
Limited Only
By Your Imagination

Leslie Solomon and Stanley Veit

The Portfolio

The easiest, most efficient way to deal with a portfolio is to secure representation by an agent of good repute in your vicinity. Obtaining such service is not so easy, however. You can be fairly certain that good agents will be extremely particular about whom they choose to represent, and ordinarily will have far too many clients before they ever set eyes on you anyway. Moreover, it is wise for *you* to be choosey about letting someone represent you. Once you're established, of course, your need for an agent's services will diminish. That is the time you will find it easiest to secure the representation you want. Getting an agent is the graphic artist's version of the union card blues: You can't get into the union without a union job, and you can't get a union job until you're a member of the union. Still, thousands of people have figured out the system, so there's no reason you can't do as well.

Initially, you'll have to represent yourself and/or your company. Most graphic artists find this to be a most hateful chore. Nonetheless, how you present yourself and your portfolio to your prospective clients will make a lot of difference in the quality and quantity of jobs you obtain. These days many art colleges and local guilds offer instruction on the best way to show a portfolio. It is worth your time to look into such courses.

For their own convenience, many agents prefer to see your work on 35mm transparencies, presented on a carousel. That's a practical method both for large items, such as illustrations, and for delicate original art such as technical drawings. But few clients are equipped to view transparencies, and the classic carrying case portfolio is the most expedient way to carry your representative efforts. Alternatively, you can seal printed samples in clear plastic, and carry them in a square briefcase-type portfolio.

Florette Leather Goods

A complete range of good-quality leather portfolios that will stand up to the considerable wear and tear they are bound to receive. Florette, suppliers to many art supply stores, will also make portfolios to order if you have special requirements.

Cost: Artist portfolios: from $25.00 to $78.00

Presentation cases: from $48.00 to $110.00

Florette Leather Goods Corp

Zero Halliburton Briefcase

Most good luggage stores will carry this aluminum case which is extremely hard wearing. Inside the rugged aluminum shell it is lined with black leatherette, with a large lap desk, flexible divider and document pockets. The extra deep interior serves well for carrying artwork, pads, samples and even a camera. Comes with combination lock and positive stay-closed catches.
Size: 13" x 18" x 5½".
Cost: $140.00

Sam Flax

Zero Halliburton

Rigid FX Carrying Case

The basic, unadorned, durable, black fibre case with metal reinforcements on each corner. An inexpensive, black box in four sizes that has heavy-duty latches, metal studs on the bottom and web interior fastener. 3" deep.
Cost: $28.15 (20" x 26")

Flax's

Canvas Portfolio

A series of heavy-duty cotton canvas portfolios that are water repellent, reinforced with straps along the sides and with a reinforced bottom. Double-stitched handles with leather grips, and heavy-duty zippers. Available in four color combinations and four sizes.
Cost: $26.50 (20" x 26")

National Specialty Manufacturing Co

Rigid FX case

Canvas portfolio

The Journal / Diary

The diary is a crucial little piece of "equipment" that serves a multitude of uses. It is fundamental in organizing both yourself and your business.

Write it down. Expenses, appointments, phone numbers, names, everything. You need to have a book especially designed for the professional, a book that looks serious and won't get lost easily. The best of all diaries, the Continental A4 size Architects and Designers Diary, is imported from England. Apart from the pages of useful data in front, it divides each week across a two-page spread, and includes sections for notes, appointments, times, and costs. It comes hard-bound with a page marker, and is simply and elegantly designed.

Cost: $11.00

Inter / Graph Ltd

Graphic 365

A bold calendar for the studio, a popular standard for designers because of its functional simplicity. The large black Helvetica letters and numbers on stark white suit most settings with its dramatic elegance. Twelve sheets, 45" x 32", bound with three metal eyelets for hanging.

Cost: $12.50

Universe Books

Professional Reference Annuals

Apart from the Yellow Pages, there are regional and national annual publications that list all the professional services in your area. One or more of these listings can prove an invaluable aid in helping you find what you need in a hurry.

The Creative Black Book

Known as the "Survival Manual," especially in the advertising business, this is a national listing of all professional services divided into sixteen categories; each category is subdivided into geographic regions. Listings are free to all major suppliers, and the book also contains many pages of high-quality advertising. It is probably the most complete and widely used directory of creative services anywhere. Its 14,000 listings include paper samples, printers, retouchers, optical labs, typographers, ad agencies, hotels, and a 1936 Stearman radial-engine byplane. A very useful tool.

Cost: $17.50

Friendly Publications Inc

RSVP

An annual collection of sample work from participating illustrators, designers, and photographers, RSVP began as the collective portfolio of the graduating students of Pratt Institute. Nowadays, it is open to all, and has become a representative portfolio of graphic art of a high standard. RSVP circulates to art buyers in advertising, publishing, design groups, and corporate departments.

RSVP is selective, and representation is limited to one page per person. RSVP supplementary services are similar to those offered by a personal representative. It's mailed to a selected and up-to-date list of buyers and offers a 24-hour, seven-day-a-week answering service for anyone included in the book. A follow up and referral service at 10% commission is offered and copies will be mailed to your own mailing list at no extra charge. RSVP will also make available 500 or so reprints of your page for a nominal fee.

The cost of inclusion in the book ranges from $125 for black and white to $250 for full color. Two-page spreads are available where necessary. RSVP will only accept same-size camera-ready art or transparencies. There is also a technical services section of listings at $25 per entry. Deadline is July 7.

RSVP

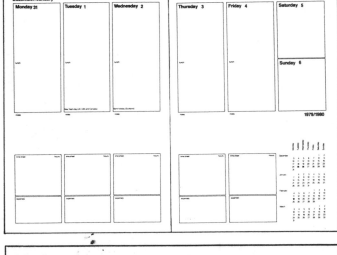

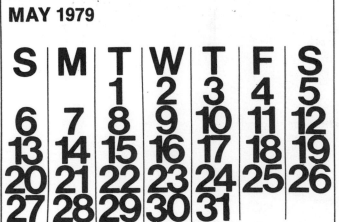

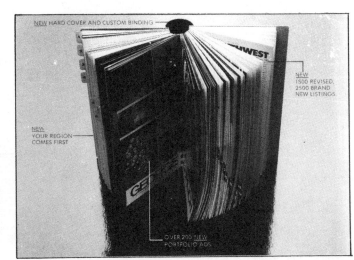

The Graphic Artists Guild Directory

Now that the Guild has gone national (see "Living by Design," p.193), this directory circulates all over the country, free to members. Designed with the art buyer in mind, it features examples of members' work. At present, it is fairly limited in concept; but as the Guild grows in numbers and strength it may become absolutely essential. Local chapters of the Guild put out their own directories and planning calendars.

Graphic Artists Guild

Creative Director

The West Coast is served by its own version of the Black Book whose 150 categories list all the creative services you may need in that geographic area. Unlike the Black Book, however, listings are not free: they begin at $15.00. Otherwise the format is essentially the same. Similar regional directories are now appearing across the county in major cities.

Cost: $16.00 (includes one free listing).

Creative Director

Washington Creative Services

No longer a small town, the Washington, D.C. area is burgeoning, and so is its creative industry with work from government, associations, businesses, plus others. A new "Directory of Washington Creative Services" offers a representation of services and their scale with six major categories including photographics, graphics, A-V, writing and editorial, graphic arts suppliers and adjacent services, plus models.

Cost: $16.50

Directory of Washington Creative Services

Artist's Market

Rather than listing talents and services, this annually revised volume lists potential graphic clients. Through the use of questionnaires, each listing describes the services he or she needs, the quantity of such services used, contact addresses and phone numbers, and so forth. The book is especially full with listings of periodical publishers, and contains information about hundreds of competitions and galleries. It is also used extensively by amateurs, however, and some of the information supplied by buyers may be suspect; so use a little caution when reviewing the information.

Cost: $12.00

Writers Digest Books

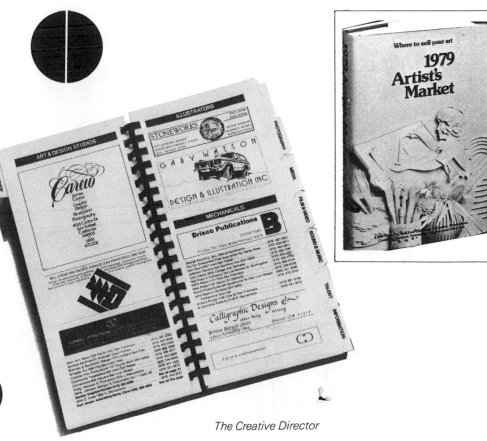

The Creative Director

F

The US Postal Service

We are all familiar with the Federal Post Office and its amazing array of regulations, constantly increasing rates, and service that never seems to improve. You can save hours of frustration by investing in your own postage scales and buying stamps in bulk. In the unlikely event that your business warrants one, get a franking machine.

The Post Office is undergoing a series of classification changes designed to speed the flow of the mail, and in 1978 it introduced the first of these: new standard maximum and minimum sizes for mail. Envelopes less than ¼" thick that are less than 3.5" high and 5" long are not accepted. Any other sizes that do not conform to their template guidelines are subject to a surcharge.

A useful manual of postal information, including rates and fees, indexed and cross-indexed, is available from several paper and envelope manufacturers, and is much easier to comprehend than the array of information sheets provided by the US Postal Service.

Cost: Free

Envelope Manufacturers Association

Delivery Services

Speedy delivery of work to or from trade service suppliers, and to or from clients, is sometimes the name of our game. All large metropolitan areas have several local messenger services (San Francisco has 40 of them), and it is wise to establish an account with one or more in your region. They are all listed in local Yellow Pages, and usually operate 24 hours a day, seven days a week. The Yellow Pages also list, under Messengers, all the long distance and air courier services in your area.

For long distance parcels, the major airlines offer small package express services with pick up and delivery. Principal long distance delivery services include Air Couriers International, Air Express International, Skycab, Emery Airfreight, Federal Express, Rocket, and UPS. The success of private delivery services has encouraged the US Postal Service to institute one of its own rare advances: "express mail" service which guarantees delivery in under 12 hours.

Become familiar with your local delivery options, find out which is best at delivering what, and to where; then, when panic strikes, you will know exactly how to deal with it.

Express Mail

The US Postal Service's next day delivery guarantee (or same day delivery in metropolitan areas) has proven extremely reliable so far. The USPS claims 95% of express mail shipments arrive on time. If the service fails to deliver on time, they offer a full refund, though the time and trouble it costs you to obtain that refund can be considerable. Express mail accepts anything up to 70 lb., with a limit on the package dimensions. Rates are determined by weight and the distance the parcel travels, and must be delivered to main post offices only, whether for local delivery or for pick up. The US Postal Service supplies a directory of all major post offices.

Cost: $5.40-$50.75, post office to post office
$7.50-$52.85, post office to addressee

US Postal Service

Federal Express

This highly sophisticated, fast courier delivery system offers four basic services and many combinations for special types of package or freight. The Standard Air Service is essentially a low-cost 48-hour delivery service; Overnight Air Service is door-to-door delivery up to 70 lbs., with guaranteed delivery next day; Courier Pak Service is a door-to-door overnight delivery system for smaller items up to five pounds, and is the most useful service of all. All of Federal's local, national, and international services and rates, discounts, and conditions are contained in their regularly revised brochure which is, in effect, a magazine.

Cost: $9.04-$82.74 (Standard Air Service)
$19.51-$82.11 (Overnight Air Service)
$16 or $22, with quantity discounts (Courier Pak)

Federal Express

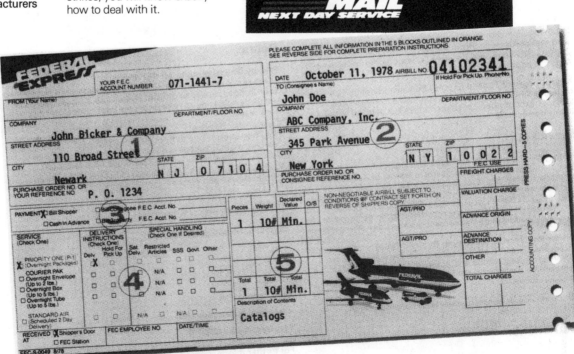

The Facsimile Connection

As the US Postal Service becomes more and more bogged down, and private mail carriers begin to reappear, the need for the electronic mail network becomes obvious. Now that some international standards have been agreed to, electronic equipment is being designed to be compatible with existing computer networks. The days of instant facsimile transmission of visual and verbal data have arrived — the cost per "fax" transmission is already down to $148. As the technology improves, with the use of fibre optics and satellites, the cost of both hardware and software will decrease significantly, usage will increase, and the momentum will have us all using the local "Fax" center, or installing our own equipment. Xerox already operates such centers, but as yet there is no small equipment we would recommend until we see how it all shakes out.

Books on Tape

Part of any business is driving, unless you live in Manhattan where that's the last thing you want to do. Whether going to or from the studio, making a delivery, or visiting clients and suppliers, you are going to spend some hours in the car with a small part of your mind driving, and a larger part endlessly going over the anxious details of personal and professional problems. The radio is often an annoying imposition.

Some people have discovered a more interesting and edifying activity to complement their hours on the road: books on tape — rented cassettes of all those books you never seem to have time to read. If you don't have an in-dash cassette player you can use a portable, which will also plug into your car's cigarette lighter. Once you get into Books on Tape, you can go on with plays, radio shows, etc., which may be available on tape from your local library.

Cost: $7.00-$8.00 per month

Books on Tape

Rent-a-Wreck

A whole new breed of car rental company has sprung up lately, simplifying the process of getting a car to drive when you cannot or do not want to use your own. For those who don't like to own cars, renting an old clunker that works fine is a wonderful alternative to Hertz, and cheaper too. These old-car companies, Rent-A-Heap-Cheap, Lease-A-Lemon, Rent-A-Wreck, and so on, will rent you the car of your choice for about $9 a day with 100 free miles and 10¢ a mile overage. You must be over 21, but then all you need is your driver's license and $100 deposit. Unlike the main car rental places, these folks accept cash.

From old Rolls-Royces to pick-up trucks, all cheap-rent vehicles are cared for to the extent that their brakes, lights, and steering are in good repair, despite their dents, scratches, and peeling paint. And, of course, you never know what will be on the lot to choose from.

Cost: $9.00 per day; $70.00 per week

Check your local Yellow Pages

Living by Design

You are now involved with the graphic design profession which is defined in the Introduction to this book. Apart from the immediate concerns of getting work, establishing yourself and your reputation, and earning a living, you have an ongoing need to learn as much as you can about the workings of the design world. Most of this education can only result from experience.

But experience can be short-circuited. There are professional organizations, clubs, and guilds set up specifically for educational purposes, all of which can make your professional life easier. They offer a kind of professional support, as well as information when you are faced with legal problems, costing and fee dilemmas, or clients who don't seem to understand what the hell "design" is, and do not see the need to pay for it.

Every area of the country has its Art Directors Clubs, Advertising Clubs, Design Associations, and, more importantly, local chapters of the national Graphic Artists Guild. Formerly based in New York, the Graphic Artists Guild has spread its wings to the far reaches of the Pacific Coast and has proved to be an authoritative force in promoting the graphic arts as a legitimate profession. (For further information on non-guild clubs and professional design-related organizations, see Section G.)

By Linda Xiques

Logo design for the publisher of this book

F

The Last Profession to Organize

 The main goal in forming local guilds with a national coordinating body is to improve the lot of the graphic artist to the point where his rights are understood and are on a par with those of other professionals. We're practically the last profession to organize—actors, musicians, lawyers and doctors, even the person who cuts your hair has an organization. It's an exciting time to be involved in this effort.

The tradition of guilds goes back to medieval times. In the 11th Century, guilds of craftsmen formed in England to protect the standards and integrity of their skills and art. Pension plans, insurance (of a sort), apprenticeshlps, and manufacturing regulations were integral parts of the guild benefits. The way we operate today is to offer the benefits package that works best for our constituency. This includes insurance, legal assistance, business contacts, and a credit union as some of the tangibles . . .

Even though the tradition of guilds has continued in Europe for centuries, it has not been firmly established in the United States; the closest we come to 'guild' is 'professional labor organization' so that's our official status with the government. We're not a union, we're a guild. Guilds are for professionals as unions are for laborers and other employed persons.

The way we try to change things is through negotiation, education—forthright persuasion if you will. We represent a *lot* of graphic artists so art buyers *do* listen to us. It's the power of the numbers we represent that we use as a tool, and the will of the majority of our membership that tells us what needs changing.

Guild membership is mostly free-lance, although we encourage staff artists to join. We eventually want to represent about half and half. Of course, it seems more free-lancers have felt burnt by the profession so it's logical that they join with less hesitation.

—Debbie Holland, Associate Director of the Graphic Artists Guild Naitonal Board. Extracted from an interview by Peter Kunz in the Graphic Artists Guild *Newsletter,* October 1978.

Why You Need a Guild

There are some basic advantages to being an individual working as a graphic artist. Your style is unique, you make your own decisions, you create your own lifestyle and your own work. But there are also some disadvantages to remaining isolated as a professional. The Guild, representing thousands of graphic artists, can approach art buyers and ask them to reconsider their policies. It can affect legislation, and can back you up on prices, ethics, and business procedures. It can supply much needed information about the rapidly changing circumstances of your profession.

In the larger sense, the Guild influences and promotes the integrity of the graphics profession, which has, in the past, been known for its isolation. The presence of the Guild encourages more open communications among its members, and also has effected some significant changes in the business ethics that apply to designers in general.

The continued growth of the communications industry is bound to strengthen the Guild. By bringing together those who produce art, the Guild becomes a consortium that regulates supply—a position of great power in any industry.

The Graphic Artists Guild is the only organization to form a not-for-profit *labor* group for graphic artists in the US. All other graphic groups in the country are educational, and legally limited in their activities to technical and creative areas only; that is, they are required to be charitable and philanthropic. However, within the national context, many of these other groups are affiliating with the Graphic Artists Guild, and offer joint membership and services.

The Guild is divided into major professional disciplines:

General Illustration
Advertising Illustration
Book Illustration
Technical Illustration
Comp Illustration
Fashion Illustration
Trade Publication Illustration
Medical Illustration
General Graphic Design
Book Design
Textile Design
Point of Purchase
Lettering
Audio-Visual Graphics
Photography
Product Design
Book Jacket Design
Retouching
Cartoons
TV-Story Boards
Mechanicals

Regular membership means an income of more than $7500; provisional membership means an income of less than $7500 and is allowed for two years only; student membership is for those who have not yet entered into the profession.

Cost: $75.00 (regular); $45.00(provisional); $20.00 (student). The cost is reduced if you are already a member of an affiliated organization.

The Graphic Artists Guild

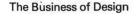

ARTISTS IN PRINT MEETING

AT LAST—
TWO YEARS IN THE MAKING—
THOUSANDS OF CHARACTERS—

GRAPHIC ARTS CONTRACTS

Credo

"A graphic artist is any person engaged or employed in the creation or production of original creative works of art intended for graphic presentation either as originals or reproductions. The term "artist" as used in this document means graphic artist as so defined. Creative works of graphic art include, without limiting, pictorial designs, drawings and painted or photographic illustrations.

Graphic artists are professionals since they are engaged in work requiring individual creative effort applied through highly developed skills and negotiate fees and prices, individually, for their work.

Graphic artists are entitled to a professional fee for consultation and services separate from, in conjunction with, or in addition to a price for the selected product(s) of their services.

As individual professionals, graphic artists are entitled to receive name credit for their work.

Graphic artists are entitled to share in the continuing economic interest derived from the additional use or resale of the products of their services.

Graphic artists are entitled to payment without unreasonable delay and to premium compensation when extraordinary service is required or requested.

Graphic artists have the right to declare, change, and/ or negotiate collectively, the minimum monetary value of their professional services and the products thereof.

The graphic art's profession is the business, concern and responsibility of the individual artist. The Guild is the collective instrument which oversees the rights and responsibilities of the artists to each other and their profession.

The Graphic Artists Guild represents graphic artists, regardless of the nature of their employment, and seeks and claims the right to negotiate on their behalf in any circumstances relating to their professional services.

The Graphic Artists Guild intends to benefit all graphic artists, their agents and representatives, and clients, and to serve all of its members in every way beneficial to them and to their profession."

—The Graphic Artists Guild

Business Seminars

Most design professionals, especially beginners, could use specific advice and guidance in the business of design. The Graphic Artists Guild has initiated ongoing workshops on important topics such as running your business, pricing, copyrights, promotion, accounting, complex contracts, leases, insurance, and representatives. The service, offered to members and non-members alike, is particularly relevant to young professionals. The first seminar, at the end of 1978, was an outstanding success. It emphasized that we must realize that as graphic artists we are in a *business,* and won't get a fair shake until we learn our rights and obligations within that business. These essential workshops are given throughout the country under the auspices of local Guild chapters. They are having considerable impact, instilling a sense of solidarity and confidence among participants, and encouraging an end to what has been a period of exploitation by the communications industries.

Cost: $55.00 (members); $65.00(non-members).

The Graphic Artists Guild

Pricing and Ethical Guidelines

This handbook, in its third edition, is the only comprehensive guide to fair business practices in every area of the graphic arts. It was compiled by practicing artists who are authorities in their special areas, and constitutes the set of standards officially accepted and adhered to by the Graphic Artists Guild — standards the Guild feels should guide practices throughout the graphic arts industry. It contains concise sections on purchase orders and contracts, sales tax, and copyright. An indispensable tool for all graphic artists, and free with membership to the Guild.

Cost: $8.00 (additional copies $5.50 to GAG members)

Graphic Artists Guild

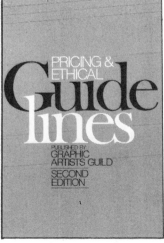

The Graphic Artists Guild Newsletter

Inspired by the Artists In Print group of San Francisco, the Graphic Artists Guild of New York now produces a large-format tabloid of at least 12 pages regularly every two months. It is virtually the only publication in the country to concern itself with the practical problems of being an artist in the commercial world. Information is collected from all over the country with some reference to international concerns, covering the topical news, features on matters of professional interest, an ethics column, reports on grievances being handled by the Guild, legal and tax advice, and business and technical information, all tailored to the needs of the free-lance designer. It is definitely an advocacy journal, with a very specific point of view.

Many regional guilds also offer their own local newsletters to members; and the national guild newsletter is available free to those members who also belong to GAG.

Cost: $1.00 donation (free to GAG members)

Graphic Artists Guild East or West

Joint Ethics Committee

This is the umbrella organization that offers mediation and arbitration services in any dispute that may arise between a buyer and producer of artwork. The Committee is composed of representatives of The Art Directors Club, Society of Illustrators, The Graphic Artists Guild, American Society of Magazine Photographers, and the Society of Photographers and Artists Representatives.

The Joint Ethics Committee bases its actions on the widely recognized Code of Fair Practice, and has long since passed its 20th year of operation and its 1000th case.

The two procedures, mediation and arbitration, have been proved both useful and popular with all segments of the communications industry, and to date, every award suggested by the Committee through arbitration has been honored. The Committee's Code has been cited as legal precedent.

The Committee also offers legal advice on contracts, copyright, bill collecting, and similar matters, and while it has neither judicial nor police powers, its prestige has made it a highly respected board. Examples of the cases with which it deals are published regularly in *Art Direction,* and full details of the workings of the Joint Ethics Committee are available in their booklet that includes the current Code of Fair Practice.

Cost: $1.25

Joint Ethics Committee

Local Guilds—An Example

Local branches of the national Guild now exist in Atlanta, Detroit, Honolulu, Los Angeles, Miami, Nashville, Portland, Greensboro, St. Louis, and Sacramento. Their recent appearance is just the beginning of a comprehensive national organization.

The best example of such a Local is San Francisco's Artists In Print (AIP), a non-profit "educational" organization formed in 1975 by a group of young designers in response to a high incidence of client rip-offs—non-payment for services rendered. Their intention was to establish ethics and standards of fair practice among the local graphic artists, and, by acting in concert, to generate a higher degree of professionalism for both graphic artists and clients alike.

Within three years, AIP became sufficiently well organized to suggest affiliating with the Graphic Artists Guild. The West Coast group adoped the national organization's ethical guidelines and legal aid service, and continued to put most of its energy into local educational efforts. They now sponsor an impressive list of seminars and programs dealing with such topics as apprenticeship, copyright law, taxes, business procedures, professionalism and creativity, and fee scales. They also run workshops in graphic communications, and provide a medical insurance program and job referral service.

AIP publishes a regular bi-monthly tabloid, *Graphiti,* and an annual Directory & Planning Calendar which is circulated among graphics buyers. It organizes 15-week "Survival Workshops" twice a year for the development of special skills of a very high order, and promotes a Community Service Program. It even issues its own certificates for those who pass its test in skills and knowledge of production for print.

For information about the guild nearest you, contact the Graphic Artists Guild, New York or San Francisco (see appendix).

Cost of membership: $20.00-$40.00 per annum

Artists in Print

Artists in Print

BALA and The Working Arts

Currently, the exemplary Bay Area Lawyers for the Arts (BALA) is the only bar association in the United States dedicated to caring for the legal needs of writers, artists, designers, and performers. During 1978 its flexible-cost referral service (free to full-rate, depending on the artist's income) handled some 1500 cases through a panel of distinguished attorneys and dedicated BALA staff.

Founded by Hamish Standison, who recently left BALA to direct a similar program for the British Government's Artlaw Project, BALA deals with all the legal problems that confront artists from copyright and contracts through nonprofit incorporation, royalty questions, and issues of basic law. BALA offers an Arbitration and Mediation Program as an alternative to the court system, and conducts legal research on artists' rights, pending and proposed legislation, and other arts law issues. The group publishes a bi-monthly newsletter, *The Working Arts,* as well as a series of low cost guides, among them "Tax and The Individual Artist," and a complete selection of books on more complicated arts law subjects such as copyright. Their educational services include conferences, seminars, and courses for both artists and attorneys.

As a non-profit organization receiving minimal funds from the State of California, BALA relies on its membership fees to pay for advocacy work, and members receive benefits and discounts whose range depends on their category of membership.

Cost of membership: from $10.00 (student) to $250.00 (patron)

Bay Area Lawyers for the Arts

Legal Guide for the Visual Artist
[Tad Crawford]

This is the best handbook available on its subject, dealing with the full range of legal problems of the visual artist: the new copyright law; general rights of artists; sales by art galleries; artists and agents; reproduction rights; publishing and dealer contracts; and model contracts. It includes listings of all artists' organizations; organizations for the arts; state agencies and lawyers; and groups which assist artists, and is free to all members of the Graphic Artists Guild.

Cost: $9.95 (additional copies $6.50 to GAG members)

Hawthorn Books

Affordable Necessary Legal Help

❝You probably think that the right time to call in a lawyer is when you've got a serious problem. Unfortunately, by then it is often too late and/or too expensive to take legal action. The right time to get advice is up front—when you're making a deal with a client, when a few minutes of guidance will save you future trouble and losses. Admittedly, in getting advance legal advice you incur an expense. "Who can afford it," you might ask. There may however be an artist/lawyer financial arrangement any professional can afford. The problem is how much does such legal advice cost? Our office has developed a plan which can hopefully be adapted, in part, for use by other legal establishments.

As you know, legal fees in general can be quite high. This is especially true in complex areas involving artists' rights, such as "copyright" and "intangible property rights." In large urban areas, such as New York, Los Angeles and San Francisco, specialists in these fields may command $60 to $125 per hour, in large measure fees attributable to skyrocketing overhead expenses for professional offices.

In deference to the financial position of most illustrators and designers, our office is attempting to deliver legal services in the range of $45 to $60 per hour during a one year experimental period. As a particular accommodation to the Graphic Artists Guild and the Society of Illustrators, members of those organizations will be charged at the rate of $45 per hour.

But the main problem is probably not the hourly rate. Rather it is the manner in which billings are handled and information conveyed. Specifically, most illustrators and other visual artists rarely have the time or inclination to write out their problem or come in for a consultation. Their attorneys on the other hand cannot afford the paper work of billing them for 10 and 15 minute phone conversations.

Given the above difficulties, our office is offering visual artists two options. Artists may of course continue to use us in the traditional way, consulting on individual matters at the special rates stated above. Or, artists may pay us a $90 fee for a total of two hours worth of consultations, which can often be handled quickly and easily by phone. This second system requires no billing on our part for each individual consultation, thus the price can be kept down. Each phone or office session, plus the recording time, will simply be marked down on the artist's ledger and subtracted from the pre-paid two hours. As a result, the visual artist might have as many as 8 or 12 such brief telephone consultations based on the $90 fee.

This is obviously a variation on the retainer system used in most law offices, but it takes into account that most visual artists are simply unable to pay a regular, substantial monthly retainer, even though most artists often have need of frequent though modest legal services.

Hopefully, other attorneys will see the merit in this advance payment or reserved time system. I'd suggest that if you've been working with an attorney for some time, the two of you might work out an arrangement along the lines of the one described above.

In any event, our office will continue to experiment with techniques for delivering information to the visual arts on an affordable basis. ❞

By Ari Kopelman, from The Graphic Arts Guild *Newsletter,* October 1978

Visual Artists Guide to the New Copyright Law
[Tad Crawford]

When they buy your art, what most clients really want is reproduction rights of one kind or another, not copyright. Nevertheless, the designer or artist frequently discovers after the fact that the publisher has legally obtained *all* rights, either inadvertently or deliberately, and for a relatively small amount of money. Knowing what rights obtain to whom under the new and improved laws is the only way for both artist and client to have a clear understanding about their arrangement.

Written expressly for the Graphic Artists Guild, this booklet is essential for all artists. Readable, practical, and thorough, it carefully explains the new law's pitfalls, including the "work for hire" provisions. It includes discussions about what may be copyright, who benefits from copyright, what the copyright owner's rights are, the proper form of copyright notice and when it must be used, how to protect your copyright, and the advantages of copyright registration. Very enlightening and useful, the booklet is free to all members of the Graphic Artists Guild.

Cost: $5.50 (additional copies $3.50 to GAG members)

Hawthorn Books

Beware the Work for Hire clause

There is a "work for hire" loophole in the new copyright law. If an artist signs a work for hire contract, he or she forfeits the right to charge for re-use or to re-sell the work, and can't even terminate the buyer's rights after 35 years as he/she can under an "all rights" contract. The work for hire provision is supposed to be applicable only to full-time employees or when a free-lance artist is contributing minimally to a collective effort and must be closely supervised.

Obviously, a work for hire contract is unfortunate and unfair because it treats a free-lancer as if he or she were a salaried employee, receiving a regular pay check and fringe benefits. And it, again obviously, flouts the spirit of creators' rights largely protected by the new copyright law.

Since the new law became effective, more and more publishing and production houses have begun to offer work for hire contracts on a take it or leave it basis. In their own defense, publishers claim that they

employ work for hire contracts only when they must closely supervise an artist's work to insure that it conforms to the specifications of the larger project. However, the work for hire clause is turning-up routinely, even when assignments are done in their own style, in their own studios, by a deadline, without special supervision. Some members have been handed *lifetime* work for hire contracts.

Tad Crawford, the lawyer for the Graphic Artists Guild and author of *The Visual Artists' Guide to the New Copyright Law,* indicated that the work for hire loophole would not have crept into the law had artists been among the framers. He expects the process of getting legislators to re-think, re-draft and re-vote a portion of the copyright law to be long and arduous. Legislators will also have to withstand the considerable lobbying apparatus of the publishers and the parent conglomerates by which more of them are now owned and controlled. The Guild has opened a legislative drive and a dialogue with publishing houses.

Watch out for euphemisms publishers are employing, which, when legally translated, still mean "work for hire."

—The Graphic Artists Guild *Newsletter,* December, 1978

"Art Work"

The first employment service for New York City artists working in all disciplines, Art Work placed 200 artists in paying jobs during its first fifteen months of operation. The placement service, funded under CETA I, a federal program, charges neither the artist nor the employer for its services.

Artists have been placed in full-time, part-time, and freelance positions, involving both fine and commercial skills, in such areas as mural painting, gallery work, graphic design and production, illustration, cartooning, silk screening, ceramics, video editing, technical theatre work and musical performance as well as instruction in dance, arts and crafts, etc. Employers include businesses, and community and arts organizations. Applicants must meet CETA eligibility standards of un- or under-employment and low-income level.

The Foundation for Community Artists also publishes *Artworker News* ten times a year.

Cost: $7.00 (10 issues)

The Foundation for Community Artists

Designers and Photographers

Photography plays a large part in design, and photographers have their own professional guild-like organization which provides them with a general set of ethics, business procedures, and pricing guidelines. When planning for photography, all designers should be aware of the ASMP fee schedules and condition of usage, available from the American Society of Magazine Photographers.

Cost: $2.00

American Society of Magazine Photographers

Women in Design

Formed in 1977, Women in Design was organized to bring more women centerstage at the Aspen International Design Conference. With that goal accomplished, WID has become a national organization whose object is to encourage women in the graphic arts professions to take leadership positions. With the overall purpose of enhancing women designers' professional development and awareness among themselves and the world community, WID sponsors seminars, meetings, and scholarships and has compiled a national speakers bureau, a directory of members, a job reference network, and a newsletter.

Their first series of seminars dealt with such topics as, "Do you have to be from New York to be pushy and successful?" "The myths that keep artists starving," "You *do* judge a book by its cover," and "Finding clients and closing in." Membership is open to men and women who earn their livings, or aspire to, in the field of design or in related areas such as writing, filmmaking, crafts and so on.

Cost of membership: $25.00

Women in Design

Living By Design
[Edited by Peter Gorb]

This is one fascinating story of what design is and how it is carried out, which clearly illustrates what it *achieves* by beautifully detailing the *process* of design. The authors and designers of this book are the renowned British partnership, *Pentagram*. They earn their living by design, and spend their time living by design. This is not so much about *Pentagram* but more about their impressive variety of work, and about their belief that design can fulfill both a social function and an economic purpose.

The book makes wonderful reading and viewing for anyone interested in the business or in the general nature of design. But it is directed principally at those who have sympathy for and interest in the subject and would like to know more about the scope of design, the ideas behind its practice, and the ways it is put to work.

Living By Design is divided into five sections devoted to the four major design areas and to *Pentagram* itself, and uses specific examples of *Pentagram's* work to explain its theory and practice of design. Acclaimed throughout Europe and the US, this is essential reading for anyone even loosely associated with design and designers.

Cost: $15.00

Whitney Library of Design, Watson-Guptill Publications

Pentagram product design: British Rail

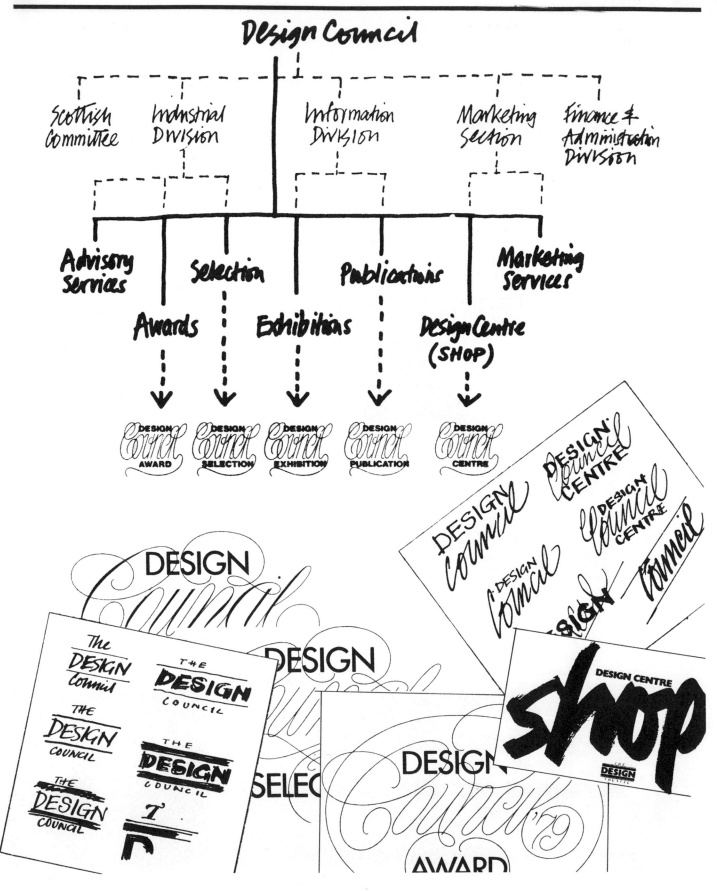

Professional Organizations and
Regular Events

COMPETITION

THE WEST-COAST SHOW, 1978

As long as there has been a cultural community in
the United States, its capital has been New York City.
New York has stood by itself as the center of the country's
most exciting experiments, and most important contributions to music, literature, theatre, and art—
especially the graphic arts.

Today, this is no longer true. While the principal
graphic arts organizations are still located in New York,
and most of the nation's major graphic industry events
take place there, more and more of the important,
award winning design and graphic work is being produced in Boston, Atlanta, Chicago, San Francisco, and
Los Angeles—anywhere, in fact, that has the resources
to attract and engage the graphics and advertising
practitioners.

One demonstration of the trend in graphic arts to
diversify geographically is the increasing prominence of
exhibits, shows, and events occurring on the west coast.
The industry roundup that follows, of the most relevant
graphics organizations and their annual shows, particularly reflects this aspect of the trend.

Our list is necessarily selective, and features only
those organizations and events which relate directly to
graphic artists on a national scale. Because of this, our
list excludes all the local art directors and illustrators
clubs which, on the whole, are locally and socially
orientated, and whose principal contributions to
members of their communities are to encourage intra-
industry contacts, and to sponsor or host important
travelling shows in their regions.

Our list begins with the two most important,
regular events in the design community: the international,
biennial ICOGRADA and the annual design conference
at Aspen, Colorado. While it is not essential for
a designer or illustrator to attend either event, it is
critical to know about them.

It is also important to attend at least one of the
major trade shows each year, since doing so is the only
efficient way to keep in touch with the rapid developments in graphic technology.

ICOGRADA Biennial

The International Council of Graphic Design Associates, formed in London in 1963, convenes every other year in one of the forty-three nations that have member associations. It met once in the United States, in Chicago, in 1978. The ninth biennial, in 1980, will meet in Leipzig, East Germany.

Non-profit and non-political, ICOGRADA's activities are financed entirely by membership fees and profits from sales of its publications. Individual membership is available. ICOGRADA also permits membership by schools, libraries, corporations, and any other institution that has interest in the wide-ranging issues, ideas, concepts, techniques, and methods of international design. Individuals can participate in the biennial through their member organizations, or by registering well in advance at a cost of about $150.

In addition to its congress, ICOGRADA maintains an audio-visual library and archive, sponsors student scholarships, studies and publishes reports on various design topics, consults with UNESCO and the Council of Europe, and maintains working relationships with many international organizations in related fields such as architecture, packaging, and printing.

ICOGRADA has become the established international exchange of design in its broadest sense — international standards, laws, regulations, customs, and other generic and specific subjects are studied and discussed under its auspices.

At the eighth biennial, in Chicago, the congress focused on "Design that Works." It attempted to clarify those factors that contribute to successful and unsuccessful design. The five-day program included a variety of exhibits and professional addresses, and over forty group sessions on a wide range of subjects, including plans to form a US National Design Association similar to the Design Council of the United Kingdom. General sessions were devoted to four case studies of design projects that failed: the Washington, DC Subway Sign Program, *Sesame Street* magazine, the British Columbia Provincial Museum Exhibition, and the Georges Pompidou Center Public Communications Program.

Considering aesthetics *vs.* function, or why design projects fail, the consensus was reached that function should take precedence over beauty, that "design that works" is design that does its job — preferably with imagination — and, correlatively, that simplicity is beautiful.

The general conclusion this particular congress reached was that national graphic design organizations are both needed and wanted. Key areas of interest for such an organization appear to be the promotion of public awareness of graphic design; raising professional standards; licensing; and improving communications among existing organizations. These findings confirmed a trend that had already surfaced in the United States.

The International Design Conference in Aspen

Every year, the design conference at Aspen seems to be more successful and relevant than the previous year's event; and now the Aspen conference is working toward becoming the second most important international design forum.

In the past, this rather informal and free ranging get together has been called a whimsical, though popular, multi-disciplinary talk-in. Although the Aspen conference has tightened its focus lately, it still speaks to the experience and nature of design, rather than the facts and procedures of design; and therein lies its unique appeal.

Aspen has rediscovered the pleasures of a design conference which concentrates on design and designing. Its last three conference themes have been "Shop Talk" (the actual business of designing), "Making Connections" (the interface between people and people, and between people and things), and "Japan In Aspen," focusing entirely on one nation, its people, and its culture.

The overriding style of the five-day IDCA event is participatory and informal. One conference includes seminars, discussion groups, forums, exhibits and presentations, feedback talks, film programs, and retrospectives; the schedules are delightfully eclectic and full of surprises. This most worthwhile international annual event always takes place in Aspen, Colorado.

Registration costs $250 (additional guest $125), and does not include food or lodging. Cassette tapes are available of the conference highlights.

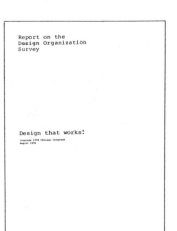

Report on the
Design Organization
Survey

Design that works!

Icograda 1978 Chicago Congress
August 1978

ICOGRADA
3-7 AUG
CHICAGO

JAPAN
in
ASPEN

A Deliberate Effort to Get Away From Nuts and Bolts

"The Aspen conference is a direct outgrowth of Walter Paecpke's (Container Corporation of America) interest in art and design. It began in 1951, when Paecpke initiated a dialogue to convince business leaders that good design was good business, and that they should pay attention to the design process.

For its first few years Aspen's theme was "Design as a Function of Management." But it wasn't long before the conference participants outgrew this modest interest and became fascinated, not just with how *industry* hinges on design, but how design is related to all life, the world, and the future of humanity. Today, the conference is concerned with the long-term aspects of cultural and environmental design.

The first time I was invited as a speaker, in 1966, the theme was "Sources and Resources in Twentieth Century Design," and I was there to talk about human potentialities, as I did again in 1970. I'm a psychologist by trade, and at that time I wasn't the least bit interested in design, except architecture. But I made so many friends at those conferences that I began to think of design in larger and larger terms.

In trying to understand human fears, I've been expanding from the individual to the constellations of groups; to the organization of the system. I got to the point where I could no longer tell where the human system fuses with the physical world, and that led me to social design. I assume it was that interest that resulted in my being asked to join the Board of the Aspen Conference.

In our efforts to come to grips with the issues that designers would find worth addressing, we arranged a mixed bag of speakers from many diverse professions, with industry still represented, along with scientists, writers, artists, philosophers and members of all the design professions.

There's no party line or philosophy—the themes are kept deliberately loose, so we leave ourselves open to do all kinds of things. But the fact that we can choose an open-ended theme, and actually build a program around it, and persuade a lot of designers to attend, may in fact raise the consciousness of designers overall. Themes like "The Rest of Our Lives" are full of futurism; and that, I think, makes designers feel differently about what they are doing, about being responsible.

Philosopher Hans Jonas has a way of talking about this. He says,"it's no longer possible to be good without being knowledgeable;" that it *used* to be possible to be good by following fundamental principles, but now, because of technology and the invisible effects of what you do, it is necessary to be increasingly knowledgeable about what those effects might be, and to be able to operate morally, ethically.

Design is not a neutral process. It is not just a matter of taste anymore, it's a matter of moral judgement. Whenever you design an ad for an automobile or a cigarette, or a middle-class ghetto, you are making a statement that is going to have ramifications well beyond any particular intent you may have had for the tasteful design that you put forth.

Who you work for, and why, and how you work for them, are all matters of serious import to the designer. And essentially those are the questions that are addressed at the conference. Thus, we'd have speakers like Bobby Seale, Rene DuBois, or Bucky Fuller talking about events that impinge on design decisions, saying things that designers can translate into their own work and lives. Ours is a deliberate attempt to get away from the nuts and bolts in order to deal with the broader problems of design: what is the role of a designer with respect to women? To education? To the social problem of growth?

The Aspen Conference is still a little provincial, but we are moving away from that rapidly. It's called the International Design Conference, and a lot of our guests are from abroad. We have begun to take the conference elsewhere, in mini-form, after the event. We went to London last year for a joint conference with the Society of Industrial Designers and the Royal Institute of British Architects. It went extremely well. We had a similar success in Oslo [1979] at the conference with Scandinavian designers. Our 1979 conference was devoted to Japan, and how Japan and the West—particularly the United States—continue to influence and change one another."

—from an interview with Richard Farson, President of the Board of Directors, *International Design Conference in Aspen*

The AIGA

The American Institute of Graphic Arts is the oldest and most prestigious graphic arts organization in the country. The AIGA addresses itself to an extremely diverse professional membership involved in the various disciplines of graphic design: books, illustrations, advertising, exhibitions, packaging, promotion, and corporate graphics.

The Institute, a rich resource of professional information and ideas, is an open university for the continuing education of professionals, and is also a training ground for students. It sponsors six major competitive exhibitions a year, for which all members are eligible. The exhibitions — or idea exchanges — are open to the public at the large AIGA gallery in New York, which also holds ongoing individual shows of contemporary interest. These exhibitions travel throughout the United States and abroad. The AIGA maintains a slide show archive of all exhibits, which is available for travel, and publishes a catalog of each show.

The AIGA calendar of events includes six Plant Tours a year to study innovative and advanced technologies in the graphics business, and five Book Clinics — plus special clinics for students — in design and technology at evening seminars. Each year the Institute honors a distinguished member of the graphics profes-

sion with a Gold Medal in recognition of his or her achievements in the field.

Expanding its activities through grants, the Institute is developing research projects like the current study for the Department of Transportation, dealing with the standardization of informational symbols and signage in the United States, and a study of the cost/efficiency benefits from design systems for the National Endowment of the Arts.

Members enjoy reduced fees and access to all AIGA facilities, reference materials, and programs. Membership costs $40 a year ($75 if you live in New York City and environs), and includes a copy of the annual *Journal* which comes in boxed form. the AIGA and the Graphic Artists Guild are the two organizations in the nation most worth your membership.

The Guilds

The Graphic Artists Guild is now emerging as a major force affecting the overall status of graphic artists in the United States. The eastern and western divisions are joining rapidly with the many local Art Directors Clubs and designers' and illustrators' societies to form a consolidated front pressing for professional ethics and practices, proper financial remuneration, and the protection of artists' rights. Through this organizing body, graphic artists have access to legal and financial advice, trade discounts, and medical insurance coverage.

Joining your local guild and local club or society, entitles you to a discounted membership in the national guild organization (see section F, p.194).

The Illustrators Guild

This guild is now affiliated with the Graphic Artists Guild, East and West, but still enjoys the distinction of a separate discipline with its own newsletter and particular concerns. Illustrator members receive all the benefits applicable to members of GAG (details of which appear in section F) and the guild also arranges their own Illustrators' Seminars annually.

Graphics In Industry

This is essentially a trade show designed for people in the printing and allied trades, and its focus is primarily on graphics reproduction technology. One of many west coast trade shows and seminars sponsored and organized by the American Seminar Institute and GII, its location varies from year to year.

The theme of the 1978 show was "New Graphics Technology . . . Simplified." It featured three days of seminars on such topics as technical illustration, computed images, graphic design, client presentation, color graphics, and portfolio presentation.

Registration for the seminars is $60 per day or $150 all three days, with the trade exhibit and West Coast Art Directors Show free. This, the best of the graphic trade shows in the west, takes place mid-June.

AIGA

Illustrators Guild
ig

Gii

MAX SEABAUGH

NEWSLETTER OF ADAC, SACRAMENTO

GRAPHICS IN INDUSTRY

The Aspen Survey

"People in the design field derive exceptional enjoyment from their work, tend to consider talent the chief requisite for success in the field, and appear to value achievement above almost anything else in life." So begins Gail Sheehey's preliminary conclusions from the results of her survey of designers at the International Design Conference at Aspen in 1977. This was probably the first major research effort to measure the attitudes of designers toward their work and their lives. It revealed, unsurprisingly, that *good education* practically never shows up as a major factor for success in the design professions— and that includes architects.

Gail Sheehey's survey, first published in the 27th IDCA's *Life Times* and to be part of a forthcoming book from William Morrow, confirms that *talent* is the number one contributing factor for success, and that this is consistent throughout all design professions—graphic design, industrial design, advertising and illustration. The next two essential ingredients for success in most designers' experience was *hard work* and *high energy*.

Among the more business-orientated designers, the *willingness to take risks* tended to replace high energy in third place. This is a somewhat different order of priorities than for other professions. Architects would rate motivation and hard work above talent, for example, and lawyers or doctors would cite good education as a major success ingredient.

But values change with age and experience. The Aspen survey showed that all designers in their early twenties rated *achievement* as the most important goal at that time in their life, followed closely by *making money* and *autonomy*. The other important value that turned up consistently, especially among illustrators, was *aesthetic and intellectual pursuits*. Autonomy becomes the primary goal as designers slip into their thirties

and early forties. The shift of focus—a concern for taking responsibility for one's own destiny in more direct ways— is a value change that has been well substantiated during the last few years.

This period of life, particularly for men between the ages of thirty and forty-four, was also found to be the time at which *family commitment* appears as a prominent concern. Over the age of forty five, particularly among the high achievers, the survey illustrated the classic evolvement of concerns beyond the self and family such as *moral integrity* and *social contribution*. This seemed to go hand in hand with a re-emphasis on "the youthful delight in aesthetic and intellectual pursuits."

The major turning points, or times of transition, were consistently described as being clustered around age thirty, or within what Sheehey calls the Deadline Decade (ages thirty-five to forty-five). These two times of crisis have long been identified in the human life cycle, with two other periods of lesser crisis being described as the late teens and around fifty.

The survey showed that most often these times of turmoil were expressed within intimate relationships rather than within professional careers, and resulted in severe disturbances to personal life. Probably the most dramatic piece of data to emerge was the number and severity of depressions and near suicides occuring in the mid-twenties. This correlates with other statistical research that pinpoints the highest suicide rate for men at age twenty-four. Other research indicates that this "point of suicide" is slipping down the age scale and beginning to occur a lot in the late teens and early twenties.

Generally, the design population sampled at Aspen in 1977 consisted of people who present themselves as being able to *cope* with crisis: "Cope while I try to solve the problem." Amongst designers between the ages thirty to forty-five, some fifteen percent preferred another way to deal with the crisis: "Plunge into more work to take my mind off my problems." Otherwise, these designers sampled derived great joy from their work and tended to insist on small-scale autonomy very early in their careers.

Keep It Simple

**Strike three.
Get your hand off my knee.
You're overdrawn.
Your horse won.
Yes.
No.
You have the account.
Walk.
Don't walk.
Mother's dead.
Basic events
require simple language.
Idiosyncratically euphuistic
eccentricities are the
promulgators of
triturable obfuscation.
What did you do last night?
Enter into a meaningful
romantic involvement
or
fall in love?
What did you have for
breakfast this morning?
The upper part of a hog's
hind leg with two oval
bodies encased in a shell
laid by a female bird
or
ham and eggs?
David Belasco, the great
American theatrical producer,
once said, "If you can't
write your idea on the
back of my calling
card,
you don't have a clear idea."**

—A United Technologies reprint from *The Wall Street Journal*

The Creativity Awards

Every year the magazine, *Art Direction,* organizes an international awards show for everyone involved in graphic communications. The show is judged, produced, and staged by the magazine, and travels to many major cities during the year. All winners appear in the annual book of the show published by *Art Direction.*

Entries in over twenty-five categories must be submitted by June 10, and produced over the previous twelve months. Entry fees range from $4 to $20, and all award winners pay additional $9 to $30 hanging fees. This show, always very fine and creative, takes place in New York every November.

Concurrent with the *Creativity* show, *Ad Directions* (see below) exhibits new products, materials, techniques, and equipment from all the major manufacturers and suppliers in the United States. *Art Direction* also plans the *Art Directors Conference,* which occurs at the same time. This theme conference is limited to art directors in a given area — for example, corporate art directors at the 1977 conference.

The Ad Directions Show

The major trade show for the advertising field since 1969, Ad Directions indicates important shifts and changes in the business of the graphics profession and in its production procedures. These days, the largest displays among some 150 exhibitors are of typesetting technology and equipment. Recent trends revealed at this exposition indicate a return to the production of larger ranges of paper, frantic development of electronic technology, and a move toward multi-service companies as distinct from specialized service firms. The counterpart to Ad Directions in the west is the Industrial Graphics International annual exhibition.

"The One Show"

This is the major media arts show of the year, sponsored by the New York Art Directors Club and Copy Club, the organization of the advertising industry that is concerned with promoting high standards of art and design. This annual awards exhibition, now in its 55th year, and its book, *Art Directors Annual,* has attained the stature of an encyclopedia of the visual communications industry. All award winners appear in the *Annual.*

Printed work produced in the United States or Canada within the previous twelve months can be submitted for The One Show in any of eighty-nine categories that comprise the ten major areas of graphic work. Deadline is December 23, and entries are accepted from anyone connected with the work. Each entry costs $8 except TV commercials, which are $15, and campaign, multiple unit, or series pieces, which are $20. Additionally, there is $50 handling charge for each entry accepted. The exhibition gives a Gold and a Silver award in each category, and every entry exhibited receives the Certificate of Merit.

Communication Arts Awards

This largest of all juried competitions is organized by *Communication Arts* magazine, whose annual awards edition contains all the winning entries and boasts a circulation of 43,000 copies. Entries are solicited internationally, although the bulk of the works submitted in fifteen categories, from Consumer Magazine Advertising to self-promotion, are from the United States. Deadline for all entries is July 1, and the work must have been produced between July 1 to June 30 in the preceding year. The *CA* Awards issue is published the following November. Handling fees per entry range from $5 to $15.

The Art Annual

This is actually part of the Communication Arts Awards (above) but specifically intended for the Illustration and Photography categories. The show is presented separately, and its awards are published in a special issue of *Communication Arts,* the *Art Annual.* Deadline is April 1 for work produced within the previous 12 months. Handling fees range from $5 to $10 per entry.

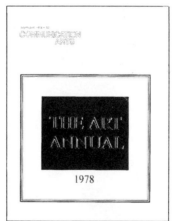

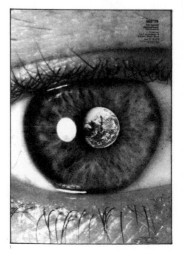

Industrial Graphics International

This annual exhibition and trade show with seminar/workshops boasts: "No longer is it necessary to travel to three or four conferences and trade shows a year — IGI has it all under one roof . . ." It is indeed the show that covers all you need for the year, sponsored by the Industrial Graphics International Society.

The highlight of the three-day event in New York is the art and design competition and exhibition that accepts entries in forty-nine categories comprising seven major areas of graphics. Deadline is April 29 for work completed within the previous twelve months. Each first entry costs $15 ($10 for IGI members), and subsequent entries, $5. Each accepted piece is charged an additional $35 hanging fee, which entitles the entrant to a free copy of *The IGI Annual.* Awards, presented at a banquet, include a trophy for first place in each major category, second, third, and fourth place awards in all categories, plus Best of Show.

The free Trade Show is one of the largest in the country with over 200 exhibits covering art supplies, typography, photography, printing, and audio-visual equipment.

The seminars and workshops deal with all areas of graphics, including technology, psychology, new materials, and art preparation. Attendance costs from $35 and up per session to $155 for all three days, with membership discounts.

Industrial Graphics International is made up of The Association of Technical Artists, the National Association of Industrial Artists, and the Technical Illustrators Management Association. Membership is open to all designers and educators who deal with the creation and preparation of visual graphics. IGI's main purpose is to merge the visual arts with commerce, industry, and the community, and it is a very active organization. Basic membership is $20 per year (less for certain categories of membership).

Illustrators Workshop

This annual summer course offers a three-week seminar and a workshop with approximately half-a-dozen distinguished illustrators. It is intended for professional illustrators, art directors, and graphic designers, as well as advanced art students.

The five-day intensive seminar is made up of presentations, discussions, and exchanges of ideas among six illustrators, their special guests, and participants. The cost of the seminar is $600, including use of gymnasium, swimming pool, and tennis courts. It is scheduled for the last week in June.

The three-week workshop, which includes the seminar, features some intensive study and practical work on a one-to-one basis with the lecturers, all geared to strengthen the participant's perceptual approaches to solving illustration problems. This instant feedback method, involving research and experimentation, has been applauded as a highly successful learning experience.

The cost of the complete three-week program (Jun/July) is $1,150, or $1,400 if you stay on the campus of Marymount College, 45 minutes from New York City.

The Type Directors Club Awards

In the past few years, the annual international show of typographical excellence has been marked by creative typographical experimentation, and informality reviving the art forms of lettering and letter design. This is definitely a show that has impact and influence. TDC awards are certificates of excellence given for each piece selected for display. For purposes of the awards, typography is defined as calligraphy, lettering, metal and film typesetting, and/ or any combination of those forms. Work can be submitted as a brochure, an advertisement, a trademark, a private press printing, a label — anything, in fact, that makes use of fine typographic design.

The show opens in New York in May, and then travels throughout the United States, Europe, and the Far East. All selected work is presented in the TDC catalogue, available for $1.25. Deadline for entries is the beginning of February for work completed within the previous twelve months, and costs $6 per entry, plus a $50 hanging fee if selected for the certificate award. All foreign entries, except Canadian, are allowed a 50% discount, and fees must be paid in United States dollars.

ARTHUR RITTER

KEN PARKHURST

*Two TDC 34 Award winners:
AlaCarte Greeting Cards and
a poster for the Los Angeles
County Museum*

The ITCA Awards

Oriented toward graphic designers rather more than the TDC, whose principle concern is the quality of production by typographic suppliers, the annual gold medal awards competition of the International Typographers Association shows the year's finest typographic design.

All entries must have been produced by an ITCA typographer during the preceding twelve month period, June 1 to May 31. There are no categories in this competition, no entry fees, and entries are not limited to printed matter. Any message, on any surface, appearing anywhere, is eligible, but a sample must accompany each entry — a photographic print is acceptable.

Entries are judged on how well typography was used as the prime design factor in communicating; the outstanding examples receive the Gold Medal Awards.

Winners are announced at the ITCA Annual Convention, where the show is first displayed before touring the United States and Canada.

Tools of the Trade Show

Tools of the Trade is aimed at professional designers in all areas of graphic communications. Presented by Pas Graphics at Anaheim, California, in late June, it features hundreds of new art products, applications, and techniques from most of the major graphic art manufacturers in the United States.

This consumer show for the graphic arts community includes seminars on a given theme. In 1979 the subject area was paper; various discussions covered paper mathematics, use of mill materials and samples, a paper trends update, and a special seminar on coated papers. At the 1979 show, following this theme, the Mead Paper Company presented two exhibits: the best 60 graphic pieces of 1978, and the best of 1979's Annual Reports. Registration for the seminars is $5 per day.

The show also has begun its own design awards competition, and the deadline for entries in over twenty categories is June 1.

The Society of Environmental Graphics Designers

The Society was formed recently to promote and formalize environmental graphic design as a professional discipline. This emerging aspect of design has been little appreciated so far, and has enormous potential to improve the quality of our built environments. The Society's basic objectives are to develop standards and ethics within the profession; to disseminate technical, educational, and intra-professional materials; to promote and aid environmentally related government graphics programs; to assist academic and training programs; and to provide a forum for both designers and materials manufacturers.

Membership is open to all designers involved with graphic elements for interior or exterior spaces, including signage systems, architectural graphics, murals, banners, and flags. Membership costs $55 per year (less for those in an allied profession, such as architecture), and includes a copy of a comprehensive guide to materials and techniques, *The Environmental Graphics Sourcebook,* as well as the SEGD's regular newsletter.

The SEGD has an annual conference, offers legislative representation and a speakers bureau, and an award program to recognize excellence on the part of *clients* of environmental graphics designers. They also distribute noteworthy literature on topics relevant to members.

Type X

Sponsored by the National Composition Association, this annual New York convention focuses entirely on typesetting, word processing, and computerized equipment. It is an intense two-and-a-half day event at the end of August, jammed with seminars and conferences on all topics of interest to the typesetting industry, placing particular emphasis on the delivery of quality products. The exhibits, sponsored by *TypeWorld*, comprise the industry's major trade show of the year.

Registration for the event is $180 ($150 for NCA members), and includes materials, receptions, meals, exhibits, and admission to all sessions.

The NCA awards for typographic production excellence are presented at the convention, and all winning entries in fourteen categories are on display. Deadline for submission is the end of July for work completed during the previous twelve months. Cost of entry is $10-$15 (members half-price).

During the year, the NCA also presents a series of seminars throughout the United States on such subjects as Production & Design, Automated Composition, and Basic Typography. These two-day seminars cost $100 per day for non-members. Within this industry, which is undergoing profound technological change that is dramatically influencing the course of graphic design, these seminars constitute the best educational programs available.

THE WEST'S BIGGEST ART PRODUCT EXPO!

Society of Environmental Graphics Designers

NCA

Envision

A major west coast annual graphic design symposium that includes workshops, demonstrations, and a trade show, Envision is sponsored by the Sacramento Art Directors and Artists Club, and held at California State University. The two-day event features speakers of national and international repute, student and speaker exhibits, and media presentations. The trade show is concerned with technical advancements in the graphics industry.

Registration for the event costs $50 ($40 for ADAC members, $30 for students), includes lunch and coffee, and is limited to 700 people.

The West Coast Show

This show has been organized by the Western Art Director's Club since 1964, and has been steadily growing in quantity and quality over the years. The West Coast Show is now a major exhibition of communications art that accepts entries nationally (including Canada), and the show travels to major cities up and down the West Coast from Seattle to San Diego.

The call for entries goes out in September and the deadline is usually in mid-October; judging in early November and the show organized for early February in San Francisco. There are 29 categories for submission, and entry fees are $10. There is an extra hanging fee of $15 for all winning entries which receive the West Cost Show certificate of merit. Entries are accepted from California, Oregon, Washington, British Columbia and Alaska only.

Package Designers Council

This is a type of guild organization for package designers. Membership is made up of professional design consultants, designers, and design directors employed by product manufacturers. Interestingly, membership is *not* open to designers working for manufacturers of packaging materials, as the Council believes that the professional designer should be free to select recommend, and specify, without bias, from all available packaging materials and processes.

The Council is concerned with visual and technical standards in packaging and other visual expressions of the corporate image, and with the constant free flow of ideas and information among designers and the industry. Its purposes include maintaining high standards of ethics and professional practice, making the designer's function known and understood by business management, protecting the designer's rights, and providing a forum for intra-professional matters. It also involves itself with design training, awards fellowships in package design, and assists young designers about to enter the profession.

Membership costs: $50 per year.

Face To Face

A three-day publishing event in New York, this annual publishing conference and exposition is the national trade show. It is the largest combined meeting of magazine and book publishers int he country, involving over 100 seminar/workshops designed to be intensive learning experiences. Included at the show is an exhibition of printing, photocomposition, word processing, paper, typography, and direct mail products which is probably the most comprehensive show in existence.

Sponsored by *Folio* magazine, the exhibition is free. Workshop/seminars cost $35 each if you sign up for more than one and register in advance. There is an additional $14 registration fee.

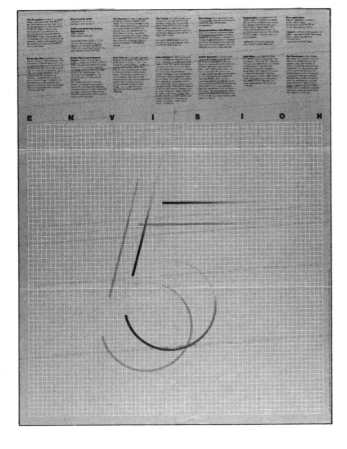

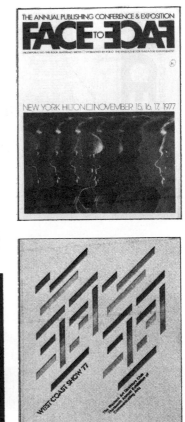

Pubmart

An annual workshop, conference, and exhibit for the book industry, including text book, trade book, and educational materials publishers and producers. Pubmart focuses primarily on books, and on all the new technology involved in their production and manufacture. It features an impressive range and quantity of participation seminars and workshops. In 1978 the three-day show involved sixty workshops that covered such topics as "New Directions in Book Graphics," "Typographic Developments," "In-house Composition Systems," and "Quality Control for Graphic Arts Buyers." A special feature, invaluable for all designers, was an intensive short course in the latest Graphic Arts technology and practice offered by the Rochester Institute of Technology.

Pubmart is spnsored by Knowledge Industry Publications, Inc. and R. R. Bowker Company. It takes place in the publishing center of the United States, New York City. Admission to the exhibits is free, but the workshops cost from $45 for one to $225 for six. Students receive a 50% discount.

Schonste Bucher aus aller Welt

Every year Germany hosts the International Book Design Exhibition in Leipzig to honor outstanding accomplishments in book design and production to present new forms of book design and publishing work, and to allow publishers from all over the world to share their bookmaking experiences.

This exhibition is concerned with only the best, and normally only those books that have already been awarded distinction in their country of origin are submitted. The exhibition and its special-theme display coincides with the annual international book trade show in Frankfurt. It takes place during most of October, although awards are handed out in March at the Leipzig Book Fair.

Sponsored by the UNESCO Commission of the German Democratic Republic, the exhibition awards the "Golden Letter," gold, silver, and bronze medals, and honorable mentions. A special award is donated by UNESCO. There is no charge for entries and all books are returned unless they receive an award, in which case they are retained.

Aperture

This is a photocommunication symposium designed primarily for photographers, but it is just as useful to anyone — particularly students — in related fields of visual communication. Several well-known professionals lead small, informal workshops and dialogues on a given theme. In 1978, the theme was "For Love and Money — Balancing Personal Growth with Commercial Realities." The speakers give their own visual presentations, and manufacturers show and demonstrate their wares and services. There is also an exhibition of photography of all sorts, for which entries may be submitted at $2 per print. Fifty are selected for the exhibit.

The program is sponsored by the American Society of Magazine Photographers, Butte College of Photography, The Fort Mason Foundation, and the Golden Gate National Recreation Area (GGNRA). It takes place at the Fort Mason Center, San Francisco, in June, costs $75, and is limited to 200 people.

International Multi-Image Festival

Sponsored by the Audio Visual Laboratory Institute, this is the showcase for the audio visual industry, presenting the best new work in the field and exhibiting equipment and new technology. The first AVL Festival took place in Vail, Colorado, in June 1979, and it is intended to be a regular event, supported by leading manufacturers and endorsed by the Association for Multi-Image (AMI).

Awards are presented for the best multi-image productions in seven categories, multi-image being defined as a synchronous presentation of concept, score, graphics and/or animation, and photography. The cost of submitting a program depends on the number of projectors used for the showing, based on $30 per projector. Deadline is the end of Aprll, and the Vail Festival, open to the public, takes place in mid-June.

Magazines, Journals and Books

Magazines and Journals

Publishers, Distributors, and
Book Clubs

A Book Selection

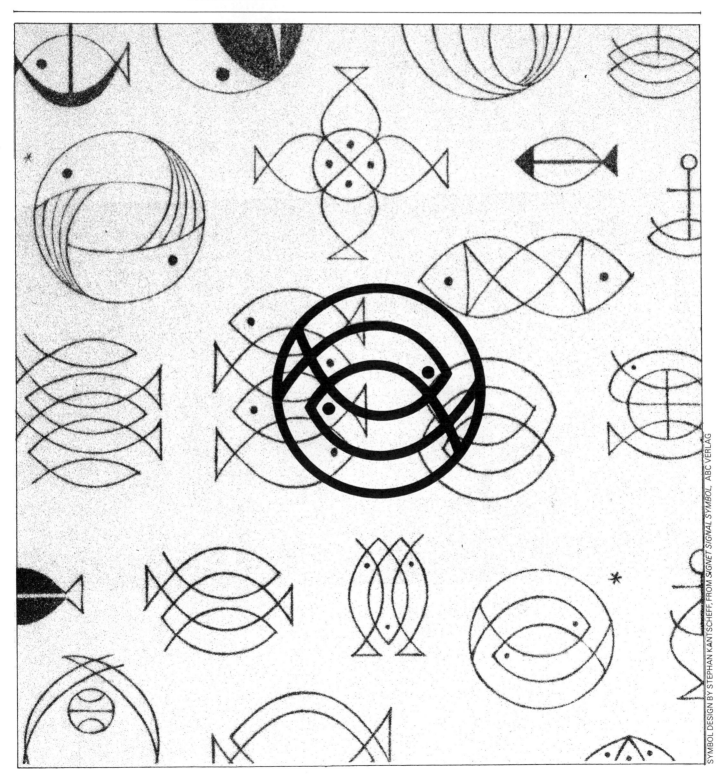

SYMBOL DESIGN BY STEPHAN KANTSCHEFF, FROM *SIGNET SIGNAL SYMBOL*, ABC VERLAG

This section of this graphics sourcebook is devoted to various periodicals and books relevant to the graphic artist / designer. The list that follows does not intend to be exhaustive, or it would be a book in itself. Besides, periodicals come and go, and books are superseded regularly, so a "complete" list would quickly become outdated. Moreover, we have excluded the vast range of *arts* publications important, but not directly pertinent, to the design profession.

Despite the high cost of producing a magazine, there are more publications available of immediate value to the designer than ever before. Reflecting the general renaissance of interest in graphics and design that has occurred since the mid-1960s, the overall quality of presentation in the print media is much improved from the standards of ten or twenty years ago.

Nonetheless, there remains a fine, general design magazine in the United States. The British journal, *Design,* is enlightening, even though it is primarily concerned with the manufacturing industries and, therefore, with industrial and product design. *Graphic Design +,* published in Japan, approaches its subject with a professional and philosophical eye. But there is nothing in the United States that compares with either of these publications, or that speaks, as they do, to design in general and design education in particular.

Delegates to the 1978 ICOGRADA conference suggested that the graphics community in the United States both wants and needs a national graphic design organization; this may herald some kind of change in this regard. Such organizations are government-sponsored in Europe—*Design* is a "government" magazine in that sense—and if the contemplated American organization actually comes into being, there is at least some reason to hope that an appropriate publication will be among its offspring. Meanwhile, the *Information Design Journal* has appeared in response to this recognized need, but that too is published in England.

Most of these remarks apply equally to books about the graphic arts. There has been an astonishing proliferation of design titles in the past few years; some are excellent; a few are execrable, and most —overpriced and superficial—seem to have the primary function of rounding out a publisher's spring or autumn list.

Even among the better design books, there is a certain amount of duplication and overlap. The not-so-careful consumer may find him or herself with four or five titles, each of which covers pretty much the same material as the others.

In compiling our own list of worthy tomes we have selected only those books we feel are the best in their particular areas of graphic concern. If your favorite title isn't here, that does not mean it is one of the books we wish no one had bothered to publish—it may be simply that we think there's another one that does the job better. Also, as with our list of magazines and journals, the list does not intend to be definitive. We cover books of general interest to people in the graphic arts, and avoid books devoted to areas of extreme specialty. This is a guide, and will give you the best possible results if you use it as such. This is *our* list. If you don't like it—to paraphrase Scoop Nisker—go out and make one of your own.

graphic design✛
グラフィック デザイン✛

Graphic Design +
(Japan)

This is one of the most satisfying of all the graphic journals, primarily devoted to contemporary Japanese work, with some pieces on related items from around the world. Editorially, the magazine approaches design from a scholarly and historical viewpoint, spotlighting the roles of designers and art directors as they deal with the demands and visual design problems of a society. As a specialized international journal, Graphic Design + has taken a critical leadership role by analyzing all areas of design including pictograms, charts, maps, landmarks, computer graphics, corporate identifications, and advertising. English translation included.

Published quarterly; $60.00 per year; single copies $17.00

Orion Books; Museum Books Inc

9

Design
(England)

An exemplary publication on all matters of design: product, environment, information, advertising, and social — Design covers them all with authority and has a refreshing advocate's point of view. Design suffers a few drawbacks on the American market — for example, it is aimed primarily at the British manufacturing industry, and refers to British people, places, and things with a familiarity the American reader cannot share. Though it focuses on British and European design issues, the magazine does include frequent features on or about the United States, and, in any case, the questions, problems, and concerns it tackles are universal in nature.

Editorially, Design exhorts manufacturers to a greater concern for the social implications of good design; applauds designers and industry alike for projects well done; and keeps its readers abreast of all the major design news in considerable, and easily readable, depth. Partly because the magazine examines its own format from time to time, Design remains exceptionally well designed, well edited, and well produced. Overall, it is the best reading material available on the broader aspects and impacts of designing.

Design is part of the British government's Design Council, which maintains a Design Index and showrooms in London to communicate about design with the public, manufacturers, and designers alike. Perhaps as an extension of this concern for good design communications, the magazine features a "Designers' Services" section, which provides regularly updated information about designers and the services they offer, and an impressive "Classified" section, with myriad advertisements of job offers for designers. Even the advertising in Design shows the best of European equipment and furniture for the studio and office.

With its concern for the education of designers, the public, and industry; its social awareness; and its uncompromising insistence on quality and professionalism, Design is the kind of journal sorely needed in the United States.

Published monthly; $40.80 per year; single copies, $4.00

The Design Council; Expediters of the Printed Word Ltd

THE AMERICAN WAY OF PRODUCT DEVELOPMENT
AND SOME CHEAPER UK ALTERNATIVES

Ossie Clark and others meet computer-aided design
Products caught in an identity crisis

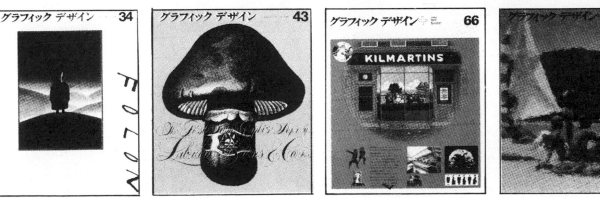

Graphis
(Switzerland)

As its subtitle says: *The* International Journal for Graphic and Applied Arts. *Graphis* is primarily a portfolio magazine for artists, shows, and exhibitions of world renown. If they are not well-known at publication time, appearance in *Graphis* frequently alters that unfortunate condition. *Graphis* occasionally covers related fields such as artifacts, crafts, folk arts, and the fine arts. It steers clear of social issues, philosophy, and advocacy, preferring to make its influence felt simply by reproducing the best in current design — which it does impeccably well. The quality of both the magazine and the work it displays is very high.

Bi-monthly: $48.00 per year, six issues.

**The Graphis Press;
Hastings House Publishers**

Communication Arts
(Palo Alto)

The American magazine most in the vein of *Graphis* and *Gebrauchsgraphik, CA* is also largely a collection of portfolios, mostly by United States designers, illustrators, and photographers. Each issue includes news items of general design interest, an editorial, new product information, and book reviews. *Communication Arts* is beautifully produced, very well edited and designed with extensive color reproductions. One of the best American graphic design journals.

Published bi-monthly; $26.00 per year; single copies $4.00, except for two special issues a year, the CA Awards issue ($14.00) and the ART Awards issue ($9.00).

Coyne & Blanchard, Inc

Novum Gebrauchsgraphik
(Germany)

For a long time this was the only design magazine graphic students could look to for inspiration, and it is still one of the foremost design journals in the world. Always interesting, *Gebrauchsgraphik* presents a mixture of designers' portfolios (mainly European), and the works of photographers, artists, and illustrators, along with in-depth articles that analyze design solutions and methods.

Published monthly in four languages, $52.50 per annum. Single issues $5.00

F Bruckman KG; Museum Books Inc

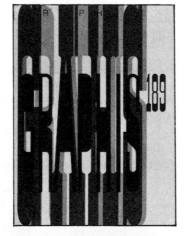

icographic
(England)

The official journal of the International Council of Graphic Design Associations (ICOGRADA) is a twice-yearly vehicle for in-depth discussions of all aspects of visual communication. As such, *icographic* fills a gap in the existing coverage of United States graphic design.

The majority of the magazine's contributors are designers themselves; others are experts in related fields, such as psychology, linguistics, and sociology.

icographic provides highly informed, erudite, critical evaluations of design, placing greater emphasis on future design directions than it does on current fashionable trends. International in scope, *icographic* pays particular attention to specialist research in a broad-based at-

tempt to compile ergonomic data similar to that collected in other design professions, such as product design. Its standing invitation to everyone to submit articles or research adds to the collective knowledge of ICOGRADA and to an increasing comprehension of the processes of visual communication.

Each issue of *icographic* is built around a theme. *icographic 12,* for example, dealt with alphabetic symbol communications, and included articles on Cyrillic Gothic typefaces, signing systems in Argentina and Yugoslavia, Japanese and French pictograms, a new sign alphabet, and design and semiotics. Overall, a very valuable publication.

Bi-annual: $10.00 per year (2 issues); free specimen copy on request

Pergamon Press Ltd

Information Design Journal
(England)

This new periodical arose to fill the need for a forum that would evaluate information-design projects and provide an ongoing arena for discussion. It offers a critical, interdisciplinary look at design, designers, design projects, design conferences, and design education courses. Editorially, it comments on design management, print technology, design theory, perception, applied psychology, design history, typography, computer applications, reading and learning, and so on. Up to the time we went to press, only the first issue was available, and this suggests a dense and wordy journal that will investigate each selected topic in considerable academic depth. Although very informative—and a little dry—throughout, it is expensive and its appeal seems limited.

Quarterly: $29.00 per year

Information Design Journal

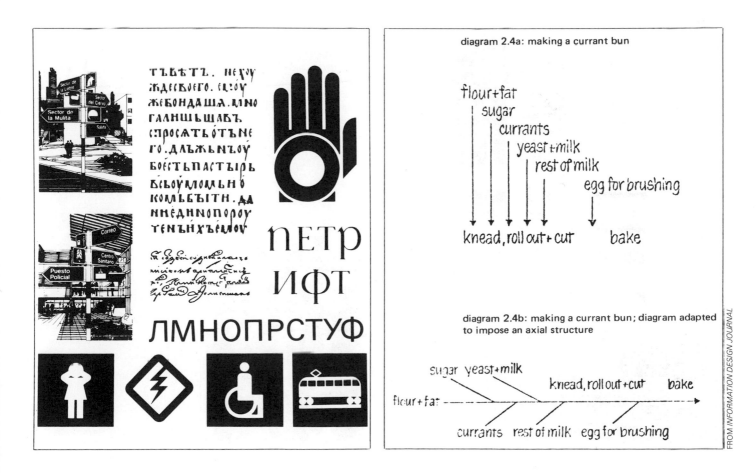

diagram 2.4a: making a currant bun

diagram 2.4b: making a currant bun; diagram adapted to impose an axial structure

Graphics Today
(New York)

Sometimes very good, this
curious graphics magazine is
invariably a let-down because it
never quite delivers on its promises to challenge, excite, and
prod creative people with useful
ideas. It lacks real panache and
is, itself, a boring and unimagi-
natively designed magazine.

Nonetheless, there is always
some worthwhile reading and
design work within these pages,
and the magazine does achieve
a useful blend of interviews and
commentary focusing on individuals' work and their approach
to their work. *Graphics Today*
attempts to communicate about
the bread-and-butter issues, by
providing background information on events, news items, and
new technology and by exploring
all the graphic specialties.

Bi-monthly; $12.00 per year;
single copies, $2.00

Syndicate Magazines, Inc

Upper and Lower Case
(New York)

Although this is ostensibly the
regular promotion piece for the
International Typeface Corporation, it is far and away the best
journal on typography and type
design in the world. The large
format, seventy-two page newsprint tabloid certainly promotes
the use of ITC typefaces — it
uses them imaginatively and
sometimes outrageously in a
wide range of contexts. *U&lc* is
slickly designed for designers,
and includes articles on myriad
topics relating to typography,
lettering, and design. It is particularly good on the subject of
new technology. It involves itself
editorially with preparing
designers and members of the
new typographic/word processing industry to cope with the
future (which has already occurred technologically) without
sacrificing typographic quality
and craft. We have entered the
era of the office with graphic arts
departments, with an almost
new profession: the Typo-
Graphic Director.

The *U&lc* Book Shop offers
access to the best design books
currently available, at retail
prices.

Published quarterly; free to
design professionals; $6.00
a year; single copies $1.50

**International Typeface
Corporation**

Typographic
(New York)

A handsomely designed and
printed sixteen-page publication
focusing on type and typography.
Its emphasis is educational and
historical, but *Typographic* is full
of typographers' ephemera,
discussions, and examples. It's
surprising that this little magazine has not expanded to
become even more substantial
than it is.

Issued quarterly,
Typographic is available free
from typography houses that are
members of the International
Typographic Association.

**International Typographic
Association**

Print
(Washington, DC)

Print magazine presents a rather confusing image, and it's unclear whom the publication is aimed at except that it is certainly about design and the graphic arts. It includes portfolios, but as a portfolio magazine — covering the same work seen in *Communication Arts* and *Graphis,* but without all the color, and without much sense of magazine design and layout — it doesn't quite make it. Fortunately, *Print*'s broader range of subject matter includes useful articles on both the business and the conceptual aspects of design. These, if less effectively conceived than similar essays in *Design,* are of greater interest in any case than the standard bios of well-known members of the profession.

Print covers areas such as exhibition design, TV and film graphics and production, commercials, and signage a little more thoroughly than it does other design areas; also, it contains information on new products and technical developments, and book reviews.

Print also publishes the annual of "The One Show," and distributes a list of worthwhile design titles (see Books, below).

Published bi-monthly; $20.00 per year; single copies $3.50.

R C Publications, Inc

Push Pin Graphic
(New York)

A showcase for illustrative and literary ideas, the journal of the renowned Push Pin Studios is filled with solid design and advertising, often presented humorously in the context of a general interest magazine for popular consumption. This is a highly innovative graphic magazine produced by graphic artists to suit their own whims and whimsey. Yet, the *Graphic* is witty, satirical, totally eclectic, and unpredictable. In this last quality lies the magazine's main appeal, since the majority of the work in it is by Seymour Chwast and the Push Pin artists, whose collective effort does have a certain sameness about it.

Published bi-monthly; $12.00 per year; single copy, $2.00

Push Pin Graphic Inc

Twen
(Germany)

Although *Twen* ceased publication in the early 1970s, in its heyday it was the classic example of a general interest magazine that is heavily subscribed to by designers. *Twen* was a forerunner of the most exciting period in modern magazine history, the 1960s; and it was the direct inspiration for the proliferation of magazines published in the 1970s. In an era when magazines were marked by intense visual imagery, large formats, extensive color, and new art techniques, *Twen* was the vanguard: a pristine example of systems-orientated, modular design principles. As we enter the era of computer-directed technology, the example of *Twen* remains; used creatively, the grid system it popularized has become a valued instrument in guiding layout through the complex production stages to reach final printed form. *Twen* is still occasionally seen in second-hand book and magazine shops, and fetches a high price.

Kindler & Schiermeyer Verlag

THE GRID FOR *TWEN*

Graphics:USA
(New York)

Primarily a trade journal for art directors, *Graphics USA* documents news at the business end of design with a sloppy graphic mixture of short items and examples of some of the latest, just completed design work. All kinds of little tidbits find their way into the magazine —news of business liaisons, new products, graphics clubs and organizations, graphics law, and people. It's easy to get hooked, particularly if you're involved with design as a *business*.

Published 11 times per year; $10.00 per year

Kaye Publishing Corp

Art Direction
(New York)

One of three magazines (the other two are *Advertising Techniques* and *Graphic Arts Buyer*) for the trade from Advertising Trade Publications, *Art Direction* is intended primarily for people in advertising agencies and related businesses. It keeps abreast of all the latest trends in advertising style, including photography, illustration, and typography; and includes book reviews, new product literature, and a valuable section on cases brought before the New York Joint Ethics Committee. The advertising, from a design standpoint, is useful as well.

Art Direction's principal appeal is that it reports very quickly on new and forthcoming work, and contains a good deal of gossip about who's doing what where. Unfortunately, rather than offering any insight into qualities of good design, and as a collection of the latest things in print, it's rather sloppily designed itself.

Published monthly, $12.50 per year

Advertising Trade Publications

Idea
(Japan)

Similar in approach to Switzerland's *Graphis, Idea* is Japan's portfolio magazine. Well produced, with a wealth of highly innovative work, it is, as its title suggests, about ideas. Its focus is Japanese and United States designers and illustrators, but it does touch on other areas of the arts as well. Occasionally an issue is built around a single person, dealing with his or her work in depth. Although the contents page and captions are in English, this magazine is really for the Japanese.

Published bi-monthly: $78.00 per year; single issues $12.00

Museum Books Inc

Picture Magazine
(Los Angeles)

An excitingly eclectic collection of contemporary photography, *Picture Magazine* has emerged as an exceptional camera-and-graphics publication of large format (13"x19") images. The selection of material covers all schools of thought, unified here by exacting reproduction, and supervised and edited by an art director run amok. Criteria for inclusion in the magazine are totally arbitrary, except that the images "must be current or future."

Published bimonthly; $30.00 per year, or $6.00 per issue

Picture Magazine

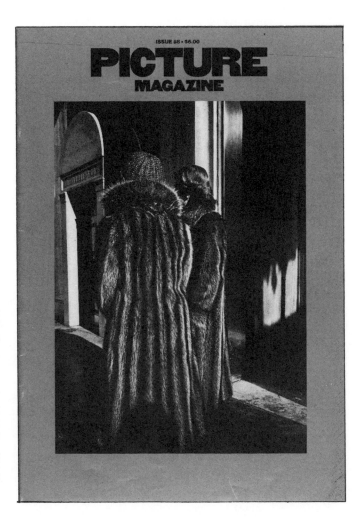

The Oregon Rainbow
(Portland)

This superb magazine is not really about design at all; but it *is* exceptionally design-conscious. Published and produced by two designers who decided to be their own clients in order to produce design of a high standard, *Oregon Rainbow* is about Oregon and its arts in the broadest possible sense of the word. Each issue is designed to hold your interest for a long time; its use of high quality paper and superb, rich, color printing take the *Rainbow* utterly out of the "disposable" class of magazines. It had won forty national and international awards by the time of its fifth issue, and, no doubt, only our press deadline keeps us from recording several more. Even its advertisements meet the *Rainbow*'s high design standards.

Still partly grant-funded, *Oregon Rainbow* is not generally available outside Oregon, Northern California and Washington.

Quarterly; $16.00 per year

Oregon Rainbow

Zoom
(France)

Subtitled "The Magazine of the Image," *Zoom* is an eclectic collection of photographic images, with beautifully produced, high quality gravure printing. Obviously of special interest to photographers, *Zoom* also intrigues designers and art directors who are frequently involved with photography because of the magazine's sophisticated awareness of photo-graphics. Unfortunately, it is still only published in French.

Monthly; $53.00 per year

Publicness

Architectural Design
(England)

Although nominally devoted to architecture, this curious and unique design magazine has a range of interest so broad that it encompasses art, design and graphics, archeology, environmental design, product design, and ecology. Blurring the edges of so many related, but ordinarily divergent, disciplines is fascinating when carried out with *Architectural Design*'s traditional style, imagination, and wit. Over the last few years, however, *AD* seems to have lost its flair for covering the creative fringe, and has been on the wane.

Published monthly; $45.00 per year, $4.00 per copy.

Architectural Design and Aeroshaw Ltd

Archetype
(San Francisco)

A brand new tabloid in the same vein as *Architectural Design;* just how far it carries the same banner remains to be seen. In any case, *Archetype* is off to a promising start. Oriented toward architecture, it explores the edges of architectural concept, which involves all the same factors and considerations that face any designer.

Published quarterly; $8.00 per year; $2.50 single copy.

Archetype

ZOOM

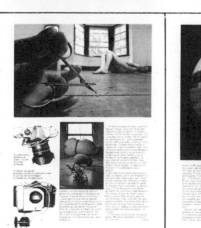

Advertising Techniques
(New York)

A potpourri of who is doing what in advertising graphics and the media, and *intended* for agency art directors. Full of examples, often badly reproduced, of the latest advertising design; stories behind the campaigns; profiles of art directors; new product reviews; and useful production tips. An entertaining look at the creative part of the advertising industry, *Advertising Techniques* is one of three magazines produced by Advertising Trade Publications. Considering their market — designers and art directors — all three are inexcusably bad examples of non-designed magazines, and surprisingly dull in their presentation.

Published 10 times a year; $6.00 per year; single copies, 85¢.

**Advertising Trade
Publications**

The Public Media Center Newsletter
(San Francisco)

The Public Media Center is a non-profit advertising agency that helps public interest groups to present their views effectively. With the help of designers and writers, the Center has coordinated and produced some dramatic campaigns for organizations that would not normally have access to the media. They provide the sort of mass communications skills that, under usual circumstances, cost a great deal.

The Center's free newsletter keeps abreast of the political aspects of media use, frequently pointing out inequities in FCC rulings, and pointing up the Advertising Council's stranglehold on public service advertising. It fills a certain information gap left by other journals involved more commercially with advertising and the media.

The Media Center also publishes a booklet, "Strategies For Access to Public Service Advertising," crammed with practical information, and highly recommended. $3.00

Public Media Center

Kodak Bulletin for the Graphic Arts
(Rochester)

Although the *Bulletin* is a trade journal for the lithography and printing businesses, knowing what's happening inside the industry that deals with your mechanicals can be a great asset to any graphic artist. The *Bulletin* updates technical information, and discusses new products and techniques for pre-press production. It is published two or three times a year, and can be obtained free from Kodak.

Eastman Kodak Co

Artworker News
(New York)

This news journal is especially valuable because it keeps a close watch on governmental developments that affect all artists. It contains continuing information reports on the health hazards posed by certain products and materials; on CETA arts programs; on legal questions; art, design, and the community; and a host of other topics important to artworkers.

Published 10 times a year; $7.00 per year

Foundation for the Community of Artists

Color Research and Application
(New York)

Perhaps *Color Research* is too highly technical and detailed a publication for most graphic artists, but it deserves mention here as *the* journal that covers color most thoroughly and objectively. It fills a void left by those diverse publications that offer only minimal coverage of this very broad subject, although to appreciate the magazine fully you need a science background. Nevertheless, it is written partly with the artist in mind, and provides an international forum for color research, endorsed by the Inter-Society Color Council, The Colour Group (UK), and the Canadian Society for Color.

Published quarterly; $35.00 per year.

John Wiley & Sons Inc

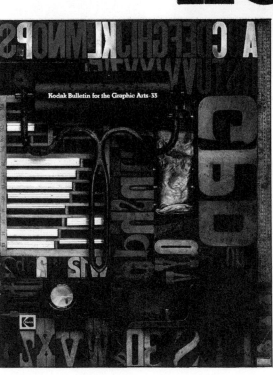

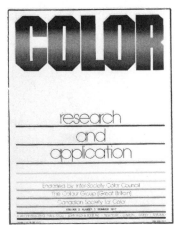

Art In America
(Marion)

Probably the best of the fine arts journals relevant to the graphic artist, *Art In America* covers contemporary art and illustration in a lively manner, making maximum use of the superb visual material that it features. To some extent, the magazine's fine arts coverage is international, including portfolios of painters, illustrators, designers, and even an occasional photographer. *Art In America* also reviews art, design, and photography books, as well as exhibitions, auctions, galleries, and the "reproducibles" business.

Published bi-monthly; $19.95 per year; single issue, $3.00.

Art In America

Publishers Weekly
(New York)

Not an essential magazine for graphic artists, but if you are involved in book or publication design, *Publishers Weekly* provides useful, up-to-the-minute information on the editorial, technological, and business ends of your trade. Four or five of the fifty-two issues a year may be of special interest to the designer, and those can usually be procured from a publishing house if necessary. *PW* records all the book illustration trends, and feeds the fascination of keeping up with current book publishing, a booming industry.

Published weekly; $30.00 per year; single copies $2.00, special issues, $4.25.

R R Bowker Co

Graphic Arts News
(Newport Beach)

A new newspaper, published by the organizer of the Tools of the Trade show (p.210), *Graphic Arts News* is designed to educate the graphic artist about supplies and equipment so that he or she may purchase wisely and save money. It's too early to tell how worthwhile this publication will be, but despite considerable potential, it has been rather shallow at the outset. It is heavy on west coast events, design news, and interviews, and it includes a professional services directory. Distributed free through major art supply stores, or direct from Newport Beach.

CAE Co

Four By Five
(New York)

Volumes of stock photography in full color, which constitute a buying guide for all the work on file at *Four By Five.* Each beautifully produced volume is a representative sample of high-quality commercial stock photography, presented as nine catalogs of subject matter all bound together. So far there are two volumes, with more promised.

Published irregularly; $30.00 per volume.

Four By Five

The Picture Reference File
(New York)

This particular pictorial encyclopedia, published in theme volumes, is the best array available of instant-access, noncopyright illustrative material. It is a resource for good quality original engravings and line illustrative material that can really save the day in a pinch or be the basis for a whole design solution. Although few compendia of pictorial graffiti are worth their cost, this ongoing edition has a higher quality of content and reproduction than the others. Volume One (of a proposed twenty-five volumes) contains more than 2,000 illustrations in ninety-six subject categories on 400 pages. It is definitely expensive.

Published regularly (apparently); $60.00 per volume.

Hart Publishing Co Inc

Office Products News
(New York)

Design studios use many of the same items used in any commercial office, and if you really want to keep up with the latest products in this vast area of manufacturing, *Office Products News* will do the trick. Every issue examines one major category of equipment, among all its listings and advertisements, and *OPN* deals regularly with word-processing products and systems, office-copying technology, and writing implements.

Published monthly, it is free if you can prove you are a big buyer of all this stuff; otherwise $7.50 per year.

Office Products News

CoEvolution Quarterly
(Sausalito)

From Soft Technology to Communications to Understanding Whole Systems, this continuing offshoot of *The Whole Earth Catalogue* offers a unique social and philosophical view of what's happening in the media, media design, crafts, and design in general. It is a genuinely eclectic addition to our selective list of regular publications, and very much in the vanguard of contemporary thought. Its selection of coevolutionary material — some directly applicable to the graphic artist, some peripherally applicable, and some applicable only in the wildest imaginings of a crazed cartoonist's nightmare — is entirely idiosyncratic, leading the reader down paths he or she had never thought to explore, bringing up questions of variable moment, and pointing out information sources that may lead the reader either to answers or to further questions. Containing reviews, cartoons, exploratory interviews, and highly personal editorials, as well as information sources such as *The Changing Information Environment,* this is a book concerned with design and information systems of the future. Predictable in attitude, but certainly not in content, *CQ* is a regular surprise package.

Published quarterly; $12.00 per year; $3.50 single copies

Point Foundation

FROM *THE PICTURE REFERENCE FILE,* VOLUME ONE

Visual Communication Books

Some of the best design books available come from the Hastings House series of titles. Hastings House publishes some themselves, and acts as the major distributor for many others. For instance, it imports all the Graphis Press annuals, which are the mainstay of the following selection.

The Art Direction Book Company

A major distributor of graphic art books, this company offers a broad, and comprehensive list of over 100 titles. They also publish a few books themselves, notably the *Creativity* annuals, the *Trade Marks* and *World of Logotypes* series.

The square, harmonic decompositions of the Golden Mean, from Geometry and The Art of Life

Print Bookstore

Best known for its unique *Print Casebooks, Print* magazine also publishes "The Best In…" series, covering all aspects of graphic communications.

Its catalog is a complete listing of nearly all titles of interest to people in the graphic arts, including fine art, architecture, and photography—over 130 books in all.

The Museum of Modern Art

Largely devoted to architecture, industrial design, and modern art, the museum's list of publications is a very special collection of source reference books. Some are not available on the general market, many are out of print, and others are distributed only through the museum, the New York Graphic Society, or the M.I.T. Press. A few of the out-of-print titles have been reissued recently by Arno Press.

Museum Books Inc

This company is a major importer and distributor of essential books for the design professions, including graphic design, color, calligraphy and lettering, packaging, photography, and printing. Its list is impressive, and Museum Books will almost certainly be able to help you find difficult-to-locate design titles. With few exceptions, all the books listed in this section are available at Museum Books, as are some of the periodicals listed above.

Designers Book Club

For a $6 membership fee, you select three books and agree to purchase four others over the year, all at reduced prices. The club offers new titles hot off the press, and—although biased toward architecture—has a consistently well-selected back list. It's a good deal. Books can be returned or exchanged if it turns out to be something other than what you expected. Quite a few of the Designers Book Club titles don't turn up elsewhere; the club does not carry the regular annuals.

Dover Publications

Well known for its collection of visual reprint material from decades past, Dover's is an inexpensive, eclectic library of graphic source material, including typefaces. They have a mass of pictorial archive titles, strange design titles, and a particularly fascinating selection of geometry-in-art-and-life type books.

For example, if you need a picture of the American Eagle, Dover has a book of 321 eagle designs. Need some odd alphabets? Dover has twenty-seven alphabet books; and so on.

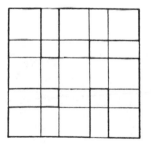
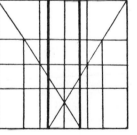
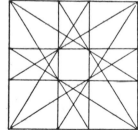

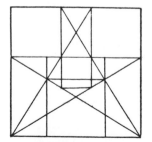
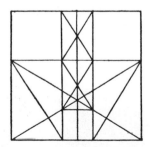
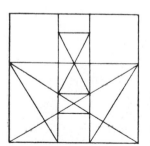

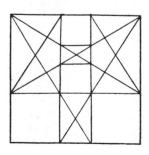
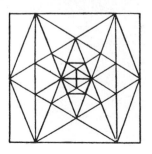
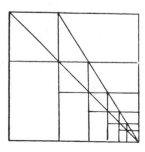

The Graphis Annual
[Edited by Walter Herdeg]

Despite ever increasing competition from other annuals, *Graphis* remains a consistent first choice for many designers as the major international roundup of award-winning graphic material. Each year Walter Herdeg makes his selections from about 20,000 submissions to make this comprehensive survey of the newest, most striking examples of visual communication in editorial and advertising art. The book is usually divided into six chapters with twenty subject groups and an index.
     Cost: $39.50

     The Graphis Press; Hastings House

Graphis Posters
[Edited by Walter Herdeg]

In 1973, Graphis initiated an annual book devoted entirely to posters, which has become the major collection of current poster work from all corners of the world. Its four sections include advertising, cultural, social, and decorative posters; like the *Graphis Annual,* it is edited by Walter Herdeg.
     Cost:$39.50

     Graphis Press; Hastings House

Graphis Packaging
[Edited by Walter Herdeg]

Another *Graphis Annual* spin off, begun shortly after *Graphis Posters, Graphis Packaging* is a collection of the best and most innovative packaging designs in the world. This annual provides eloquent proof that despite the vast amount of insultingly *bad* packaging we see every day, packages that satisfy marketing requirements can also be attractive, functional, and even things of beauty.
     Cost:$42.50

     Graphis Press; Hastings House

Graphis Annual Reports
[Edited by Walter Herdeg]

There is no indication as yet that *Annual Reports* will become a regular publication, though it may well be updated from time to time. This is not so much a collection of the best, but, rather, a "How To" manual that covers everything you need to know about preparing an annual report, with emphasis on its graphic design aspects. It's a beautifully designed, thorough work that pays attention to the newest techniques of design and manufacturing.
     Cost: $35.00

     Graphis Press; Hastings House

Graphis Record Covers
[Edited by Walter Herdeg]

Not an annual, but a definitive look at the best examples in a highly innovative, expressive, and eclectic art form.
     This comprehensive survey of album art presents a fascinating cross-section of work from the early stages of record cover design up to the most recent achievements in the field. A terrific collection; one of a series of square, "international reference" books.
     Cost: $28.00

     Graphis Press; Hastings House

Film + TV Graphics 2
[Edited by Walter Herdeg]

This third in the *Graphis* square book series is the second edition of a widely acclaimed collection of film and TV animation and graphics. It surveys the new techniques and ideas that have swept through those media in the past few years, and leaves one wondering why so little of this rich development is actually *used.* The book itself is divided into six sections: entertainment, film, television film, sponsored film, commercials, titles and captions, and experimental.
     Cost: $39.50

     Graphis Press; Hastings House

Graphis Diagrams

An exciting, thorough survey of all the methods and techniques by which abstract data may be rendered in diagram and chart form, ranging from obvious and very simple solutions to highly sophisticated design concept work. In an area of design that constantly tests ingenuity and visualization skills, this volume is a goldmine of ideas and solutions to spark the imagination.
Cost: $31.00

Graphis Press; Hastings House

PhotoGraphis

To complete the wonderfully produced international Graphis series, PhotoGraphis is the most comprehensive compilation of the world's successfully applied photography. The book is divided into eleven sections that cover advertising, annual reports, book jackets, editorial, magazine and record covers, packaging, calendars, house journals, booklets, and television.
Cost: $39.50

Graphis Press; Hastings House

The *Print* Casebooks

Every year *Print* magazine publishes a set of books that are more than just examples of the year's best design. *The Casebooks* examine in detail each of the successful designs chosen, exploring their problems, the influencing factors, the thinking behind the concepts, marketing, why each design succeeds, and where it fails.

The greatly informative post mortems on design projects are divided into six categories and six volumes: advertising; annual reports; book/magazine/record album covers and posters; environmental graphics; exhibition design; and packaging. Although clearly and neatly presented, the discussions of 250 problem-solving designs are generally poorly reproduced. The volumes are available separately or as a boxed set.
Cost: $13.50 each; $74.95 complete set

RC Publications Inc; Watson Guptill Publications

The *Creativity* Annual

One of the major design annuals in the United States, this book is made up of the award-winning entries to *Art Direction*'s annual media arts show, the Creativity Awards. Its emphasis is clearly advertising, the best of whose art and design it documents. As a yearly publication this annual lacks the verve apparent in some of the other annuals listed here.
Cost: $22.50

Art Direction Book Co

Print *Casebooks*

The Art Directors Annual

One of the best known of all
the United States annuals, the
ADA's collection of advertising
design ideas is made up of all
the winners of the New York Art
Directors Club show. This comprehensive catalogue covers
work in all areas of the media
arts from newspaper ads to letterheads and is, of course, lovely
to look at, delightful to hold.
Cost: $24.75

Watson-Guptill Publications

The Penrose Annual
[Edited by Clive Goodacre]

Sometimes brilliant, and more
often rather dull, this English collection of essays pretends to be
a state-of-the-art, end-of-the-year
wrap-up. It is not so much a mirror of the year, though, as it is an
idiosyncratic anthology of more
or less technical articles on all
aspects of printing and design.
Oriented toward the industry,
Penrose used to be *the*
innovative graphic arts annual.
Its orientation remains the same,
but the presentation of material
seems somewhat anachronistic
by now. Still and all, though
most of the book is of peripheral
interest to many readers, nearly
everyone will find something of
value in it. If one major design
article per volume does not
make this annual worth the
price, get a copy at the library.
Cost: $30.00

**Lund Humphries; Hastings
House**

Computer Animation
[Edited by John Halas]

Seventeen United States and
British experts explore the latest
techniques, methods, and systems for computer made film
and graphics. The writings,
photographs, and diagrams
form a source of information invaluable to anyone involved with
animation, and are a fascinating
assessment of the collaboration
among designer, artist, and
machine.
Cost: $20.00

Hastings House

Design & Art Direction

This is the annual showcase for
British talent that corresponds to
the *Creativity* annual in the United
States. For some indefinable
reason, the overall quality of the
work in the *D&Ad* annuals is consistently higher than *Creativity;*
possibly their selection process
is more rigorous. *D&Ad* is a
record of the year's best work —
distinctly European in style, flavor,
and humor — divided into six
principal sections: advertising,
photography, television advertising and graphics, movie
advertising and graphics,
packaging, and editorial and
environmental design.
Cost: $39.50

Hastings House

Illustrators Annual
[Edited by Robert Hallock]

The annual from the Society
of Illustrators' national exhibition
presents the work of all the
award winners. It is known as
the standard publication of contemporary United States illustration, and certainly appears to be
the most comprehensive work
available on the subject. It is a
sumptuous production, and a
sourcebook for much of the best
illustration talent at the vanguard
of graphic style, imagination,
and technique.
Cost: $26.50

Hastings House

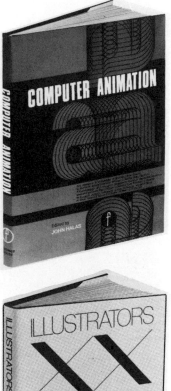

European Illustration
[Edited by E Booth-Clibborn]

Drawing its material from the wide range of European mass media, this illustration annual covers all media, and is the unparalled showcase for current European art, and appears to improve on itself each year. Commercial illustration, in its broadest sense, is a multifaceted art form rapidly gaining the status and respect it so obviously deserves.

Cost: $42.50

Hastings House

The Complete Guide to Illustration and Design
[Edited by Terence Dalley]

A thorough and comprehensive guide to all the various types of illustration design in media, and how they are used. This is not just another encyclopedia of graphic arts stuff, but a real attempt to cover in-depth every possible topic within illustration and design and their related skills. Every type of illustration is described for all media — pen & ink, painting, print-making, technical illustration — complete with the tools, techniques and history of each medium.

Cost: $19.95

Mayflower Books, Inc

Basic Principles of Design

A four volume paperback set of the famous Foundation Program offered at the School of Design in Basel, Switzerland — one of the most highly regarded basic-design programs in the world. The books contain fundamental design training exercises in drawing, color, space, and form that are dynamically impressive in their simplicity. Each of the four volumes is a complete unit in itself, and constitutes a compact reminder of the basic purpose of design, with a wealth of detailed visual material. Volume One is about drawing; Volume Two about perspective, lettering, and advanced drawing; Volume Three about materials, texture, and color; and Volume Four about graphic exercises, dimensional design, and color.

Cost: $36.00 (boxed set)

Van Nostrand Reinhold

The Arts and Crafts Movement
[Gillian Naylor]

The Arts and Crafts Movement was inspired by a crisis of conscience. Based on aesthetic values that derive from the conviction that a society produces the art, design, and architecture it deserves, the book is an excellent summary of the Modern Movement that appeared to shatter with the disolution of the Bauhaus in Germany just prior to World War II. It contends that we are still conditioned by the efforts of those 19th Century reformers in our attempts to create a world fit to live in.

The concerns of The Arts and Crafts Movement resurface constantly in differing forms, and this visual volume promotes the ideal, as defined by Moholy-Nagy: "To lay down the basis for an organic system of production whose focal point is man, not profit."

Cost: $8.00

The MIT Press

Art In Society
[Ken Baynes]

A marvelous compendium of society's essential icons that taps the roots of cultural symbology and mythology without laboring its point. *Art in Society* offers a cohesive overview of graphics as a social activity, exploring work, worship, war, sex, and other basic themes, illuminating the fundamental human need to communicate about universal mysteries. It is a collection of Jungian matrix, commercial art, fine art, environmental design, folk arts and crafts, and signage covering everything from ancient artifacts to comics and movies.

Cost: $35.00

Graphics Books

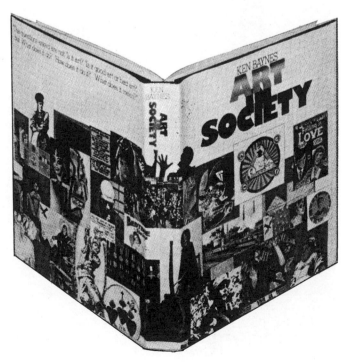

Grand Design
[George Gerster]

This general, inspirational book on design has been called the most magnificent visual book of our times. A vision of man and nature from above—the truly *grand* design—it contains the superb photography of George Gerster, the renowned Swiss aerial photographer.

Its scope of pattern and color create powerful effects, and illustrate some of the concepts discussed in the more abstract titles listed above. The original hardcover edition is hard to find anymore, but an abridged paperback edition is in print.

Cost: $60.00 (hardcover)
$10.95 (paperback)

Paddington Press

Images of an Era

Banned at the Moscow Book Fair, and probably the most comprehensive collection in book form of any art mirroring its time, this is the book of the American Poster collection at the Smithsonian Institution covering the era 1945-1975. It is an assemblage of over 300 representative posters reflecting American social and political concerns during those years, including cultural and purely graphic endeavors. The books includes posters from political campaigns, rock concerts, the Vietnam War protest movement, ecological issues, and the Bicentennial. All the well-known poster designers of the age are represented.
Cost: $15.00

The MIT Press

Geometry and Design

The much—and deservedly—praised Dover Publications has a series of books that deal with all aspects of the relationship between geometry and art, nature, human design, and even life itself, which reveal the principles by which all things are related. They explain some of the reasons that certain proportions are effective and "correct," while others lead to chaos. This, of course, is the subject area where design meets mathematics, philosophy, and the universe. Together, these books constitute an excellent background course in the *reason* of design, and provide a host of basic principles that have utilitarian applications. None of the books requires a geometry background, and all are written clearly and simply with lots of diagrams and illustrations.

The Geometry of Art and Life, cost $2.75

The Elements of Dynamic Symmetry, cost $2.50

Pattern Design with Dynamic Symmetry, cost $2.50

The Divine Proportion, cost $2.50

Dover Publications

The Language of Pattern
[Albarn, Smith, Steele and Walker]

Picking up where the previously listed titles leave off, *The Language of Pattern* is a much needed synthesis of the organic and the geometric; of subjective and objective understandings of nature and design. A visual inquiry into the qualitative values inherent in design, the book cuts through the confusions of design influenced by a rapidly developing technology.

The Language of Pattern explores the richness of invention based on order, beginning with the basic systems of numbers and patterns, and ending with structure. It is essentially a plea for wholesomeness and unity. Throughout its pages of diagrammatic progressions, there is an underlying challenge to preset ways of thinking that emphasizes the character and quality of the perceptual experience.
Cost: $5.95

Harper & Row, Publishers

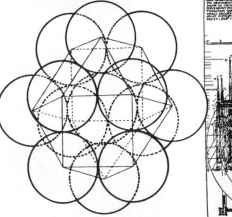

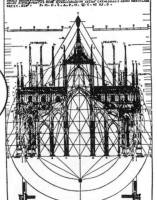

THE GEOMETRY OF ART AND LIFE

Layout
[Allen Hurlburt]

Allen Hurlburt, an art director of international repute, presents a stimulating analysis of the principles that govern the architecture of the printed page. Hurlburt's book pretty well summarizes the creative aspects of the design profession with excellent guidelines. From style to the principles that determine form, it explores the elements of successful layout, and delves into the process of communication involving the psychology of perception and illusion. In his thoughtful and articulate survey, Hurlburt covers all the necessary design principles.
   Cost: $17.95

Watson-Guptill Publications

The Grid
[Allen Hurlburt]

An analysis in depth of one small element of *Layout,* the grid modular layout system is explained and illustrated in Hurlburt's lucid text. For this book of applications, the work of eighteen top designers is reproduced and analyzed to study exactly how each has applied his own modular rules — and broken them selectively. A very useful reference work that includes a glossary and a technical hardware appendix.
   Cost: $16.95

Watson-Guptill Publications

The Art of Advertising
[George Lois]

A stimulating, and even exciting book on creative advertising by one of the game's masters, George Lois, who cleverly wraps all the aspects of this communication field into a lively textbook of possibilities. Every piece reproduced in this volume has been exposed to a mass audience, and most are classic examples of imaginative, successful advertising. Together they make up a picture book whose copy alone demands attention. This is about the *art* of advertising, and it's the only book worth having on the subject.
   Cost: $45.00

Harry N Abrams Inc

Graphic Design International
[Igildo G Biesele]

The inpeccable Swiss design publishing house, ABC Editions of Zurich, produces a series of square international reference books such as this collection of the best works from twelve leading design colleges in Germany, France, England, the United States, Holland, Italy, Japan, Poland, Czechoslovakia, Canada, and Switzerland. The book is impressive both in its high standard of design, and in the extreme range of creative ideas from young designers. The international comparisons are, of course, fascinating.
   Cost: $47.50

ABC Editions; Hastings House

Signet Signal Symbol
[Walter Diethelm]

This first volume of a two-part series is an extremely instructive and informative source and reference book containing an abundance of ideas about all forms of symbolizing. It includes an analysis of sign conception, and demonstrates the systematic development of signs as a language linking the world. One of the best, most succinct books on the subject.
   Cost: $47.50

ABC Editions; Hastings House

Form + Communication
[Walter Diethelm, Marion Diethelm-Handl]

Part two of *Signet Signal Symbol* further explores methods of international communication, studying more sign systems, experimental letter usage, pictographs, symbols, and film, television, and computer designing. It provides a wealth of information for handling this most precise of all creative graphic tools — the symbol.
   Cost: $47.50

ABC Editions; Hastings House

Trade Marks
[Edited by David E Carter]

This series of regular publications constitutes an annual of United States commercial symbols and logos, except for volume six, which is international in scope. A valuable reference source, *Trade Marks* summarizes the best of each year's new designs with at least 1,000 examples — most obviously successful solutions, and some classic examples of badly conceived symbolism.

Cost: $12.95, volumes 1-3; $16.50, volumes 4-6.

Art Direction Book Co

Trade Marks & Symbols
[Yasaburo Kuwayama]

A two-volume set of logo designs from all over the world — one of the best of many such collections of symbols. Very comprehensive and totally visual, this set makes an excellent reference source, showing some of the world's cleverest commercial cyphers and trademarks. Volume one deals with alphabetical designs, volume two with ideogrammatic designs.

Cost: $19.90 each

Van Nostrand Reinhold Co

Designing Corporate Symbols
[Edited by David E Carter]

A useful little book that tries to convey just how much work, thought, and research goes into the creation of a symbol that concisely and accurately portrays the personality and function of a company. 148 examples include the story of their creation — the problems, limitations, and successful solutions.

Cost: $11.50

Art Direction Book Co

Corporate Identity Manuals
[Edited by David E. Carter]

The first compendium of corporate identity manuals that shows the complete program, fully illustrating all the considerations that have to be taken into account when designing these complex projects. The "house-styling" projects cover a wide range of types of corporation, and include a mine of detailed graphic information that is not easily available anywhere else.

Cost: $30.00

Art Direction Book Co

The Symbol Sourcebook
[Henry Dreyfuss]

Unparalleled. An exceptionally thorough, encyclopedic, reference work by Henry Dreyfuss that represents over twenty years of collecting and codifying graphic symbols as they are used in all walks of life throughout the world. This major sourcebook is practical and easy to use; many of the original symbols have been redrawn for the sake of consistency. The book has been applauded the world over for its contribution toward the international develoment of clear and unambiguous signage, and that is the main orientation of this incredible compendium of symbols.

Cost: $30.00

McGraw Hill Book Co

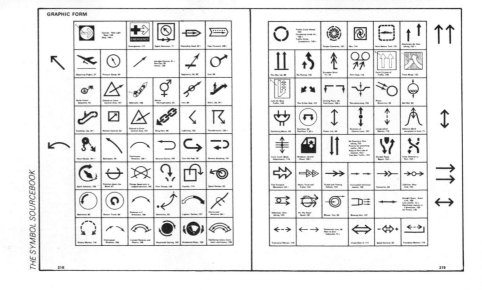

The Elements of Japanese Design
[John W Dower]

An unusual sourcebook, focused entirely on the sense of symbolism and graphic design inherent in a culture famous for its inventiveness and its tradition, its variety and its elegance. The Japanese tradition is heraldic, and its symbols are at one and the same time products of a great art form and mementoes of a dramatic history. The history and heraldry, and their related symbolism, are arranged here in logical thematic sequences with an informative text running parallel to the 2,715 designs. One wondrous facet of the Japanese symbol tradition is that it has survived for centuries to the present time as part of that nation's exquisite sense of beauty and form.
Cost: $15.00

John Weatherhill, Inc

Two Books of Signs

Two inexpensive but valuable reference works, one general and one specific. The first, *Hornung's Handbook of Designs and Devices,* is a totally visual, encyclopedic comparison of fifteen major basic design motifs — the circle, line and band, triangle, square, diamond, cross, swastika, pentagon, hexagon, octagon, star, scroll and curvilinear motif, interlacement, fret and rectangular motif, and the shield — their extensions, and their combinations. Each page contains nine uniformly drawn designs, all of which are discussed in the notes section. Drawn from cultures all over the world, this is a basic collection of reference material from which to develop your own extensions and combinations.
The Book of Signs is Rudolf Koch's calligraphic treatise on signage: 493 symbols used from ancient times, through the middle ages to the present. A beautifully prepared little history book, with Koch's fine calligraphy and Fritz Kredel's woodcuts.
Hornung's Handbook, cost: $3.00
The Book of Signs, cost: $2.00

Dover Publications, Inc

Graphic Science and Design

In its third edition, this standard reference work for technical illustrators brings the study of engineering drawing and graphics to full professional standing. A definitive, complete, and highly relevant handbook, it emphasizes documentary communication for all engineering fields. This is not a beginner's book, nor even a "how-to" manual, since it delves into science in some depth. However, the publisher has two companion volumes — *Mechanical Drawing* and *Manual of Engineering Drawing for Students and Draftsmen* — which cover the more fundamental aspects of technical illustration. All these titles are regularly updated.
Cost: $18.00

McGraw-Hill Book Co

Album Cover Album
[Christopherson, Howells]

This Dragon's World Production is far and away the most complete and informative of the several books that have been published on the subject. An amazingly eclectic collection of design and art, that is packed with examples and wonderfully designed and produced.
The introduction is a history of album art up to the explosion of creativity in this form that occurred in the second half of the 1960s. The book is divided into seven sections, with a detailed appendix on the process and politics of album cover designing, and a detailed index. Every album shown (at least 3,000 of them) includes a list of credits.
Cost: $10.95

A & W Visual Library

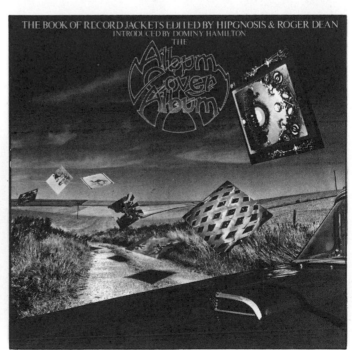

How To Wrap Five More Eggs
[Hideyuki Oka]

One of the best available books on traditional Japanese packaging, that illustrates everything desirable in the essential craft of wrapping things up. *Eggs* goes to the heart of the problem—how materials may determine form and aesthetics—and demonstrates how the humblest of materials can be transformed with breathtaking panache. The ancient Japanese art of packaging may inspire modern mass-market packagers to create objects of singular visual splendor. The photographs in the book are as fine as the subjects themselves.

Cost: $15.00

John Weatherhill, Inc

Optical Art

A standard volume on the theory and practice of using optical illusion pattern without the aid of computers—although it is interesting to observe just how accurately the classical op artists anticipated computer derived patterning. This book studies optical art from its inception in the early 1900s, with the formation of the Gestaltists, up until the use of the computer, and contains all the best examples of the optical art of this century.

Cost: $9.95

Van Nostrand Reinhold

Perspective

Subtitled "A New System for Designers," this book on perspective supersedes all earlier books on the subject by using a system based on just three technical relationships between observer and object. The author, Jay Doblin, discovered that traditional methods of mechanical and freehand perspective permitted enormous error. His easy-to-learn system which this book explains in detail, allows you to draw any three-dimensional concept with only basic drafting equipment.

Unlike most older methods, Doblin's incorporates a demand for artistic judgment while encouraging drawing skills, which makes *Perspective* a unique book, as well as an informative and useful one for designers, illustrators and draftspeople.

Cost: $10.95

Designers Book Club

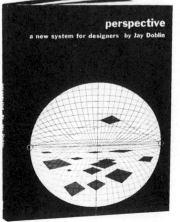

Book Design
[Stanley Rice]

Probably even more useful to book editors than to book designers, these two volumes help organize and systematize the repetitive aspects of book production. The first volume, *Systematic Aspects,* goes into considerable detail explaining how to organize all the routines so that they coordinate; it is heavily illustrated with charts and forms. Full of tips and practical advice, this is part of the "art" of design—procedural organization that creates more time for creative work.

Volume two, *Text Format Models,* is a visual reference catalogue for different types of text design problems, each a model solution on which to build on or from which to adapt. This is the sort of information that any book designer would put together for him or herself, if time allowed. Each volume is complete with detailed specifications.

Cost: $17.50 each

R R Bowker

Letterheads
[Edited by David E Carter]

Letterheads/1—probably the first in a new series of books on a graphic design subject—is a collection of more than 3,000 letterheads from around the world, all produced actual size. Letterhead design, like logo design, is an exacting art with many particular limitations, and this is a great volume to have around to remind you of possibilities.

Cost: $30.00

Art Direction Book Co

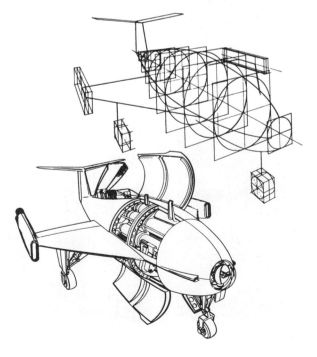

Basic Typography
[Ruedi Ruegg, Godi Frohlich]

A major handbook of typography that explains simply but thoroughly all the present day typesetting techniques and their range of applications from hand composition to the latest electronic installations. Throughout, the emphasis is on typesetting as design — typography — and how to use the symbols creatively. This is one area of design where technical knowledge is a tremendous asset.
Cost: $47.50

ABC Editions; Hastings House

Typography
[Emil Ruder]

This fundamental treatise on typographical design by Emil Ruder, director of the Basle Technical School, has been around for many years, yet it is still one of the standard works on its subject — especially with regard to the strict, basic-design, Swiss school of thought. Often stunning in its simplicity and severity, it is surely one of the most intelligent and attractive manuals on typographic design, its applications, and its usage.
Cost: $30.00

Hastings House

Type and Typography

A complementary volume to a typeface encyclopedia, this basic arsenal of facts is a practical workbook for the graphic artist or designer. Its main feature is that it shows basic typeface family groups in all sizes from 72pt to 16pt as complete alphabets, and 14pt to 6pt as text settings with varying line spacing. The book includes a measure of perspective on the history, origins, and traditions of type, and some very general technical data.

Type and Typography makes no claim to being comprehensive; it is simply an important day-to-day tool that provides instant visual comparisons of type sizes and settings, and is complete enough to be very useful.
Cost: $9.95

Van Nostrand Reinhold

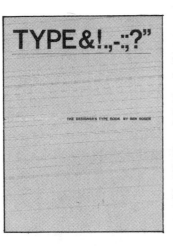

Designing With Type
[James Craig]

An excellent basic course focusing on a creative understanding of typography. Contemporary in viewpoint and heavily visual, *Designing with Type* is a work tool that provides a concise understanding of this art form. Each chapter — ranging from a history of type origins to the working tools of the designer — concludes with design exercises and projects.
Cost: $15.00

Watson-Guptill Publications

An Atlas of Typeforms

This is a beautiful book on type, dynamic and superbly presented in a large 10" x 16" format. Using illustrations rather than words, the atlas shows the main changes in type forms through over 500 years of printing. Shapes are enlarged more than 500% for detailed comparison, and the type is also shown in its original setting at the same size. Thus, the book is full of huge letters and beautiful facsimiles of old printed pages, beginning with the calligraphy of the Book of Kells and including all the significant stages of typography up to the work of William Morris' Kelmscott Press.
Cost: $45.00

Lund Humphries

The Lettera Series
[Armin Haab]

Page after page of letter forms in complete alphabets make up this excellent three-volume sourcebook on letter design. Armin Haab has selected the best of the useful, often decorative, alphabets and presented them ready for studio use or adaptation.

Cost: $25.00 per volume

Hastings House

Letraset Typen

This is a most unusual type specimen book, ring-bound with all the pages slit into horizontal thirds. As you turn the pages, or thirds of pages, you create new combinations of display and text typefaces on the right, and new human faces on the left. Example of Letragraphic and Instant lettering, in sizes 60-144pt, appear on the upper strip of the type pages. The middle strip displays subheads in sizes 36-48pt, and the lower strip shows body types to be combined with the display types above. All the typefaces are identified in this remarkably clever and very useful visual workbook.

Cost: $10.00

Upper & Lower Case Books

Computer Age Copyfitting
[Leslie Raspberry]

A step-by-step manual that really takes advantage of the electronic calculator, and outlines a method of copyfitting using simple procedures that do not even require a knowledge of math. The book deals with fitting elements other than type and with complex fitting problems, and comes with two pads of proportion and typefitting charts to get you into the habit of the system.

Cost: $8.95

Art Direction Book Co

The Roman Alphabet
[Arthur Baker]

An excellent selection of fine calligraphy alphabets and letterform construction, all based on the traditional Roman capitals. The author, Arthur Baker, is a well known typeface designer; and it comes as no surprise that his collection of beautifully designed pen and brush letters is a masterful, personal example of refined utilitarian craftsmanship. Though not an instruction manual, this book will certainly be an inspiration to designers concerned with original alphabets.

Cost: $15.00

Art Direction Book Co

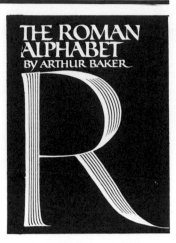

The Encyclopedia of Typefaces

A typeface encyclopedia is an essential studio tool. There are many such volumes on the market, of which this, regularly reprinted and revised, is probably the most useful. It includes a very wide selection of typefaces as complete alphabets, classified under the British Standards Classification system with succinct notes on each typeface.

Cost: $30.00

Barnes & Noble

Solotype's Cheap Catalog

We are including this newsprint catalog of a commercial typesetters since it is an unusual collection of strange, crazy and hard-to-find types dating from the beginning of the century and earlier. Solotype has been long known for their collection of Victorian, art nouveau and type styles that they have constantly added to, and this sixty-four-page resume shows 1000 of their odd typefaces.

Solotype provides all the normal custom services such as type reproportioning, italicizing, bending and twisting to any predetermined shape, perspective and tapering, and — their specialty — outlining, contouring, shadowing and antiquing.

Some of the collections of types published by Dover Publications are prepared by Solotype.

Cost: free

Solotype Typographers

Early Egyptian Eye Chart
as imagined by Solotype

The Graphic Arts Encyclopedia

[George A Stevenson]

A helpful book to have around, this encyclopedia gives more than mere definitions , and tries to impart a working knowledge of all the latest products, processes, equipment and techniques within the graphic arts professions. But this is a vast area to cover, and the alphabetical entries are by necessity brief, and not as well illustrated as they could be. Nevertheless, it is thorough and up-to-date (this is a second edition), packed with neatly presented information on products and tools, types of imagery, kinds of materials and their uses; all cross-indexed, and discussed in the light of actual working experience rather than a parroting of catalog descriptions that refer to ideal or "typical" situations.

This encyclopedia shoud be particularly useful to beginners or students, and to those working on the fringes of the graphic arts or attempting to use a method or process for the first time.

Cost: $24.95

McGraw-Hill Book Co

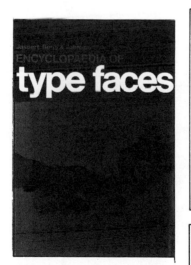

The Colorpedia

This is not really a book on design so much as it is a huge, overwhelming volume of design work. It is the *Random House Encyclopedia* — an incredible visual project which, to an experienced designer, is a mind boggling example of design planning and supervision carried to the nth degree. Designed and prepared in England, this colorpedia is dense with illustrations and diagrams that do not simply illuminate word oriented ideas, but are, themselves, the primary means of communicating information. The bulk of the 14,000 illustrations are fine examples of information design carried out by hundreds of designers, illustrators, and technical draftspeople who convey information on complex subjects such as a bird in flight, how a watershed functions in nature, and the workings of a nuclear generator.

An extensively illustrated encyclopedia is not a new concept — it was done a lot in the nineteenth century; but this modern edition is a definitive example of the state of the art while explaining the increasing complexity of our technological age. The colorpedia includes an 820-page Alphapedia, a 48-page Time Chart, and an 80-page Atlas.

The Colorpedia is, of course, a rich and abundant design reference source.

Cost: $69.95

Random House, Inc

The Dover Pictorial Archive Catalog

Once in a while Dover prepares a visual newsprint catalog of all its pictorial books in print, which total at least 250. It is all visual reference material and largely copyright-free, providing an inexpensive source of hundreds of thousands of motifs, emblems, costumes, patterns, symbols, alphabets, engravings, and illustrations. Some of it is plain junk, but every Dover title includes material that is authentic, original, and valuable, and it is invariably well reproduced. Since the books really are cheap by today's standards, finding just one needed piece of design reference is worth the price of the book, and on the average you get illustrations for one cent each here. There are so many useful titles in the *Pictorial Archive* collection that, rather than list them here, we simply advise you to send for their catalog. For ever after you'll receive packets of information on Dover books.

Cost: free

Dover Publications, Inc

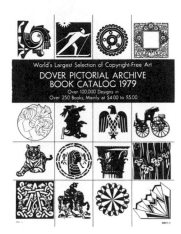

The anatomy of birds

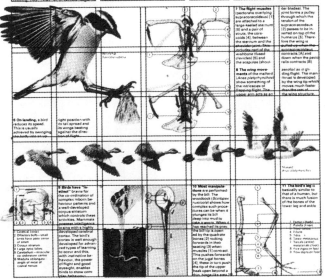

Appendix

Lamp Selector Guide

Addresses of Manufacturers
and Distributors

UNIVERSAL DRAWING STATION INVENTED BY G BOUDRIOT, 1880

The Lamp Selector Guide and lighting performance data shown here indicate the wide range of available lamps — and their performance — that may be used in various fixtures. Lamps are available with narrow, medium and wide beam spreads from 25 to 500 watts.

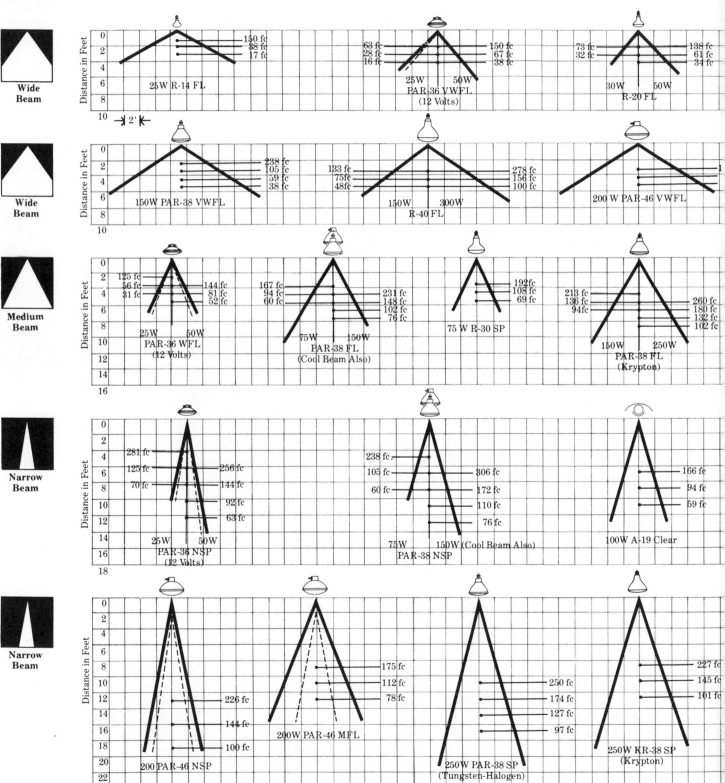

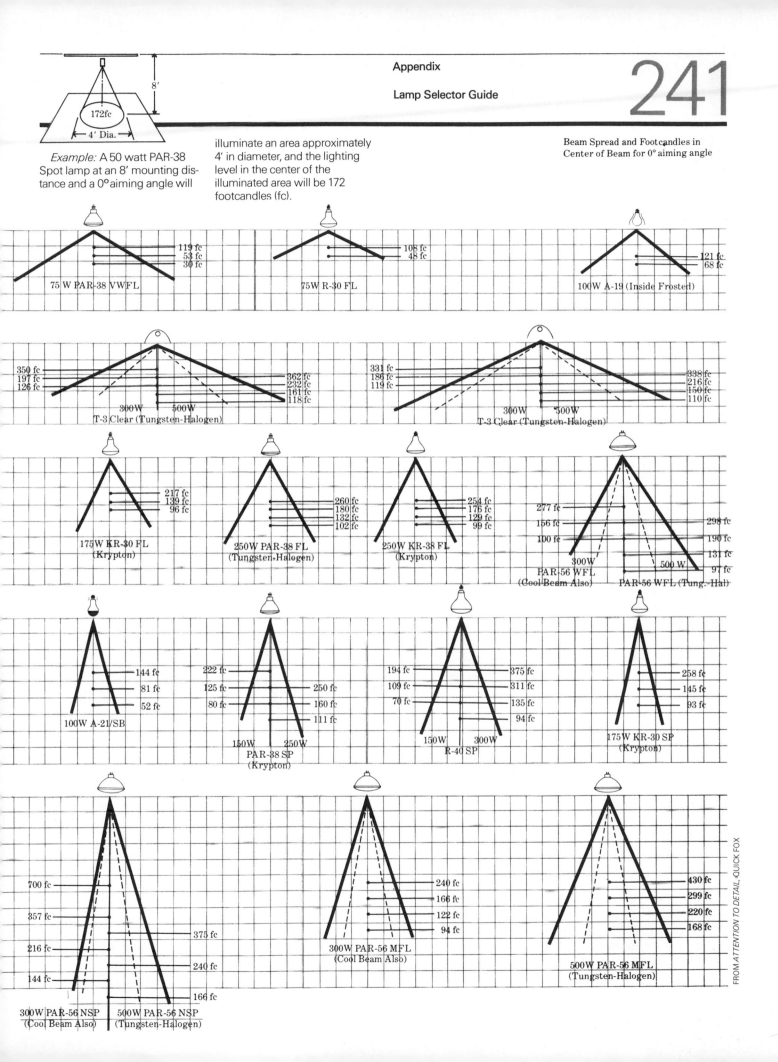

Example: A 50 watt PAR-38 Spot lamp at an 8′ mounting distance and a 0° aiming angle will illuminate an area approximately 4′ in diameter, and the lighting level in the center of the illuminated area will be 172 footcandles (fc).

Beam Spread and Footcandles in Center of Beam for 0° aiming angle

75 W PAR-38 VWFL — 119 fc / 53 fc / 30 fc

75W R-30 FL — 108 fc / 48 fc

100W A-19 (Inside Frosted) — 121 fc / 68 fc

300W / 500W T-3 Clear (Tungsten-Halogen) — 350 fc / 197 fc / 126 fc — 362 fc / 232 fc / 161 fc / 118 fc

300W / 500W T-3 Clear (Tungsten-Halogen) — 331 fc / 186 fc / 119 fc — 338 fc / 216 fc / 150 fc / 110 fc

175W KR-30 FL (Krypton) — 217 fc / 139 fc / 96 fc

250W PAR-38 FL (Tungsten-Halogen) — 260 fc / 180 fc / 132 fc / 102 fc

250W KR-38 FL (Krypton) — 254 fc / 176 fc / 129 fc / 99 fc

300W PAR-56 WFL (Cool Beam Also) — 277 fc / 156 fc / 100 fc

500W PAR-56 WFL (Tung.-Hal) — 298 fc / 190 fc / 131 fc / 97 fc

100W A-21/SB — 144 fc / 81 fc / 52 fc

150W / 250W PAR-38 SP (Krypton) — 222 fc / 125 fc / 80 fc — 250 fc / 160 fc / 111 fc

150W / 300W R-40 SP — 194 fc / 109 fc / 70 fc — 375 fc / 311 fc / 135 fc / 94 fc

175W KR-30 SP (Krypton) — 258 fc / 145 fc / 93 fc

300W PAR-56 NSP (Cool Beam Also) / 500W PAR-56 NSP (Tungsten-Halogen) — 700 fc / 357 fc / 216 fc / 144 fc — 375 fc / 240 fc / 166 fc

300W PAR-56 MFL (Cool Beam Also) — 240 fc / 166 fc / 122 fc / 94 fc

500W PAR-56 MFL (Tungsten-Halogen) — 430 fc / 299 fc / 220 fc / 168 fc

FROM *ATTENTION TO DETAIL*, QUICK FOX

A

A&W Visual Library
95 Madison Avenue
New York, NY 10016

Abbeon Cal, Inc
123-55A Gray Avenue
Santa Barbara, California 93101

ABC Editions
8021 Zurich, Switzerland

Academy of Art
540 Powell Street
San Francisco, California 94108

Ad Directions Show
19 West 44 Street
New York, NY 10036

Adjusto Equipment Co
20163 Hawkins Road
Bowling Green, Ohio 43402

Advertising Techniques
19 West 44 Street
New York, NY 10036

Advertising Trade Publications
19 West 44 Street
New York, NY 10036

S B Albertis
5 Tudor Place
New York, NY 10017

Alvin & Co, Inc
Box 188
Winsor, Connecticut 06095

Alvin & Co, Inc
Box 1975
San Leandro, California 94577

American Artist
1 Astor Plaza
New York, NY 10036

American Bankruptcy Council
(see *Yellow Pages* for local offices)

American Institute of Graphic Arts
(AIGA)
1059 Third Avenue
New York, NY 10021

American Society of
Magazine Photographers
60 East 42 Street
New York, NY 10017

Arbitare
Messaggerie Internazionali
4 Via Gonsaga
20123 Milano, Italy

Architectural Design (AD)
Aeroshaw Ltd
7/8 Holland Street
London W8, England

Archetype
25 Osgood Place
San Francisco, California 94133

Arenson Inc
919 Third Avenue
New York, NY 10022

Arizona State University
College of Fine Arts
Tempe, Arizona 85281

Atlantic & Pacific Industries, Inc
18662 MacArthur Boulevard
Irvine, California 92715

The Art Annual
Communication Arts
410 Sherman Avenue
Palo Alto, California 94303

Art Center
College of Design
1700 Lida Street
Pasadena, California 91103

Art Direction
19 West 44 Street
New York, NY 10036

Art Direction Book Co
19 West 44 Street
New York, NY 10036

Arthur H Gaebel, Inc
Box 5
East Syracuse, New York 13057

Art in America
542 Pacific Avenue
Marion, Ohio 43302

Artists In Print
Building 314
Fort Mason Center
San Francisco, California 94123

Artograph, Inc
529 South Seventh Street
Minneapolis, Minnesota 55415

Artworker News
280 Broadway
New York, NY 10007

Audio Visual Laboratories
500 Hillside Avenue
Atlantic Highlands
New Jersey 07716

Autotype USA, Inc
523 West Golf Road
Arlington Heights, Illinois 60005

Autotype USA, Inc
523 West Golf Road
Arlington Heights, Illinois 60005

B

Badger Air-Brush Co
9128 West Belmont Avenue
Franklin Park, Illinois 60131

Banker's Box
1789 Norwood Avenue
Itasca, Illinois 60143

Barnes & Noble Books
10 East 53 Street
New York, NY 10022

Bates Manufacturing Co
Orange, New Jersey 08805

Baumwell Graphics
461 Eighth Avenue
New York, NY 10001

Bay Area Lawyers for the Arts
Building 310
Fort Mason Center
San Francisco, California 94123

Bell Springs Publishing
Box 322
Laytonville, California 95454

Berol USA
Danbury, Connecticut 06810

Bieffeplast
Box 406
Padova, Italy

Bienfang Paper Co, Inc
Metuchen, New Jersey 08840

Blair Art Products
Memphis, Tennessee 38122

Books on Tape
Box 7900
Newport Beach, California 92660

Borden Chemical Co
New York, NY 10017

Boston University
School of Visual Arts
855 Commonwealth Avenue
Boston, Massachusetts 02215

R R Bowker Co
Box 1807
Ann Arbor, Michigan 48106

Brady Adhesives & Graphics
727 West Glendale Avenue
Milwaukee, Wisconsin 53201

Brookstone Co
127 Vose Farm Road
Peterborough
New Hampshire 03458

C

California Air Environments
1299 Bayshore Highway
Burlingame, California 94010

California College of Arts & Crafts
Division of Design
5212 Broadway
Oakland, California 94618

California Polytechnic State
University
School of Applied Art & Design
San Luis Obispo, California 93407

Canon Electronics
10 Nevada Drive
Lake Success, NY 11040

Carnegie-Mellon University
Department of Art
Schenley Park
Pittsburgh, Pennsylvania 15213

Charles Scribner's Sons
597 Fifth Avenue
New York, NY 10017

Charles T Bainbridge's Sons, Inc
808 Georgia Avenue
Brooklyn, New York 11207

Champion Papers
Marketing Services
245 Park Avenue
New York, NY 10017

Charrette Corporation
31 Olympia Avenue
Woburn, Massachusetts 01801

Charrette
212 East 54 Street
New York, NY 10022

Charrette
44 Brattle Street
Cambridge, Massachusetts 02138

Charrette
1 Winthrop Square
Boston, Massachusetts 02110

Chartpak Graphic Products
One River Road
Leeds, Massachusetts 01053

Clear Light Productions
Box 391
Newton, Massachusetts 02158

Clearprint Paper Co
1482 67 Street
Emeryville, California

CoEvolution Quarterly
Point Foundation
Box 428
Sausalito, California 94965

College Board Publication Orders
Dept C12, Box 2815
Princeton, New Jersey 08540

Collier Books
Macmillan Publishing Co, Inc
866 Third Avenue
New York, NY 10022

Color Research and Application
John Wiley & Sons
605 Third Avenue
New York, NY 10016

Communication Arts
Coyne & Blanchard, Inc
410 Sherman Avenue
Palo Alto, California 94303

Communication Arts Awards
410 Sherman Avenue
Palo Alto, California 94303

Compugraphic Corporation
80 Industrial Way
Wilmington
Massachusetts 01887

Conran's
160 East 54 Street
New York, NY 10022

Consul & Mutoh, Ltd
519 Davis Street
Evanston, Illinois 60201

Cooper Union School
of Art & Architecture
41 Cooper Square
New York, NY 10003

Copyright Office
Library of Congress
Washington, DC 20559

Creative Director
21456 Salamanca
Woodland Hills, California 91364

Creativity Awards
30 East 37 Street
New York, NY 10016

Crown Zellerbach
Communications Department
9 Bush Street
San Francisco, California 94119

C-Thru Graphics
6 Britton Drive
Bloomfield, Connecticut 06002

D

Dahle USA, Inc
Commerce Drive
Danbury, Connecticut 06810

David R Godine, Publisher
306 Dartmouth Street
Boston, Massachusetts

Dazor Lamp Corporation
310 Canal Street
New York, NY 10013

Design
The Design Council
28 Haymarket
London SW1Y 4SU
England

Design Center Books
The Design Council
28 Haymarket
London SW1Y 4SU
England

The Design Schools
Time Life Building, #777
1271 Avenue of the Americas
New York, NY 10020

Designers Book Club
2160 Patterson Street
Cincinatti, Ohio 45214

Design Research
(Out of Business)

Dial-A-Color
Box 157
Prospect Heights, Illinois 60070

Dick Blick
Box 1267
Galesburg, Illinois 61401

Dictaphone Corporation
105 Oak Street
Norwood, New Jersey 07648

Directory of Washington
Creative Services
1609 Connecticut Avenue, NW
Washington, DC 20009

Door Store
210 East 51 Street
New York, NY 10022

Dot Pasteup Supply Co
1612 California Street
Omaha, Nebraska 68102

Dover Publications, Inc
180 Varick Street
New York, NY 10014

Drake University
College of Fine Arts
25th Street
Des Moines, Iowa 50311

E

Early Financial Aid
Planning Service
Box 2843
Princeton, New Jersey 08541

Eberhard Faber, Inc
Crestwood
Wilkes-Barre
Pennsylvania 18703

Eberhard Faber, Inc
Crestwood
Wilkes-Barre
Pennsylvania 18703

E B Eddy Forest Products Ltd
1335 Carling Avenue
Ottawa, Ontario K1Y 4L5
Canada

Eden Press
Box 667
Clarkdale, Arizona 86324

Eico Electronic Instrument Co
(Eico Security Control Center)
283 Malta Street
Brooklyn, New York 11207

Emerson Electric Co
Rittenhouse Division
Honeyeye Falls, New York 14472

Envelope Manufacturers
Association
1 Rockefeller Plaza
New York, NY 10020

Envision
Art Directors and Artists Club
3400 J Street
Sacramento, California 95816

Expediters of the Printed
Word Ltd
527 Madison Avenue
New York, NY 10020

F

FaberCastell Corporation
551 Spring Place Road
Lewisburg, Tennessee 37091

Faberhults Industri Ab
S-560 40 Habo
Sweden

Face To Face
Folio Magazine Publishing Corp
125 Elm Street
New Canaan, Connecticut 06840

Federal Express
(see *Yellow Pages* for local offices)

Fine Print
2107 Van Ness Avenue
San Francisco, California 94109

Flax Art Supplies
250 Sutter Street
San Francisco, California 94108

Flax Art Supplies
10852 Lindbrook Drive
Los Angeles, California

Flax Art Supplies
180 Wabash Avenue
Chicago, Illinois

Flax Art Supplies
4554 N Central Avenue
Phoenix, Arizona 85012

Flax Art Supplies (discount)
1699 Market Street
San Francisco, California 94105

Flax Art Supplies (discount)
510 East El Camino Real
Sunnyvale, California

Florette Leather Goods
40 West 17 Street
New York, NY 10011

Ford Industries Inc
Portland, Oregon 97206

Fototype, Inc
1414 West Roscoe Street
Chicago, Illinois 60657

Foundation for the Community
of Artists
280 Broadway
New York, NY 10007

Four by Five
485 Madison Avenue
New York, NY 10022

Al Friedman, Inc
37 West 53 Street
New York, NY 10019

Al Friedman, Inc
25 West 45 Street
New York, NY 10036

Friendly Publications, Inc
80 Irving Place
New York, NY 10003

Friends of Calligraphy
555 Cedarberry
San Rafael, California 94903

G

Geographics, Inc
2339 South 2300 West
Salt Lake City, Utah 84119

George Kovacs, Inc
831 Madison Avenue
New York, NY 10021

Global Equipment Co
2255 Sunset Boulevard
Los Angeles, California 90028

Grade Finders, Inc
Box 444
Bala-Cynwyd,
Pennsylvania 19004

The Graphic Artists Guild East
30 East 20 Street
New York, NY 10003

The Graphic Artists Guild West
Building 314, Fort Mason Center
San Francisco, California 94123

Graphic Artists Guild Locals

Atlanta
1144 Crescent Avenue, NE
Atlanta, Georgia 30309

Detroit
Campbell-Isbell Alphabet
2359 Liverois
Troy, Michigan 48084

Greensboro
The Design Center
2909 Baltic Avenue
Greensboro
North Carolina 27406

Honolulu
Box 37932
Honolulu, Hawaii 96827

Los Angeles
1533 Wilshire Boulevard
Suite 202
Los Angeles, California 90017

Miami
2230 South West 23rd Street
Miami, Florida 33145

Nashville
1101 Kermit Drive
Nashville, Tennessee

Portland
3312 SW Veterans Hospital
Medical Graphics Department
Portland, Oregon 97201

Sacramento
Box 15192
Sacramento, California 95813

St Louis
4515 Maryland
St Louis, Missouri 63108

Graphic Arts News
CAE Company
3950 Campus Drive
Newport Beach, California 92660

Graphic Design +
Kodansha, Ltd
2-12-21 Otowa, Bunkyo-ku
Tokyo, Japan

Graphic Products Corporation
Rolling Meadows, Illinois 60008

Graphics Books
120 East 56 Street
New York, NY 10022

Graphics In Industry
American Seminar Institute
311 California Street
San Francisco, California 94104

Graphics Today
Syndicate Magazines, Inc
6 East 43 Street
New York, NY 10017

Graphics USA
Kaye Publishing Corp
120 East 56 Street
New York, NY 10022

Graphis
The Graphis Press
107 Dufourstrasse
CH 8008 Zurich
Switzerland

Griffin Manufacturing Co, Inc
Webster, New York 14580

GRS Instruments, Inc
8730 King George Drive
Dallas, Texas 75235

M Grumbacher, Inc
460 West 34 Street
New York, NY 10001

H

Harper & Row Publishers, Inc
10 East 53 Street
New York, NY 10022

Harry N Abrams, Inc
110 East 59 Street
New York, NY 10022

Hastings House Publishers
10 East 40 Street
New York, NY 10016

Hawthorn Books
260 Madison Avenue
New York, NY 10016

Headliners International, Inc
1000 Sansome Street
San Francisco, California 94111

Heinemann, Ltd
c/o Museum Books, Inc
48 East 43 Street
New York, NY 10017

Henniker's
779 Bush Street
San Francisco, California 94120

Henry Schein, Inc
39-01 170 Street
Flushing, New York 11358

The House of Grids
135 East York Street
Akron, Ohio 44314

Howard W Sams & Co, Inc
4300 West 62 Street
Indianapolis, Indiana 46268

Hunt Manufacturing Co
Bienfang Paper Division
1405 Locust Street
Philadelphia, Pennsylvania 19102

I

IBM Corporation
Office Products Division
590 Madison Avenue
New York, NY 10022

ICOGRADA
Warren House
St. Paul's Cray Road
Chislehurst, Kent BR7 6QA
England

Icographic
Pergamon Press
Fairview Park
Elmsford, New York 10523

Idea
Museum Books, Inc
48 East 43 Street
New York, NY 10017

Idea Seminars
1612 California Street
Omaha, Nebraska 68102

The Illustrators Guild
Graphic Artists Guild, Inc
30 East 20 Street
New York, NY 10003

The Incredible Slidemakers
23 East 73 Street
New York, NY 10021

Industrial Graphics International
7835 Eastern Avenue
Silver Spring, Maryland 20910

Information Design Journal
4 Maurice Walk
London NW11 6JX
England

Illustrators Workshop, Inc
Box 280
Easton, Connecticut 06425

Instant Type, Inc
99-19 70 Avenue
Forest Hills, New Jersey 11375

Inter/Graph, Inc
2345 Vauxhall Road
Union, New Jersey 07083

International Book Design
Exhibition
DDR
Postfach 146
701 Leipzig
West Germany

International Design
Conference at Aspen (IDCA)
Box 644
Aspen, Colorado 81611

International Multi-Image
Festival
Box 272
Fair Haven, New Jersey 07701

International Paper Corporation
220 East 42 Street
New York, NY 10017

International Typeface Corporation
216 East 45 Street
New York, NY 10017

International Typographic
Composition Association
2233 Wisconsin Avenue, NW
Washington, DC 20007

Itoya of America
1835 Centinela Avenue
Santa Monica, California 90404

J

Japan Interior Design
Japan Publication Trading Co
1255 Howard Street
San Francisco, California 94103

Jasper Seating Co
Box 111
Jasper, Indiana 47546

Jobec Inc
Route 1, Box J
Goleta, California 93017

John Weatherhill, Inc
10 Cleveland Avenue
Rutland, Vermont 05701

John Wiley & Sons
605 Third Avenue
New York, NY 10016

Joint Ethics Committee
Box 179, Grand Central Station
Grand Central Station
New York, NY 10017

K

Kansas City Art Institute
Department of Design
4415 Warwick Boulevard
Kansas City, Missouri 64111

Kent State University
School of Art, Division of Design
Kent, Ohio 44242

Keuffel + Esser Co
20 Whippany Road
Morristown, New Jersey 07960

Kodak Publications
Eastman Kodak Co
Department 454
343 State Street
Rochester, New York 14650

Koh-I-Noor Rapidograph, Inc
100 North Street
Bloomsbury, New Jersey 08804

Krueger Corporation
Box 8100
Green Bay, Wisconsin 54308

L

Lectro-Stik Corporation
3721 North Broadway
Chicago, Illinois 60613

Lee's Art Shop
220 West 57 Street
New York, NY 10019

Levolor Lorentzen Inc
720 Monroe Street
Hoboken, New Jersey 07030

Light, Inc
417 Bleecker Street
New York, NY 10014

Lightolier, Inc
346 Claremont Avenue
Jersey City, New Jersey 07304

Loew Cornell, Inc
131 West Ruby Avenue
Palisades Park, New Jersey 07650

Lowell-Light Manufacturing Co
421 West 54 Street
New York, NY 10019

Lund Humphries
12 Bedford Square
London WC1
England

Luxo Lamp Corporation
Monument Park
Port Chester, New York 10573

Lyon Metal Products, Inc
1933 Montgomery Street
Aurora, Illinois 60507

M

Macmillan, Inc
866 Third Avenue
New York, NY 10022

Magic Marker Corporation
Cherry Hill Industrial Park
Cherry Hill, New Jersey 08003

Market Forge
35 Garvey Street
Everett, Massachusetts 02149

Markline Co, Inc
Box 1750F
Waltham, Massachusetts 02154

Martin Instrument Co
13450 Farmington Road
Livonia, Michigan 48150

Maryland College of Art & Design
10500 Georgia Avenue
Silver Spring, Maryland 20902

Matrix/Leedal, Inc
2929 S Halsted Street
Chicago, Illinois 60608

Mayflower Books, Inc
575 Lexington Avenue
New York, NY 10022

,Mayline Corporation, Inc
619 North Commerce Street
Sheboygan, Wisconsin 53081

McGraw Hill Book Co
330 West 42 Street
New York, NY 10036

Medicon Corporation
333 Fell Street
San Francisco, California 94102

The Merchant Taylor Corporation
25 West 45 Street
New York, NY 10036

Mergenthaler Linotype
Corporation
Mergenthaler Drive
Plainview, New York 11803

Metacolor, Inc
855 Sansome Street
San Francisco, California 94111

Methods Research Corporation
Ashbury Avenue
Farmingdale, New Jersey 07727

Metro Supply Co
1420 47 Avenue
Sacramento, California 95822

Midwest Publishers Supply Co
4640 North Olcott Avenue
Chicago, Illinois 60656

Minolta Corporation
101 Williams Drive
Ramsey, New Jersey

The MIT Press
28 Carleton Street
Cambridge, Massachusetts 02142

3M Energy Control Centers
(see local *Yellow Pages*)

Mobius Design
2475 Linden Avenue
Boulder, Colorado 80302

Modern Supply Co
19 Murray Street
New York, NY 10007

Modern Tint
2403 De La Cruz Boulevard
Santa Cruz, California 95050

The Monotype Corporation
Salfords, Redhill, Surrey
England

The Monotype Corporation
3620 G Street
Philadelphia, Pennsylvania 19134

Morgan Adhesives Company
Stow, Ohio 44224

Mountain West Alarm Co
4215 North 16 Street
Phoenix, Arizona 85064

Museum Books, Inc
48 East 43 Street
New York, NY 10017

Museum of Modern Art
Bookshop II
23 West 53 Street
New York, NY 10019

N

National Art Education
Associaton
1916 Association Drive
Reston, Virginia 22091

National Art Industries, Inc
Allendale Park
Allendale, New Jersey 10028

National Association of
Schools of Art
11250 Roger Bacon Drive
Reston, Virginia 22090

National Business Furniture
222 E Michigan Street
Milwaukee, Wisconsin 53202

National Speciality
Manufacturing Co
Chicago, Illinois 60610

Nationwide Photolamp Supply Co
Lighting Supplies, Inc
Box 206
Norfolk, Virginia 23501

New York Central Supply Co
62 Third Avenue
New York, NY 10003

New York State University
Art & Art History Department
3435 Main Street
Buffalo, New York 14214

Normagraphics
20 Whippany Road
Morristown, New Jersey 07960

North American Publishing Co
401 North Broad Street
Philadelphia, Pennsylvania 19108

Northwood Publications, Ltd
93-99 Goswell Road
London EC1V 7QA
England

Novum Gebrauchsgraphik
F Bruckmann KG
D-8 Munchen 20
West Germany

Office Products News
Box 619
Garden City, New York 11530

Ohline Corporation
1930 West 139 Street
Gardena, California 90249

Olivetti of America
500 Park Avenue
New York, NY 10022

The One Show
The Art Directors Club, Inc
488 Madison Avenue
New York, NY 10022

Oregon Rainbow
213 Southwest Ash Street
Portland, Oregon 97204

Paasche Airbrush Co
1909 West Diversey Parkway
Chicago, Illinois 60614

Package Designers Council
Box 3753, Grand Central Station
New York, NY 10017

Paddington Press
95 Madison Avenue
New York, NY 10016

Pantheon Books
Random House, Inc
201 East 50 Street
New York, NY 10022

Pantone, Inc
55 Knickerbocker Road
Moonachie, New Jersey, 07074

Parsons School of Design
66 West 12 Street
New York, NY 10011

PAS Graphics, Inc
3950 Campus Drive
Newport Beach, California 92660

PAS Graphics, Inc
1292 E Colorado Boulevard
Pasadena, California 91106

Patton Electric Co
Box 9340
Fort Wayne, Indiana 46809

Pentel of America
Torrence, California 90503

Pentalic Corporation
132 West 22 Street
New York, NY 10011

Peregrine Smith, Inc
1877 East Gentile Street
Layton, Utah 84041

Pergamon Press, Ltd
Fairview Park
Elmsford, New York 10523

Photo & Sound Co
116 Natoma Street
San Francisco, California 94105

Picture Magazine
3818 Brunswick Avenue
Los Angeles, California 90039

Pickett Industries
Rio Rico Industrial Park
386 North Frontage Road
Nogales, Arizona 85621

The Picture Reference File
Hart Publishing Co, Inc
15 West 4 Street
New York, NY 10012

Pilot Corporation of America
41-15 36 Street
Long Island City, New York 11101

Plan Hold
17621 Von Karman Avenue
Irvine, California 92714

Polaroid Corporation
280 South Birne Street
Cambridge, Massachusetts 02139

Portage Newspaper Supply
Box 5500
1858 Akron Peninsular Road
Akron, Ohio 44313

Pratt Institute
School of Art & Design
Brooklyn, New York, NY 11205

Print
RC Publications, Inc
6400 Goldsboro Road, NW
Washington, DC 20034

Print Bookstore
6400 Goldsboro Road
Washington, DC 20034

The Printing Industry of the
Carolinas Foundation (PICA)
301 Hawthorn Lane
Charlotte, North Carolina 28204

The Public Media Center
2751 Hyde Street
San Francisco, California 94133

Publishers Weekly
R R Bowker Co
Box 1807
Ann Arbor, Michigan 48106

Pubmart
Knowledge Industry
Publications, Inc
2 Corporate Park Drive
White Plains, New York 10604

Push Pin Graphic
207 East 32 Street
New York, NY 10016

Quick Fox
33 West 60 Street
New York, NY 10023

Qyx Systems
264 Welsh Pool Road
Lionville, Pennsylvania 19353

Radio Shack
Tandy Corporation
Fort Worth, Texas 76102

Random House, Inc
201 East 50 Street
New York, NY 10022

Record-O-Phone
Quasar Microsystems, Inc
448 Suffolk Avenue
Brentwood, New York 11717

Rhode Island School of Design
Division of Design
2 College Street
Providence, Rhode Island 02903

Richard Marek, Publishers
200 Madison Avenue
New York, NY 10016

Ridley Enslow, Publishers
60 Crescent Place
Short Hills, New Jersey 07078

RitaSue Siegel Agency, Inc
60 West 55 Street
New York, NY 10019

Richard Schlatter Design
265 Capital Avenue, NE
Battle Creek, Michigan 49017

RSVP
Box 314
Brooklyn, New York, NY 11205

Robert Sonneman Associates, Inc
37-50 57 Street
Woodside, New York 11377

Rochester Institute of Technology
College of Fine & Applied Arts
One Lomb Memorial Drive
Rochester, New York 14623

Saint Heironymous Press
1705 Grove Street
Berkeley, California 94709

Sam Flax
551 Madison Avenue
New York, NY 10022

Sam Flax
55 East 55 Street
New York, NY 10022

Sam Flax
15 Park Row
New York, NY 10013

Sam Flax
25 East 28 Street
New York, NY 10022

Sam Flax
2606 Oaklawn Avenue
Dallas, Texas 75219

Sam Flax
1515 Spring Street
NW Atlanta, Georgia 30309

Seal Art Materials Group
Derby, Connecticut 06418

Sears/Roebuck Co
(see local *Yellow Pages*)

Scheafer Machine Co
Box 512, Boston Post Road
Clinton, Connecticut 06413

School of Visual Arts
Department of Media Arts
209 East 23 Street
New York, NY 10010

SMC Corporation
831 James Street
Syracuse, New York 13203

Sharp Electronics
Box 588
Paramus, New Jersey 07652

Shenandoah Manufacturing Co
Box 839
Harrisonburg, Virginia 22801

Sid Diamond Furniture Design
964 Third Avenue
New York, NY 10022

Sierra Club Books
530 Bush Street
San Francisco, California 94108

Solar Age Press
Indian Mills, West Virginia 24949

Society of Environmental
Graphics Designers
228 North La Salle Street
Chicago, Illinois 60601

Solotype Typographers
298 Crestmont Drive
Oakland, California 94619

J S Staedtler, Inc
Box 787
Chatsworth, California 91311

J S Staedtler, Inc
Box 65
Elk Grove Village, Illinois 60007

Strathmore Paper Co
Westfield, Massachusetts 01085

Tactype
127 West 26 Street
New York, NY 10001

Taplinger Publishing Co, Inc
200 Park Avenue South
New York, NY 10003

Taylor & Ng
Embarcadero Center
San Francisco, California 94113

Teledyne National Tracing Paper
Indianapolis, Indiana 46206

Testrite Instrument Co, Inc
135 Monroe Street
Newark, New Jersey 07105

Tools of the Trade Show
CAE Co
3950 Campus Drive
Newport Beach, California
92660

The Type Aids Co
238 Merrydale Road
San Rafael, California 94903

Type Directors Club
12 East 41 Street
New York, NY 10017

Type X
National Composition Association
1730 North Lynn Street
Arlington, Virginia 22209

The Ulano Companies
210 East 86 Street
New York, NY 10028

Union Rubber & Asbestos Co
Trenton, New Jersey 08608

Universe Books
381 Park Avenue South
New York, NY 10016

University of California Press
223 Fulton Street
Berkeley, California 94720

University of Chicago Press
5801 Ellis Avenue
Chicago, Illinois 60637

Upper and Lower Case
International Typeface
Corporation
216 East 45 Street
New York, NY 10017

Van Nostrand Reinhold Co
430 West 33 Street
New York, NY 10001

Vemco Corporation
766 South Fair Oaks Avenue
Pasadena, California 91105

Virginia Commonwealth
University
Communication Arts & Design
325 North Harrison Street
Richmond, Virginia 23284

Visual Communication Books
Hastings House Publishers
10 East 40 Street
New York, NY 10016

Visual Graphics Corporation
VGC Park
North West 94 Avenue
Tamarac, Florida 33321

Watson-Guptill Publications
2160 Patterson Street
Cincinnati, Ohio 45214

The West Coast Show
Western Art Directors Club
Box 996
Palo Alto, California 94302

Western Michigan University
Department of Art
Kalamazoo, Michigan 49001

Whitney Library of Design
Watson-Guptill Publications
2160 Patterson Street
Cincinnati, Ohio 45214

William Clowes & Sons, Ltd
Dorland House
14-16 Lower Regent Street
London SW1, England

Wingbow Press
2940 Seventh Street
Berkeley, California 94710

Winsor & Newton, Inc
555 Windsor Drive
Secaucus, New Jersey 07094

Women in Design
530 Howard Street
San Francisco, California 94107

Workman Publishing
1 West 39 Street
New York, NY 10018

Writers Digest Books
9933 Alliance Road
Cincinnati, Ohio 45242

X-acto Corporation
45 Van Dam Street
Long Island City, New York 11101

Xerox Corporation
Xerox Square
Rochester, New York 14644

Yasatumo & Co
24 California Street
San Francisco, California 94111

Zipatone, Inc
150 Fencl Lane
Hillside, Illinois 60162

Zoom
2 Rue du Faubourg Poisonniere
75010 Paris, France

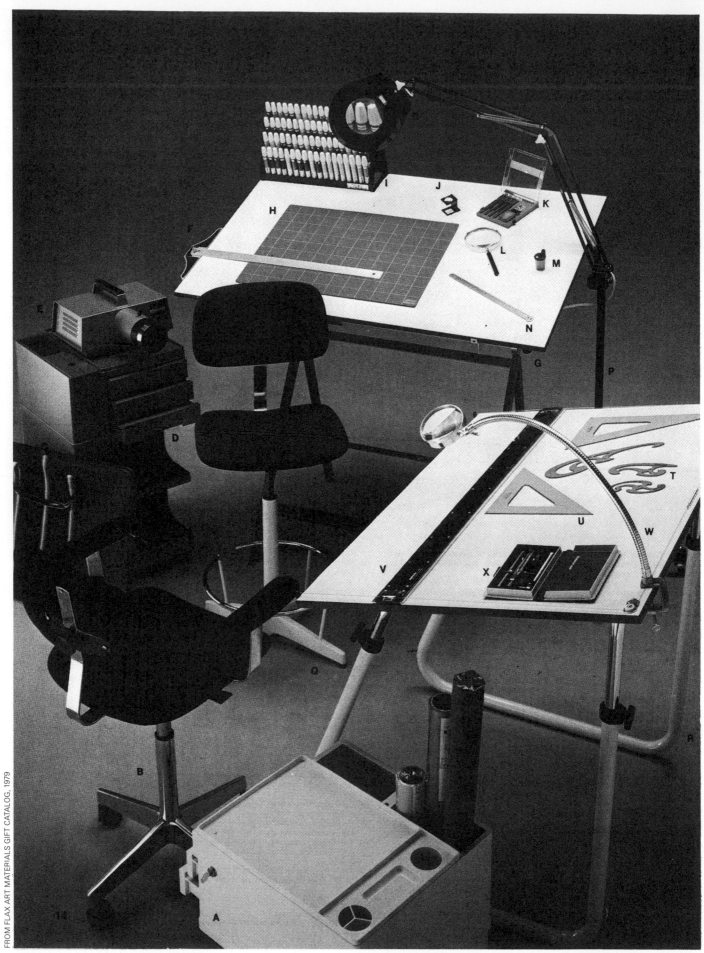

By Design:

Jon Goodchild is a book designer living up country on the West Coast, working for *Sierra Club Books* and many New York and San Francisco publishers. From a London design partnership and early involvement with the underground press, he moved to San Francisco to work with *Rolling Stone* and to help create *Straight Arrow Books.* His book design work has since earned him numerous book awards.

Bill Henkin is a freelance writer and editor based in San Francisco, whose wide-ranging interests have resulted in books about aging, ceramics, psychology, film, and contemporary literature. Since 1968, when he worked with Lawrence Levy on William Gass' AIGA award-winning novella, *Willie Masters' Lonesome Wife,* he has been particularly concerned with the graphic presentation of books.

The type was photoset by Community Type and Design of Fairfax, California, in 11/12½ pt Univers 55 and 9/10pt Univers 45 on Compugraphic equipment. All the line and 120-line halftone photostats were made by Negatorium, San Francisco, and the camera-ready boards prepared by Craig DuMonte. The Book was printed and bound at Crest Litho Inc, Albany, New York on 60lb Doecote uncoated opaque.